METHUEN'S MANUALS OF MODERN PSYCHOLOGY
EDITED BY C. A. MACE

# A Short History of British Psychology
## 1840–1940

# A Short History
# of British Psychology
# 1840 - 1940

BY
## L. S. HEARNSHAW

METHUEN & CO LTD
11 NEW FETTER LANE LONDON EC4

*First published 1964*
*© 1964 by L. S. Hearnshaw*
*Printed in Great Britain*
*by Butler & Tanner Ltd*
*Frome and London*

# Preface

In more ways than one psychologists today are in the public eye. Their work is frequently referred to in the press, on the air, even in Parliament, and it excites a variety of reactions and prejudices. Psychologists themselves are no longer rare specimens in the community. There are nearly one thousand Fellows and Associates of the British Psychological Society resident in Great Britain, all of them professionally qualified, and nearly all of them earning their livings as psychologists. In addition there are many practitioners in the allied professions of psychiatry and psychiatric social work. Apart from the universities and research institutes, jobs are available for psychologists in the civil service, on the staffs of local authorities and hospital boards, and in a number of industrial and commercial organizations. Nearly all the universities of the country now have independent departments of psychology which are attracting an increasing number of students, and extra-murally psychology is among the most popular subjects of study with adult audiences.

This growth has almost entirely taken place during the last hundred years. It was just over a century ago that the first stirrings began which led eventually to the separation of psychology from the parent stem of philosophy. To understand and to evaluate properly the work that psychologists are doing today one must understand the main outlines of the developments which have transformed a largely abstract philosophical study pursued by a small number of individuals into an independent, if rudimentary, science, with many practical applications and the beginnings of a professional organization. The aim of the present book is to trace the development of psychology in Great Britain from the middle of the nineteenth century to the time of the Second World War, during which period this transformation took place.

It is, of course, to some extent unreal to chronicle the development of psychology in this country in isolation from the rest of the Western world. Psychology, like all sciences, is international. The progress of psychology in Great Britain has not taken place behind closed frontiers and has been much dependent on advances made elsewhere. Reference must be made even in a history of British psychology to the impact of ideas

v

from abroad. Provided this is done there are some grounds which perhaps justify a national history.

First, we commonly tend to underestimate the important role which British psychologists and scientists have played in shaping the development of psychology, particularly in the early years. The French psychologist Ribot, writing in 1870, held that "since the time of Hobbes and Locke England has been the country which has done most for psychology". Leadership soon afterwards passed first to Germany, and then to the United States. But it is well to remember that psychology is not, as it is sometimes considered to be, something alien and un-British, but in its roots a largely native growth. It is rather the resistances to psychology which to a great extent are alien and spring from an imported idealist philosophy which became increasingly influential from 1870 onwards.

Secondly, there is a great deal to be said for making a special study of the development of psychology within the framework of one's familiar native culture. Ideas can be related to their social background; the books that British psychologists wrote are readily available in libraries; the departments and institutes that they founded, or in which they worked, still in many cases survive; and the traditions of their work and personalities still influence us today.

Finally there are names which have a rightful place in the history of the development of British psychology and which deserve to be remembered, but which are necessarily relegated to the background, or passed over entirely, in broad general histories. Moreover while several good general histories of psychology exist no history of British psychology has as yet been written.

The limits of historical time that I have set myself also need some justification. British psychology is older than Bain; but Bain is perhaps the first man who might claim to be first and foremost a psychologist. He represents, therefore, the beginnings of psychology's independence; and it is the development of an independent psychology that I wish to trace. Hence 1840 is the date at which this history begins. It ends in 1940. The Second World War and its aftermath brought such a large expansion of psychology, both applied and academic, that an account of it could not conveniently be compressed within these pages, nor adequately covered by one author. Moreover since 1940 British psychology has become much more fully merged with international, particularly American, movements, and the special characteristics which previously marked it have diminished in importance. Today the young British student of psychology is brought up largely on American textbooks, and his gods, if he has any, are probably American. 1940 was in more ways than one the end of an epoch.

This short history is intended for the general reader as well as for students of psychology. It is only an outline, and aims in the first place to bring out broad trends rather than to introduce an excessive load of minute and technical detail. Enough detail has, I hope, been included to give the book some substance without making it unduly specialized. I make no apology for including a good deal of material on sciences closely related to psychology. The development of psychology is unintelligible apart from the concomitant developments in medicine, physiology, biology, sociology, anthropology, and statistics, and apart from the changes in the prevailing philosophic climate. In the closely related discipline of psychiatry (the branch of medicine that is concerned with mental disorders) I have attempted to sketch some of the main lines of progress, but not technical developments of purely medical interest.

I am most grateful to all those who have assisted me by answering queries and providing information, sometimes in more detail than I have been able to incorporate in the present work. In particular my thanks are due to Sir Frederic and Lady Bartlett, Mr R. J. Bartlett, Sir Cyril Burt, Dr C. B. Frisby, Professor G. Humphrey, Mr J. C. Kenna (Archivist of the British Psychological Society), Professor Sir Aubrey Lewis, Emeritus Professor T. H. Pear, Mrs Winifred Raphael, Mr J. C. Raven and Dr R. R. Rusk.

*Department of Psychology,*  L. S. HEARNSHAW
*University of Liverpool.*

# Contents

x  *Contents*

## Contents

Contents

# CHAPTER I

# Bain and his Background

## 1. Background to Bain

To commence a history of British psychology with Bain is misleading if it in any way suggests that Bain was the founder and fountain head of psychological enquiry in Great Britain. Just two hundred years earlier Hobbes was writing about human nature and the human mind in a manner which we recognize as characteristically psychological and characteristically British; and in the two centuries which intervened between Hobbes and Bain a succession of English and Scottish philosophers contributed a great deal to the foundations of psychology. Yet Bain has been described as "the first psychologist" and as "the author of the first textbook of psychology written in the modern manner".[1] It is only necessary to compare Bain's *The Senses and the Intellect* and *The Emotions and the Will* with the psychological works of his immediate predecessors to recognize that there is much justice in these ascriptions. Thomas Brown's *Lectures on the Philosophy of the Human Mind* (1820) are in manner, method and scope very different from Bain's books. His lectures are rhetorical in style and embellished with copious quotations from poets, both English and Latin. His method is wholly introspective: for the student of the human mind "no costly apparatus is requisite – no tedious waiting for seasons of observation. He has but to look within himself to find the elements which he has to put together, or the compound which he has to analyse, and the instruments that are to perform the analysis or composition."[2] The analysis of mind is only one part of the story. "When we know that man has certain affections and passions, there still remains the great inquiry as to the propriety or impropriety of those passions"; and the philosopher of mind must go on to consider "the nature of our spiritual being . . . the ties which bind us to our fellow-men and to our Creator; and the prospect of that unfading existence of which life is but the first dawning gleam".[3] In spite of his medical training there is little physiology in Brown's lectures.

The other major psychological treatise of the half century preceding

---

[1] J. C. Flugel *A Hundred Years of Psychology*, 79–80.
[2] T. Brown op. cit., lect. II.       [3] op. cit., lect. I.

the publication of Bain's first book was James Mill's *Analysis of the Phenomena of the Human Mind* (1829). This gaunt and bloodless work propounds an extreme form of associationism, in which all man's complex intellectual and moral states are analysed into combinations of "sensations, ideas, and trains of ideas", and human action is shown to be wholly dominated by what Mill's teacher, Bentham, called "two sovereign masters, pain and pleasure". Although in some ways a *tour de force* Mill's *Analysis* is essentially a speculative construction supported by analytic reasoning and casual introspective observation. As his son J. S. Mill points out in the second edition, which he edited with the help of Bain, the book is marred by "a certain impatience of detail"; and also by its inadequate physiology. A good deal of the contents, moreover, might more appropriately be classed as logical rather than psychological.

When we compare Bain with his predecessors three things strike us: first, the scope of psychology has been much more clearly defined; secondly, the physiological foundations of psychology are beginning to be accurately laid; and thirdly, the requirements of scientific method are better understood.

There is not much in Bain's books which cannot be regarded as properly falling within the province of psychology. And this can be said of none of his British predecessors. It is plausible to argue that the introduction of the term 'psychology' into Great Britain in the early part of the nineteenth century may have had something to do with the sharper definition of its scope. The term 'psychology' is, of course, not an ancient one. It is, however, older than the term 'biology' which was proposed by Lamarck in 1802. It originated in Germany in the sixteenth century, but was not widely used until after the publication of Wolff's *Psychologia Empirica* (1732). On the continent it soon became accepted; Bonnet, for example, the Swiss naturalist and philosopher, wrote an *Essai de Psychologie* in 1754, which was, incidentally, published in London. The first employment of the term 'psychology' in Great Britain would seem to have been among a group of Aberdeen philosophers towards the end of the eighteenth century. George Campbell, Principal of Marischal College, used the word in his *Philosophy of Rhetoric* (1776), and Dr Beattie, Professor of Moral Philosophy, entitled the first part of his *Elements of Moral Science* (1790) 'Psychology'. Possibly Thomas Reid, who held the chair of philosophy at King's College, Aberdeen, from 1752 to 1764 and was secretary of the Aberdeen Philosophical Society (the "Wise Club"), was responsible for its introduction, for we know that he was familiar with Wolff's treatise. However, it is to Coleridge more than to any other man that we owe the naturalization of the word 'psychology' into English. In the years 1798–9 Coleridge spent nine months in Germany; he learned German and steeped himself in German philosophy. Among other things he attended Blumenbach's lectures on psychology at Göttingen. In *Biographia Literaria* some years later (1817) he makes frequent use of the term. "Metaphysics and psychology have long been my hobby-horse", he declares. And in a footnote to 'psychological' in *A Treatise on Method* he writes: "We beg pardon for the use of this *insolens verbum*; but it is one of which our language stands in great need. We have no single term to express the philosophy of the Human Mind; and what is worse, the principles of that philosophy are commonly called 'metaphysical', a word of very different meaning." The word, however, did not catch on quickly, and when Sir William Hamilton was appointed to the chair of logic and metaphysics in Edinburgh in 1836 he still had to apologize for using "an exotic, a technical name", and to spend almost half a lecture period on listing the advantages of the term 'psychology'.[1] It was, he pointed out, now the ordinary expression for the doctrine of mind in the philosophical language of every other European nation. The value of having a single word, with a convenient adjectival form, was great. Most other branches of philosophy were designated by Greek technical names. And if 'psychology' were not generally adopted, there was a danger of inappropriate terms like Brown's 'physiology of mind', used to denote a wholly psychological analysis, and still more impossible terms like 'intellectual physics', which had actually been used for the title of a book, gaining currency. Hamilton's advocacy was no doubt a powerful one, for he was recognized as the most learned British philosopher of his day, and though his lectures were not published until after his death, his influence was considerable. In 1843 Mill's *System of Logic* appeared; and Mill in this widely read work not only argues that "there is a distinct and separate Science of Mind", but names this science "Psychology".[2] In 1848 *The Journal of Psychological Medicine and Mental Pathology* was first issued and in 1855 with the publication of Spencer's *Principles of Psychology* the word 'Psychology' appeared in the title of a systematic text-book written in English and published in England.[3] The battle for the term 'psychology' was won, even though to the average Englishman

[1] W. Hamilton *Lectures on Metaphysics*, lect. VIII.
[2] J. S. Mill *System of Logic*, bk. VI, ch. 4.
[3] Several books on 'psychology' were published in America in the 1840's. See Roback's *History of American Psychology*. And in 1854 Sir Benjamin Brodie produced a volume of dialogues called *Psychological Inquiries*.

it for long retained – and perhaps still retains – an 'exotic' flavour, and to psychologists themselves its definition was destined to be the cause of many controversies in the future. Bain was perhaps slower than some of his contemporaries to employ the word. It appears only gradually and mainly in his later writing. But he must have been, from his early post-graduate years, familiar with it, for he read Mill's *Logic* in manuscript before its publication. The empirical 'science of mind' as something distinct from the wider 'philosophy of mind' was, therefore, appreciated by him; and this appreciation determined the scope of his psychological treatises.

The second advantage Bain had over his predecessors was in the much firmer basis of physiology that was available to him. The first edition of Quain's *Anatomy*, of which Bain made extensive use, appeared in 1828. In 1842 an English translation of Johannes Müller's *Handbuch der Physiologie des Menschen* (1833–40) was published, and this opened up a new era in the study of physiology. Müller had in particular made important investigations into the workings of the nervous system and sense organs. A number of basic discoveries had not long previously been made in this country. Sir Charles Bell in his *A New Idea of the Anatomy of the Brain* (1811) had propounded the differences between sensory and motor nerves; and in 1832 Marshall Hall of Nottingham published a paper "on the reflex function of the medulla oblongata and medulla spinalis", in which the non-conscious, non-voluntary nature of reflexes was clearly established. When Bain wrote, new knowledge on the brain and nervous system was rapidly growing, and the pseudo-science of phrenology, which had enjoyed a wide vogue between about 1820 to 1840, was on the decline. "The mind", wrote Thomas Brown in 1820, "in that central brain in which it is supposed to reside, communicating with all these extreme branches, has been compared, by a very obvious but a very beautiful similitude, to the parent Ocean, receiving from innumerable distances the waters of its filial streams:

> Ac uti longinquis descendunt montibus amnes
> Velivolus Tamisis . . . etc." [1]

Bain in 1855 could be more precisely factual.

Finally Bain benefited from the serious attempt which was made in England from about 1830 to analyse the nature of scientific knowledge. As Hamilton points out in his article on 'Logic' in the *Edinburgh Review* this study had for a century and half experienced "combined perversion

[1] Thomas Brown *Philosophy of the Human Mind*, lect. XIX.

and neglect".[1] The revival began with the publication of *The Elements of Logic* (1829) by Richard Whately, Archbishop of Dublin, and former Fellow of Oriel College, Oxford. Two years later Sir John Herschell, the astronomer renowned alike for his telescope construction, his mathematical work, and his celestial observations, published his *Preliminary Discourse on the Study of Natural Philosophy* (1831) in which he showed how the discoveries of science were made, and how its generalizations were arrived at. William Whewell's works on the inductive sciences were more important. Whewell was professor of mineralogy at Cambridge from 1828 to 1832, and of moral philosophy from 1838 to 1855. He became Master of Trinity College in 1841. He wrote a comprehensive *History of the Inductive Sciences* (1837) and followed this up by a *Philosophy of the Inductive Sciences* (1840) in which he analysed the methods employed in the natural sciences. These writings stimulated Mill and were among the influences that shaped his *System of Logic* (1843). What makes Mill's *Logic*, however, of peculiar importance to the psychologist is his inclusion in it of a section "on the logic of the Moral Sciences" in which he inquires "how far the methods, by which so many of the laws of the physical world have been numbered among truths irrevocably required and universally assented to, can be instrumental to the formation of a similar body of received doctrine in moral and political science".[2] The backward state of 'the moral sciences' Mill regards as a "blot on the face of science";[3] he argues that man and society can become the subject matter of true empirical sciences and that "the same process through which the laws of many simpler phenomena have by general acknowledgement been placed beyond dispute must be consciously and deliberately applied to those more difficult inquiries". Mill made a distinction between psychology and ethology, or the science of character, which has not generally been adopted, but which nevertheless foreshadows the much later development of a psychology of personality. His analysis of the methodology of the moral sciences in general shows remarkable perspicacity, and is even today of the greatest interest to psychologists. It gave Bain, who was a close adherent of Mill, a solid grounding in methodology.

For these reasons then Bain can rightly be regarded as opening a new chapter in the history of British psychology—a new chapter, not a new book; for in recognizing Bain's advances on his predecessors, we must

---

[1] *Edin. Rev.*, 1832, reprinted in Sir William Hamilton's *Discussions on Philosophy etc.*
[2] Mill op. cit., Preface.   [3] op. cit., bk. VI, ch. 1.

not underestimate his debts to them. Behind him lay the whole history of British associationist psychology, adumbrated by Hobbes and Locke, and worked out more elaborately by the admirable Hartley (1705-57), whose *Observations on Man* (1749) are systematic, thorough, and, as far as the knowledge of his day permitted, factual. Behind him, too, was the century-old tradition of Scottish philosophy, derived from Reid (1710-96) and essentially psychological in character, with its long-winded accounts of the intellectual and of the active powers of human nature. Though he disagreed with the Scottish school on fundamentals Bain borrowed from it in details. We may suspect, too, the influence of the eighteenth-century moral philosophers, Shaftesbury, Hutcheson, Butler, Adam Smith and others, who in the course of their moral enquiries analysed the passions of man, and, in contrast to the intellectualism of the dominant philosophical schools, sketched the beginnings of a dynamic psychology. Bain was thoroughly acquainted with their work and incorporated detailed summaries of it in his *Mental and Moral Science*. In one respect, and one respect only, does Bain seem to have been influenced by German philosophy. He accepted Kant's threefold division of the mind into cognitive (knowing), affective (feeling) and conative (willing) aspects, and he derived this not directly from German sources but from Sir William Hamilton, who was one of the first to introduce Kantian theories to British philosophers.

In his own day Bain naturally allied himself with the philosophical radicals, whose two leading figures Bentham and James Mill had died in 1832 and 1836 respectively, and whose mantle was being carried from the 1840's onwards by J. S. Mill. But cracks in the edifice of the utilitarian-empirical school were already appearing and the cracks half a century later were to lead to an almost complete collapse of the edifice. J. S. Mill perceived something of the limitations of the Benthamite school. "All the more subtle workings both of the mind upon itself and of external things upon the mind, escaped him", he wrote of Bentham.[1] In a striking chapter of his *Autobiography* Mill describes the emotional crisis he passed through during the years 1826-8 and his discovery of the romantic poets, which permanently modified his outlook on life. At the centre of this new movement in British thought was Coleridge (1772-1834). Bentham and Coleridge are called by Mill "the two great seminal minds of England in their age". "Every Englishman of the present day is by implication either a Benthamite or a Coleridgian", he states in his

---

[1] J. S. Mill 'Essay on Bentham', *London and Westminster Review*, Aug. 1838.

essay on Coleridge.[1] Whatever the influence of Coleridge on British thought in general in the second and third decades of the nineteenth century, it cannot be said that he influenced British psychology until much later, and even then the changes that took place in British psychology were due rather to direct contacts with German thought than to Coleridge. Nevertheless Coleridge is a figure of profound interest to British psychologists. Not only his account in *Biographia Literaria* (1817) of how he turned from the associationism of Hartley and of how he derived inspiration from German philosophers, but even more the jottings in his notebooks on psychological topics deserve to be better known. As a recent critic has pointed out, "he was naturally a psychologist, abnormally aware of and curious about the happenings in his own mind".[2] He rejected the atomism and the passivity of the older associationists. "What is a thought? What are its circumscriptions, what the interspaces between it and another? Where does it begin? Where end? Far more readily could we apply these questions to an ocean billow, or the drops of water which we may imagine as the component integers of the ocean. As by a billow we mean no more than a particular movement of the sea, so neither by a thought can we mean more than the mind thinking in some direction." [3] Coleridge indeed stressed the underlying unity and activity of the mind, and the role of feeling. "Association depends in a much greater degree on the recurrence of resembling states of feeling than on trains of ideas." [4] Above all Coleridge was interested in the active powers of imagination, "my shaping spirit of imagination", which he distinguished from the passive associative principle he terms "fancy", and in the products of the imagination, which he saw not merely in poetry, but in dreams, visions, and the supernatural. He penetrated deeply into his own mind and the minds of others. "Perhaps all my faulty actions", he notes, "have been the consequence of some dread or other on my mind; from fear of pain or shame, not from prospect of pleasure." "Could we emancipate ourselves from the be-dimming influence of customs, and the transforming witchcraft of early associations, we should see as numerous tribes of fetish-worshippers in the streets of London and Paris, as we hear of on the coasts of Africa." [5] But, however much influenced by his imagination, Coleridge was no mere mystic. He believed that the separation of

---

[1] J. S. Mill 'Essay on Coleridge', l.c., March 1840.
[2] I. A. Richards *Coleridge on Imagination*.
[3] Quoted by I. A. Richards l.c.      [4] Quoted by I. A. Richards l.c.
[5] Quoted from K. Coburn *Inquiring Spirit*.

psychology from physiology was fatal, depriving the former of all root and objective truth, and reducing the latter to a mere enumeration of facts and phenomena. He deplored "the gloomy and hopeless opinions concerning insanity" and "the exquisite superficiality of treatises on the passions".[1] And he coined the term 'psycho-somatic' to describe the unitary theory towards which he was working.

There was indeed more in Bain's background than Bain ever realized! But he realized enough to make his work a milestone in the development of British psychology.

## 2. Alexander Bain (1818–1903)

The name of Bain is indissolubly connected with Aberdeen. He was born in Aberdeen; he was educated at the University of Aberdeen; he held the chair of logic there; and after a life spent mainly in Aberdeen, he died in 1903 in the countryside just outside the city. Bain's father was a weaver of humble circumstances, a hard and severe man with narrow religious views. Of his eight children three died in infancy and apart from Alexander, the second child, the others were all failures in life. In his academic career Alexander got little sympathy and no assistance from his home. Leaving school at the age of eleven he worked for seven years, first as an errand boy and then as a weaver, educating himself by attending the Mechanics Institute in the evenings and by reading. He was able, persistent and thoughtful. He early became critical and sceptical of religion; he concentrated his studies on mathematics and physics, and made such good progress that he was awarded a small bursary at Marischal College, now one of the constituent colleges of the University of Aberdeen. In 1840 he graduated equal top in his year in an examination which embraced classics, mathematics, science and philosophy.

This success was followed by twenty years of academic frustration. Bain's agnosticism was a serious obstacle to academic appointment and he applied in vain for numerous chairs. He made a living by writing, casual teaching, and examining. For a time he lived in London. He became intimate with the philosophical radicals, particularly J. S. Mill and George Grote. For three years he held the post of assistant secretary to the Metropolitan Sanitary Commission under Chadwick, the distinguished pioneer of public health. And from 1851–4 he lectured to the young ladies of the newly founded Bedford College in London on mental and moral philosophy. Above all during three years of struggle he

---

[1] Quoted from K. Coburn l.c.

was composing his major psychological work, the two-volume treatise *The Senses and the Intellect* (1855) and *The Emotions and the Will* (1859), upon which his fame mainly rests.

At length in 1860 on the union of the two Aberdeen colleges a new chair of logic was founded, to which Bain was elected. The duties were strenuous and involved teaching English grammar, composition and rhetoric, as well as logic, moral and mental philosophy. Bain undoubtedly had to spread himself too widely during these years, and none of the numerous books he wrote on all the subjects he was responsible for teaching compare in importance with his earlier treatise on psychology. In 1880 he retired in a state of general exhaustion, which fortunately proved only temporary. He became a distinguished elder statesman in Aberdeen University circles, a protagonist of university reform, and was twice elected rector of the university, on the second occasion defeating Lord Randolph Churchill. He continued to write on psychological topics, mainly for *Mind*, the journal which he had founded in 1876 and of which he was proprietor until 1892. He was invited, but declined, to stand for parliament by the radicals of Sheffield. In 1892 he attended and gave a paper at the Second International Congress of Psychology held in London. During the last eight years of his life his health rapidly failed, and from 1895 he ceased to play a direct part in the intellectual life of the day.

As a psychologist Bain is in more ways than one a transitional figure: he stands halfway between the mental philosophy of the eighteenth and early nineteenth centuries and the scientific psychology of the twentieth; he moved at least part of the way from the older intellectualism and associationism to the activist and hormic psychologies which supplanted it. It is usual to classify Bain as an associationist and it is true that the law of association played a large part in Bain's psychology. He believed that complex thoughts, emotions and actions could be analysed into simpler components, which cohered as the result of associations formed in the course of experience. But a simple label such as 'associationism' far from adequately describes the complex and by no means wholly consistent structure of Bain's psychology. Bain was certainly not an extreme or uncompromising associationist. He did not regard association as the whole story. "No enumeration of these laws (of association) expresses everything that is properly included under intellect." [1] The most fundamental property of intellect is not association but discrimination, a point of view which seems to imply the existence of a prior indiscriminated

[1] *Mind*, 1887.

continuum, and which is commonly upheld by psychologists with 'Gestalt' proclivities. Nor did Bain believe that all compound mental structures are built up from experience: he allowed room for primitive or innate combinations. Muscular movements, for example, were generally grouped, and the organization of movements involved in walking was "an original endowment". Both the feelings and the will play a part in determining the passage of ideas in our minds, nor is motivation wholly confined to the pursuit of pleasure and the avoidance of pain. These are not the statements of a diehard associationist.

Bain's two-volume treatise is indeed a rich mine of ideas and observations which is still of more than antiquarian interest. Some forty years after the publication, Stout, the representative of a very different school of thought, wrote that "Bain's two great books appear even more valuable and suggestive the more they are studied".[1] At the time of their appearance J. S. Mill was almost lyrical. "The sceptre of psychology", he exclaimed, "has decidedly returned to this island. The scientific study of mind . . . is now nowhere prosecuted with so much vigour and success as in Great Britain." [2] If Bain's books are rarely read by psychologists today it is no doubt partly due to their great length. The two volumes together comprise 1330 pages. The only other British textbook of comparable length is the second edition (1870) of Spencer's *Principles of Psychology*. In this country the progress of psychology would seem to have gone hand in hand with a reduction in the size of textbooks! Bain, too, it must be admitted, is often ponderous and verbose. He lacks the vivacity of William James, whose great textbook, though as long as Bain's, is in consequence still recommended as "of lasting value" in the book lists. Nevertheless there is a massive strength about Bain's work. He may sometimes be ridiculous, particularly in his prosaic analyses of our emotional life. It was easy for James and McDougall to gibe at him. Yet he was often an acute observer, and a powerful reasoner. Many of his conclusions have been confirmed or re-stated by later psychologists. Consider for example his account of conscience. "Conscience is the imitation within ourselves of the government without us . . . it is moulded upon external authority as its type";[3] and the formative period is early childhood.

How did Bain go about his work? He described his method as "the natural history" method. He observed both himself and others in the

[1] G. F. Stout *Analytical Psychology*, 1896, Preface.
[2] J. S. Mill 'Bain's Psychology', *Edin. Rev.*, Oct. 1859, 'Discussions', vol. III.
[3] *The Emotions and the Will*, ch. 15.

ordinary circumstances of life. The observation of others he regarded as "much superior to the discrimination of individual self-consciousness"; so it is quite wrong to label his psychology 'introspectionist' even if he did hold that introspection is indispensable, since "it is only my own mind that I know directly". Bain's books are the generalized distillation of his observations and reflections. They contain many acute analyses, often, apart from terminology, of surprising modernity. Every now and again the observations are precise and detailed; of an infant, for example, suckling at the breast, or of the movements of twin lambs for twenty-four hours after their birth. Bain believed in detailed analysis; he saw the need to "resist the totalizing influences of the complex object", and no doubt if mental philosophy had not been by tradition a rather generalized discipline he could have presented the world with fine individual case studies.

Bain indeed in several respects was on the verge of much more revolutionary progress than he in fact made. He believed in principle in experimentation: "In science meditation and speculation can do much, but in practice a disposition to try experiments is of the greatest service." Bain himself, however, never experimented. He believed, too, in quantitative methods, and saw that "the inability to estimate quantity with precision is a serious defect in any department of knowledge", including psychology. Quantitative methods he regarded as not impossible of application in psychology, though he was not very sanguine about them. Graduations of mental states can be estimated, their durations and rapidity of succession measured, while vital and social statistics can supply data of psychological value. In all this no doubt he was following the Benthamites with whom he had been closely associated. But his psychology never became a quantitative one, and even in the later editions of *The Senses and the Intellect* he does not refer to Fechner's psychophysical methods. Bain never quite made the transition from the mental philosopher to the scientific psychologist. His analyses often remain unduly verbal, and he failed to realize that the greatest value of the natural history method lay in the field of comparative psychology, and particularly in the field of the abnormal. The case studies which enlivened James's *Principles of Psychology* are entirely absent from Bain, whose observations of generalized normal human beings lack the tang of life and the spice of individuality.

Perhaps Bain's principal claim to remembrance in the history of British psychology is that his is the first systematic physiological psychology based on a reasonably sound physiology. "The time has now come", wrote Bain, "when many of the striking discoveries of physiologists relative to the nervous system should find a recognized place in the science of mind." [1] So *The Senses and the Intellect* contains a long chapter on the brain and nervous system and detailed accounts of the sense organs; while the physical basis of all emotion is stressed in *The Emotions and the Will*. Bain's knowledge of physiology was by no means perfunctory or second-hand. While in London he had attended Sharpey's lectures on the brain and nervous system at University College. But he was handicapped by his imperfect knowledge of German, and of the work of the great German physiologists of his time. On the physiological side his account of the senses does not compare in lasting importance with the great researches of Helmholtz, whose *Physiological Optics* began to appear in 1856, only one year after the publication of Bain's book. It is in his insistence on the value of physiology to the psychologist that Bain is important rather than in his detailed contributions. Bain indeed went further than this, and it would not be a misrepresentation to say that for him all psychology was in principle physiological. "The mind is completely at the mercy of the bodily conditions; there is no trace of a separate, independent, self-supporting spiritual agent, rising above all the fluctuations of the corporal frame";[2] or as he put it elsewhere more succinctly, "no currents, no mind".[3] Thought no less than feeling and sensation has a physical basis. "For every act of memory, every exercise of bodily aptitude, every habit, recollection, train of ideas, there is a specific grouping, or co-ordination of sensations and movements, by virtue of specific growths in the cell junctions." [4] Mind and body are indeed but two aspects of a unitary sentient organism.

Bain's other really important contribution to psychology was his stress on movement and activity. He held strongly, and adduced many arguments to show, that the organism was active in its own right, not merely reactive. "Movement precedes sensation, and is at the outset independent of any stimulus from without." [5] "The nervous system may be compared to an organ with bellows constantly charged, and ready to be let off in any direction, according to the particular keys that are touched. The stimulus of our sensations and feelings, instead of supplying the inward power, merely determines the manner and place of the discharge." "There is a central fire that needs no stirring from without." [6]

---

[1] *The Senses and the Intellect*, Preface.        [2] *Mind and Body*.
[3] *The Senses and the Intellect*. By 'currents' of course Bain means 'nerve currents'.
[4] *Mind and Body*.        [5] *The Senses and the Intellect*.
[6] *The Senses and the Intellect*, 298.

This is a great advance over the careful hedonic calculus of the utilitarians. Bain realized that pleasure and pain for all their importance were far from an adequate explanation of motivation. Not only the drive of the organism's never-dying spontaneity, but habits, fixed ideas, and the upsurge of passions are all recognized by Bain.

Bain's psychology is indeed full of 'seminal ideas' which he failed to develop himself and the significance of which he probably did not fully recognize. He writes of "the grand process of trial and error" long before experimental work with animals made this a key concept in the psychology of learning. In a lecture at the Royal Institution in 1867 he first promulgated the distinction between 'molar' and 'molecular', which appealed to Herbert Spencer, who was in the audience. He recognized the importance of social influences. "The working of human beings collectively is wholly different from their individual actions; a new set of forces and influences are generated." [1] He not merely recognized the part played by emotional drives in human behaviour, he spoke of the malevolent principle – "the perennial fountain of malevolence in human beings" – and the role of inner conflict – "the inner life of every one is a sort of battleground or scene of incessant warfare". But Bain had read his Shakespeare and professed to have heen helped by him "to psychological results both intellectual and emotional"; so perhaps his tentative if imperfectly developed insight into the dynamics of behaviour is not altogether surprising. Finally, Bain was groping towards the applications of psychology. Psychology he regarded as "the largest chapter in the science of education"; but in this, of course, he was by no means original, for Herbert, in Germany, had paved the way towards a scientific pedagogy, and James Mill in his *Encyclopedia Britannica* article on education (1818) had also stressed the relevance of psychology. Bain, however, hints at wider applications. He saw that psychology might elucidate the circumstances which aid the acquisition of skills in industry, military training and sport. He early recognized the importance of individual diffcrences and their assessment. "The discriminating knowledge of individual character is a primary condition of much of the social improvement that the present age is panting for. The getting the right man into the right place is mainly a problem of the judgement of character." [2] Bain was clearly interested in the practical problems of the assessment of ability and character. In *The Emotions and the Will* he draws up a scheme for the diagnosis of character – almost an outline for compiling case histories, though he did not employ that term. In his

[1] *Education as a Science.*      [2] *Science of Character.*

*Science of Character* he makes some tentative suggestions for testing aptitudes. "A boy might be tested for business by being asked the prices of a great number of things that he may have himself bought, or seen others buy, in the course of his life, and the places where they were obtained. If this information is found to cling to him by nature, and before he has any special motive of application, he has a true bent for trade." It was a good many years before suggestions like this were taken seriously and attempts made to validate them empirically.

Just before his retirement Bain rendered one further service to British psychology, which would have entitled him to lasting remembrance, even if he had done nothing else. He was the prime mover in establishing the journal *Mind*, and he undertook the publishing risks. Bain gave an account of the negotiations, which led to the publication of *Mind* in January 1876, in his Memoir on his pupil, Croom Robertson, who became the journal's editor. *Mind* was the first journal devoted to the study of philosophy and normal psychology in Great Britain, and its influence on the development of both these disciplines was considerable. The early volumes were less chastely philosophical than they are today, and contained a good deal of psychological material, including surveys of contemporary German developments in psychology, articles by Wundt, Helmholtz and others, occasional experimental reports, and, of course, reviews of all the important books published in Europe or America. The British, henceforth, had no valid excuse for being psychologically or philosophically insular or ill-educated. This first and necessary step in the establishment of psychology as a profession – the establishment of a journal – we owe to Bain.

Even before Bain's death his influence waned under the impact of new movements which we shall be examining later. His psychology after the turn of the century was largely forgotten and disowned in the country of its origin. His true successors were Thorndike and the American learning theorists. Indeed Bain's psychology has not untruly been referred to as one of the main foundation stones of contemporary learning theories. So the wheel has turned, and Bain's work seems far more in tune with present-day notions than some of the psychologies which superseded it at the end of the nineteenth century. Perhaps British psychology would have advanced more rapidly and more surely if it had more closely followed Bain!

# CHAPTER II

# Physiological and Abnormal Psychology to 1875

## 1. Mesmerism and Phrenology

We can appreciate neither the essential sanity and integrity of Bain, nor some of the later developments of, and public reactions to, psychology in Great Britain without a knowledge of the wave of mystery-mongering and credulity which swept through the country in the 1840's and culminated in what has been termed "the mesmeric mania of 1851".[1] In the previous year two itinerant Americans who styled themselves 'professors' of a new art they termed 'electro-biology' toured the land, claiming that by means of a secret influence derived from a disc of silver and copper, held in the subject's hand and steadily gazed on, even the most determined will could be brought under subjection. According to J. H. Bennett, Professor of Clinical Medicine in the University of Edinburgh, "fashionable parties have been converted into scenes of experiments on the mental functions. Noblemen, members of the learned professions, and respectable citizens have been amusing themselves in private, whilst public discourses and exhibitions to an unusual extent have been got up for the entertainment of the public . . . the result of this excitement has been an increased degree of nervousness in many individuals. . . . Several instances are known to me where intelligent young men – students in this university – have, for a longer or shorter time, been incapacitated from following their ordinary occupations, and obliged from want of attention and mental power to absent themselves from their classes."[2] 'Electro-biology' was only one of several similar movements. In the same year (1850) a translation of Baron Reichenbach's *Researches on Magnetism in relation to Vital Force* gave an impetus to the belief in his so-called 'odylic force', a mysterious influence developed by certain crystals, magnets and the human body, and existing throughout the universe. Persons sensitive to the force saw luminous phenomena near the poles of magnets and the heads of gifted individuals. The 'odylic force' was supposed to show itself among other ways by the movement of suspended buttons, and, according to

[1] See J. H. Bennett's pamphlet of that title.    [2] J. H. Bennett op. cit.

Carpenter,[1] to whose work we shall be referring later, at this time "no inconsiderable portion of the British public was amusing itself with swinging buttons and rings from its finger ends".

Even more disturbing was the sudden incursion of modern spiritualism into Great Britain in 1852. Although spiritualistic manifestations go back to the dawn of human history, modern spiritualism was born in America in 1848, when Mr and Mrs Fox and their two daughters were troubled by unexplained knockings. Kate Fox believed that the cause of the sounds was intelligent and that communications were being received from the spirit of a murdered pedlar. Thus Kate Fox and her sister became the first modern mediums, professing to be able to communicate with lost relatives. The spiritualistic movement spread like an epidemic, and table-tapping and table-turning became yet another popular pastime. The movement reached England in 1852 when Mrs Hayden, a professional medium from Boston, arrived in the country. Three years later D. D. Home, who was born near Edinburgh in 1833 but brought up in America, returned to Great Britain. He gave numerous seances which were attended by many prominent people. Robert Browning's impression of Home in the poem "Sludge the Medium" is well known. Nearly twenty years later, however, he convinced Crookes of his genuineness, though Faraday in 1853 had devised a simple apparatus which conclusively demonstrated that the movements in table-turning were due to unconscious muscular action.[2] Nevertheless spiritualism continued to spread and soon became a religious movement with a newspaper of its own, published in Keighley, the *Yorkshire Spiritual Telegraph*. Serious scientific study of so-called 'psychic' phenomena had to wait until the establishment of the Society for Psychical Research in 1882. But the Cambridge 'Ghost Society' founded by E. W. Benson, who later became Archbishop of Canterbury, made a small beginning as early as 1851.

Many of the phenomena which so excited the public in the 1840's and 1850's were soon recognized to be 'hypnotic', a term which James Braid of Manchester coined in 1843 to describe the essential feature of animal magnetism or mesmerism, which was introduced into England in 1828 by an Irish gentleman, Richard Chevenix, F.R.S. Chevenix resided in Paris where he became acquainted with mesmerism. In 1828 he visited London and demonstrated mesmeric phenomena to several persons including John Elliotson, who became shortly after Professor

[1] W. B. Carpenter *Mental Physiology*, 286.
[2] M. Faraday, letter to *The Times*, 30 June 1853.

of the Principles and Practice of Physic at University College, London. Elliotson, who was a distinguished physician and a Fellow of the Royal Society, was at first not greatly interested, but in 1837, after the visit of a French mesmerist, he became a convert, and began to employ mesmerism during surgical operations at University College Hospital. This led to a conflict with the hospital authorities and he was forced to resign his position. The hypnotizing of patients about to undergo surgical operations might possibly have overcome professional opposition had not Sir James Simpson discovered the anaesthetic properties of chloroform in 1847. After this discovery hypnosis ceased to be of practical importance to the surgeon. In 1843 Elliotson began editing the *Zooist* "a journal of cerebral physiology and mesmerism", which appeared for thirteen years and had a considerable influence in the spreading of mesmeric ideas and encouraging mesmeric experiments. In spite of his scientific and medical attainments Elliotson was curiously emotional and uncritical. He believed that the strange mixture of mesmerism and phrenology which he propounded in the *Zooist* would "give new life to the world",[1] and he accepted the cardinal mesmeric faith in occult forces. It was left to Braid, who first investigated animal magnetism in 1841 as a complete sceptic, to dissociate the phenomena entirely from occult emanations and clairvoyance, and to attribute them to "a kind of derangement of the state of the cerebrospinal centres".[2] It was to distinguish his views from those of the mesmerists that Braid coined the terms 'hypnotism', 'hypnotize' and 'hypnotist'. Braid believed that hypnotism was an extremely valuable therapeutic agency in the cure of a large range of disorders. In spite of numerous case studies in Braid's books, and demonstrations by Braid himself, the medical profession was in general not persuaded of the value of hypnosis. It was not until 1892 that a committee of the British Medical Association reported favourably upon it after a searching inquiry.

Although Braid's approach to hypnotic phenomena was far more scientific than that of many contemporary enthusiasts we are not altogether surprised, as we read his books, that his findings were greeted with incredulity in scientific circles. Take, for instance, the alleged proof of the phrenological location of faculties in the brain through hypnotism. "I placed a cork endways", relates Braid, "over the organ of veneration, and bound it in that position by a bandage passing under the chin. I now hypnotized the patient and observed the effect which was precisely the same for some time as when no such appliance was

[1] *Zooist*, I. 135.        [2] See J. Braid *Neurypnology*, 1843.

used; after a minute and a half had elapsed an altered expression of the countenance took place, and a movement of the arms and hands, which later became clasped as in adoration, and the patient now arose from the seat and knelt down as if engaged in prayer." [1] Braid frequently produced what he termed "phreno-hypnotic phenomena" from the time of his first attempt in Liverpool in April 1842; he was satisfied that his subjects knew nothing of phrenology. The marriage between hypnotism and phrenology, which we have already noted in Elliotson's *Zooist,* was a conspicuous feature of the 1840's. It was the main note of H. G. Atkinson and Harriet Martineau's *Letters on the Law of Man's Nature and Development* (1851). It was indeed the way in which the dying system of phrenology attempted to keep itself alive. The principal phrenological tenet was that psychological traits, aptitudes and propensities were located in distinct brain locations, and could be quantitatively assessed by an inspection of the shape of the skull. Introduced into England by Gall's principal disciple Spurzheim, who settled in London in 1814 and who lectured assiduously in many parts of the country till his death in 1832, phrenology gained a considerable hold on scientific and medical opinion in the 1820's and 1830's. In 1832 there were no less than twenty-nine phrenological societies in Great Britain. In 1836 a representation, signed by numerous medical men and persons of standing in the academic world, including Richard Whately, the logician, then Archbishop of Dublin, was sent to Lord Glenelg, Secretary for the Colonies, urging that convicts shipped to New South Wales should be selected on phrenological principles by a qualified officer. "In the hands of enlightened governors, phrenology will be an engine of unlimited improving power in perfecting human institutions and bringing about universal good order, peace, prosperity and happiness", asserts the memorandum. These pretensions were accepted, however, neither by leading medical men, such as Sir Charles Bell and Sir Benjamin Brodie, nor by philosophers, such as Thomas Brown and Sir William Hamilton. Phrenology, with its arbitrary list of mental 'faculties', and its arbitrary location of them in the brain, was non-progressive. The suspicious claim was being made by George Combe (1788–1858) of Edinburgh, upon whom the mantle of Spurzheim fell after his death, that "it is only phrenologists who are capable of reporting . . . pathological cases calculated to establish the functions of different parts of the brain".[2] The most honest non-phrenologist was incapable of doing so. Meanwhile

---

[1] J. Braid *Neurypnology*, 99–100.
[2] G. Combe *A System of Phrenology*, 5th ed., vol. I. 101–3.

scientific research into brain functions was rendering phrenology increasingly untenable. The *Phrenological Journal* which had appeared for twenty-four years ceased publication in 1847. When Queen Victoria summoned George Combe to Buckingham Palace in 1850 to discuss the education of the royal children in the light of phrenological assessments she was slightly behind the times! By then the new and more scientific physiological psychology of Carpenter and his school was in the ascendant, and whatever good phrenology had done, by suggesting the importance of the physiological basis of mind and stimulating investigation into brain anatomy, had been absorbed into the accepted corpus of knowledge. The balanced and lucid writings of Carpenter no doubt did something to calm the rather hectic enthusiasms which culminated around 1851.

### 2. W. B. Carpenter (1813–1885) and Physiological Psychology

The leader of the new school of physiological psychology, W. B. Carpenter, the son of an eminent Unitarian minister, Dr Lant Carpenter, was brought up in Bristol, and received his training at the medical schools of Bristol, University College London, and Edinburgh. He never practised as a physician and early devoted himself to the study of physiology and zoology. He became Fullerian Professor of Physiology at the Royal Institution in 1845 and a Fellow of the Royal Society. From 1856 to 1879 he was Registrar of London University and had an important part to play in the development of scientific and medical education in London. The administrative business of the university was not so heavy, however, as to preclude the continuance of his scientific work. Particularly in the field of marine biology he made distinguished contributions to knowledge, and he played a large part in the dispatch of the famous 'Challenger' expedition which contributed so much to oceanography. In 1872 he was President of the British Association, and on several occasions Vice-President of the Royal Society. His physiological writings, *General and Comparative Physiology* (1838) and *Principles of Human Physiology* (1842), were not highly original, but they were remarkably able syntheses of the new knowledge of the day and written with beautiful lucidity. For many years they were almost without a rival in the London medical schools. The fourth edition (1852) of the *Human Physiology* was completely re-written and contained a large section on physiological psychology. This was later expanded into a separate book, *Principles of Mental Physiology* (1874), which contains the final and definitive statement of Carpenter's psychological views.

It deserves to rank as one of the classics of British psychology. Though more restricted in coverage, in readability and general interest it is almost the equal of James.

Carpenter's school was in no sense a formal organization, but a group of talented medical men who all saw the possibility and the importance of a physiological psychology. The senior member of the group was Sir Benjamin Brodie (1783–1862), court surgeon to George IV and William IV, Professor of Comparative Anatomy and Physiology at the Royal College of Surgeons, and President of the Royal Society from 1858 to 1861. He was one of the leading medical men of his day and first President of the General Medical Council. His *Psychological Enquiries* (1854) written in dialogue form were published anonymously. Sir Henry Holland (1788–1873) was the most sought after fashionable doctor of early Victorian London. He numbered six prime ministers among his patients, and was also physician to Queen Victoria. He was convinced of the importance of the psychological factor in disease – "Scarcely can we name a morbid affection of body in which some feeling or function of mind is not concurrently engaged" – and wrote a series of papers which were collected in book form as *Chapters on Mental Physiology* (1852). The most learned member of the group, apart from Carpenter, was probably T. Laycock (1812–76) who became Professor of the Practice of Physic at Edinburgh in 1855. He had studied medicine in London, Paris, and Göttingen, and was far more influenced by philosophical ideas than Carpenter or the others. He was the only one to attempt in *Mind and Brain* (1859) a systematic treatise. His relations with Carpenter were at times distinctly strained owing to a dispute over priority in propounding the concept of 'unconscious cerebration'. The two other principal members of the school were R. Dunn (1799–1877) of Guy's and St Thomas's Hospitals who wrote *An Essay on Physiological Psychology* (1858), and D. Noble (1810–85) of Manchester, who was converted by Carpenter from the phrenological views he expressed in *The Brain and its Physiology* (1846), and in his later book, *Mind and Brain* (1858), adhered closely to Carpenter's general standpoint. He was also the author of *Elements of Psychological Medicine* (1855).

In a rather different category, but linked to the group both by reason of his friendship with Carpenter, and because he also believed that psychology must be investigated in the manner of a natural science and in close conjunction with physiology, was J. D. Morell (1816–91). Morell was for most of his life a nonconformist inspector of schools. After a philosophical training in Glasgow he studied under Fichte in

Germany. He wrote an influential *Historical and Critical View of the Speculative Philosophy of Europe in the 19th Century* (1846) and then turned for a time to psychology. His *Elements of Psychology* (1853) was the first book published in England actually to be called 'Psychology'. He followed this up with *An Introduction of Mental Philosophy on the Inductive Method* (1862), in which he combines the teachings of Carpenter with German psychological and philosophical work of the early nineteenth century. Morell's psychology is hardly more than an outline sketch – an empirical psychology without the empirical data to fill it out – but it is a highly suggestive sketch, which shows a ripe appreciation of the complexity of intellectual and emotional development. The final result is in broad outline not unlike the psychology of Piaget; and like Piaget he saw the verification of his theories in the facts of child development. "It is only when the mind verges towards maturity that the powers of abstraction and generalization become fully developed . . . each particular season of life up to the full bloom of our maturity exhibits the culmination of some particular sphere of mental activity." [1]

Enough has been said to show that the move to establish a physiological psychology emanated not from a narrow clique of obscure eccentrics, but from a group comprising some of the most eminent medical and scientific figures of the day.

The principal conviction of the group was that medicine and biology, not metaphysics, were the proper foundation for psychology. "Medical practitioners", writes Brodie, "are necessarily led to contemplate the mind, not simply in the abstract, as is the case with the mere metaphysician, but in connexion with the physical structure with which it is associated." [2] Cerebral physiology was the only sound basis for "a mental science from which all mysticism will be as effectually excluded as it now is from physical science".[3] Not introspection, but detailed observation of the human species must provide the data. "What I have ventured to call 'the science of human nature' ", to quote Brodie again, "is a department of knowledge, in which I will not say we recognize no leading principles, but in which we recognize none that will supersede the necessity of minute observation and an extended individual experience." [4]

All the members of the school, too, stressed the mutual interactions

---

[1] J. D. Morell *Elements of Psychology.*
[2] Sir Benjamin Brodie *Psychological Enquiries*, 1st series, 216.
[3] Laycock *Mind and Brain*, x.      [4] Brodie op. cit., 240.

of mind and body. Mind influenced body both through emotional influences and through the power of attention. Holland's paper on "The Effects of Mental Attention on Bodily Organs" [1] discussed "the peculiar effects which depend on the act of concentrating the attention" and was influential in giving the doctrine of attention a central place in the school. It was this doctrine that enabled its members to escape from the dread bogey of 'materialism'. At the same time mental functioning depended intimately upon physiological conditions, in particular the conditions of the brain and nervous system – a view which all Carpenter's associates could support with abundant clinical evidence. Laycock went further and propounded a doctrine of temperamental differences "founded on the laws of embryology" (thus long anticipating Sheldon!).

The phrenological scheme of brain location was decisively rejected. The death-knell of phrenology was sounded by Carpenter's review of Noble's book on the brain in the *British and Foreign Medical Review* (1846). Carpenter replaced the spurious localization of the phrenologists by a broad theory of levels. He distinguished the spinal level of what, following Marshall Hall, he termed 'excito-motor reflexes'; the level of the sensory ganglia, or 'sensorium' (situated in and round the thalamus), where 'sensori-motor' reflexes had their location; and the level of the cerebrum, where intellectual and volitional actions had their origin. But Carpenter believed, and in this belief he was anticipated by Laycock, that cerebral actions might also be of a reflex or automatic nature. For these reflex actions of the cerebrum Carpenter coined the term 'ideo-motor'. The seat of consciousness was not the cerebrum but the sensorium, and this could be excited either peripherally from the sense organs, or centrally from the cerebrum. Carpenter used this scheme for explaining abnormal phenomena, hallucinations, dreams and automatisms. Within the cerebrum Carpenter advocated no precise localization of functions, but in the appendix of his *Mental Physiology* he indicated that he was prepared to accept Ferrier's investigations into the results of faradic stimulation of the cortex, an account of which was published after Carpenter had completed writing the main body of his book.

Very largely due to Carpenter's advocacy the doctrine of unconscious cerebral functioning became generally accepted. Lecky, the historian, writing in 1865, notes "it is now fully established that a multitude of events which are so completely forgotten that the statement of them calls up no reminiscences, may nevertheless be, so to speak, embedded

[1] Sir Henry Holland *Chapters on Mental Physiology*, ch. II.

in the memory, and may be reproduced with intense vividness under certain physical conditions . . . it is in connexion with these facts that we should view that reappearance of opinions, modes of thought, and emotions, belonging to a former stage of our intellectual history, which is often the result of the automatic action of the mind, when volition is altogether suspended".[1] We have Carpenter's explicit statement that he arrived at the idea of 'unconscious cerebration' in ignorance of Sir William Hamilton's exposition, which was, of course, directly derived from Leibniz. Laycock, who as early as 1837, after watching the mesmeric manipulation of two girls at University College Hospital, arrived at his theory of 'the reflex action of the brain', did not actually use the term 'unconscious'. But Carpenter ultimately conceded him priority so far as the idea was concerned.

The main value of the theory of the unconscious was that it made room for abnormal phenomena within the ambit of psychology. Carpenter indeed maintained "that scientific study of the various forms of abnormal mental activity . . . is probably the most promising field of psychological enquiry".[2] For Carpenter his theory led on to the study of hypnotism, sleep, dreaming, spiritualism, intoxication, delirium and insanity. Holland, too, pointed to the importance of these phenomena and the light that might be thrown on the nature of both mind in general and insanity in particular. "Dreaming – insanity in its many forms – intoxication from wine or narcotics – and the phenomena arising from cerebral disease, are the four great mines of mental discovery still open to us. . . . By the curtailment or suspension of certain functions, by the excess of others, and by the altered balance and connexion of all, a sort of analysis is obtained of the nature of mind, which its waking and healthy acts cannot equally afford, either to individual consciousness or the observation of others. . . . If it were an object to obtain a description of insanity which might apply to the greatest number of cases of such disorder, I believe this would be found in the conditions which most associate it with dreaming – viz. the loss, partial or complete, of power to distinguish between unreal images created within the sensorium and the actual perceptions drawn from external sources . . . and secondly, the alteration or suspension of that faculty of mind by which we arrange and associate the perceptions and thoughts successively coming before us." [3]

[1] W. E. H. Lecky *History of Rationalism*, vol. I. 101.
[2] W. B. Carpenter *Mental Psychology*, ix.
[3] Sir Henry Holland *Chapters on Mental Physiology*, 109 and 113.

Neither with Carpenter, however, nor with any of his associates was there any suggestion that human action was ultimately controlled from the unconscious. To reflex automatism and unconscious cerebration he opposed voluntary action. Though the will strictly can originate nothing, by its control of attention it can indirectly act on the effector mechanisms. Years before the Würzburg psychologists Carpenter noted the existence of determining tendencies.[1] "The will is constantly initiating movement or directing movement without any present consciousness of motives; this initiation or direction being, in fact, the expression of a remotely formed determination deliberately made and systematically acted on." Will, for Carpenter, was not a transcendental force but something formed gradually by habit and experience. There is indeed throughout Carpenter's psychology an emphasis on development through experience. He noted the importance of infancy, and spoke of "that very earliest stage of infant education, which lays the foundation for the intellectual and moral habits of the conscious life".[2] Carpenter noted too the slow development of perceptual powers in cases of congenital cataract cured by operation – several such operations having been carried out by J. B. Estlin of Bristol, and carefully observed by Carpenter himself.[3] There was, therefore, nothing mystical about Carpenter's theory of volition, which was based on many detailed observations, though his psychology, and even more that of Laycock, was in the last resort teleological. For Carpenter remained throughout his life a deeply religious man and he believed firmly in a divine ordering of the world.

Though present-day psychologists have largely forgotten Carpenter and his school, and few direct references to its members are to be found in contemporary works, both British and American psychology owe more than is commonly realized to Carpenter. James for one was considerably influenced by him, and even American textbooks published since the Second World War contain anecdotes and diagrams taken unconsciously and at second- or third-hand from Carpenter! In the words of T. H. Huxley, "Dr Carpenter contributed in no small degree to the foundation of a rational, that is to say, a physiological psychology."

### 3. Henry Maudsley (1835–1918) and the Pathology of Mind

Though Carpenter and the school of physiological psychologists recognized the importance of mental pathology, they were, with the

---

[1] W. B. Carpenter *Mental Physiology*, 418.
[2] op. cit., 353.        [3] op. cit., 180–1.

exception of Laycock, too much on the fringes of the subject to be able to integrate the physiology and pathology of mind. They lacked the intensive first-hand experience of mental disorder which comes from the study and treatment of the insane, while the asylum doctors tended very much to be a group on their own. The association between psychology and psychiatry, which in Germany goes back to the first decade of the nineteenth century with the publication of a medico-psychological journal by Reil and Hoffbauer, did not take place in this country till forty years later, when Forbes Winslow (1810–74) issued his *Journal of Psychological Medicine* (vol. I, 1848). This journal, which appeared until 1863 and then again in a new series from 1875–83, was a serious attempt to bring together psychology and mental pathology. It contained not only clinical reports and technical articles, but philosophical discussions, for example on Kant's psychology and Hamilton's lectures on metaphysics. It has the distinction of being the first nonpartisan psychological journal to be published in this country, uncommitted like the *Phrenological Journal* or the *Zooist* to particular causes, though it was, of course, essentially medical and designed primarily for medical practitioners.

To the asylum doctors themselves Forbes Winslow's journal no doubt seemed in parts somewhat remote from reality. They were already beginning to feel a consciousness of their professional identity. In 1841 an Association of Medical Officers of Asylums and Hospitals for the Insane was established. This became in 1865, on Henry Maudsley's suggestion, the Medico-Psychological Association (since 1926 the Royal Medico-Psychological Association). In 1855 they began to issue a journal, *The Asylum Journal of Mental Science*, which expressly excluded the "higher branches of metaphysical science". In 1858 its title was changed to the *Journal of Mental Science*, which title it still retains.[1] Not until Maudsley became editor in 1862 did the scope of the journal broaden out to include psychological and even some philsophical articles.

In the background of these new developments in psychological medicine were the great reforms in the treatment and care of the insane which culminated in Lord Shaftesbury's Lunacy Acts of 1842 and 1845. The conditions in the madhouses of the eighteenth century have often been described. "They comprise almost every species of cruelty, insult and neglect, to which helpless and friendless people can be exposed, when abandoned to the charge of ignorant, idle and ferocious

[1] [The journal was re-named *The British Journal of Psychiatry* in 1963.]

keepers, acting without conscience or control", stated the lunacy commissioners in 1847. The example of Pinel and Esquirol, who introduced more humane methods of treating the insane in France; the establishment of the Retreat by the Quakers in York (1792), which was the beginning of reform in this country; a series of commissions and Acts, all led up to Shaftesbury's legislation, and set the pattern of the nineteenth-century asylums. In 1839 Conolly, resident physician to Hanwell Asylum, the largest in England, discontinued every form of mechanical restraint, and by 1854 when the commissioners in lunacy circulated a questionnaire nearly all the county asylums had ceased to employ restraint. The visit of the American philanthropist and reformer, Dorothea Dix, to Scotland in 1855, led to rapid reforms in the Scottish asylums. The nineteenth-century asylum may seem in retrospect a grim institution, but we perhaps tend to underestimate the aims and ideals of the pioneers of that time. Both Conolly and his son-in-law, Maudsley, were believers in individual treatment. The value both of occupation and recreation was widely recognized. And when the Association of Medical Officers of Asylums was founded in 1841 one of its recommendations was "that by members of this association the terms 'lunatic' and 'lunatic asylum' be abandoned except for legal purposes and that the terms 'insane person' and 'hospital for the insane' be substituted".[1]

The standard work on mental disorders at this time was J. C. Prichard's (1786–1848) *Treatise on Insanity* (1835). Prichard, whose main claim to fame is as an ethnologist and anthropologist (he is really the founder of these sciences in this country), was a physician in Bristol with a special interest in nervous and mental diseases. He was deeply influenced by the new French school ¦of Pinel and Esquirol. He is chiefly remembered in psychiatry for his description of 'moral insanity'. "There is likewise", he writes, "a form of mental derangement in which the intellectual faculties appear to have sustained little or no injury, while the disorder is manifested principally or alone in the state of the feelings, temper or habits." [2] Prichard's approach is admirably scientific; he notes the importance of constitutional predisposition, of temperamental differences, of education and upbringing, and of social factors as well as of physical causes. "Care and anxiety, distress, grief and mental disturbances", he believes, "are by far the most productive causes of insanity." [3] But he suspects there is always some concomitant

---

[1] *Journal of Mental Science*, Historical sketch, 1879.
[2] J. C. Prichard *Treatise on Insanity*, 4.          [3] op. cit., 182.

inflammation of the brain. When Bucknill and Tuke published their *Manual of Psychological Medicine* (1858) there had been relatively few major advances in psychiatric theory. They were more sceptical than Prichard of the value of classifications of mental disorders; more sure that organic conditions were invariably responsible, but less certain that these related to the circulatory system or inflammation of the brain. They stressed the value of drug treatment, particularly of opium, "the sheet anchor of the alienist physician".[1] Yet the 'moral' factor and psycho-therapeutics were not ignored, and Tuke in his *Influence of the Mind upon the Body* (1872) provided much data to support the importance of psychological factors. However, his book, which is in effect a treatise on psychosomatics, lacks any adequate background of psychological theory and is not much more than a catalogue. Both J. C. Bucknill (1817–97) and D. H. Tuke (1827–95) were able men who consolidated, if they did not greatly advance, the psychiatry of their day. The limitations of the psychology with which they worked are well brought out in Bucknill's essays *The Psychology of Shakespeare* (1859).

Henry Maudsley (1835–1918) had a more forceful mind and a more penetrating psychological insight. He was widely read not only in contemporary British and German physiological psychology but in the older philosophical and psychological classics. He made the first serious attempt in this country to unite normal and abnormal psychology. As he puts it in the introduction to his principal work *The Physiology and Pathology of Mind* (1867) his aim was "to bring the manifold instructive instances presented by the unsound mind to bear upon the interpretation of the obscure problems of mental science". His success in this endeavour was perhaps limited. The two parts of his book, the physiology and the pathology, scarcely blend, and eventually Maudsley published them as separate books. But he did later use his knowledge of the abnormal in the interpretation of many of the phenomena of religious belief, and his *Natural Causes and Supernatural Seemings* (1886) is an important essay in religious psychology – because of Maudsley's agnostic standpoint, a precursor of Freud's *Future of an Illusion* rather than of James's *Varieties of Religious Experience*. For Maudsley had a trenchant, acid, sceptical mind. As a person he is described as "difficult" making "tart replies and scathing judgements".[2] Above all he hated shams, particularly "melodious words which express

[1] J. C. Bucknill and D. H. Tuke op. cit., 2nd ed., 515.
[2] Aubrey Lewis *Journal of Mental Science*, XCVII. 259–77.

no definite ideas but are pleasing discharges of vague and incontinent emotion".[1] He could write well; and he had breadth. He believed in the 'multi-discipline' approach to the science of mind. "Man as a whole is a larger affair than any single method of minute inquiry – be it chemical, physical, pathological, microscopical or psycho-physical – will ever unfold. . . . There is work enough for as many methods of the study of mind as are rationally based." [2] Not only child and comparative psychology, physiology and psychopathology must provide materials for a science of mind, but biography and history also cannot be neglected. Maudsley himself very early became interested in insanity. After a medical training at University College Hospital, London, he took a post at Wakefield Asylum. He became medical superintendent of Cheadle Royal, Manchester, at the early age of 23. From 1869 to 1879 he was Professor of Medical Jurisprudence at University College, London, and from 1862 to 1878 editor of *The Journal of Mental Science*.

In his psychology Maudsley totally rejected anything metaphysical or subjective. He regarded self-consciousness as "utterly incompetent to supply the facts for the building up of a truly inductive psychology";[3] for "consciousness gives no account of the essential material conditions which underlie every mental manifestation and determine the character of it".[4] His main emphasis was on the concept of organization. "The mind is not like a sheet of white paper which receives just what is written upon it, nor like a mirror which simply reflects more or less faithfully every object, but by it is connoted a plastic power ministering to a complex process of organization in which what is suitable to development is assimilated, what is unsuitable is rejected." [5] The organizing power works largely unconsciously, and builds up organized structures which Maudsley terms 'residua' (clearly something very like the 'schemata' of later writers). Maudsley accepts Carpenter's theory of levels – spinal, sensory, ideational. Volition is not an independent power, but a name for the higher co-ordinations, and "the different forms of insanity are not actual pathological entities, but different degrees or kinds of the degeneration of the mental organization".[6] The mind is not a single function, but "a federation of functions . . . bound together into the organic unity of the whole".[7] One of the most inter-

[1] Henry Maudsley *Natural Causes*, 134.
[2] Henry Maudsley *The New Psychology* quoted from A. Lewis l.c.
[3] Henry Maudsley *Physiology and Pathology of Mind*, 11.
[4] op. cit., 13.    [5] op. cit., 106.    [6] op. cit., 369.    [7] *Natural Causes*, 82.

esting features of Maudsley's psychology was his doctrine of imagination. Imagination was for him "the productive force in mind", and like the generative force in nature of which it is a portion "it is prolific, it is pleasant, it is prophetic".[1] The roots of imagination lie deep in the personality; in fact they touch "the multitudinous infraconscious vibrations of the organic nature". But Maudsley did not hypostatize the imagination in the way that Freud later hypostatized his libido. He regarded it only as a general term which included a great number and variety of particular imaginations.

There was according to Maudsley a gradual transition from the everyday observations of the imagination (as in dreams or religious beliefs) to the hallucinations and delusions of insanity. Fundamentally, however, insanity was dependent on physical, organic changes. "Every moral cause operates through the physical changes which it produces." [2] Maudsley had too penetrating an insight not to recognize the role of psychological and social factors. He was outspoken on the part played by sexual factors in the aetiology of mental disorder, and by social factors such as "the extreme passion for getting rich".[3] He was convinced from the study of family histories of the importance of hereditary predisposition, "the insane temperament". He was particularly interested in childhood insanity, and in his studies of childhood had noted the occurrence of sexual phenomena in infancy. Maudsley was critical of the asylums of his day; he wanted treatment to be undertaken early, and as far as possible in the community. Treatment should be "specially directed to the character and the circumstances of the individual case" [4] – a thing impossible in overgrown and overcrowded asylums. Not surprisingly, therefore, when in 1907 Sir Frederick Mott, the psychiatrist and a former pupil of Maudsley, after a visit to Kraepelin's clinic in Munich, urged the establishment of a university psychiatric hospital for early treatment and research, Maudsley offered £30,000 to the London County Council for the realization of the plan. The Maudsley Hospital in London was the result. The building was not completed until 1915 and not fully opened until 1923, some years after Maudsley's death. Through the distinguished work carried out there, both in psychiatry and psychology, Maudsley's name has become still more widely known than during his lifetime, though his reputation was even then international.

---

[1] *Natural Causes*, pt. I, ch. III.     [2] *Physiology and Pathology of Mind*, 227.
[3] op. cit., 232 ff.     [4] op. cit., 502.

## 4. Juvenile Delinquency

Juvenile delinquency is a problem that has exercised so many psychologists that some mention must be made of the first systematic attempts in this country to understand and to cope with juvenile offenders. In the person of Mary Carpenter (1807–77), the elder sister of W. B. Carpenter, a direct link between the study of delinquency and psychology was established from the very beginning. The growth of delinquency in the 1840's in the rapidly developing industrial towns began seriously to alarm the public. There was then no universal public system of education. As Mary Carpenter pointed out, "The only school provided in Great Britain by the State for her children is the gaol."[1] So-called 'ragged schools' sprang up in considerable numbers as a result of voluntary efforts for children excluded from Sunday and day schools because of their filthy condition. But the problem was already too large to be dealt with haphazardly. Between 11,000 and 12,000 juveniles were passing through the prisons of England and Wales annually. The 'ragged schools', generally giving only two evenings of instruction a week, dependent on uncertain voluntary teachers, and often indifferently run, could not cope. Hence the passing of the Reformatory Schools Act of 1854 and the Industrial Schools Acts (1856, Scotland; 1857, England and Wales), the former type of school dealing with offenders up to the age of 16, and the latter instituted for preventive treatment. These schools were the direct ancestors of the present Approved Schools, which were first so named in the Children and Young Persons Act of 1933.

Mary Carpenter had herself been concerned with juvenile problems in Bristol, and was responsible for the establishment of the Kingswood Reformatory in 1852. The publication of her two books, *Reformatory Schools* (1851) and *Juvenile Delinquency* (1853), had much to do with the legislation which followed in 1854. It is impossible to read them even today without admiring both her factual knowledge and her psychological understanding. She held that "to all who engage in education it is most important thoroughly to study the nature of the mind".[2] Reformation, she urged, must be based not on sentiment but on knowledge of the child. Her work with juveniles had made her realize that the uneducated juvenile was incapable of abstract reasoning, and unsuited, therefore, to the kind of bookish education prevalent at the time. She advocated practical occupations, group recreations, and the

---

[1] Mary Carpenter *Reformatory Schools*.          [2] ibid., 77.

organization of reform schools on the family principle. She was strongly opposed to punishments of a degrading or revengeful nature, and was satisfied of the ineffectiveness of corporal punishment. The work of reformation must be individual work, and its guiding principle must be love. Her views on the importance of maternal love in infant care were no doubt being expressed by her brother, W. B. Carpenter, when he wrote, "It is the experience of those who have endeavoured to awaken any dormant sense of good, which may not have been crushed out from the nature of the most hardened criminals by a life of brutal indulgence in every bad passion, that if they retain any recollection of a mother's love, this affords a loop-hole through which what remains of their better nature may be reached, though the wall of sullenness and obstinacy within which it was shut up may at first seem utterly impenetrable."[1]

It was more than two generations before psychologists began to catch up with the insight which Mary Carpenter expressed in the early 1850's. By then reformatory and industrial schools had become associated with punishment and repression, and it required more psychological pioneering to open the way to further reforms. These newer movements are still fresh in our minds, but the older work of Mary Carpenter and her recognition of the importance of psychology also deserves to be remembered.

[1] W. B. Carpenter *Mental Physiology*, 360.

CHAPTER III

# Evolution and Psychology

## 1. The Rise of the Evolutionary Theory

Bain's psychology, which we examined in the first chapter, was in its fundamentals pre-evolutionary. *The Emotions and the Will*, the second part of his two-volume textbook, was published in 1859, the same year as Darwin's *Origin of Species*, and only in its later editions did Bain's book take into account the implications of Darwin's theory. There was indeed nothing surprising about this. Although evolutionary speculations go back a long way in the history of philosophy, and although in the latter half of the eighteenth and the first half of the nineteenth centuries they became, with Erasmus Darwin in England and Lamarck in France, increasingly firmly supported by factual evidence, we have it on T. H. Huxley's authority that the joint paper of Darwin and Wallace which announced the modification of species by natural selection in 1858 took the biological world by surprise,[1] and that the special creation hypothesis seemed in that year more impregnable than ever. Not only were the theologians and their numerous camp-followers, the faithful, wholly opposed to evolution and wholly in favour of the arguments for the special creation of the world and of all its strange inhabitants, which had been so lucidly set forth by Paley, the Cambridge divine, in his *Natural Theology* (1802), but the leading scientists themselves with few exceptions were antagonistic. Even after the publication of Darwin's *Origin of Species* it required courage and independence to hold this "anti-scriptural and most debasing theory . . . standing in blasphemous contradiction to Biblical narrative and doctrine", as a reviewer of Huxley described it. Before Darwin had assembled the evidence only an individualist as radical as Herbert Spencer dared to speak openly in evolutionary terms. Lyell, the geologist, whatever he thought, tactfully held his peace in order not to arouse the prejudices of the powers that be. The author of *The Vestiges of the Natural History of Creation* (1844), a popular scientific work which advocated evolution and the transmutation of species, chose discreetly to remain anonymous. The book had a wide circulation and went through many editions. Prince Albert even

[1] T. H. Huxley *Collected Essays*, vol. I. 100.

32

ventured to read it aloud to the young Queen Victoria. Only much later, when the twelfth edition was published in 1884, after his death, was he identified as Robert Chambers, the publisher. In spite of its lack of scientific caution and its factual inaccuracies, and though its reception by reviewers, both scientific and lay, was almost wholly unfavourable, Darwin believed that the *Vestiges* did something to remove prejudices and prepare the ground for later developments. A much more important preparation, however, was the work of the geologists, in particular of Sir Charles Lyell.

For evolution needed time; and time was the gift of the geologists. Orthodox theology granted to the earth a past of only a few thousand years, and a future perhaps even shorter. This precluded evolution on temporal grounds alone. Hartley, for instance, in 1749 argued that owing to the shortness of time since the flood language and writing must necessarily have been given by direct miraculous agency.[1] The French naturalist, Buffon, in his *Époques de la Nature* (1778), presented the first reasoned chronology based on scientific grounds, giving the earth's age as about 75,000 years and the past duration of life as some 15,000 years. The geologists extended this estimate enormously, and Lyell in his *Principles of Geology* (1830–3) writes of "an indefinite lapse of ages". True, later the physicists led by Lord Kelvin cut this down to a meagre 20–40 million years, but more recent estimates based on radioactivity have extended this again to some 4000 million, which appears to satisfy the needs of contemporary biologists. The earth has at any rate lasted long enough for evolution to be within the bounds of the possible.

Nor, argued Lyell, has the earth's extended history been punctuated by the periodic catastrophes, in which the majority of geologists in 1830 believed, "a succession of destructions and creations" in which life was wiped off the globe and re-created. Lyell was a 'uniformitarian'; that is he held that the features of the earth's surface were due to the slow working of uniform causes during untold ages. "No causes whatever", he stated, "have from the earliest time to which we can look back to the present ever acted, but those that are now acting."[2] Lyell's importance in the history of the doctrine of evolution, however, goes further than his setting of the stage. He realized that his views led naturally on to "a principle of incessant change in the organic world", and he

---

[1] D. Hartley *Observations on Man*, Prop. 83.
[2] Sir Charles Lyell, letter to Murchison, quoted by Judd *The Coming of Evolution*, 59.

devoted the third part of his book to biology and the problem of species. He posed many of the questions to which Darwin was shortly to propound new answers. He was the direct and avowed inspiration of all the leaders of evolutionary thought, of Darwin, Wallace, Spencer and Huxley. Lyell's *Principles of Geology* was one of the few books that Darwin took with him on the voyage of the *Beagle*, and he dedicated the second edition of his journal of that voyage to Charles Lyell "as an acknowledgement that the chief part of whatever scientific merit this journal and the other works of the author may possess has been derived from studying the well-known, admirable *Principles of Geology*".

The science of geology was not, however, sole forerunner of evolutionary biology. It was but one of many contributory streams. Comparative anatomy, embryology, palaeontology, prehistoric archaeology, and other new disciplines, all sprouted vigorously during the early half of the nineteenth century. We tend to forget how recent was the discovery of much of the basic data of the biological sciences. The manlike apes, for example, were not scientifically described until the late eighteenth century, though the subject of travellers' tales from 1600 onwards. It was not till 1835 that Owen, later Director of the Natural History Museum, first examined the skeleton of an adult chimpanzee. The remains of the giant reptiles were revealed to an astonished world in the 1820's and 1830's, and in what has been called 'the heroic period' of palaeontology some kind of system was gradually imposed upon the extraordinary panorama of ancient life. In Germany the researches of von Baer between 1819 and 1837 "first clearly demonstrated the great events in a life history", and laid the foundations of embryology. His work was one of the formative influences upon Spencer, and when related to the discoveries of the palaeontologists led to the formulation of the law of recapitulation, which saw in the development of the individual a re-enactment of the main stages in the development of the species. Finally man himself was shown to have an 'antediluvian' pre-history first by the discovery in 1846 of flint instruments at Abbeville in France which were unquestionably of great antiquity, and then by the discovery in 1857 of the Neanderthal skull. The theory of evolution alone could make sense of these numerous discoveries.

## 2. Charles Darwin (1809–1882)

Charles Darwin's reputation as a biologist is so great, and his influence on many branches of science has been so extensive, that it is easy to forget that he was in his own right a considerable psychologist. The Copernican revolution which he effected in the biological sciences was bound to have profound consequences for psychology. Darwin realized that this must be so. "In the future I see open fields for far more important researches. Psychology will be securely based on the foundations already well laid by Mr Herbert Spencer, that of the necessary acquirement of each mental power and capacity by gradation. Much light will be thrown on the origin of man and his history."[1] Less than nine years after the publication of *The Origin of Species* in 1859 Darwin himself began to till these fields. He notes in his diary for 4 February 1868, "began work on man". This work led to two books, first, *The Descent of Man* (1871), which contained a long comparative study of the mental powers of man and the lower animals, and, in connexion with the theory of sexual selection, an account of the courtship behaviour of animals and of psychological differences between the sexes in both animals and men; and second, *The Expressions of the Emotions in Man and Animals* (1872), a wholly psychological work which remains even today an outstanding study on the psychology of emotion. In addition to these two major contributions to psychology Darwin wrote on animal instinct, and carried out some admirable observations on the development of his own children, one of the earliest accurate studies of infant behaviour ever made.

There was little in Darwin's early life to suggest his future eminence either as a biologist or as a psychologist. His ancestry was indeed distinguished. His paternal grandfather, Dr Erasmus Darwin (1731–1802), who has already been mentioned for his evolutionary theories along Lamarckian lines, was a scientist, poet and physician of some note in his day. His maternal grandfather Josiah Wedgwood (1730–95) was famous as a potter. But Charles Darwin showed little aptitude at the grammar school in Shrewsbury, where his father had a medical practice. "The school as a means of eduction to me was simply a blank" he wrote later in his *Autobiography*, and his father complained that "he cared for nothing but shooting, dogs and rat-catching".[2] Sent to Edinburgh University as a medical student he found the lectures "intolerably dull" and after two years withdrew. His residence at Christ's College, Cambridge, where it was proposed that he should study for the ministry, was hardly more successful. Nevertheless he got a degree, made the acquaintance of some able Cambridge men, who saw something out of the ordinary about him, trained his powers of observation through assiduous beetle collecting, and read some books which permanently influenced him, in particular the *Personal Narrative* of von Humboldt,

---

[1] *The Origin of Species*, 668.     [2] *Autobiography*, 7.

the great German naturalist and traveller, and Sir J. Herschel's *Intro-duction to the Study of Natural Philosophy*. These works "stirred up in me", he relates, "a burning zeal to add even the most humble contribu-tion to the noble structure of natural science".[1] On leaving Cambridge he was lucky enough to get a job as naturalist (unpaid) on H.M.S. *Beagle*, a small survey ship of 235 tons, that was about to start on a voyage round the world. The voyage began in 1831 and lasted five years. Darwin describes it as "by far the most important event in my life. . . . I have always felt that I owe to the voyage the first real training or education of my mind".[2] On his return to England he settled at Down in Kent, and, thanks to private means, was able to devote himself wholly to scientific work. Few scientific lives have been more assiduous or more brilliantly productive.

The conclusions set forth in the most famous of all Darwin's works, *The Origin of Species*, had been reached by him many years before their publication, and it is characteristic of Darwin's scientific caution that he should have devoted so long to their patient verification. He jotted down some short notes on the main theme in 1842, and a longer sketch in 1844. But it was not until 1858 when the naturalist and collector, A. R. Wallace, then in the East Indies, sent him a paper em-bodying almost identical ideas, that he made his views known. At a meeting of the Linnaean Society on 1 July 1858 papers by both Darwin and Wallace on the theory of evolution by means of natural selection were read. Darwin realized that he could no longer withold a fuller statement, and *The Origin of Species* was published on 24 November 1859. The importance of the book was grasped immediately both by the scientific world and by the public. The first edition was sold out on the day of publication and a second edition appeared on 7 January 1860.

The book was indeed epoch-making, for it brought the whole king-dom of life, and by implication, of course, Man himself, within the province of natural science. If the central question of the work, the origin of species, is a biological problem of no direct concern to the psychologist, the explanatory concepts it employed and its point of view are as pertinent to psychology as to biology; necessarily so, for from now on psychology becomes basically a biological science. Mind has evolved like every other piece of organic equipment; it is subject to the laws of variation and inheritance; it is one means by which organisms adapt themselves in the struggle for existence and reveal their fitness to survive. The process of natural selection, nature's way of sifting the

[1] *Autobiography*, 30.　　　　　　　　　[2] ibid., 36.

fit from the unfit, operates upon mental no less than upon physical qualities. The wonderful intricacies of instinctive behaviour, the development of the higher qualities of intelligence, animal and human, and the survival of apparently arbitrary rudiments and vestiges of previously serviceable behaviour find for the first time a plausible explanation in Darwin's theory.

In details the theory has been challenged and modified by subsequent investigators. Darwin may have exaggerated the element of struggle in the biological world[1] – an idea he borrowed from Malthus' *Essay on Population* (1798) – and the formative influences of "the war of nature, famine and death".[2] He knew little of the complexities of genetics, a science unborn at the time he wrote. Yet in its broad outlines the Darwinian theory of evolution seems more widely accepted today and more firmly founded than ever. Only three years after *The Origin of Species* was published the discovery of Archaeopteryx provided a remarkable confirmation of Darwin's main argument. Described by Sir Gavin de Beer of the Natural History Museum as "probably the most precious, the most beautiful, and the most interesting fossil hitherto discovered in the world, . . . it is a mosaic in which some characters are perfectly reptilian and others no less perfectly avian".[3] Evidence of this sort has accumulated in vast quantities during the past hundred years, and the fact of evolution has become incontestable.

The application of the evolutionary theory to the human species and the human mind followed soon and inevitably. In 1863 T. H. Huxley took up the "burning question of the position of the human species in zoological classification" in his lectures on *Man's Place in Nature*. He rebutted the arguments put forward by Richard Owen the anatomist so recently as 1857 for the separation of the human genus from all other mammals, and maintained that Linnaeus in the eighteenth century was right in grouping man, apes and monkeys in a common order, Primates. "If man had not been his own classifier", wrote Darwin a few years later, "he would never have thought of founding a separate order for his own reception." [4] Not all those who upheld evolution in general, however, were prepared to go as far as Huxley. Wallace believed that "a superior intelligence has guided the development of man in a definite direction and for a special purpose";[5] and Lyell in the last of his great

---

[1] See G. G. Simpson *The Meaning of Evolution.*
[2] *The Origin of Species*, 669.
[3] *British Association*, 1954, Pres. address, Section D.
[4] *The Descent of Man*, 231.
[5] A. R. Wallace *Contributions to the Theory of Natural Selection* (1870).

works argued that "man must form a kingdom by himself if once we permit his moral and intellectual endowments to have their due weight in classification".[1] Darwin with courageous unconcern for the consequences went ahead, and in *The Descent of Man* (1871) presented evidence to suggest that "man is the co-descendant with other mammals of some unknown and lower form",[2] and in particular "that the mental faculties of man and the lower animals do not differ in kind, though immensely in degree". Thus Darwin, though anticipated in a somewhat philosophical way by Spencer, became the founder of comparative psychology.

In this new field Darwin had little to guide him, and had largely to create his own methodology. He had no taste for the introspective analysis of the philosophical psychologists. His methods were objective and factual. He realized that even so there were unusual difficulties in the way, and his short methodological discussion in the introduction to *The Expression of the Emotions* is of particular interest. "The study of expression is difficult," he writes, "owing to the movements being often extremely slight, and of a fleeting nature. A difference may be clearly perceived, and yet it may be impossible, at least I have found it so, to state in what the difference consists. When we witness any deep emotion, our sympathy is so strongly excited, that close observation is forgotten or rendered almost impossible; of which fact I have had many curious proofs. Our imagination is another and still more serious source of error: for if from the nature of the circumstances we expect to see any expression, we readily imagine its presence." [3] His data he collected from many sources: he observed infants and animals; he obtained reports upon the insane; he sent 'printed queries' to missionaries and others in contact with primitive peoples with the instruction: "General remarks on expression are of comparatively little value; and memory is so deceptive that I earnestly beg it may not be trusted. A definite description of the countenance under any emotion or frame of mind, with a statement of the circumstances under which it occurred, would possess much value."[4] Darwin, however, in spite of his considerable reflection on methodological problems, could not escape from the terminology and the frames of reference of his time. Even the dangers he saw, he did not wholly avoid. In describing animal behaviour he slipped readily into anthropomorphism, though he admitted "the impossibility of judging

---

[1] Sir Charles Lyell *Antiquity of Man*, (1863) 495.
[2] *The Descent of Man*, 226.
[3] *The Expression of the Emotions*, 14.       [4] ibid., 18.

what passes through the mind of an animal".[1] Yet "when a dog sees another dog at a distance, it is often clear that he perceives that it is a dog in the abstract": "it is certain that associated animals have a feeling of love for each other" and "dogs possess something very. like a conscience". Nor is Darwin anything like careful enough about the anecdotes he regards as reliable evidence. There is, therefore, a good deal in his writing on comparative psychology that will not bear rigorous examination.

Nevertheless Darwin was a suberb observer. His *Biographical Sketch of an Infant*,[2] written down in diary form in 1840, is a masterpiece of concise, accurate and objective reporting. *The Expression of the Emotions* is full of acute observations, many of them made in the ordinary circumstances of everyday life. Moreover both with his own children and with animals Darwin frequently had recourse to simple experiments to check his theories and his observations. For example he took stuffed snakes, and a live snake in a paper bag, to the zoo to experiment on the monkeys.[3] Or take this incident. Darwin was enquiring into the cause of the obliquity of the eyebrows under suffering. By chance "on a very bright day with the sun behind me I met whilst on horseback a girl whose eyebrows, as she looked up at me, became extremely oblique, with the proper furrows on her forehead. . . . On my return home I made three of my children, without giving them any clue to my object, look as long and as attentively as they could, at the summit of a tall tree standing against an extremely bright sky." The same eyebrow movement was observed, and Darwin was able to arrive at an explanation of the expression in which he was interested.[4] It is because it is so full of acute and detailed observations that Darwin's work on emotions is still so well worth perusal. Whether he is dealing with gestures like the shrugging of the shoulders or the wagging of the head in denial; unintentional actions like trembling, the erection of hair, or blushing; or the major emotional expressions of anxiety, anger and joy, Darwin always presents a wealth of factual evidence and ingenious, sometimes too ingenious, explanations. But his explanations, even if not always convincing, are a large advance upon those of his predecessors. Sir Charles Bell in his *Anatomy and Philosophy of Expression* (1806, 3rd ed. 1844), a work to which Darwin was much indebted, could only explain emotional expression as due to 'special provision'; and for Dr Burgess who wrote in 1839 on *The Physiology or Mechanism of Blushing*,

[1] *The Descent of Man*, 126.  [2] *Mind*, II, 1877.
[3] *The Descent of Man*, 109.  [4] *The Expression of the Emotions*, 192–7.

blushing was designed by the creator in order that the soul might display the emotions of the moral feelings. Darwin in the light of his general theory was often able to account for emotional expressions as the vestiges of once serviceable modes of behaviour, and give a rational explanation of much that was previously obscure.

The outcome of Darwin's investigations in comparative psychology was a considerable body of evidence to support the psychological kinship between man and animals. On the one hand human behaviour often showed evidence of its animal ancestry; on the other animal behaviour showed signs of incipient reasoning and intelligence. There was a difference in degree, but not of kind. Even man's use of language and his moral sense did not constitute impossible barriers between man and the animal kingdom. For language "owes its origin to the imitation and modification of natural sounds",[1] and the social and parental instincts constitute the matrix of the moral sense. Man could no longer be regarded as a mainly rational creature carefully weighing up the consequences before he acted; he often acted impulsively "from instinct or long habit, as does probably a bee or ant, when it blindly follows its instincts".[2]

Darwin's influence on psychology extended, indeed, far beyond the special field of comparative psychology. He introduced a new way of looking at mind, as something functional and dynamic, as something deeply involved in the struggle for existence and the process of adaptation to the environment. He pointed to the significance of individual differences and inherited variations, and thus opened the way for the development of differential psychology. He scotched finally the theory that 'savages' were degenerate backsliders from civilization, which the versatile 8th Duke of Argyll had maintained in his book *Primeval Man* as recently as 1869, and inaugurated a new era in the study of primitive peoples. A good many of the developments in psychology during the following half-century sprang directly from Darwin's work.

### 3. Herbert Spencer (1820–1903)

In retrospect Darwin now seems so much more considerable a figure than Spencer that he is naturally given priority of treatment. Yet as an evolutionist Spencer was in fact first in the field. In an article on *The Development Hypothesis* in 1852 he advocated development by successive modifications rather than special creation, and put forward a Lamarck-

---

[1] *The Descent of Man*, 132.          [2] ibid., 184.

ian explanation in terms of the inheritance of acquired characters. In his *Principles of Psychology* (1st ed. 1855) he maintained that "mind can be understood only by showing how mind is evolved".[1] For Spencer, as for Darwin, psychology was only a secondary field of interest, but Spencer's work in psychology was far more systematic than Darwin's. It was a serious attempt to found psychology from first principles upon an evolutionary basis, and to conceive mind as being functionally involved in the business of living, which Spencer defined as "the continuous adjustment of internal relations to external relations".[2] Before Darwin, he linked psychology firmly to biology, though he did not deny that "under its subjective aspect Psychology is a totally unique science".[3] Spencer was indeed a man of striking independence and originality of mind. He sprang from the new urban middle class of the industrial towns. Both his father and his grandfather were schoolmasters in Derby. His father was a strange character with an attitude of repugnance to all authority and orthodoxy, carried to such an extreme that he even refused to take off his hat to anyone. His teaching method was that of self-help in all directions. In this atmosphere Herbert Spencer grew up prepared to scrap the past and to work out something new from basic scientific principles. Unencumbered by tradition he was able to reflect the growing points of his own age.

His limitations, however, are conspicuous. Only twenty years after his death McDougall could write of "the forlorn figure of Herbert Spencer".[4] Few persons today take Spencer seriously as a philosopher; few students of psychology consult his *Principles of Psychology*. The huge two-volume revised edition (1870–2) is to modern taste hopelessly indigestible. Spencer's pretentious system-building has quite gone out of fashion. His vast scheme of synthetic philosophy was founded on the scientific ideas current in the 1840's and 1850's, on von Baer's developmental law, Lyell's *Principles of Geology*, and Mill's *Logic*. The superstructure was architectonic, and an expression of Spencer's obsessional love of system. "It has been a source of frequent elation to see each division, and each part of a division, working out into a congruity with the rest – to see each component fitting into its place, and helping to make a harmonious whole." [5] Such system building is, of course, not science. Spencer was not a scientist, but a man obsessed by certain

---

[1] *Principles of Psychology*, 2nd ed., 129.　　　[2] *Principles of Biology*, 30.
[3] *Principles of Psychology*, 56.
[4] William McDougall *Outline of Psychology*, 29.
[5] *Autobiography*, II. 450.

scientific ideas. These ideas developed gradually in his mind. "It has never been my way to set before myself a problem and puzzle out an answer. The conclusions at which I have from time to time arrived have not been arrived at as solutions of questions raised; but have been arrived at unawares – each as the ultimate outcome of a body of thoughts which slowly grew from a germ . . . thus, little by little, in unobtrusive ways, without conscious intention or appreciable effort, there would grow up a coherent and organized theory." [1] What brought Spencer's constructive processes to rest – to a state of equilibration, as he would have termed it – was usually a verbal formula. His works are a succession of magnificent abstract verbal formulae, such as his well-known definition of evolution as "a change from an indefinite, incoherent homogeneity, to a definite, coherent, heterogeneity, accompanying the dissipation of motion and the integration of matter".[2] What these formulae mean is sometimes a puzzle. "An afferent nerve communicates a wave of isomeric transformation to the vesicle at its inner end." "Ideas arise when compound co-ordination passes into doubly compound co-ordination." But they appeared to satisfy that streak in Spencer which he described as "a dash of the artist".

Spencer's psychology was no more scientific than the rest of his work. It was based neither on research nor on reading. "The data for the subjective part, which was dealt with after a manner unlike that commonly adopted, were lying ready internally: and the views taken of the objective part were so little alien to those of preceding psychologists, that no extensive study of their writings was necessary." [3] Spencer had shown no early curiosity in psychology. His education was an incomplete one, and after formal instruction had closed at the age of sixteen, he spent ten years as a civil engineer on the railways, and some years as a journalist. His interest was turned to philosophy and psychology by reading G. H. Lewes' *Biographical History of Philosophy* (1845–6). But he could not read the philosophers themselves, and put aside Plato and Kant with disgust. So when he came to write his own book on Psychology in 1855 it was almost completely lacking in historic roots. The first edition was written largely outdoors in Wales. "The weather being fine my writing in Wales was done almost wholly out of doors. Furnished with a pocket inkstand I daily started off, manuscript in hand, for a ramble among the hills or along the banks of the Llugwy; and from time to time finding a convenient place, lay down and wrote a paragraph

[1] *Autobiography*, I. 399–400.   [2] *First Principles*, 138.
[3] *Autobiography*, II. 171.

or two." [1] The largely reconstructed second edition (1870–2) was dictated to an amanuensis while reclining in a boat on the Serpentine.[2] Yet in spite of this apparently casual mode of composition Spencer's psychology does not lack importance. Its value lies in its key ideas, which were strikingly original and novel, not in their detailed exemplification. When these key ideas were absorbed into the general body of psychological doctrine, the work that gave them birth had fulfilled its usefulness. But it is well that we should remember that when they first appeared they were highly revolutionary. As Spencer relates in the preface to the second edition of the *Principles of Psychology*: "When in 1855 the first edition was issued it had to encounter a public opinion almost universally adverse. The doctrine of evolution everywhere implied in it was at the time ridiculed in the world at large, and frowned upon even in the scientific world."

There is no need to follow the Spencerian scheme – data, inductions, analysis, synthesis, corollaries – into which his psychology, like the other parts of his synthetic philosophy, was poured. Spencer accepted the associative principle which was current at the time he wrote. He analysed the components of mind into 'feelings' and 'relations between feelings'. Feelings as we experience them, however, are in fact composite, and made up of more elementary 'mental shocks' which correspond to unitary 'nervous shocks'. The development of intelligence proceeds by the establishment of the relations of likeness and unlikeness. "A feeling cannot form an element of mind at all except it is associated with predecessors more or less the same in nature." [3] Thus assimilation or classification becomes the principal psychological operation. "Every perception of an external object implies either the identification of it as a particular thing, or the ranging of it with certain kindred things",[4] and "the highest reasoning is one with all the lower forms of human thoughts, and one with instinct and reflex action . . . the universal process of intelligence is the assimilation of impressions . . . differences [are] consequent on the increasing complexity of the impressions assimilated." [5] Fundamentally Spencer believed that this is nothing but association by similarity. Spencer's main addition to the associative scheme was his theory that the concatenations of experience are not necessarily effected in the life-time of the individual, but may be inherited from his forebears. Thus space perception may be *a priori* for

[1] *Autobiography*, I. 465.   [2] *Autobiography*, II. 201.
[3] *Principles of Psychology*, 115.
[4] op. cit., 314.   [5] op. cit., 381.

the individual, though *a posteriori* for the entire series of individuals.[1]

Perhaps the two most valuable features of Spencer's psychology were his description of developmental levels, and his application of dynamic concepts to the study of mind. Successive processes of differentiation and integration give rise to a series of distinguishable levels, commencing with the reflex level, and passing through instinct, "which may be described as compound reflex action", and memory (which is Spencer's term for learning) to the highest level, reason. There is, however, no complete break between these levels, and fundamentally the *modus operandi* is identical. Spencer also allowed for regression. "Under a lowered condition of the nervous system failure is first manifested in the highest intellectual co-ordinations, and in the highest emotional co-ordinations. Speaking generally each step in mental evolution results in a faculty by which the simpler pre-existing faculties have their respective actions so combined that each aids in regulating or controlling the others, and the actions of all are harmonized." [2] Psychologically the mark of evolution is not merely greater heterogeneity, but the development of representativeness. The 'presentative' passes by successive stages to the 'presentative-representative', the 'representative', and finally the 're-representative' – a beautiful example of Spencer's verbal formularies! All he means is that the 'correspondences' of mind, as he terms them, extend further afield in space and time and increase in abstractness. Spencer expected that as a result of this increase in representativeness the aesthetic impulse would probably play an increasing part in human life; and for this, too, he had a formula: "the highest aesthetic feeling is one having the greatest volume, produced by due exercise of the greatest number of powers without undue exercise of any".[3] And so we reach the topmost level of conceivable perfection!

The whole of Spencer's synthetic philosophy is essentially a dynamic philosophy. The object of philosophy and of the sciences is to explain change within the realm of the knowable, which Spencer distinguished from the ultimately unknowable. Every object no less than the aggregate of all objects undergoes constant alterations of state; the human mind and human societies are no exception. They are part of the dynamic system of the world and obey the same dynamic laws as the rest of the world. All dynamic processes show a tendency towards equilibriation, or a balancing of forces; in the case of living organisms this means a balancing of internal relations with external relations, in other

---

[1] *Principles of Psychology*, 332.     [2] *Autobiography*, I. 487.
[3] *Principles of Psychology*, 539.

words an adjustment or adaptation of the organism to the environment. "All the processes by which organisms are fitted to their environments must be equilibriations of one kind or another."[1] Psychologically these equilibriations take place on the symbolic plane and are termed 'correspondences': as we have seen, intelligence for Spencer is "an adjustment of inner to outer relations that gradually extends in Space and Time, that becomes increasingly special and complex, and that has its elements ever more precisely co-ordinated and more completely integrated".[2] From the primary dynamic laws, which were simply the laws of matter, motion and force, Spencer derived a number of principles which he applied to psychology. The idea of system pertained to mental as well as to physical forces; "every thought involves a whole system of thoughts, and ceases to exist if severed from its various correlatives. As we cannot isolate a single organ of a living body, and deal with it as though it had a life independent of the rest; so from the organized structure of our cognitions, we cannot cut one, and proceed as though it had survived the separation".[3] The law of least effort applies to mind as well as to matter, and "a volition is an incipient discharge along a line which previous experiences have rendered a line of least resistance".[4] The conflict of forces not in equilibrium gives rise to rhythm and oscillation, and these are observable in a variety of mental states. "The current of mental energy that shows itself in such modes of bodily action as dancing, poetry and music is not continuous, but falls into a succession of pulses."[5] The laws of the conservation, transformation and equivalence of forces apply to mental forces: indeed no idea of feeling arises save as the result of some physical force,[6] though how the metamorphosis from physical or mental takes place is a mystery which it is impossible to fathom. These dynamic concepts which Spencer introduced into psychology have by no means even yet outlived their usefulness.

For Spencer psychology was only a prolegomenon to other studies. His earliest and his most enduring interest was in 'the politico–ethical question'[7] – what are the duties of the state, and what are not its duties? Towards the end of his life, handicapped and at times quite incapacitated by a psychosomatic disability, he skipped large portions of his projected work and hastened to complete *The Principles of Ethics* (1892–3). With this work we shall not be concerned. But his *Principles*

---

[1] *Principles of Biology*, 168.   [2] *Principles of Psychology*, 126.
[3] *First Principles*, 39.   [4] op. cit., 79.   [5] *First Principles*, 86.
[6] op. cit., 71.   [7] *Autobiography*, II. 273.

*of Sociology* (3 vols. 1876–96) contains a long section on the psychology and beliefs of primitive man; and his earlier essays on *Education: Intellectual, Moral and Physical* (1861) are of some importance in the history of educational thought. A consideration of these we leave to later chapters.

### 4. George Henry Lewes (1817–1878)

Among the almost forgotten figures of nineteenth-century British psychology few are more interesting, or better repay study, than George Henry Lewes. From time to time, Lewes is acclaimed and re-discovered. Sully spoke highly of his stimulating qualities; Lloyd Morgan judged him to be far ahead of his time. In Warren's dry *History of Association Psychology* Lewes is the one psychologist who appears to arouse enthusiasm. "Lewes", writes Warren, "deserves far more study than has been accorded him by recent writers; and especially does he deserve the attention of genetic psychologists." [1] More recently Hayek, whose theoretical views are in some respects strikingly like those of Lewes, notes that Lewes' writings "never seem to have received the attention which they deserve". [2] This is indeed true. In the standard general histories of psychology Lewes gets not even a mention except from Brett. He has passed almost completely into oblivion. [3] Yet he had a mind of great subtlety, originality, and erudition. His fluency in German and his profound knowledge of German physiological research gave him a great advantage over Bain; and his wide philosophical reading made him far less naïve than Spencer; but he has not been accorded the status of either Bain or Spencer in the history of British psychology. In part this is perhaps due to the fact that Lewes' principal psychological work, *Problems of Life and Mind* (1874–9), appeared later in time, when the British empirical tradition was on the point of being submerged in the idealistic flood. In part it is possibly a result of the inadequacy of the labels with which Lewes has been marked. He has been described as a materialist (by Ward), an associationist (by Warren), a positivist (by Ribot) and sometimes he is classed as an evolutionist. With Lewes such labels are more than usually misleading. A more important reason for Lewes' neglect is, no doubt, defects in Lewes himself. He is repetitious, verbose, and unsystematic. His physiology, which was detailed and

[1] Warren *History of Association Psychology*, (1921) 152.
[2] F. Hayek *The Sensory Order*, (1952) 152.
[3] The fact that it was a Russian translation of Lewes' *The Physiology of Common Life* that first turned Pavlov's attention to physiology would alone make him worthy of remembrance.

based on much first-hand study, soon became out-of-date; his theoretical views passed out of fashion. In the year when the final volumes of Lewes' *Problems of Life and Mind* were posthumously published (1879) Wundt opened his psychological laboratory in Leipzig. A new world appeared to be emerging for psychologists to explore, and Lewes was not of this world.

George Henry Lewes was a Londoner by birth. His grandfather, Charles Lee Lewes, was a prominent eighteenth-century actor, and George inherited both his talent for and interest in the stage. His education was irregular, and his vocation for long uncertain. He tried commerce, then medicine; he wrote novels, and appeared on the stage. In 1840 he married, after a long stay in Germany, and supported himself and his family mainly by journalism and writing. His scholarship was already wide and his philosophic grasp considerable; combined with his early love for the theatre and a lively mind these qualities gave the dramatic criticisms which he contributed to the press high merit. But philosophy became increasingly his major interest, and the French philosopher Comte his god. In 1845–6 Lewes published his *Biographical History of Philosophy* which reviewed the course of western philosophy to its culmination in Comte! It was widely read in its day, and included by Sir John Lubbock in his collection of the world's hundred best books. Probably the best known of Lewes' writings however is his *Life and Work of Goethe* (1855) which went through many editions and is still listed as one of the principal studies of Goethe. In 1850 Lewes became acquainted with Herbert Spencer. The meeting was momentous for both men, and a close friendship sprang up between them. It was the reading of Lewes' *History of Philosophy* that aroused Spencer's interest in psychology. It was Spencer who turned Lewes to biology and physiology. From 1855 onwards he concentrated more and more on scientific and biological work. The result was the publication of a book called *The Physiology of Common Life* in 1859; *Studies in Animal Life* in 1862; and an intensive study of the physiological basis of mind which found expression in his later psychological writing. But more than this it was the stimulation of Spencer's theorizing that set Lewes moving. "His intense theorizing tendency was contagious", says Lewes,[1] "and it was only the stimulus of a theory which could then have induced me to work." Another consequence of the meeting with Spencer was Lewes' introduction to Miss Marian Evans, then assistant-editor of the *Westminster Review*, later to achieve fame as the novelist

[1] Quoted by J. W. Cross *George Eliot's Life*, vol. I. 454.

'George Eliot'. In 1854 Lewes left his wife, and from then until his death lived with Miss Evans. Although never officially married they regarded each other as man and wife, and on the manuscript of *Adam Bede* (1859) George Eliot inscribed the words "To my dear husband, George Henry Lewes, I give the MS. of a work which would never have been written but for the happiness which his love has conferred on my life". For both it was intellectually and emotionally an ideal union, marred only by its discord with the canons of Victorian morality. For Lewes it meant in his own words "a new birth". To George Eliot it gave the companionship of one whom she describes as "a very airy, bright, versatile creature" [1] – a judgement which accords with Spencer's account. "As a companion", says Spencer, "Lewes was extremely attractive. Interested in and well informed upon a variety of subjects – full of various anecdotes, and an admirable mimic; it was impossible to be dull in his company. Nowadays he is chiefly known by his contributions to philosophy in his *Problems of Life and Mind*; but his reputation was then mainly that of an extremely versatile man – a critic, writer on general literature, a novelist, a dramatist, an actor, an expositor of philosophy." [2] Lewes wrote with facility. Spencer relates that on one occasion Lewes, T. H. Huxley, and himself were discussing together their habits as writers. Lewes said he had no difficulty in getting into the swing of writing. "I never hesitate. I get up steam at once. In short I boil at low temperatures." To which Huxley, who had an acid wit, retorted, "Well, but that implies a vacuum in the upper regions." Yet Lewes was neither empty-headed nor a dilettante. His psychological ideas, to which we must now turn, were based on hard thinking and a range of knowledge as extensive as that of any English thinker of his time.

Psychology for Lewes was in its foundations a biological science to be pursued by the methods common to all the sciences. He had no use for the traditional "absurd notions respecting the nature of the mind, its simplicity, autonomy, independence of the organism, and its equality in all men". [3] Yet psychology was more than a branch of physiology, for it must embrace the study of social influences. Though Lewes did not use, he would thoroughly have approved of, the term 'biosocial', which perhaps best describes his standpoint. Yet unlike Comte, from whom he increasingly diverged, he did not reject introspection as a source of psychological data. He had indeed too sensitive a mind to become a

---

[1] J. W. Cross op. cit., 519.     [2] Herbert Spencer *Autobiography*, vol. I.
[3] *Problems of Life and Mind*, III. 1. 44.

'tough' behaviourist. "The fact is", he writes, "that the mind does observe its own operations – and precisely in the same way that it observes any other operations. Because they are felt and re-felt under varying conditions, and are capable of being discriminated, classified, generalized, and experimentally modified, they are data for scientific constructions." [1] At the same time he was aware of the limitations of introspection, and "there is something naïve in the idea that simply watching the changes in consciousness will reveal the complexities of the phenomena and the laws of change, to say nothing of the conditions which determine the phenomena". [2]

The physiological aspects of Lewes' psychology to which he devoted the second series of his *Problems of Life and Mind* entitled *The Physical Basis of Mind* (1877) inevitably dated more rapidly than the more theoretical parts. Only seven years afterwards in 1884 Sherrington's first papers on the nervous system began to appear, and before long these were destined to throw much new light on nervous functioning. Nevertheless Sully found it worthwhile to issue a new edition of *The Physical Basis of Mind* as late as 1893. Lewes' physiological work was marked by thoroughness and penetration. He was sceptical of widely accepted views and deplored the "false persuasion of knowledge" which was common at the time. His own suggestions were often perspicacious – his criticisms, for example, of the doctrine of specific energies – but the value of his work was necessarily limited by the amateur character of his own experimental investigations. The main burden of his physiological psychology was to dispute the adequacy of the purely mechanistic view of reflexes. He urged that sensibility of a kind – and sensibility was something wider than consciousness – was present at the reflex level, and he differentiated reflex action from purely mechanical action. He produced experimental evidence to disprove the idea of fixed reflex pathways. He extended the properties of mind to the reflex level, and protested against the correlation of mind and brain. "It is the man and not the brain, that thinks; it is the organism as a whole, and not one organ that feels and acts." [3] He disliked Carpenter's neat theory of functional levels. His own point of view he described as 'organicist'. The organism could not be treated as a mosaic, nor is the mind made of separable pieces. Each piece has significance only in its relation to others. [4] The organism constitutes a dynamic system and "every sensation and every action depend on the lines of least resistance, which in turn depend on

---

[1] l.c., 89.        [2] l.c., 99.        [3] *The Physical Basis of Mind*, 441.
[4] *Problems of Life and Mind*, 3rd series, I. 179.

the poise of the whole system".[1] The relation between physiology and psychology he considered to be the relation between process and product. Physiology dealt with processes and conditions of productions; psychology with the products and their relations. No observation of products could of itself provide an understanding of process.

Where Lewes differs from some later schools of 'organicists' is in his emphasis on the historical factor and on experience. He did not to be sure deny the existence of innate structure. The notion of a *tabula rasa* was unbiological. But the primary emphasis was on the role of experience; and in this respect, of course, Lewes showed himself to be a true follower of the English empiricist tradition. The residua of past experience became grouped and organized and account not only for our perceptions and 'motor intuitions', as Lewes termed them, but for personality and intelligence. Lewes was perhaps the first British psychologist to employ the term personality in approximately its modern sense. Intelligence he regarded as "the sum of all our various registered experiences" [2] and not therefore an inherited product. The combination and recombination of impressions into experiences, of experiences into groups, and of groups into higher groups leads to increasing 'innerness'. "The Inner Life thus represents the whole of our experience. Developing with the evolution of experience, it becomes a logical and co-ordinating system which enlarges perception and regulates action, rendering us more and more independent of the immediate stimulus." [3]

The fundamental law of mental action was grouping. All nervous functioning at all levels involved a threefold process: physiologically this could be described as stimulation, co-ordination, and discharge; psychologically as sensible affection, logical grouping, and impulse. Lewes therefore equated co-ordination in physiological terms with logical grouping in psychological terms. As consequences of the continuity of Lewes' system and its application to all levels of nervous complexity we find that Lewes spoke on the one hand of logic at the sensory level and on the other hand of the motor element of thought. The threefold process was a universal rubric. Sensation was a resultant, a function of the three variables, stimulation, grouping and motor impulse. The quality of each sensation was a result of the grouping of neural units, of their quantity and configuration. We have here a clear anticipation of Hayek's theory already referred to. The co-ordinating processes in which the elements were sensations, perceptions,

---

[1] *Problems of Life and Mind*, 3rd series, II. 44.          [2] ibid., III. 392.
[3] l.c., 86.

images, appetites, instincts and emotions Lewes, borrowing the phrase from Comte, termed "the Logic of Feeling". He distinguished this from "the Logic of Signs" which operated with symbols, mostly verbal.

Thought was not something wholly different from feeling. The thinking process, the logical process, Lewes regarded as common to all psychical phenomena: thinking in the narrower sense, however, was concerned with symbols rather than directly with feelings. Symbols or ideas were not, like images, reinstatements of prior feelings, but substitutes for them. The relation between the logic of signs and the logic of feeling Lewes compared to the relation between algebra and arithmetic. Algebra and arithmetic employed the same operations – grouping, inclusion, exclusion – but different symbols. Lewes noted a quarter of a century before the Würzburg psychologists that "the greater proportion of all men's thinking goes forward with confident reliance on the correctness of logical operations and with only an occasional translation of symbols into images".[1] But thought always involved a motor element though it might be in almost complete occultation. In particular "to think by means of words is to think by means of certain definite motor feelings".[2]

It was at this point that Lewes brought in the social factor. Human language, unlike animal language, was a social not an individual product. Although Lewes unfortunately did not develop the theme of the social component of human nature at length, he laid great emphasis on it. "Man is distinctively a social being; his animal impulses are profoundly modified by social influences, and his higher faculties are evolved through social needs. By this recognition of the social factor as the complement to the biological factor, this recognition of the Mind as an expression of organic and social conditions, the first step is taken towards the constitution of our science."[3] Lewes, therefore, clearly saw the importance of the social factor; more than this he saw, what few social psychologists have even yet seen, that the study of society means the study of history. "We must always", he wrote, "take history into account . . . the objective data of psychology are furnished by zoology and history . . . if we follow the development of thought on the large scale of history we see how the mind acquires new powers and possibilities with new conceptions."[4] Had Lewes developed his theory more fully a key place would have been taken by language, for "Language is to the social organism very much what the nervous system is to the

[1] l.c., 479.    [2] l.c., 350.    [3] l.c., 3rd series, I. 5–6.    [4] l.c., I. 152–4.

body – a connecting medium which enhances all functions".[1] Because of his emphasis on the social life of man Lewes did not hope for much illumination of the central problems of psychology from the study of animals.

It would be wrong to give the impression that Lewes' psychology centred round logical and symbolic processes. True his writing was unsystematic and he devoted little space to a consideration of motivation. But he fully recognized its importance. "Important as sensation and ideation are, they are less important than the appetites, instincts, emotions and sentiments."[2] Images and ideas are, he maintained, at all times signals, not motors. "The actions of men are determined by motives, but the motives are determined by motors lying deep down in the mental structure."[3] The nature of these 'motors' he did not discuss; but they were buried in the unconscious regions of the mind which he conceived to "play by far the greater part in mental life",[4] dismissing Mill's objection to unconscious mental processes as merely verbal. Translating these deeper motors into conscious terms Lewes set out certain laws of mental operation. According to the law of interest, "we only see what interests us, or has once interested us. We only know what is sufficiently like former experiences to become incorporated with them."[5] In the field of perception Lewes termed this 'preperception', a term which both James and Ward borrowed from him with acknowledgements. By preperception Lewes implied a direction of perceptual attention by the residua of past experience. "The new object presented to sense must be soluble in old experiences, be recognized as like them, otherwise it will be unperceived."[6] This was more broadly conceived as an aspect of orientation. The organism is perpetually taking its bearings. We work to landmarks and standards, to known points, by which the signals of sense or intellect are located. This conception Lewes applied both to "the subjective landscape of thought", and to overt movements. "Motor intuitions enter as components into that general picture of the organism and its activities which we carry about with us, and regard as contradistinction to our mind"[7] – a sort of body schema, or body image, as it might now be termed, serving as an orientating framework and a general background of all particular movements. Each movement is preceded by a 'motor intuition', and the results of each muscular contraction are reported back to consciousness and serve as a stimulus to the next contraction.[8] This is interesting, even though Lewes was

[1] l.c., IV. 495.   [2] l.c., IV. 444.   [3] l.c., II. 138.   [4] l.c., II. 17.   [5] l.c., II. 106.
[6] l.c., II. 108.        [7] l.c., III. 336.        [8] *The Physical Basis of Mind*, 407.

writing before Sherrington and did not grasp the nature of the mechanism. He thought in terms of backward impulses along the motor nerves themselves.

Perhaps even today, however, and in spite of those features in his work which date, we can endorse Sully's judgement on Lewes. *"The Problems* are pre-eminently the work of a *modern* thinker, one versed in the newest developments of philosophic thought, keenly sensitive to all superficiality and one-sidedness of view, critical of mere abstractions, and resolute in keeping speculation in vitalizing touch with concrete realities." [1]

## 5. Samuel Butler (1835–1902)

It would be a mistake to take Butler too seriously as a psychologist. He would have laughed at us and lampooned us were we to do so. He was even more of an amateur than G. H. Lewes. Not only did he lack scientific training and the scientific attitude, he lacked also the patience and persistence needed for scientific endeavour. Sheep farming in New Zealand, painting, music, travel, and above all writing, all engaged his active interest and employed his considerable talents. Nevertheless his brilliant shafts and intuitions. acrimonious and warped though they were, often proved psychologically perceptive. In *The Way of All Flesh* (1903), his one novel, largely autobiographical in content, he provided a classic case-study of the 'Oedipus' family complex, which partly explains his own career. "My most implacable enemy from childhood onward has certainly been my father",[2] he commented in his notebooks. The aggression generated in his conflicts with parental authority was projected against all that was orthodox and pontifical, against society and its institutions in *Erewhon* (1872), and against the new scientific creed of Darwinism in *Life and Habit* (1877), *Evolution, Old and New* (1879), *Unconscious Memory* (1880) and other works. His contemptuous attitude to Darwin aroused the ire of his scientific contemporaries, and his cavalier disregard for scientific accuracy their scorn.

As far as evolution was concerned Butler campaigned against the Darwinian view that chance variations could explain continuous development. There must, he held, be "a definite and persistent principle underlying them", a sort of purposive life-force or immanent deity. "Our own progress, or variation, is due not to small fortuitous inventions or modifications which have enabled their fortunate possessors

---

[1] J. Sully, Preface to the new edition of *The Physical Basis of Mind* (1893.)
[2] *Butleriana* (1932).

to survive in times of difficulty, not in fact to strokes of luck . . . but to strokes of cunning, to a sense of need, and to study of the past and present which have given shrewd people a key with which to unlock the chambers of the future." [1] These speculations, unsupported by evidence, would be of little concern to us had they not led Butler on to follow the German physiologist, Hering, into further speculations on memory. Here he got on to some issues that are psychologically relevant. He held with Hering that in some sort of way all storing of information involved a common principle, that heredity was in fact a form of memory. "Plants and animals only differ from one another because they remember different things." [2] His evolutionary views, therefore, were Lamarckian; acquired characters could be transmitted to, or were remembered by, as he preferred to put it, subsequent generations. "Each embryo takes note of, remembers and is guided by the profounder impressions made upon it while in the persons of its parents." [3] There was thus no real break between the generations; instincts were racial habits, ancestral memories which had become unconscious, just as well established memories in the individual operated unconsciously.

To support these views Butler produced some quite sound psychological observations. "We draw the inference, therefore, as regards pianoforte or violin playing, that the more the familiarity or knowledge of the art, the less is there of consciousness of such knowledge." [4] "Men invariably put the same leg first into their trousers – this is the survival of memory in a residuum; but they cannot until they actually put on a pair of trousers remember which leg they *do* put in first; this is the rapid fading away of any small individual impression." [5] Butler had reached here something closely similar to the doctrine of unconscious schemata – "the memory of many past performances strikes a sort of fused balance in the mind, which results in a general method of procedure with but little conscious memory of even the latest performances, and with none whatever of by far the greater number of the remoter ones". [6]

The individual personality was thus largely constituted by a cluster of such buried memories, and this meant that it was a complex and imperfectly integrated structure. "This 'we' which looks so simple and definite is a nebulous and indefinable aggregation of many component parts which war not a little among themselves." [7] And because

[1] *Life and Habit*, 248.    [2] op. cit., 298.
[3] *The Deadlock in Darwinism* (1890).    [4] *Life and Habit*, 5.
[5] op. cit., 157.    [6] op. cit., 158.    [7] op. cit., 78.

# CHAPTER IV

# Galton and the Beginning of Psychometrics

## 1. Sir Francis Galton (1822-1911)

The philosopher who spoke of Freud as psychology's one man of genius either overlooked Sir Francis Galton, or must have attached to him some other label than psychologist. For Galton was unquestionably a genius; and, though his genius manifested itself in most varied fields, among the most important was psychology. Galton was the first to investigate and measure individual differences in psychology; he was the first to provide evidence that psychological traits might be inherited in man; and he was the first to employ the statistical technique of correlation to assess the relationship between measured qualities. His work is fundamental to very large areas of contemporary psychology.

Francis Galton, like his cousin Charles Darwin (Galton's mother was a daughter of Erasmus Darwin), inherited sufficient worldly means to be able to live without paid employment, and like Darwin he devoted his whole life to scientific work. Both his grandfather and his father were well-to-do Birmingham manufacturers, and Francis, the last child in a family of nine, was brought up in a cultivated and lively home. He was a child of extraordinary precocity; he knew his capital letters when 12 months old; could read at the age of $2\frac{1}{2}$ years, and just before his fifth birthday he could write "I am four years old, and I can read any English book. I can say all the Latin substantives and adjectives and active verbs besides 52 lines of Latin poetry. I can cast up any sum in addition and can multiply by 2, 3, 4, 5, 6, 7, 8 and 10. I can also say the pence table. I read French a little and I know the clock."[1] On the basis of evidence of this sort Terman has estimated Galton's I.Q. as 200! In spite of this precocity Galton's school and university career was undistinguished, and his most important work was not carried out until he was in his sixties. He started but never completed a medical training; and at Trinity College, Cambridge, where he read mathematics, he had a breakdown in health and ended up with a pass degree. It was twenty years after he left Cambridge before he found his life's work as a result of reading *The Origin of Species*. Meanwhile, however, his original and

[1] Letter to his sister, quoted by K. Pearson *Life of Galton*, I. 66.

enquiring mind had already shown its powers in more ways than one. As a medical student his curiosity incited him to take small doses of all the drugs included in the pharmocopœia – commencing with the letter A! "I nearly got to the end of the letter C," he relates, "when I was stopped by the effects of Croton oil." [1] Some years later he engaged in an adventurous balloon flight at night because "I was eager to know the sensations of ballooning".[2] In 1850 his pioneering bent settled down to serious exploration, and in an expedition to tropical south-west Africa he opened up large tracts of arduous country never before visited by Europeans. Galton was a highly intelligent traveller, keen in his observations, fertile in contrivances, and cool in the face of danger and difficulty. His *Art of Travel* (1855), which went through several editions, is full of practical wisdom and 'boy scout lore'. His interest in geography was lifelong, and he was a member of the council of the Royal Geographical Society from 1854–93. The scientific work accomplished on his travels brought him various distinctions, including a Fellowship of the Royal Society. His journeys also aroused his interest in meteorology and anthropology. Meteorology was another of the sciences to which Galton made important contributions. Galton was the first to draw up weather maps, and the first to notice the existence of high-pressure systems which he christened 'anticyclones'. For nearly forty years Galton was intimately associated with the development of meteorology in this country, and was a member of the Meteorological Committee until 1901. It was Galton who supplied the first weather map to *The Times* on 1 April 1875. From 1860 onwards, however, these interests became overshadowed by Galton's growing devotion to anthropology and psychology. His travels had sown seeds; Darwin's *Origin of Species* caused them to germinate. From now on Galton's main concern was with the inheritance of human qualities, physical and psychological, and his investigations, anthropometric, psychometric, statistical, eugenic, were subordinated to this major purpose. His laborious studies, for instance, on composite portraiture and on fingerprints sprang directly from his work on inheritance, and to the eugenic movement Galton devoted the last decade of his life with almost religious fervour. As a man and a scientist Galton was highly respected by the scientific world of his day. He was twice invited, but declined, to become President of the British Association, a position which his cousin, Sir Douglas Galton, held in 1895. He was for four periods a member of the Council of the Royal Society. He was honoured by both Oxford and Cambridge

[1] *Memories of My Life,* 37.  [2] l.c., 115.

Universities. And we learn from Beatrice Webb's *My Apprenticeship* that he made a profound impression on the young. "Amongst these scientists," she writes,[1] "the one who stays in my mind as the ideal man of science is, not Huxley or Tyndall, Hooker or Lubbock, still less my guide, philosopher and friend, Herbert Spencer, but Francis Galton. . . . Even today I can conjure up . . . that tall figure with its attitude of perfect physical and mental poise. . . . Fascinating to me was Galton's all-embracing but apparently impersonal beneficence. But to a recent and enthusiastic convert of scientific method, the most relevant of Galton's many gifts was the unique contribution of three separate and distinct processes of the intellect; a continuous curiosity about and rapid apprehension of individual facts, whether common or uncommon; the faculty of ingenious trains of reasoning; and more admirable than either of these, because the talent was wholly beyond my reach, the capacity for correcting and verifying his own hypotheses by the statistical handling of masses of data." We may compare with this youthful impression the mature judgement of his disciple and biographer, Karl Pearson, who in the preface to his monumental *Life of Francis Galton* asserted that "the ramifications of Galton's methods are producing a renaissance in innumerable branches of science, which will be as epoch-making in the near future as the Darwinian theory of evolution was in biology". In psychology it could be maintained without undue exaggeration that this prophecy has come true.

Galton's contributions to psychology were brilliant but unsystematic. As Pearson points out "he left others to settle and develop; his joy was in rapid pioneer work in a wide range of fields".[2] Yet there is in Galton's psychological inquiries a unifying theme, "the varied hereditary faculties of different men". His great contributions to psychology consist in his realization of the importance of individual differences, and his forging of the tools to deal with them. In theoretical background Galton's work, like that of some of his psychometric successors, was weak; it was enormously suggestive and original in its techniques. It is only possible to get hints here and there of the conceptual framework of Galton's psychology. "Talent and character are exhaustive," he affirms in his first psychological article, "they include the whole of a man's spiritual nature so far as we are able to understand it." [3] Both talent and character are largely inherited, and they are closely bound up with physical qualities. Even if Galton had been a great reader, which he was not, he could not

[1] op. cit., 134–5.        [2] op. cit., II. 25.
[3] 'Hereditary Talent and Character', *Macmillan's Magazine*, 1865.

have got much help from the psychology of his day towards the analysis of talent and character. He got little further than defining character as "a definite and durable 'something' ", and realizing that trait names were possibly deceptive. "We must guard ourselves against supposing that the moral faculties which we distinguish by different names, as courage, sociability, niggardliness, are separate entities." [1] For a classification of temperament he made use of the old traditional four temperaments – nervous, sanguine, bilious, lymphatic. In default of a better theory of talent and character Galton tended to over-emphasize the importance of physical qualities. He regarded powers of sensory discrimination as a measure of intelligence – hence his interest in psychophysical experiments and in apparatus, like his whistles, for testing sensitivity. In the anthropometric laboratory which he set up at the International Health Exhibition in London in 1884, and continued at the Science Museum, South Kensington, until 1891, he laid emphasis on measures of physical energy, sensory discrimination and reaction time. Energy he regarded as the most important quality. It was the quality which above all others characterized the eminent men of science to whom he sent a questionnaire and whose 'nature and nurture' he discussed on the basis of their replies in *English Men of Science* (1874). There are indications, nevertheless, in some of Galton's articles, that had his interest remained focused on the psychometric field he would have advanced much farther. In 1886 he visited asylums with Bain and Sully to test the 'prehension' of idiots by means of memory span;[2] in his *Inquiries into Human Faculty* (1883) he suggests that "the powers of quickly seizing and easily manipulating ideas of a very abstract nature" is the best test of intellectual capacity;[3] and in his article on "The Measurement of Character" he makes a number of acute suggestions. "Character ought to be measured by carefully recorded acts, representative of conduct. An ordinary generalization is nothing more than a muddle of vague memories of mixed observations. . . . It is the statistics of each man's conduct in small everyday affairs, that will probably be found to give the simplest and most precise measure of his character." And he goes on to propose that "Emergencies need not be waited for, they can be extemporized; traps, as it were, can be laid . . . a sudden excitement, call, touch, gesture, or incident of any kind evokes in different persons a response that varies in intensity, celerity and quality."

Galton's deficiencies in psychological theory were to some extent

---

[1] 'The Measurement of Character', *Fortnightly Rev.*, 1884.
[2] *Mind*, XII (1887), 79–82.          [3] op. cit., 144.

compensated by his psychological insight. He had a highly developed gift for introspection, and a vivid realization that other minds might differ qualitatively from his own and from each other. He endeavoured not merely to measure but to understand the diversity of human nature. His researches on mental imagery, colour association and number forms led him to an appreciation of "the vast variety of mental constitution", and showed "how impossible it is for one man to lay his mind strictly alongside that of another".[1] In his experiments on association he succeeded in recording faint and fleeting early memories. Well before Freud had turned his attention to the psychology of the unconscious, Galton had discovered that "whole strata of mental operations that had lapsed out of ordinary consciousness admit of being dragged to light"; he noted the prominent place of childish incidents in these uncovered recollections, and observed that "they lay bare the foundations of a man's thoughts with curious distinctness and exhibit his mental anatomy with more vividness and truth than he would probably care to publish to the world".[2]

Another penetrating enquiry was an introspective analysis of free-will. Continuously for a period of six weeks and episodically for several further months Galton observed the occasions when he caught himself "engaged in a feat of what might be called free-will"[3] and he noted any circumstances that might have influenced his decision. Most of his actions seemed to him to be within the province of normal cause and consequence. Free will appeared to be associated with cases of irresolution, and these cases occurred only about once a day. "I suspect that much of what we stigmatize as irresolution is due to our self being by no means one and indivisible." A subconscious region exists from which ideas may arise as suddenly as the head of a seal above the surface of still water. "Those who introspect and those who study the genesis of dreams", he adds, "succeed in discovering plain causes of numerous images and thoughts that had seemed to have arisen spontaneously."

These experiments and observations made Galton realize the importance of the abnormal. "No professor of metaphysics, psychology, or religion can claim to know the elements of what he teaches unless he is acquainted with the ordinary phenomena of idiocy, madness and epilepsy."[4] There was in Galton's view no hard line of division between sanity and insanity – "I often feel", he wrote, "that the tableland of san-

---

[1] *Inquiries into Human Faculty*, 112.      [2] op. cit., 131–47.
[3] *Mind*, IX (1884).      [4] *Inquiries into Human Faculty*, 47.

ity upon which most of us dwell is small in area, with unfenced precipices on every side, over any one of which we may fall."[1] In the *Memories of My Life* (1908), from which this last statement is taken, Galton reports a number of attempts he made earlier on to obtain a first-hand understanding of the abnormal.[2] On one occasion he adopted the plan of investing everything he met with the imaginary attributes of a spy. In the course of a morning stroll every horse even seemed to be watching him, and it took hours before the uncanny sensation wore off. On another occasion he took the figure on the cover of *Punch* as a fetish object and pretended it had divine attributes. The experiment gradually succeeded and for a long time he retained for Punch's image a "large share of the feelings a barbarian has for his idol".

These examples of Galton's psychological insight and imagination are important because they remind us of a side of his genius which is sometimes overlooked. His major contributions to the development of psychology relate to hereditary differences and to statistical method. As we turn to an account of these it is perhaps worth emphasizing that Galton himself, the real founder of the psychometric school, would not have denied that statistical methods are complementary to a subtle insight into the dynamics of mental functioning.

When Galton in the 1860's turned his attention to the inheritance of psychological characters in man the idea of the hereditary transmission of limited human powers was unfamiliar. As Galton pointed out in the preface to the Second Edition (1892) of *Hereditary Genius*, "the human mind was popularly thought to act independently of natural laws and to be capable of almost any achievement if compelled to exert itself by a will that had power of imitation". The words 'hereditary' and 'inheritance' were of legal origin, and had only comparatively recently been introduced into biology. Certainly no one before Galton had carried out any systematic enquiry into the inheritance of ability in man. Galton, struck during his ethnological work by family resemblances in mental qualities, and inspired by the theories of his cousin, Charles Darwin, made an examination of the kindred of about 400 eminent men. The results of this enquiry, published in *Hereditary Genius* (1869), convinced him that 'genius', by which term he meant 'exceptionally high ability', was inherited.

In order to establish this Galton had to devise some method of classifying ability according to a standard scale, to compare the members of successive generations, and to show that environmental influences were

---

[1] *Memories of My Life*, 38.　　　[2] op. cit., 276–7.

not primarily responsible for the results. Quetelet, the Belgium astronomer, had shown in his *Lettres sur la théorie des probabilités* (1845, Eng. tr. 1849) that the distribution of human stature closely approximated to the Gaussian curve of probability, to what we now term a 'normal distribution'. Galton, on the basis of what must be regarded as rather slender evidence, went a step further and argued "if this be the case with stature, then it will be true as regards every other physical feature ... and thence, by a step on which no physiologist will hesitate, as regards mental capacity".[1] So far from human beings being equal "there is a continuity of natural ability reaching from one knows not what height and descending to one can hardly say what depth".[2] The gaps in Galton's evidence may seem to us glaring, but a momentous step had been taken. The normal distribution curve had for the first time been applied to psychological data. Grading natural ability into sixteen equal grades and employing Quetelet's tables of probability Galton estimated the number of persons in each grade of ability in the population of England. Taking his top grade with a frequency of 1 per million, and his next two grades with combined frequencies of 247 per million, he found these to agree remarkably closely with his count of 'illustrious' and 'eminent' men derived on the basis of predetermined criteria from works of reference.

Next Galton undertook an extensive historical and biographical research into the kinsmen of his 'illustrious' and 'eminent' men in various walks of life. Taking, for instance, the records of the judges of England from 1660–1865 he found that eighty per cent of Lord Chancellors and thirty-six per cent of the remaining judges had eminent relations. Combining all his groups of statesmen, soldiers, authors, scientists, artists, scholars, etc., he estimated that illustrious or eminent men had in thirty-one per cent of cases illustrious or eminent fathers, and in forty-eight per cent of cases illustrious or eminent sons, and decreasing percentages with more distant relationships. Galton concluded that 'genius' was strongly hereditary. A recent follow-up of Galton's study covering three subsequent generations has closely corroborated his findings on the frequency of eminent relations.[3]

By modern standards of evidence, however, Galton undoubtedly underestimated the difficulty of separating hereditary from environmental influences. Galton pointed, in favour of the hereditarian argument, to the fact that individuals advanced by nepotism remained

[1] *Hereditary Genius*, 28.      [2] op. cit., 22.
[3] B. S. Bramwell *Eugenics Review*, vol. XXXIX (1948).

curiously undistinguished, while genius had a way of overcoming adverse circumstances. But these arguments are certainly not decisive, and if we believe in the role of genetic factors in determining psychological characters it is on the basis of much more cogent evidence, in particular from investigations into the characteristics of twins.[1] We must remember, however, that in the study of twins Galton was once again the pioneer.

At the time these studies of Galton were carried out there was no scientific understanding of the mechanism of inheritance. Mendel's papers published in 1866 and 1869 in an obscure local journal in Austria remained unknown to the scientific world until 1900. In 1868 Darwin propounded a theory of 'pangenesis' to account for hereditary transmission which now seems wholly fanciful.[2] Galton's own hypotheses in comparison were acute and not entirely mistaken. Partly from his studies of family trees and animal pedigrees, partly on the facts of experimental work with rabbits and sweet peas, Galton arrived at the concepts of particulate inheritance ("we seem to inherit bit by bit, this element from one progenitor that from another"),[3] of latent characteristics ("skipping a generation"),[4] and of discontinuity in evolution. He realized that remote ancestors, as well as parents, contribute to an individual's genetic make-up, and propounded a law of ancestral inheritance which stated the proportionate contribution of each generation.

From the very beginning Galton's interest in heredity was practical as well as theoretical. In *Hereditary Genius* he asserted that it is "most essential to the well-being of future generations that the average standard of ability of the present time should be raised".[5] With prophetic insight he foresaw that an increasingly complex technical civilization would make heavier and heavier demands on the limited pool of native talent. He believed this pool could and must be increased by positive measures. He named these measures 'eugenic'; and defined eugenics as "the study of agencies under social control which may improve or impair the racial qualities of future generations either physically or mentally".[6] He devoted the last decade of his life largely to eugenics; and was instrumental in founding both the Eugenics Society, which since 1907 has done a great deal to spread a knowledge of heredity particularly through the medium

[1] *Inquiries into Human Faculty*, 155–73.
[2] Charles Darwin *The Variation of Animals and Plants under Domestication*, 1868.
[3] *Natural Inheritance*, 7.      [4] ibid., 12.
[5] *Hereditary Genius*, 332.
[6] Quoted K. Pearson's *Life of Galton*, vol. IIIa. 222.

of its journal the *Eugenics Review*; and the Eugenics Laboratory at University College, London, where a succession of distinguished men, Karl Pearson, R. A. Fisher and L. S. Penrose, has occupied the Galton chair.

But perhaps none of the consequences of Galton's work on heredity have been as far-reaching as the statistical developments that sprang from it. Statistical methodology has transformed large areas of science, including psychology. The ideas of Galton, elaborated and systematized by Pearson and his school, underlie most modern developments in statistics. Though Galton himself was by no means an expert mathematician – his Cambridge training had been incomplete, and his mathematical attainments, such as they were, allowed to rust – he saw the importance of quantitative methods and was often able to grasp the essentials of a problem. "Until the phenomena of any branch of knowledge have been submitted to measurement and number, it cannot assume the status and dignity of a science." [1] And the advice, which he adopted himself on every possible occasion, was "whenever you can, count". "Some people", he writes later, "hate the very name of statistics, but I find them full of beauty and interest. Whenever they are not brutalized, but delicately handled by the higher methods, and are warily interpreted, their power of dealing with complicated phenomena is extraordinary. They are the only tools by which an opening can be cut through the formidable thicket of difficulties that bars the path of those who pursue the science of man." [2]

Galton's two major contributions to statistics were the method of ranks and the method of correlation. His 'proposed statistical scale' was first explained at a Royal Institution lecture in 1874 and followed by a letter to *Nature*.[3] If the members of a population are ranked a statistical scale is established, and the place of any individual can be determined by the percentage of the whole population who stand above him on the scale. Galton referred to these determinations as 'centisimal grades', now usually called 'percentiles'. The mid point of the scale was later termed by Galton the 'median', and the seventy-five per cent and twenty-five per cent grades the quartiles.[4] The real measures corresponding to each percentile rank when graphically represented produced an 'ogive' curve. Galton held that "we can lay down the ogive of any quality, physical or mental, whenever we are capable of judging which of any two members of the group we are engaged upon has the larger

---

[1] 'Psychometric Experiments', *Brain*, II (1879).
[2] *Natural Inheritance*, 62–3.          [3] *Nature*, IX. 342.
[4] *Natural Inheritance*, ch. V.

amount of that quality".[1] Statistical techniques could, therefore, be employed even when precise measurements were impossible.

Galton's method of 'ogives' and percentiles has to a considerable extent been superseded by newer techniques; not so the method of correlation. Galton's paper on 'Co-relations and their Measurement' [2] has been described by Pearson as "in its permanent influence perhaps the most important of his writings". In spite of anticipations by Gauss and by Bravais, Pearson argues that Galton was the true discoverer of correlation. He was the first to devise a coefficient of correlation.[3] Galton was brought to the concept of correlation by his work on inheritance. He was confronted with a situation in which the character of the offspring was partially, but not wholly, determined by the character of the parents, and he required a measure to express this partial relationship. In default of precise data for successive human generations Galton experimented with sweet peas, and measured the diameter of the seeds in mother and daughter plants. He plotted the measures and noted that the mean diameter of the daughter seeds was positively related to the mean diameter of the parent seeds, but that it tended to be nearer to the general mean. Galton termed this phenomena 'regression' and the line joining the means on his diagram the 'regression line'. He had not yet, however, arrived at the concept of correlation.

Galton was driven to take the next step by problems arising from Bertillon's system for identifying criminals by measurement of head length, foot length, stature, etc. Galton doubted Bertillon's claim that these various measures were virtually independent of each other. He saw that the problem of establishing their non-independence was similar to the problem of determining hereditary relationships, but he was troubled by the fact that the slope of the regression line varied with the varying dispersion and the different units of the characters being measured. After puzzling for thirteen years on this problem Galton suddenly found the solution during a country walk. Each measure must be expressed by terms of its deviation from the average, taking the semi-interquartile range of each distribution as a standard unit. If this is done the slope of the regression line becomes the coefficient of correlation.

In his paper on 'Co-relation' [4] Galton sums up his results as follows: Let $x$ be the deviation of the subject, and $Y_1$, $Y_2$, $Y_3$ etc. the corresponding deviations of the correlative, all deviations being reduced to their

[1] *Inquiries into Human Faculty*, 33–38.  [2] *Royal Society Proc.*, XLV (1885).
[3] K. Pearson 'Notes on the History of Correlation'. *Biometrica*, XIII (1920).
[4] l.c., 1885.

proper unit of variability, also let the mean of the $Y$ deviations for the given $x$ be $\overline{Y}x$, then we find (1) that $\overline{Y}x = rx$ for all values of $x$; (2) that $r$ is the same whichever of the two variables is taken for the subject; (3) that $r$ is always less than 1; (4) that $r$ measures the closeness of the correlation. "It will be seen at once", writes Pearson, "that we have here the first fundamental statement as to the correlation coefficient and its properties." [1]

Meanwhile Galton had been collecting human data. In 1884 he offered £500 in prizes for the best "record of family faculties", and received 150 returns. He also had the measurements collected in the anthropometric laboratory, and the returns of a special enquiry into 783 brothers. This gave him just enough data for statistical purposes, and he published the results of his analysis in *Natural Inheritance* (1889), in some ways his most influential book, in that it inspired Pearson, Edgeworth and others to study correlation, and led to the foundations of the school of mathematical statistics. "The methods of *Natural Inheritance* may be antiquated now", observes Pearson, "but in the history of science it will ever be memorable as marking a new epoch, and planting the seed from which sprang a new calculus, as powerful as any branch of the old analysis, and valuable in just as many fields of scientific endeavour." [2]

There can be no question that Galton's work is one of the foundation stones of modern psychology; and that both differential psychology and psychometrics largely derive from it. Before Galton died in 1911 he saw under the rigorous leadership of Karl Pearson an extensive development of his own tentative statistical endeavours, and though Pearson was no psychologist his influence on psychology has been sufficiently important to justify a brief account of his achievements.

## 2. Karl Pearson (1857-1936) and the Biometric School

Trained in mathematics at Cambridge, where he was third wrangler in 1879, Karl Pearson at the early age of 27 was appointed to the Chair of Applied Mathematics at University College, London. He remained at the college until his retirement in 1933, transferring in 1911 to the new Chair of Eugenics which Galton endowed. He was from the first a whole-hearted devotee of science and scientific method, and, as his well-known book *The Grammar of Science* (1892) showed, he believed that science rightly understood and rightly handled was competent to solve all problems. "The material of science is coextensive with the whole life,

[1] K. Pearson *Life*, vol. IIIa, 56.    [2] K. Pearson op. cit., IIIa. 58.

physical and mental, of the universe." [1] Galton's extension of quantitative methods to the biological and human sciences fitted in admirably with Pearson's creed, and after reading *Natural Inheritance* it became the main purpose of his life to apply statistical method to the study of heredity and evolution. Much better equipped mathematically than Galton, he placed Galton's statistical methods on a firmer mathematical basis, and greatly extended their range and scope. In other ways, too, Pearson continued Galton's work, particularly in the field of heredity and eugenics. He and his pupils contributed numerous papers on inheritance, including the inheritance of mental characteristics in man, both to *Biometrika* (founded by Pearson in 1901 with Weldon, the zoologist, as co-editor and Galton as consulting editor) and to *The Annals of Eugenics* (which he founded in 1925). Pearson was also responsible for the vast *Treasury of Human Inheritance* (1909–33) which provided data in the form of pedigrees for the measurement of all aspects of human heredity. But it is by reason of his work in statistics that Pearson is mainly important to the history of psychology.

Pearson's chief contributions to the theory and technique of statistics were made between 1893 and 1907, principally in an important series of papers entitled *Contributions to the Mathematical Theory of Evolution*. Galton's *Natural Inheritance* (1889) had roused an interest in correlation in several persons. The zoologist Weldon carried out intensive correlational measurements on crabs and shrimps in 1892. He replaced the medians used by Galton with means, and also suggested the possibility of negative correlations, which had not occurred to Galton. In the same year Edgeworth, the economist, coined the phrase 'coefficient of correlation' (Galton had used the term 'index', and Weldon the expression 'Galton's functions') and adumbrated the theory of multiple correlation. Pearson, using for the first time the terms 'normal curve' and 'standard deviation' (1892–3), entirely abolished the measurement of deviation by probable errors or quartiles. He showed that the best formula for correlation was the one suggested by Bravais in 1846, and he named this the 'product-moment' formula (1896). He worked out the method of multiple correlation (1896),[2] the formula for the probable error of a correlation coefficient (1898), methods for calculating correlation from data classed into broad or qualitative categories (1900), the correlation ratio for dealing with non-normal distributions and

---

[1] *Grammar of Science*, 18.
[2] In 1897 G. Udny Yule, who worked in Pearson's department from 1893–9, devised the partial correlation coefficient.

non-linear regression (1903), and the method of biserial correlation (1909). For Pearson correlation was not merely a technique but an idea which illuminated the whole field of scientific method. In the third edition of *The Grammar of Science* (1911) he wrote: "We have tried to subsume all things under a perfectly inelastic category of cause and effect. It has led to our disregarding the fundamental truth that nothing in the universe repeats itself; we cannot classify by sameness, but only by likeness. Resemblance connotes variation, and variation marks limited not absolute contingency. How often when a new phenomenon has been observed do we hear this question asked: what is the cause of it? A question which it may be absolutely impossible to answer, whereas the question: to what degree are other phenomena associated with it? may admit of easy solution and result in invaluable knowledge."[1]

But the technique of correlation was not Pearson's only achievement in statistics. In 1900, in what has been described as one of his greatest single contributions to statistical theory, he introduced the $\chi^2$ test for goodness of fit, a criterion which has been almost as extensively used, and perhaps abused, in psychological work as the correlation coefficient. Finally in 1904 he devised the contingency coefficient to assess the relationship of qualitative attributes which can be classified but not scaled. From a perusal of the dates when these methods were introduced it becomes clear that as the twentieth century dawned, psychologists had been provided by Pearson and his school with a wholly new set of statistical tools. They were not slow, either in this country or America, to take advantage of them.

[1] op. cit., 170.

CHAPTER V

# Developments in Neurology
# and Neurophysiology

Great Britain was backward in developing the systematic and specialized study of neurology and physiology in its medical schools and hospitals, and in the middle of the nineteenth century lagged behind the most advanced continental countries. But in the latter half of the century two notable centres of research were established, the National Hospital for the Paralysed and Epileptic in Queen Square, London, and the Cambridge school of physiology; and in close conjunction with these centres sprang up the necessary learned societies and journals to provide an outlet and meeting place for those engaged in the new disciplines. The journal *Brain* was founded in 1878, and the Neurological Society (which later became the Neurological Section of the Royal Society of Medicine) in 1886. The Physiological Society was founded slightly earlier in 1876, and the *Journal of Physiology* commenced publication in 1878. The results of these developments for psychology, not only in Great Britain but throughout the world, have been far-reaching. For however much psychology in its higher flights may extend beyond the domain of neurology and neurophysiology its foundations must surely be laid upon these biological sciences. The work carried out at Queen Square, London, and the Cambridge school of physiology, and by those who, like Sherrington and Head, derived their inspiration and training largely from these sources, has inevitably affected the outlook of all subsequent psychological work. It is necessary, therefore, briefly to review these developments in neurology and neurophysiology.

## 1. Queen Square Neurologists

In 1860 as the result of the efforts of a maiden lady, who possessed almost no resources of her own, the National Hospital "for the relief of paralysis, epilepsy and allied diseases" was opened in a single house in Queen Square, London. In the eighty-eight years which passed before it was absorbed by the National Health Service it grew enormously in size, and became a world centre of neurology. This was above all due to a large succession of brilliant neurologists who served unpaid on its professional staff. From the very beginning it was fortunate in attracting men of outstanding ability, whose breadth of mind and philosophical grasp made their teachings and discoveries as important to psychologists as to neurologists: Brown-Séquard (1817–94), William Gowers (1845–1915), H. Charlton Bastian (1837–1915), Victor Horsley (1857–1916), and above all Hughlings Jackson (1835–1911) and David Ferrier (1843–1928), to mention only the principal celebrities of its early years. Jackson and Ferrier we must look at more closely.

a) *Hughlings Jackson* (1835–1911)

Hughlings Jackson is now generally accounted the foremost of nineteenth-century neurologists. Even in his lifetime Sir William Broadbent could say "we accord to him unanimously the first place among those who have contributed to neurology as a science"; and at his centenary celebrations in 1935 the distinguished German neurosurgeon, Foerster, proclaimed "There is scarcely a single neurological problem which was not illuminated and elucidated by his prophetic ingenuity. Hughlings Jackson's writings are the Bible of Neurology." Born of a Yorkshire farming family, John Hughlings Jackson spent nearly his whole working life in London, and the Queen Square Hospital was the focus of his activities. The year he came to London (1859) was the momentous one when *The Origin of Species* was published. Hughlings Jackson was deeply and permanently influenced, and indeed the theory of evolution can be regarded as the major premise of all his thinking. He had already become a devotee of Spencer's *Principles of Psychology* (1855) and at one stage was on the point of abandoning his medical training for a career in philosophy. He was dissuaded from doing this, but Spencer's theories left their mark on all his future work; in his writings he constantly quotes Spencer and Spencer is acknowledged as the source of many of his working hypotheses. Another powerful influence was Laycock (see Chapter II) under whom Hughlings Jackson worked in York before coming to London, and who, like Spencer, was something of a systematizer.

Jackson's own strength rested on a rare combination of philosophic grasp and clinical observation. His mind was essentially deductive, and he constantly urged the importance of hypotheses. "The use of hypothesis is the method of science. To suppose that we can make discoveries by the Baconian method is a delusion . . . an hypothesis is not a conclusion, it is only the starting point for methodical observation and experiment." At the same time he was an acute and systematical observer who held that "for the scientific study of insanities a very wide clinical knowledge is necessary". Certainly both the neurologist and the psychologist can study with profit the methodology of Jackson's work; it was his methodology that enabled him to bring system and order into the confused descriptive neurology of his time.

Though philosophically a parallelist Jackson believed that when approaching the study of nervous disease it was necessary to be "brutally materialistic". He held that terms like 'will', 'memory', and 'emotion' were only words, and in fact that "all psychological explanations are merely verbal".[1] It was essential to get behind these words to the sensori-motor co-ordinations underlying them. For this was a basic tenet of Jackson's creed – and here Laycock's influence is apparent – "All centres are supposed to be sensori-motor – the highest as certainly as any lower. In a word the nervous system is to be thought of as a sensori-motor machine." The nervous system he conceived as a representing system, and what it represented was sensori-motor co-ordinations. Centres, therefore, could not be divided into sensory centres, motor centres, ideational centres, etc. All centres were concerned with sensori-motor co-ordination. When Jackson put forward this theory in the early 1860's it was a revolutionary departure from the commonly accepted views of Flourens, who had taught that the cerebral hemispheres and cerebellum were not irritable and could not produce movements: this was the job of lower centres. Jackson was indeed the first to postulate the existence of a motor cortex; and he did this on the basis of clinical observations some years before first Fritsch and Hitzig in Germany and then Ferrier in this country provided experimental demonstrations. But Jackson went further than merely postulating a motor cortex; he showed that in the 'march' of an epileptic attack "the order in which the different parts of the body became involved reveals the arrangement of the corresponding foci in the precentral convolution". Though Jackson was never a believer in what he called 'abrupt localization' he nevertheless was a pioneer in the field of cerebral localization.

His other main theoretical contribution was the concept of levels, borrowed no doubt from Spencer, but buttressed in Jackson's writing with a wealth of observational data. Jackson recognized three main levels of nervous organization: the lowest reflex level; that of the 'middle centres'; and the highest voluntary level, which he suspected of being non-cortical. The function of the highest level not only included the most complex co-ordinations, but control and inhibition of lower

[1] *Selected Writings*, vol. I. 454.

centres. When the highest centres were damaged there was a release of lower functions. In normal functioning the highest centres were 'protected' and partially insulated from the lower; in cases of brain damage they were the first to suffer dissolution.

These general principles of sensori-motor representation, localization, and levels of organization were used by Jackson to explain a great many neurological observations, particularly in the two fields of epilepsy and aphasia in which his major achievements lay. No doubt Jackson's greatest claim to fame is as the founder of modern views of epilepsy. Prior to Jackson the general opinion was that epilepsy was a reflex discharge originating in the medulla, and epilepsy proper, which involved a loss of consciousness, was sharply distinguished from all other convulsive phenomena. Jackson's essential achievement was to class all convulsive phenomena together and to locate the principal discharges in the cerebral hemispheres. "Epileptic discharges are occasional, abrupt and excessive discharges of parts of the cerebral hemispheres." There could be all kinds and degrees of epileptic seizures. "A paroxysm of red vision, a strong smell in the nose, a paroxysm of vertigo, a spasm in certain parts of the body . . . are all epilepsies." Methodologically Jackson insisted that it was necessary to study the simpler forms of convulsive phenomena first; in particular he studied those convulsions since commonly called 'Jacksonian' which begin in one side of the body usually in a thumb or finger and spread in a distinct sequence to other parts. His first reported case (in 1864) was a case of right unilateral convulsion followed by a temporary defect of speech. The reflections provoked by this case not only led Jackson to his theories of cortical localization but aroused a lifelong interest in the phenomena of aphasia.

In his treatment of aphasia Jackson's strength again rested on the combination of general principles and accurate observation. He cut through the jungle of official terminology (amnesia verbalis, agnosia tactalis, etc.) which, he held, merely obscured the facts. His golden rule was "put down what the patient does and avoid all such terms as amnesia". The physical basis of a word was a sensori-motor nervous arrangement. Internal speech was identical in form and nature with uttered speech. Images were something quite different. Speaking like other forms of movement could take place at various levels: in aphasia the most complex and highly organized forms of speech suffered first, while conventional and emotive language might be retained. As speech was always what Jackson termed 'propositionizing' (i.e. the organization of words into meaningful groups) he insisted that speechlessness was not wordlessness, and that the aphasic was not usually deprived of all use of words. Nor was he deprived of all power of thinking, because speech is only a part of thought. Jackson's views on aphasia, through the influence of Henry Head, who revived and extended them, have had a considerable influence on psychology particularly in this country. Because of their acute analyses and observations his papers are still worth consulting in the original. What could be better, for example, than his account of the skill of doing up buttons in his *Lectures on Convulsive Seizures* (1890)? [1] And there was prescience in his paper on 'The Psychology of Joking' (1887) in which he saw that jokes throw light on the working of the mind, both normal and abnormal. In his own field of neurology he paved the way for most subsequent work, including the physiological researches of Sherrington.

## b) *Sir David Ferrier* (1843–1928)

If Jackson was largely influenced by Spencer, Ferrier, who was an Aberdonian, was influenced by Bain. Before taking up medicine he got a degree in classics and philosophy, and Bain was one of his teachers. His great book *The Functions of the Brain* (1st ed. 1876; 2nd ed. 1886) was partly directed to students of psychology. Though primarily attached to King's College Hospital, where he held the Chair of Neuropathology, he was for many years a consulting physician at Queen Square.

His fame rests on his early experimental work on the localization of function in the brain and in particular on his clear demonstration that movements of the limbs could be excited from certain areas of the cortex (1873). He improved the technique of electrical stimulation by employing a faradic current, and in his extirpation experiments, by utilizing the antiseptic methods of his colleague, Lister, he was able to avoid the secondary encephalitis and the extension of the lesions which often vitiated earlier work involving surgical interference with the brain. He used many species of animal in his investigations (monkeys, dogs, jackals, cats, rabbits, guinea pigs, rats, frogs, fishes, etc.) and insisted on the importance of considering both the species of animal and its age in drawing conclusions. Thus he pointed out that dogs showed a much greater recovery of functions after cortical lesions than either monkeys or men.

Ferrier was one of the first to observe "the extraordinary absence of any discoverable physiological defect after entire removal of the prefrontal lobes, or anterior half of the frontal lobes".[2] But he noted alterations in the behaviour and character of his experimental monkeys which

---

[1] *Selected Papers*, vol. I.          [2] *Phil. Trans. Roy. Soc.*, II, 1875.

he said were difficult precisely to describe. The monkeys instead of being actively interested in their surroundings and displaying curiosity remained apathetic and dull, responding only to the sensations of the moment or showing purposeless activity.

The work of Ferrier had as one of its direct consequences the establishment of modern neurosurgery by Sir Victor Horsley (1857–1916) who, inspired by Ferrier's work, carried out in May 1886 at Queen Square the first operation on the human brain. The patient happened to be a Scotsman, and this was the famous occasion on which Hughlings Jackson whispered to Ferrier (both were watching the operation), "Awful, awful"; and when asked "why?" explained "he opened a Scotsman's head and failed to put a joke in it".

Ferrier also had a direct and considerable influence on Sherrington. He had indeed noted that "when the spinal centres form only a part of the whole cerebro-spinal system, stimuli which excite reflex action also affect the whole nervous system, cerebral as well as spinal".[1] It is not altogether surprising, therefore, that Sherrington should have dedicated his classic work on *The Integrative Action of the Nervous System* "to David Ferrier, in token of recognition of his many services to the experimental physiology of the central nervous system".

c) *H. Charlton Bastian* (1837–1915)

Brief mention, finally, deserves also to be made of Bastian if only for the sreason that it was he who coined the term 'kinaesthesis'. Though les sure in his judgement than his colleagues Hughlings Jackson and Ferrier, he too was eminent as a neurologist. He took an independent line and refused to accept Ferrier's conclusions as to the motor functions of the cortex. He held that the cortex was the 'end-station' for ingoing impulses, and that the highest motor centres were in the corpora striata and cerebellum. It followed that he could not accept Jackson's views on aphasia and in his own *Treatise on Aphasia* (1898), in many ways an influential book, postulated the existence of visual, auditory, and kinaesthetic word centres. He was perhaps the chief of the 'diagrammakers' whom Head was later to castigate, and his views paved the way for the concepts of 'word deafness' and 'word blindness'. His views of the 'muscular sense' were put forward in an early article published in 1869.[2] He controverted the theories of Bain and Wundt which depended on awareness of motor impulses, exposed the confusions of the term 'muscular sense', and suggested that the term 'kinaesthesis' should

[1] *Functions of the Brain*, 2nd ed., 69.        [2] *Brit. Med. J.*, Apr. 1869.

be used to denote a separate endowment of a complex kind whereby we are made acquainted with the position of our limbs, and enabled to guide their movements. His views on this and other matters were expounded systematically in his book *The Brain as an Organ of Mind* (1880), in which he showed himself equally versed in the neurological, anatomical, biological and philosophic theories of his time.

## 2. Cambridge Physiologists

The beginnings of physiology in Cambridge date from 1870 when Michael Foster (1836–1907), who for some years had been assisting William Sharpey at University College, London, was persuaded to migrate to Cambridge, as the result of the establishment of a Praelectorship in Physiology at Trinity College. The principal movers in bringing about this new development were George Henry Lewes and 'George Eliot'. Though Foster himself was not an active research worker he was outstandingly successful in attracting and stimulating others, and he played the major part in establishing physiology as a scientific discipline in this country. He was one of the founders of the Physiological Society in 1876, and the first editor of the *Journal of Physiology* which began to appear in 1878. His *Text Book of Physiology* (1877) superseded all other British textbooks. The brilliant achievements of the Cambridge school of physiology are largely due to the sound foundation which Foster laid in the single room in Trinity College which in 1870 served him both as laboratory and lecture room. Not all these achievements, of course, were relevant to psychology, but in the period before the First World War two lines of work, on the autonomic nervous system and on the conduction of the nervous impulse, were fundamental contributions to the foundations of physiological psychology, and as we shall see later Cambridge psychology itself was on one side the child of Cambridge physiology.

### a) *The autonomic nervous system*

The role of the autonomic nervous system in emotional behaviour and in the production of many psychosomatic phenomena is a commonplace of contemporary psychology. Our understanding of its structure and its mode of functioning is largely the result of the work of two Cambridge physiologists, W. H. Gaskell (1847–1914) and J. N. Langley (1852–1925), who succeeded Foster in the chair of physiology and as editor of the *Journal of Physiology*. In the years 1886–9 Gaskell, who had already achieved fame through his demonstration that the contraction of the heart arose in the muscular tissue itself independently of nerves, produced the first definite evidence that the visceral nerves left the central nervous system in three outflows, the cranial, thoracic, and sacral. He was the first to realize that the sympathetic nervous system did not receive branches from each spinal nerve. Langley continued Gaskell's investigations and clarified many points that Gaskell had left obscure. He discovered that the influence of adrenaline was confined to effects caused by stimulating sympathetic fibres, while other drugs caused effects more or less akin to the stimulation of cranio-sacral nerves. In 1903 he suggested the term 'parasympathetic' for this latter group of nerves. He had already (1898) introduced the term 'autonomic' to describe what Gaskell had called the 'visceral' or 'involuntary' nervous system. The term 'autonomic' was intended to imply a 'local autonomy of function'. Langley's terminology has now become the standard usage. Langley himself wrote a brief account of his discoveries in a monograph on *The Autonomic Nervous System* (1921).

b) *The conduction of the nervous impulse*

Perhaps of even greater significance were the researches initiated between 1904 and 1914 by Keith Lucas (1879–1916), who was tragically killed in a flying accident while carrying out work on aircraft design. Lucas's researches on the conduction of the nervous impulse, together with the earlier work of Gotch (1853–1913) who preceded Sherrington at Liverpool, threw the first light on the nature of the electrical changes which accompany the nerve impulse and indicated the kind of information which could be transmitted by such nerve fibres. Almost from the beginning Adrian was a collaborator with Lucas and after Lucas's death it was Adrian who edited his book on *The Conduction of the Nervous Impulse* (1917).

It had already been established by German investigation that even the shortest nervous discharge consisted in fact of a group of impulses, and that each impulse was a discrete event. Gotch discovered (1899) that these impulses were separated by a 'refractory phase', or period of incomplete recovery, when the fibre could not transmit. Lucas and Adrian (1912) distinguished three periods in the recovery of a nerve fibre; an absolute refractory period when it was inexcitable; a relative refractory period, when it gradually returned to normal; and a supernormal phase, when it showed increased excitability. Lucas (1909) had previously shown that the force of a muscle contraction did not alter when the stimulus was increased, that it was an 'all-or-nothing' phenomena, and that the strength of the contraction could be varied only by varying the number and frequency of the impulses. It was established by Adrian (1912) that the energy for the passage of the nerve impulse was supplied by the nerve itself and not by the stimulus which excited it. Thus were laid the foundations of present-day neurophysiology upon which Adrian and others were to build after the war. We shall return to Adrian in a later chapter.

Meanwhile two other Cambridge men, Sherrington and Head, were clarifying the nature of reflex action and sensation respectively, and making discoveries of fundamental importance to the psychologist.

## 3. Sir Charles Sherrington (1857–1952)

The long life of Sir Charles Sherrington spans nearly the whole of the period covered by this history; he was certainly one of its dominating figures. After a preparatory phase in Cambridge, at St. Thomas's Hospital, London, and in Germany, his life was spent at the Universities of Liverpool (1895–1913) and Oxford (1913–35) as Professor of Physiology. Almost from its foundation in 1881 the University College of Liverpool, as it then was, distinguished itself in neurophysiology. Its first physiologist Richard Caton (1842–1926) long anticipated Berger's discovery of electrical potentials from the cortex of the brain. Francis Gotch, who preceded Sherrington both in Liverpool and Oxford, we have already noted as the discoverer of the refractory phase. At the same time the nearby mental hospital at Rainhill was also a notable centre of research, numbering among its distinguished staff A. W. Campbell (1868–1937) whose *Histological Studies on the Localization of Cerebral Function* (1905) are classical, F. W. Mott, and Henry Head.

Of all those centred on Liverpool Sherrington, who became President of the Royal Society (1920–5) and a Nobel prizewinner (1932), was the most illustrious. Indeed it has been said that his work did for the nervous system what William Harvey in the seventeenth century did for the circulatory system. Sherrington laid the foundations of our understanding of nervous functioning, the foundations, therefore, of the neurophysiology of 'mind'. His importance for psychology is obvious; but he was besides a good friend to psychology and did much to help the early growing pains of the experimental approach in this country. This brief account of his work must necessarily be highly selective and confined to those aspects of it with a direct bearing on psychology.

A main theme runs through the whole of Sherrington's prodigious output. "Behaviour is rooted in integration." It consists of "a single pattern of pieces all subordinate to one keypiece"; the organism carries out "one main thing at a time" even at the spinal level; the integrated motor act is "the earliest nurse of infant mind"; higher consciousness merely increases the range, finesse, and adaptability of motor control. How does integration take place? That was the problem to which Sherrington addressed himself. What are the mechanisms involved in the integrative action of the nervous system?

Perhaps no single discovery of Sherrington's is more illuminating to the psychologist than his discovery in 1893–4 that many of the nerves supplying muscles were afferent in function and that muscle spindles were sensory end-organs. In modern terminology what Sherrington discovered was that there is a 'feed-back' mechanism in muscles themselves which acts in the first place reflexly and plays a large part in the regulation both of posture and of movement. Such a mechanism had been postulated by Sir Charles Bell and others, but up to Sherrington's demonstration the nature of 'the muscular sense' was a matter of controversy, Bain and Wundt, for example, both holding that muscular sensations were connected with the innervation of outgoing motor fibres. We now know that all self-regulated behaviour, whether in organism or machine, depends on 'feed-back'. Sherrington was the first to provide the experimental evidence for 'feed-back' in the animal nervous system, and he coined the word 'proprioceptive' for all those sensations from muscles, joints, etc., concerned with muscular regulation. Of particular interest to the psychologist was Sherrington's investigation into the role of afferent impulses from the eye-muscles in the perception of visual space. This was not a purely visual matter, but the result of a fusion of retinal sensations with eye-muscle posture sensations. Also, of course, in the perception of the vertical, sensations from the labyrinth were involved.

Sherrington's early work on reflex co-ordination was summarized in his book *The Integrative Action of the Nervous System* (1906) – a classic which must still be considered obligatory reading for the student of psychology. The reflex arc may be taken as the unit mechanism of the nervous system, but the reflex is a purely abstract conception, since in the living animal reflex arcs always comprise one or more junctions (for which Sherrington coined the now well-known term 'synapse'). It is what happens at these junctions that determines the motor outcome; here stimuli are summated, and here blocking occurs. There is one 'final common path' to the muscle fibre along which all impulses must ultimately travel. Contradictory messages cannot reach muscle; the messages have been integrated and the contradictions ironed out in the motor nerve centres. A common form of integration is reciprocal innervation, for example the reciprocal excitation of the flexor muscles of a limb accompanied by the reflex inhibition of the antagonistic extensor muscles. This reciprocal inhibition is a central process, not something that takes place in the muscle itself. There are no efferent nerve fibres in the higher animals which directly inhibit contraction of skeletal muscle, as is the case with the visceral muscles and in lower organisms. In spite of the immense complexity of the rich and intricate tangle of branching fibres comprising the nervous system, Sherrington held that even complex reflex patterns and sequences could be analysed in terms of the mechanisms discovered in simple reflex co-ordination.

A particularly interesting section of *The Integrative Action* to the psychologist is that in which Sherrington invalidates the James-Lange theory of emotion, the theory that emotion is a derivation of, and secondary to, visceral and vascular changes. By transecting the spinal and vagal nerves of a dog Sherrington removed the pathways of visceral and vascular impulses; nevertheless emotional behaviour persisted. He concluded that "the visceral expression of emotion is secondary to the action occurring with the psychical state".[1] Emotional states in decorticated animals, on the other hand, he described as 'pseudaffective' and lacking in the persistence and directness of true emotion.

A good deal of Sherrington's work from his discovery in 1896 of the condition of 'decerebrate rigidity' was concerned with the problems of the reflex maintenance of posture and muscle tonus. Sherrington showed that the rigidity and increased muscle tonus of the decerebrate animal was dependent on afferent impulses from the muscles and was a reflex affair. This led him to consider the whole mechanism of posture and tonus and to postulate two separate systems of muscular innervation, a 'tonic' system concerned with the maintenance of muscular tension and postural attitude, and a 'phasic' system concerned with action and movement. The proprioceptors were particularly closely associated with posture and tonus, and these were 'plastic' in the sense that they were modifiable by afferent impulses from the muscles themselves. Sherrington's final achievement in this field was his elucidation of the basic 'stretch reflex' in 1924. He showed that the mechanical stretching of the muscle itself supplies adequate stimulus to the muscle receptors, that stretch reflexes could be excited by gravity, and that reflex standing could be explained in these terms. The 'knee-jerk' (a term coined by Sir

[1] *Integ. Action*, 266.

William Gowers) which Sherrington had begun to study in 1891 was now shown to be a fractional manifestation of a stretch reflex. Sherrington himself was quick to see the implication for psychology that all movement takes place against a background of posture and tonic contraction; attitude is as significant as action, psychologically as well as neurologically.

The last phase of Sherrington's experimental work, which it is convenient to consider here, though it relates mainly to the inter-war years in Oxford, was devoted to the clarification of the roles of excitation and inhibition at the synaptic junctions. The discovery of reciprocal innervations (1897) had led Sherrington on to an unravelling of the roles of excitation and inhibition in co-ordinated action. It became clear that inhibition was an active process, not simply a cessation of nervous discharge nor the result of interference. Excitation and inhibition, though polar opposites in function, were equal in standing and presented many parallels in their *modus operandi*. From 1925 onwards Sherrington extended and refined this conception. In the first place he sought to explain the variations in quantity and duration of effect in 'moto-neurones' (as he now termed the motor units, each controlling teams of several hundred muscle fibres) from one and the same stimulus. He postulated persisting excitatory and inhibitory effects from subliminal impulses, and termed these respectively 'central excitatory state' and 'central inhibitory state'. Excitations and inhibitions could sum and balance each other to give graded effects; moreover the neurones themselves were not merely passive transmitters of impulses but contributed their own rhythmic discharges. Sherrington summarizes the main findings of this last phase of his experimental work in the Rede lecture on *The Brain and its Mechanisms* (1933) and there, as if to apologize for his preoccupation with the motor act, he writes, "I may seem to stress the preoccupation of the brain with muscle. Can we stress too much that preoccupation when any path we trace in the brain leads directly or indirectly to muscle? The brain seems a thoroughfare for nerve-action passing on its way to the motor animal. It has been remarked that life's aim is an act, not a thought. Today the diction must be modified to admit that, often, to refrain from an act is no less an act than to commit one, because inhibition is coequally with excitation a nervous activity."

This alone would be a momentous conclusion for psychology. But Sherrington's influence on psychology has been both wider and more specific than this. First and foremost must stand his elucidation of the main principles of neural functioning; for these must lie at the foundations of any scientific psychology. The behaviour and experience which psychology endeavours to understand are the resultants of, and indissolubly correlated with, the action of the nervous system. It must be admitted that Sherrington himself remained obstinately a dualist, and that he even expressed a doubt whether reference to the brain helped in the study of mind. Nevertheless the contemporary psychologist tends to think in terms of neurological models or even mechanical analogies, and leans heavily on Sherrington.

And Sherrington himself, in spite of the dualism and the scepticism as to the possibilities of a scientific psychology expressed in *Man, on his Nature* (1940), not only contributed to psychology, but went out of his way to back its development. His own enquiry on binocular flicker was encouragingly contributed to the first number of the *British Journal of Psychology* (1904) of which he became, and long remained, a member of the advisory panel. At Liverpool he pioneered the teaching of experimental psychology, and a succession of three lecturers was appointed in his department, W. G. Smith (1905) who afterwards proceeded to Edinburgh to found the George Combe laboratory, H. J. Watt (1906) who moved on to Glasgow to set going the study of psychology there, and Cyril Burt (1907–12) who became the first psychologist to the London County Council. Unfortunately on Sherrington's translation to Oxford this promising development at Liverpool itself was allowed to lapse. Nevertheless experimental psychology in Great Britain owes a good deal to Sherrington's support.

Finally Sherrington backed the beginnings of industrial psychology. During the First World War he had himself worked for some weeks in a munitions factory. He played a prominent part on the Health of Munition Workers Committee which inaugurated studies into industrial psychology and physiology; and after the war he became chairman of the Industrial Fatigue Research Board. He was also a vice-president of the National Institute of Industrial Psychology.

British psychology may justifiably feel proud and grateful for the support of so great a scientist and so great a man as Sir Charles Sherrington.

## 4. Sir Henry Head (1861–1940)

Head's theories have stood the test of time less well than those of Sherrington; nevertheless Head had an important and direct influence on British psychology and particularly on Cambridge psychologists. He worked in conjunction with Rivers, was a close friend of C. S. Myers, and in his later work was assisted by F. C. Bartlett. Head himself was trained in the Cambridge school of physiology, where he was especially influenced by Gaskell. After carrying out research in Prague under Hering, he returned to Cambridge to complete his medical degree. For a time he was clinical assistant at Rainhill Asylum, near Liverpool; finally he was appointed to the London Hospital, where he came into contact with Hughlings Jackson, as whose disciple he may justifiably be regarded. From 1910 to 1925 he was editor of *Brain*. For the last fifteen years of his life he was increasingly incapacitated by illness and was forced to lead a secluded existence until his death in 1940. Like Sherrington, Head published verse of his own and was a man of wide interests and a cultivated mind.

Head's work falls into two fields, cutaneous sensibility and speech disorders. He early became interested in sensation, his Cambridge M.D. being awarded in 1892 for a thesis "On disturbances of sensation, with especial reference to the pain of visceral disease". This study of 'referred' cutaneous pain associated with visceral disease gave rise to an investigation of the distribution of the posterior spinal roots. Head was the first to establish the segmental distribution of the afferent fibres. These studies led him on to the comprehensive studies of cutaneous sensibility which were subsequently collected together in *Studies in Neurology* (1920). Head traced and analysed sensory impulses from their origin, through the spinal cord, to the thalamus and the cortex. In the course of their passage to the brain Head insisted that complex groupings and integrations took place, so that an introspective analysis of the end product in the psychological manner could throw remarkably little light on the nature of sensations. "The day of the *a priori* psychologist is over as far as sensation is concerned," asserted Head. "A man can no longer sit in his study and spin out of himself the laws of psychology by a process of self-examination. For we have been able to show that, at a level deeper than any he can reach by introspection, are prepared those states, which condition the nature and characteristics of the ultimate sensation." [1] Yet Head in his studies of sensation borrowed from the more precise methods of the psychological laboratory, and one of his more important advances was the application of quantitative techniques to clinical material, and the devising of a series of tests which, as he put it, "stand midway between the rough and ready examination of the clinician and the elaborate observations of the psychologist in his laboratory".

Head's studies of injury to peripheral nerves and the disturbances of

[1] *Studies in Neurology*, II. 741.

sensation which resulted from them led him to the conclusion that the traditional accounts of the loss and return of cutaneous sensibility were erroneous. He determined to check his conclusions by observations on himself. On 25 April 1903, therefore, the radial and external cutaneous nerves of his left arm were divided in the neighbourhood of the elbow, and for over four years a detailed examination of the resulting loss and return of sensibility was carried out with the assistance of W. H. R. Rivers. In this classic experiment very detailed observations were made and careful experimental precautions observed. On the basis of these observations Head postulated three systems of sensibility: first, deep sensibility, responsive to pressure and certain forms of movement; secondly, a form of crude cutaneous sensibility he termed 'protopathic', responsive to pain, extremes of heat and cold, and showing imperfect localization; and thirdly, a so-called 'epicritic' sensibility, accurate and discriminating.

In putting forward this theory, which for a time gained some acceptance among neurologists and psychologists in this country,[1] Head was much influenced by Hughlings Jackson's doctrine of evolutionary levels. He regarded the two forms of cutaneous sensibility, protopathic and epicritic, as respectively more primitive and more developed forms, the more developed epicritic sensibility overlying and masking the protopathic in the intact human being. There is now no doubt that Head was unduly theoretical in the interpretation of his observations, and the protopathic-epicritic distinction has been wholly rejected. It was indeed early called in question by Trotter and Davies[2] in this country and by Boring in America, who repeated the experiment of nerve section but did not confirm Head's conclusions.[3] Walshe in his critical review[4] has shown conclusively that the theory is quite incompatible with what is known of nervous functioning, and that cutaneous sensory impulses do not undergo the kind of changes that Head postulated before they reach the brain. Nevertheless, Head's detailed observations are still a valuable storehouse of information.

In subsequent papers Head followed the sensory impulses first into the spinal cord, investigating their groupings, and then up into the brain. Here again his conclusions have not entirely proved acceptable. He postulated, for instance, special groups of fibres concerned with tactile

[1] See for example, C. S. Myers *Experimental Psychology*, 1911; W. H. R. Rivers *Instinct and the Unconscious*, 1920; J. S. B. Stopford *Sensation and the Sensory Pathway*, 1930.
[2] *J. Physiol.*, 1909.   [3] *Q.J. Expt. Phys.*, 1916.
[4] F. M. R. Walshe *Brain*, LXV (1942).

localization and with tactile discrimination, and his sharp distinction between thalamic and cortical functions is too simple to fit the facts now revealed by psychosurgery. For Head held that the thalamus was occupied mainly with the affective side of sensation, while the cortex was concerned with fine discriminations, appreciation of similarity and difference, projection in space and recognition of sequence in time.

It was when considering cortical functions that Head propounded his doctrine of 'the schema' [1] which was adopted with modifications by F. C. Bartlett and by Wolters and which has played an important role in British psychology. Head formulated his doctrine to explain the capacity of the normal human being to appreciate bodily position and the direction of bodily movement. Head saw that some sort of reference point was needed, and that visual images were incapable of doing the job. Hence 'the schema' which he defined as a "combined standard against which all subsequent changes of posture are measured before they enter consciousness". "By means of perpetual alterations in position", he added, "we are always building up a postural model of ourselves which constantly changes. Every new posture of movement is recorded on this plastic schema, and the activity of the cortex brings every fresh group of sensations evoked by altered posture into relation to it. . . . Such schemata modify the impressions produced by incurring sensory impulses in such a way that the final sensations of position or of locality, rise into consciousness, charged with a relation to something that has happened before." These schemata Head regarded as functioning at the physiological level; but unfortunately he merely adumbrated his doctrine, and never worked it out in any detail. So, as subsequent critics have pointed out,[2] the theory, though suggestive, is in many respects extremely vague. Nevertheless it has been regarded as "a significantly novel contribution to psychological theory".

Head's second major work was the monumental *Aphasia and Kindred Disorders of Speech* which appeared in 1926. Head had been interested in aphasia since 1886 when he first treated an aphasic patient, but his main investigations were carried out a good deal later on patients suffering from war injuries. Head had early become dissatisfied with the theories of Bastian and the 'diagram-makers'. The papers of Hughlings Jackson on aphasia had largely been forgotten; Head rediscovered them and was at once impressed. His own views were largely a development of Jackson's, and it is to Head that the revival of interest in this aspect of

[1] *Studies in Neurology*, II. 604–7.
[2] See C. Oldfield & O. L. Zangwill *Brit. J. Psychol.*, XXXII, XXXIII (1942–3).

Jackson's work is largely due. In the valuable historical sketch which forms the first part of Head's book a large place is given to an exposition of Hughlings Jackson's theories. Head himself did three main things. He devised a series of quantitative tests for the study of aphasic patients; he introduced a new classification; and he expounded a novel theory which is of exceptional interest to psychologists.

Once again, however, Head's work, though stimulating, has not withstood detailed criticism. He was undoubtedly right in demanding more precise quantitative tests in place of vague clinical labels, but the tests he employed have been criticized on a number of grounds. They were imperfectly graded, and some of them too difficult except for persons of above average intelligence. His classification has not proved acceptable in practice, though it endeavoured to break away from the unsatisfactory division into 'motor', 'visual', and 'auditory' defects of speech, and rests on sounder psychological foundations. In particular Head's 'semantic aphasia' in which there is "a want of power to combine mentally into a single act a series of relevant details" is psychologically important. Theoretically Head's views were too simple. He regarded all types of aphasia as disturbances in one form or another of the function of 'symbolic formulation and expression', a concept which bears some resemblance to Hughlings Jackson's 'propositionizing'. But as Weisenburg and McBride point out in their work on aphasia symbolic disturbances do not explain all forms of aphasia, and certainly not many disturbances in non-verbal responses which Head regarded as dependent on faulty inner verbalization.

In the final part of the expository volume on aphasia – the second volume is devoted to detailed reports of clinical cases and constitutes an immensely valuable record – Head introduced his concept of 'vigilance' This was a novel and most suggestive concept, though once again it was not developed by Head in detail. It refers to states of high-grade physiological efficiency in which "mind and body are poised in readiness to respond to any event external or internal". The way a human being behaves and the kind of responses he makes depend not only on structural factors but also on his general condition of 'vigilance'. As Head left it 'vigilance' is a sort of physiological counterpart of attention. Like some of Head's other concepts it has become incorporated into psychology and had a directive influence on subsequent psychological research.[1]

[1] See for example, N. H. Mackworth 'Researches on the Measurement of Human Performance', *Medical Research Council Special Report No. 268*, 1950.

## CHAPTER VI

# The Rise of Comparative Psychology

## 1. Naturalists and Anecdotalists

The systematic observation of animals and their ways begins in modern times with the early naturalists, and in this country goes back to the seventeenth century, and to the 'father' of British naturalists, John Ray (1628–1705), who wrote a number of zoological works in addition to his better-known botanical treatises. Ray had two major interests, the classification of species, and the collection of evidence demonstrating *The Wisdom of God as manifested in the Works of the Creation*, as he entitled one of his principal works (1691). Ray's influence on naturalists was long-lived, and the Ray Society for the publication of works on natural history was founded in his honour in 1844; his interests remained their principal interests until Darwinian times. Animal behaviour, like other phenomena in the natural world, was directly ordered by God, and demonstrated his miraculous power.

This viewpoint was well illustrated by one of the famous Bridgwater Treatises "on the power, wisdom, and goodness of God as manifested in the creation", the seventh treatise, by the Rev. William Kirby, F.R.S., *On the History, Habits, and Instincts of Animals* (1835). Its author, whose long life (1759–1850) was almost wholly spent as rector of Barham in Suffolk, was a first-rate naturalist, and the *Introduction to Entomology* (1815–26), of which he was joint author with W. Spence, long remained a standard work. Kirby believed that instinct was the characteristic mode of animal behaviour. Intellect and instinct were distinct, though, unlike many natural theologians, Kirby held that animals gifted with the ordinary organs of sensation had intellectual powers which they could employ in the routine of their instinctive activity. Typically, however, instincts were neither the result of instruction, nor of experience, but due to the action of some external agency upon the animal's organization, which is fitted by the omniscient creator to respond to its action.[1] The aptness of organization and external agent could only have come about by design, and in his plan God was concerned with the benefit of man, his supreme creation, as well as of the animals themselves. Thus

[1] *Treatise*, vol. II. 238.

the instinct to migrate was nicely contrived not only for the welfare of the migrants, but also for the gratification of the palate of man "by multiplying and varying his food".

The naturalists of this period had indeed only two ways of explaining animal behaviour. In so far as it was instinctive it was divinely ordained; in so far as it was intelligent, it was to be interpreted anthropomorphically. In the numerous collections of animal 'anecdotes' published in the nineteenth century anthropomorphic interpretation proliferated. It would be tedious to review this now outdated literature, and the book by the Rev. J. S. Watson on *The Reasoning Power of Animals* (1867) may be taken as fairly typical. Watson set out to show that "the inferior animals have a portion of that reason which is possessed by man", and he collected anecdotes to show that dogs, for example, could communicate their thoughts to each other, could understand not merely human words of command, but "whole sentences expressing many ideas", and have moral feelings and knowledge of duty. Whether or not the anecdotes were true, the interpretations were usually uncritical and incautious. "Great circumspection", wrote Watson, "was shown by a dog which was in the habit of stealing from a kitchen that had two doors opening into it; for he would never indulge his thievish propensity if one of them was shut, but if both were open, he understood that the chance of escape was doubled, and readily seized what he could."[1] Oddly enough monkeys and apes Watson credited with inferior reasoning powers to dogs or elephants, perhaps because at that time suitable anecdotes were harder to come by. But pigeons "in their conjugal relations" were capable of behaving "exactly as a husband and wife among mankind".[2]

It would be unjust, however, to dismiss this early period of natural history and anecdotalism as wholly valueless. The ground had been prepared for more critical studies, and every now and then a naturalist of genius would pioneer experimentally. Thus D. Barrington, the correspondent of Gilbert White of Selbourne, communicated to the Royal Society in 1773 his observations and experiments on the learned modification of bird song, and Dr E. Jenner, of vaccination fame, carried out experiments, also communicated to the Royal Society (1824), to prove that swallows go back to the same nest, besides being the first to elucidate the habits of the cuckoo. But these anticipations should not excite our surprise, for after all even in antiquity Galen had experimented on the feeding habits of young kids!

[1] *Reasoning Powers*, 74.          [2] ibid., 383.

## 2. Darwin and the Early Experimentalists

The birth of comparative psychology proper dates from Darwin and his theory of evolution. This theory we have already examined; suffice it here to say, that it provided the hypotheses which directed observation to the critical problems of animal behaviour, and by replacing divine with naturalistic explanation it paved the way for experimentation. Anecdotalism and anthropomorphism were not immediately exorcised – Darwin himself, as we have noted, showed not infrequent lapses – but gradually they gave way before the advance of the more rigorous methodology of science.

Consider Darwin (1881) on worms.[1] "As I was led to keep in my study during many months worms in pots filled with earth I became interested in them, and wished to learn how far they acted consciously, and how much mental power they displayed. I was the more desirous to learn something on this kind, as few observations have been made, as far as I know, on animals so low in the scale of organization, and so poorly provided with sense-organs as are earthworms." In the course of his observations Darwin was struck by the manner in which the worms plugged their burrows with leaves. As a rule the leaves were drawn in with the stalks protruding and this seemed to imply intelligence and not to be merely a matter of instinct. First Darwin experimented with the leaves of English plants which might have been familiar to the worms. In the pots in which the worms were kept he pinned down leaves to the soil, and at night observed the manner in which they were seized. Of 227 withered leaves of various kinds pulled out of the worm's burrows

181 were drawn in by the tips, with stalks protruding;
20 were drawn in by the stalk, with tips protruding;
26 were drawn in by the middle, transversely.

"This is almost sufficient to show that chance does not determine the manner in which leaves are dragged into the burrows", adds Darwin. Had he been familiar with modern statistical tests he would have been even more confident that it was not a matter of chance. Similar results were obtained with leaves from exotic trees, and with elongated paper triangles scattered on the ground. Of 303 paper triangles, sixty-two per cent were drawn into the burrows by the apex, fifteen per cent by the middle, and twenty-three per cent by the basal part – again clearly a result significantly different from chance. With objects like these the worms could not have been equipped to deal by instinct alone, nor on

[1] C. Darwin *The Formation of Vegetable Mould through the Action of Worms.*

the basis of previous experience. Darwin argues that some degree of intelligence, "some notion of the general shape of the objects, which is probably gained by touching" is involved. In this interesting account we see both the experimental testing of a hypothesis and a simple statistical tally of the results.

Darwin, however, was not the sole comparative psychologist in the 1870's to experiment. Recently J. B. S. Haldane has rescued from undeserved oblivion a young investigator, Douglas Spalding (c. 1840–77), of whom he writes "had he lived even to the age of 50, there can be little doubt that he would be recognized as the principal founder of what is now called ethology".[1] Born of humble parents in London, Spalding worked as a slater in Aberdeen and attended Bain's lectures on psychology. Later he became tutor to the sons of Lord Amberley. The younger son, Bertrand Russell (b. 1872), was however not old enough at the time of Spalding's early death to have received any formal instruction from him.

Spalding was quite unconvinced by Bain's attempt to explain away the facts of instinct and attribute them to learning and imitation, and he set out to prove experimentally that Bain was wrong.[2] Several of his experiments were carried out with chicks. He hooded them on emerging from the egg and kept them hooded for up to three days. When able to see "their behaviour was in every way conclusive against the theory that the perceptions of distance and direction by the eye are the result of experience . . . in from 2 to 15 minutes they pecked at some speck or insect, showing not merely an instinctive perception of distance, but an organized ability to judge, to measure distance, with something like infallible accuracy". Chicks, too, responded instinctively to the cluck of the hen during the first few days of life, though if reared separately for from 8–10 days, they no longer did so. Spalding showed moreover that their fear of sparrow-hawks was innate. "Having procured a young hawk able to take only short flights," he relates, "I made it fly over a hen with her first brood, then about a week old. In the twinkling of an eye most of the chickens were hid among grass and bushes." To show that the flight of birds was the result of maturation, not of learning, Spalding shut up young swallows, tits and wrens in a box small enough to prevent them exercising their wings.[3] On their release the birds flew in a nearly

[1] J. B. S. Haldane. Introducing Douglas Spalding, *B. J. Animal Behaviour*, II (1954).
[2] Douglas Spalding *Macmillan's Magazine*, XXVII (1873), 282–93; reprinted in *B. J. Animal Behaviour*, l.c.
[3] Douglas Spalding *Nature*, vol. XII (1875), 507–8.

or completely normal manner. His experiments were not only conducted with birds. He blinded young piglets with blinkers immediately after birth, and showed that when some days later their eyes were uncovered their behaviour was normal. One piglet kept in a bag in darkness for several hours responded immediately to the mother on release. Spalding rejected anecdotalism, and believed in experimenting. Of dogs, he stated, "though volumes of marvellous stories have been written, I am not aware that any careful experiments have been tried"; and experiments should be carried out, he urged, under natural conditions. "I am inclined to think that students of animal psychology should endeavour to observe the unfolding of the powers of their subjects in as nearly as possible the ordinary circumstances of their lives."

Between Spalding and his contemporary, Sir John Lubbock (1834–1913), there was little in common except their interest in animal psychology. Lubbock came from a wealthy banking family and was educated at Eton. He became M.P. for Maidstone, a Fellow of the Royal Society, Vice-Chancellor of London University, President of the British Association, Chairman of the L.C.C. and ended his life as the first Lord Avebury. He won popular fame as the father of Bank Holidays and of Early Closing Days for shops; for his selection of "The Hundred Best Books", and for an anthology *The Pleasures of Life* which was translated into many languages. Yet in spite of this diverse activity he made original and important contributions both to comparative psychology and to anthropology.

His work on insects, published in a series of papers between 1874 and 1882 and in the book *Ants, Bees and Wasps* (1882), pioneered in methods and techniques. Lubbock kept colonies of ants for long periods, up to 15 years in some cases, in special nests designed to facilitate observation; moreover he marked individual ants (being the first to do this) so that detailed records of their movements could be made. His aim was to experiment, not merely to observe. "My object", he said, "has been not so much to describe the usual habits of these insects as to test their mental condition and powers of sense." He carried out a number of ingenious experiments, paying attention to design and the statistical assessment of results. He showed experimentally that ants could distinguish between members of their own colony and members of other colonies; and that they could recognize their kin even if removed from the nest during the pupal stage and brought up by strangers. He put to the test the hypothesis that ants had a kind of language by means of which they could communicate with each other – a hypothesis which Kirby and

Spence believed to be supported by observation – and came to the conclusion that it was possible for them to convey information about the quantity of larvae to be carried back to the nest. He devised detour experiments to test the intelligence of ants, observing that "there was no better way to test their intelligence than to ascertain some object which they would clearly desire, and then to interpose some obstacle which a little ingenuity would enable them to overcome". By means of a runway in which a moving turntable was included Lubbock proved that an ant's sense of direction was dependent on its awareness of the incidence of light. If the turntable was shifted with an ant on it under normal conditions the ant immediately changed direction to compensate for the movement of the turntable. It still continued to do this when the turntable was replaced by a hat box which prevented the ant getting its bearings visually from surrounding objects. When a lid was put on the hat box ants generally did not change direction when the hat box was rotated; and when the light source was shifted during the experiment their sense of direction was usually confused. The results were not invariable and Lubbock carefully noted the statistical trends. His experiments on colour vision were also statistically assessed. He had observed that ants disliked light in the nest and tended to congregate in the darkest part. He shaded the nest with yellow, red, green and violet glass (moving the glasses at intervals "so that each should by turns cover the same portion of the nest"), and counted the number of ants congregated under each colour. The results were:

|  |  |  |
|---|---|---|
| Under red glass | 890 ants |
| „ green „ | 544 „ |
| „ yellow „ | 495 „ |
| „ violet „ | 5 „ |

Thus ants reacted differently to different colours, and seemed to show a marked sensitivity to violet. In further experiments Lubbock proved that ants were sensitive to ultra-violet light. These experiments were the first carried out on animal vision with the exception of those of Bert a few years earlier in Germany. Lubbock later followed up his own researches with a systematic survey of all the work on the sense organs of animals (*The Senses of Animals*, 1888). After that, although he remained interested in scientific work to the end of his life and wrote on botanical subjects, his numerous other duties prevented him from continuing his experimental work with insects, except perhaps as *Punch* observed on Bank Holidays!

How doth the Banking Busy Bee
Improve the shining hours,
By studying on Bank Holidays
Strange insects and wild flowers.[1]

### 3. G. J. Romanes (1848–1894)

Romanes can properly be described as the first systematic comparative psychologist. The contributions of Spalding and Lubbock were isolated and limited. Romanes went further; he experimented and he collected observations, but he also attempted to map the territory of animal psychology descriptively and theoretically. Largely on the basis of his popular writings he has been labelled an 'anecdotalist', and his work regarded as unscientific, while his experimental investigations have mostly been forgotten. It is time that Romanes was rehabilitated, and his contributions to psychology given their due recognition.

George J. Romanes was descended from an old Scottish family, and inherited considerable wealth. He never had to earn his living, and the only post he ever held was a part-time lectureship at Edinburgh University which involved a fortnight's residence a year. Although his father, the Rev. George Romanes, was at the time of his birth Professor of Greek at Kingston, Ontario, his own education was desultory and unsystematic. He entered Cambridge in 1867 "half-educated, utterly untrained, with no knowledge of men or books". He left in 1872 a capable biologist and physiologist, dedicated to science, and ready to mix with the leading scientific men of the day, with Darwin, Huxley, Spencer, G. H. Lewes, Galton, Michael Foster and others. The winters from then onwards he spent in London or Oxford; during the summer he migrated to the sea-coast of Eastern Ross-shire, where he had his own well-equipped marine laboratory "thrown open to the sea breezes" and magnificently situated. In a short working life of twenty years he wrote more than half a dozen books and many papers; at his death he left piles of notebooks and plans for experimental projects and the outline of an ambitious work on human psychology. "All my best work was to have been published in the next 10–15 years", he lamented just before his death. His name is commemorated in the 'Romanes Lectures' which he instituted at Oxford; but his work, though cut short, is his best memorial.

So far from being a mere 'anecdotalist' Romanes "lost no opportunities of observing and experimenting for himself". Moreover he recog-

[1] *Punch*, 1883.

nized the importance of theory: "it is indispensable to the continuity of advance", he believed, "that we should be prepared to supplement observation with hypothesis". As a theorist, perhaps, he was not particularly original; he was an ardent Darwinian, and psychologically a follower of the British associationist tradition; but he gave this tradition an experimental turn which neither Bain nor Spencer had been able to give it.

His most important work was on medusae (jelly-fish) and the echinoderms (star-fish and sea-urchins). Originally published in Royal Society papers it was summarized in book-form in *Jelly-Fish, Star-Fish and Sea-Urchins* (1885). When Romanes wrote, it was uncertain whether medusae had a nervous system at all. Romanes elucidated both its structure and functions, employing excision and section, electrical and other forms of stimulation and drugs of various kinds. He used kymograph recording, and measured the time course of responses with (for those days) some accuracy. This led him on to some quite important discoveries on latency and summation of stimuli. "Suppose that a paralysed Aurelia has been left quiet for several minutes in sea-water at 45° and that it is then stimulated by means of a single induction shock; the response contraction will be comparatively feeble with a very long period of latency, viz. $\frac{5}{8}$ sec. If another shock of the same intensity be thrown in as soon as the tissue has relaxed, a somewhat stronger contraction with a somewhat shorter latency period will be given. If the process is again repeated the response will be still more powerful with a still shorter period of latency; and so on, perhaps for eight or ten stages when the maximum force of contraction of which the tissue is capable will have been attained." [1] Romanes went on to suggest that this 'summation of stimuli' might apply throughout psychology. The temporal properties of responses, Romanes realized, had a bearing on their coordination. He noted that there had to be an interval between successive stimuli for responses to take place, and saw that by preventing 'antidromic' (i.e. backward) impulses in the nerve fibres this served to promote the rhythmic patterning of responses. In a normal intact organism spontaneous rhythmic contractions occurred; this could be slowed down by removal of parts of the organism, Romanes thought, because of the removal of "some influence of an afferent character". Certain excisions and sections led to complete paralysis; in other cases the intact parts functioned vicariously, and Romanes commented on "the astonishing extent to which neuro-muscular tissue may be mutilated without destroying physiological continuity".

[1] *Jelly-Fish etc.*, 53.

Romanes' experimental work embraced many animal species from medusae to the chimpanzee, Sally, in the London Zoo, whom he taught to count up to five. Sally learnt to associate numbers with their names and to present the right number of pieces of straw when asked. If more than one straw was asked for she was taught to hold the others in her mouth until the required number was complete and then deliver the whole at once. "After having consigned them to her mouth", Romanes observed, "she never looks at the straws, and therefore her estimate of their number must be found either by the feeling of her mouth or by retaining a mental impression of the successive movement of her arm in picking up the straws." It is impossible to tell from Romanes' account whether all the necessary precautions were taken to provide an un-equivocal answer, but Romanes did take some precautions, for instance against "possible error arising from her interpretation of vocal tones", and his experiment was probably one of the first of its kind. Romanes also got his sister to keep a detailed diary of the behaviour of a Cebus monkey kept in the house for a period of ten weeks. The observations are not without their interest – on motivation, for instance, the "remark-able thing is that he should take so much trouble to do that which is no material benefit to him. The desire to accomplish a chosen task seems a sufficient inducement to lead him to take any amount of trouble. It is not the desire of praise, as he never notices people looking on; it is simply the desire to achieve an object for the sake of achieving an object, and he never rests nor allows his attention to be distracted until it is done."

Among other experiments carried out by Romanes were experiments on direction-finding in cats, which were taken in bags and released several miles from their homes, experiments on hearing among lepi-doptera, on olfaction in crabs and lobsters, on the homing of bees, and on the effects of isolation on the acquisition of animal cries. In the last of these experiments carried out just before his final illness Romanes used his influence in high places to persuade Mr A. J. Balfour, a prominent member of Lord Salisbury's second ministry, to allow him to use light-houses on lonely rocks and islands as places of isolation for chicks, pup-pies, and other young animals. The question he sought to answer was whether animals reared in complete isolation would reproduce the sounds natural to their kind. The answer he got was indecisive, but Romanes was not satisfied that the isolation was complete, and he was unable to repeat the experiment.

How, it may well be asked, in spite of all this experimental work on animals, and yet further experimentation on human subjects, did

Romanes acquire the label 'anecdotalist'? It was largely the result of one popular book *Animal Intelligence* (1882), in which, in an endeavour to give an all-embracing account of the psychology of animals, he "fished the seas of popular literature as well as the rivers of scientific writing"; and perforce fell back on anecdotes in default of more reliable material. Romanes was not by the standards of the day uncritical in the anecdotes he accepted – he laid down criteria of acceptability – but he was not critical enough. He was too free in his use of anthropomorphic expressions, such as "the emotional life of spiders"; was too prone to look for "instances of the display of unusually high intelligence" before discounting simpler modes of explanation, and he "allowed to pass" some anecdotes which seem to us highly incredible, like the story of the cat which deliberately scattered crumbs to attract birds! And it is hard for us not to smile when he describes a dog's "scientific spirit overcoming his sense of the mysterious" on being confronted with a soap bubble, or when he talks of a dog showing "an inherited antipathy to butchers"!

In all this Romanes was guilty of two mistakes: he was incautious in his use of analogy from human experience; and in his attempt to bridge "the psychological distance which separates the gorilla from the gentleman" he scaled the gorilla up rather than the gentleman down. Nevertheless Romanes included in his work the two essential ingredients of a scientific psychology at least in some measure, namely experimental techniques and a conceptual framework. His conceptual framework was evolutionary, and consisted in a developmental scheme worked out in some detail and linking the simplest manifestations of mind, indicated by "antecedent uncertainty of adjustive action", to the highest level of conceptual thinking. All adjustive action involved the discrimination and classification of stimuli. At the simplest level the habituation of the sea-anemone to disturbances in the water indicated a capacity for discrimination between stimuli to which it was already habituated and new stimuli. Even the most primitive perception was partly generic and involved classificatory processes. Romanes' main task was to trace the genesis of conceptual thought from the non-conceptual antecedents. The most important intermediate step Romanes termed the 'recept'. This he defined as a "spontaneous association formed unintentionally as what may be termed an unperceived abstraction". Recepts did not involve symbolism and could be acquired by animals and infants; they correspond approximately to the 'preconcepts' and 'learning sets' of contemporary psychology. The power of translating ideas into symbols Romanes regarded as the essential distinction between man and animals.

many of the influences that affect us derive from others Butler did not hesitate to write of "the parasites that abound within us".[1]

How much influence all this had on subsequent psychology it is hard to say. Percy Nunn was apparently indebted to Butler in propounding his concept of 'mneme'; other psychologists perhaps indirectly and only rather slightly. It is indeed for *Erewhon* and *The Way of All Flesh* that Samuel Butler is likely to be remembered rather than for *Life and Habit* and *Unconscious Memory*.

[1] op. cit., 100.

Language was the needful condition for the attainment of conceptual thought. Lower concepts could be regarded as 'named recepts'. Language, however, was not necessary in the handling of familiar concepts and shorthand thinking could take place wordlessly. In his *Mental Evolution in Man* (1888) a considerable amount of space was devoted to the evolution of human language through various stages of complexity.

In providing a conceptual framework for the study of mental development Romanes was not being wholly original. He was doing what Spencer for one had already done. But there were differences between him and Spencer. Romanes' scheme was much more firmly grounded empirically than Spencer's; and instinct was differently located. While Spencer regarded instinct as an intermediate stage between reflex action and intelligence, Romanes regarded it as an independent line of development from the common stem of perception. In the interpretation of animal behaviour he gave to instinct a large place, explaining it, like Darwin, in terms of natural selection, though he did not altogether rule out the theory that instincts could originate from habits.

As the first comparative psychologist who combined experimental method and systematic theory Romanes has a secure place in history in spite of his mistakes of interpretation. Had he lived he might well have gone on to make a useful contribution to the developmental study of the human individual.

### 4. C. Lloyd Morgan (1852-1936)

The methodological mistakes of Romanes were spotted and corrected by Lloyd Morgan. Though only four years younger than Romanes, Lloyd Morgan went on living for more than forty years after Romanes' death and his work in comparative psychology was almost wholly subsequent to that of Romanes. For Romanes as a man and for much of his work Lloyd Morgan had the greatest admiration. In the preface to a selection of Romanes' essays, which he edited, he commented on "the range of his (i.e. Romanes') thought and the versalility of his mind" and remarked that the man was even greater than his works. "His conversation was so suggestive, his personality so genial and lovable, that we cannot but feel how inadequate is the printed page." These observations are worth noting because Lloyd Morgan did not spare his criticisms. He objected to "the little gratuitous unwarrantable human touch which is so often filled in, no doubt in perfect good faith, by the narrators of anecdotes", including Romanes. When Romanes wrote of his pet monkey discovering "the mechanical principle of the screw", Lloyd Morgan regarded this as "an unsatisfactory misuse of terms"; nor was he prepared to credit our dumb companions with a single sentiment. "A sense of beauty, a sense of the ludicrous, a sense of justice, and sense of right and wrong – these abstract emotions or sentiments, as such, are certainly impossible to the brute." [1] The principles underlying these criticisms Lloyd Morgan summed up in the canon for which he is chiefly famous: "In no case may we interpret an action as the outcome of the exercise of a higher psychical faculty, if it can be interpreted as the outcome of the exercise of one which stands lower in the psychological scale."[2] The enunciation of this canon has been an enormously important guide to all subsequent work in comparative psychology. It sounded the death knell of the anecdotal period; from now on anecdotes ceased to be admissible even as subsidiary evidence. As Lloyd Morgan went on to state, problems had to be settled "not by any number of anecdotes, but by carefully conducted experimental observations, carried out as far as possible under nicely controlled conditions".[3]

Lloyd Morgan's own experimental work was not extensive, and was less important than his contribution to methodology. His experiments were mainly devoted to clarifying the roles of innate and acquired factors in behaviour. To this end he hatched various species of bird – chicks, ducks, moorhens, partridge, pheasant, etc. – in an incubator and carefully observed their behavioural equipment. In the case of chicks he satisfied himself that pecking, walking, scratching themselves, scratching the ground, preening, stretching up and clapping their wings, squatting down and dusting themselves, scattering and crouching when alarmed, making the danger churr and other sounds, as well as numerous minor activities were instinctive. He did not, however, fully agree with Spalding's conclusions. Though pecking was innate in chicks, there was not such perfect accuracy of aim on the first occasion as Spalding implied. Practice was necessary, and also discriminations had to be learned. At first chicks would peck at almost any small object, and if small enough almost anything was eaten, or at least tasted – grain, sand, crumbs, bits of chopped up wax match, buttons, beans, cigarette ash, etc. Lloyd Morgan also doubted if Spalding was right in speaking of a chick's innate specific fear of sparrow-hawks; he regarded it rather as a manifestation of a more general fear response to strange sights and sounds. On more complex matters such as migration Lloyd Morgan admitted a profound sense of ignorance. "I should be inclined to surmise", he says, "that while the migrating impulse is innate and perhaps there is an instinctive tendency to start in a given direction, yet the element of traditional guidance may be effectual, in the migration stream as a whole, in some way that we have hitherto been unable to observe." [1] In his study of instinct Lloyd Morgan focused his attention on the instinctive act; the question of an underlying impulse he regarded as a metaphysical not a scientific matter. Commenting on his own divergence from McDougall's theory of instinct he said: "Instinct is not something that through impulsive force and motive power, drives bodily or mental processes towards their end; it is a concept in terms of which we can in some measure interpret these processes as facts presented in nature."[2]

Lloyd Morgan's observations of chicks soon led him on to the study of acquired behaviour. His young birds rapidly profited from experience, and when in flocks learned also by imitation. Imitation, for instance, accounted for some feature, of bird song, and Lloyd Morgan noted that it was much easier to bring up young birds if older birds were setting an example of eating and drinking. Lloyd Morgan's analysis of the process of learning was a very detailed one, and some of the key terminology of learning theory can be traced back to him. Chicks learned by "the method of trial and error", there was conscious "reinforcement of successful modes of response", and "inhibition of the unsuccessful"; all this before Thorndike and his work on animal learning, of which indeed Lloyd Morgan was somewhat critical, regarding the experimental situations as too artificial. Perhaps Lloyd Morgan's own most detailed observations were on the acquired discrimination made by young chicks between small worms and cinnabar moth caterpillars which were presented to them on their third day of active life. There was no instinctive acquaintance with the difference between a nice worm and a nasty caterpillar, but after a few trials the chicks profited by experience, some kind of associative link was formed between sight and taste, and subsequent actions guided accordingly.[3] Some of Lloyd Morgan's other observations – for example those on his fox terrier and how it learned, at first by chance, the trick of unlatching the front gate – were less fully controlled. But the facts were carefully observed and cautiously interpreted. His caution led Lloyd Morgan to doubt whether there was at that time any experimental evidence for any kind of reasoning in animals as distinct from associative learning. "Animals deal with difficulties by the method of trial and error . . . the perception of relations as such is not necessary

[1] *Habit and Instinct.*     [2] *Instinct and Experience.*
[3] See *Habit and Instinct,* 148 ff.

to the performance, and is therefore by our canon of interpretation excluded." [1] And, Lloyd Morgan added, "the fuller and more careful the investigation the less is the satisfactory evidence of processes of reasoning".[2] Nevertheless he did not dogmatically rule out the existence of reasoning in animals and admitted that some recorded performances were difficult to explain wholly in terms of associative learning. It is, too, interesting, in the light of subsequent developments, to note that Lloyd Morgan allowed for two main kinds of learning: "there are two important processes", he wrote, "which fall under the head of acquisition. We acquire experience, and we acquire skill. The first involves the correlation of incoming data from the special senses, from the motor organs, and from the viscera. The second implies the more or less accurate co-ordination of outgoing impulses to the viscera and to the motor organs."[3] Somehow in the process of acquiring experience and skills Lloyd Morgan believed that consciousness played a part. The loop-line to higher centres upon which control depended and with which consciousness was associated worked through the inhibition of some, and the reinforcement of other activities. The chapter on "Automatism and Control" in which Lloyd Morgan expounds his views on these matters is a remarkable example of his clear-headed analysis of the complexities of behaviour.[4]

All these interesting observations and formulations were made by Lloyd Morgan in the late 1880's and 1890's. In America, where he lectured on comparative psychology in Boston, New York, and Chicago, he made a deep impression. In Great Britain where the associationist viewpoint had become unfashionable he made less impact, and his ambition to see a chair of comparative psychology established in this country with an attached experimental station was unfortunately never realized, and to this day remains unrealized. Lloyd Morgan himself in 1887 became Principal of the University College of Bristol, a post he held until 1910 when the college became a university. Administrative duties naturally occupied a great deal of Lloyd Morgan's time, and when he retired at the early age of 58 his interests had turned more and more towards his first love – philosophy. Although he continued to write on comparative psychology, he had ceased serious experimentation, and his books, which contain little new material, became increasingly garrulous in style. His theory of emergence, however, which he expounded in his Gifford Lectures on Emergent Evolution (1923), is of

---

[1] Introd. to Comp. Psychol., 254.    [2] l.c., 304.
[3] Habit and Instinct.    [4] Introd. to Comp. Psychol., ch. 11.

some importance psychologically. The term 'emergent' he borrowed from G. H. Lewes; and the theory itself he regarded not so much as philosophic speculation as a description of the scientific facts. Consciousness itself was an emergent quality in the sense that it was something new in evolutionary development, something which could not have been predicted from earlier developments, any more than the emergence of life from the inorganic could have been predicted from an analysis of inorganic properties. Emergence, however, though involving genuine novelty did not involve the intrusion of external agents. Lloyd Morgan rejected 'entelechies', the '*élan vital*', or 'psychic entities' as animistic and unscientific. Emergence meant an emergence within the natural order. Lloyd Morgan's philosophy was fundamentally a monistic one. Within the psychological domain what Lloyd Morgan's doctrine really achieved was to place in a wider theoretical framework the doctrine of mental levels. There were three main distinguishable stages in the emergence of human consciousness which he termed percipient, perceptive and reflective. Whereas percipient consciousness was shut up within the passing moment, as higher levels emerged revival and expectancy played an increasingly important role.

There was all through Lloyd Morgan's theorizing a certain disharmony and ambivalence. He objected to Romanes' definition of instinct because it introduced the criterion of consciousness; he threw doubt on the validity of animal study not based on objective methods; he introduced the term 'behaviour' as an appropriate description of his field of study. Yet he regarded introspective psychology as an "essential preliminary to comparative psychology"; believed that consciousness was an effective agent of control; and philosophically he maintained a phenomenalist viewpoint according to which the objective world was a symbolic construct.

In spite of this ambivalence and uncertainty his contribution to comparative psychology, particularly in the field of methodology, was of enduring importance. He had a keenly analytic mind that could cut through to essentials, and a desire, as he put it, "to get down to bed-rock in the pure science of psychology". Nor should we forget that Lloyd Morgan was the first person to be elected to a Fellowship of the Royal Society for psychological work, and the first President of the psychological section of the British Association, which he addressed in Edinburgh in 1921 on "Consciousness and the Unconscious". In more ways than one he was a link between the early developments of the Darwinian era and the contemporary world of psychology.

## 5. L. T. Hobhouse (1864-1928)

Hobhouse, the last of the pioneers of British comparative psychology, was only incidentally a psychologist. He has been described as "after Spencer the most encyclopaedic mind among British philosophers". He was the author of many books on epistemology, ethics, politics and sociology – long and often rather abstract books which have passed out of fashion with the liberal faith that inspired much of Hobhouse's thinking. Commencing his working life as an Oxford philosophy tutor, Hobhouse took up first journalism with the *Manchester Guardian*, and then came to rest as the Martin White Professor of Sociology at the London School of Economics. His work on comparative psychology was an episode carried out during the Manchester period to confirm certain general theories. It involved a good deal of experimental work with animals, much of it at the Manchester Zoo. The ground had been prepared while Hobhouse was still at Oxford not only by a philosophical analysis of the nature of knowledge but more practically by an intensive study of physiology and biochemistry in J. S. Haldane's laboratories. The theories and the findings were published in *Mind in Evolution* (1901).

All Hobhouse's work was based on the fundamental philosophical position which he expounded in *The Theory of Knowledge* (1896). Knowledge and truth resided in the systematic interconnection of judgements. This mutual interdependence of the parts within the whole he termed 'consilience'. The evolutionary nisus was a movement towards greater connectedness, towards unities of wider and wider scope. In this process developing mind played a guiding role. Hobhouse's studies of mind in evolution were an attempt to provide factual confirmation of his theories from the study of animal behaviour. Not only were his animal studies, coming when they did, of a pioneering nature, but they are notable as precursors of many features of what later became 'Gestalt psychology'. Though in a sense Hobhouse, even more than most other British psychologists of his day, was only an amateur psychologist, he was a remarkably successful one. Perhaps he succeeded because he approached comparative psychology with a clear-cut set of hypotheses, with the conviction that scientific verification demanded experimental tests, and with the sturdy belief that (as he put it some years later) "radical behaviourism is the one and only method of all psychology".[1]

[1] Article on 'Comparative Psychology', *Ency. Brit.* (1929).

Hobhouse's theory of evolving mind was in some respects not unlike Lloyd Morgan's and his 'stages of correlation' bear a resemblance to the latter's emergent series. Mind Hobhouse regarded as being founded upon organic adaptability, which was basically what today we should term 'homeostatic'. Hobhouse stated it thus: "every organism is so built, on mechanical principles or not, that every deviation from the equilibrium point sets up a tendency to return to it" [1] – a process some- what analogous, as he pointed out, to the regulation of a steam engine by a governor. Thus "the living organism is distinguished by its tendency to maintain itself through process and against change".[2]

The advent of mind is the advent of a new form of correlation, by which Hobhouse means the organization and inter-connexion of parts within a whole, guided and directed to an end. The simplest forms of correlation are hereditary, consisting of reflex action and instinct. Reflex action is a response to a present sensory stimulus; instinct involves rather more, namely a permanent internal disposition of 'enduring interest' determined by heredity. As mind evolves correlations become increasingly based on individual experience. In the lower animal species experience is 'assimilated' without clear discrimination of what is being assimilated and action is guided by momentary perceptual conscious- ness. In associative learning, upon which Hobhouse placed rather little emphasis, ideas are discriminated but fortuitously linked. Properly associated it should be regarded as a limiting case of 'practical judge- ment' in which the apprehension of relation is reduced to a minimum. For Hobhouse held that animals below the primates were capable of 'practical judgement' and perceptual learning. He was critical of Thorndike's experimental work with cats and his conclusions on the random nature of the learning process, and produced evidence to show that the slope of the learning curve was not always as gradual as Thorn- dike had maintained. Some cats and dogs could learn in a very few trials. "What we may call the sensi-impulse theory of association implies that an animal can only learn to do a thing by doing it, and so getting the pleasure of success associated with the doing. Now if one puts an animal through an act to show him how it is done, and if he can learn in this way, the theory breaks down." [3] It was in an endeavour to verify the existence of this kind of learning that Hobhouse carried out his first series of experiments on a variety of animals, cat, dog, otter, elephant and monkey. The animals were confronted with problem situations in which they had to obtain food in a novel manner. For example a piece of

---

[1] *Mind in Evolution*, 24.        [2] l.c., 35.        [3] *Mind in Evolution*, 151.

meat was placed on a card to which a string was tied and then placed on a shelf. The first reaction of the dog to which this was presented was to leap up and paw wildly. After a time Hobhouse pulled the card down by means of the string, when he was satisfied that the dog was attending, and demonstrated how the problem could be solved. The experiments did not always succeed, but when they did there was a sudden change in the behaviour of the animals. "It became clear that the animal was abandoning these (its own) methods and adopting mine." The transition was not a gradual one, and what was once acquired was rarely lost. Moreover what had been learned was not a stereotyped set of movements, but an acquirement that could be varied to meet changed circumstances. Thus alternative routes to a goal might be adopted if the usual route was blocked. In some of Hobhouse's tests the animals were presented with two or more strings to pull, or boxes or drawers to open, and he showed (several years before Yerkes in 1907 devised his discrimination apparatus) that they could make discriminations. He also showed that they were capable of what are now called 'stimulus generalizations', or as he put it: "the more intelligent animals not merely learn to react appropriately to a certain kind of sense stimulus but from knowledge of the concrete and perhaps highly complex object, they learn to deal suitably with another object of the same class".[1] The animals were guided by class resemblances, "a similarity in which many elements are concerned and in which the relation between the elements is perhaps the determining feature".[2] In spite of all this Hobhouse nevertheless made it clear that, in his opinion, none of his animals showed the least understanding of the how and why of their actions. At the most they attained, in the case of monkeys and chimpanzees, to what he called 'articulate ideas'. A chimpanzee could, for example, learn to use a short stick to reach a longer stick with which to obtain a banana. To do this seemed to imply a clearer, more articulate grasp of the relational structure of the situation confronting the animal. To test this hypothesis Hobhouse carried out a number of experiments with tied ropes, a bolt fastened by a hook, chains, stools and so on, and came to the conclusion that monkeys were capable of grasping the plan of simple structures in an articulate manner, that they could "apply one object to another", and were to some extent freed from slavery to the perceptual order. Concepts proper, however, were still beyond them. Concepts imply a still higher abstraction from the perceptual setting and are peculiar to man. Man, through conceptual, and later systematic, thought, finds himself in a new world in which the

[1] l.c., 255.　　　[2] l.c., 257.

realization of self identity, the conception of other selves, social institutions and tradition gives rise to new forms of experience and behaviour. Throughout all its stages, however, at whatever level, the mind works in fundamentally the same way, by correlating experience.

With the uses to which Hobhouse put these conclusions we are not here concerned. He went on to expound a comprehensive philosophy of evolution in *Development and Purpose* (1913), and to apply his philosophical and psychological principles to sociology. In his passage through the domain of comparative psychology he made by the way a very suggestive and valuable contribution to experimental animal study. Unfortunately it was the last important original piece of work in comparative psychology in Great Britain for some time. Hobhouse moved off to other fields; Romanes was dead; and Lloyd Morgan was claimed by administration and philosophy. No one took up the work so brilliantly commenced. The virtual cessation of this promising line of development is perhaps one of the most lamentable occurrences in the history of British psychology.

# CHAPTER VII

# The Foundations of Social Psychology

Social psychology as a distinct discipline is a twentieth-century creation. But its foundations were laid in the social philosophy of the eighteenth and early nineteenth centuries, in the new sociology of the middle nineteenth century, and in the social anthropology of its final decades. It is at these foundations that we must now look.

## 1. Social Instincts

British social philosophy of the eighteenth and early nineteenth centuries was predominantly individualistic. It was concerned to justify the political rights of the individual against the authority of the absolute monarch, and the economic rights of the entrepreneur against the restrictions imposed by the state. Not unnaturally, therefore, it was concerned to uphold the rationality and practical wisdom of the individual rather than to expose the mixed and sometimes irrational manner of his actual social behaviour. John Locke in his *Treatises on Civil Government* (1690) conceived the state as an aggregate of equal individuals each possessing inalienable natural rights to life, liberty and property, behaving for the most part rationally, and contractually delegating certain limited functions to the community. The founder of economic science, Adam Smith, in his classic treatise *The Wealth of Nations* (1776) showed how "the natural effort of every individual to better his own condition" led to the maximum benefit to society, and to certain regularities of economic behaviour which could be scientifically codified. These individualistic principles were accepted by Bentham and his followers whose utilitarian social philosophy was influential in this country throughout the early part of the nineteenth century.

To the individualists and utilitarians there were no special problems involved in social behaviour. J. S. Mill put the matter with dogmatic directness:[1] "Human beings in society have no properties but those which are derived from and may be resolved into the laws of the nature of individual man". It was against the background of this tradition that psychology as a separate science first emerged, and not surprisingly

---

[1] Mill *Logic*, VI. 7.

social psychology was, as a result, slow in gaining recognition. Nevertheless in the theories of social instinct which can be traced back to the eighteenth century we can see the beginnings of what was later to become social psychology.

The moral philosophers Shaftesbury (1671–1713) and Hutcheson (1692–1752) recognized the role of human instinct in human conduct, and in particular the existence of a social instinct. Man was not wholly self-centred and egoistic. These views were adopted by Hume (1711–76) whose trenchant mind saw through the unhistorical assumptions of the contract theory of society. The basis of society was not intelligent self-interest, but instinct. Not all action could be accounted for by self-love: rather "everything which contributes to the happiness of society recommends itself directly to our approbation and good will".[1] Not only is there a natural "propensity to company and society"[2] but there is a natural impulse of sympathy which serves as the cement of society. Moreover "the human mind is of a very imitative nature, nor is it possible for any set of men to converse together without acquiring a similitude of manners".[3]

The doctrine of social instinct, propounded in succession by Adam Ferguson (1723–1816), Dugald Stewart (1753–1828) and other philosophic writers, was placed on a biological foundation by Darwin. Man was a social animal and like other social animals "would inherit a tendency to be faithful to his comrades and obedient to the leader of his tribe". Such an instinct Darwin regarded as innate and resulting from natural selection. Galton's vivid description of gregariousness in cattle[4] lent observational support to the theory of a social instinct, and, by analogy, to the explanation of man's 'slavish' tendency to social conformity in terms of his gregarious propensity.

The doctrine of sympathy, borrowed perhaps by Hume from the French philosopher, Malebranche, was adopted by Adam Smith and played a major role in his *Theory of Moral Sentiments* (1759) though carefully kept out of his later economic theories. A striking feature of Smith's account was the recognition that social interaction is necessary for any kind of self-knowledge. "Were it possible that a human creature could grow up to manhood in some solitary place without any communication with his own species he could no more think of his own

---

[1] Hume *An Enquiry concerning Human Understanding*, (1748).
[2] Hume *Essays*, XXI.
[3] l.c.
[4] Galton 'Gregariousness in Cattle and Man', *Macmillan's Magazine*, 1871.

character, or the propriety or demerit of his own sentiments and conduct, of the beauty and deformity of his own mind, than of the beauty
or deformity of his own face."[1] Bain, Spencer, and McDougall all incorporated sympathy in their psychologies; but in the harsh light of the
twentieth century it seems practically to have vanished from the psychological scene.

Imitation has fared more propitiously. One of the most brilliant of
Victorian minds, Walter Bagehot (1826–77), became its advocate. Editor
of *The Economist* from 1860 till his death and famous for his classic
books on *The English Constitution* (1867) and *Lombard Street* (1873),
Bagehot in *Physics and Politics* (1869) made one of the first psychological
analyses of society. Moving in high governmental and city circles he
was intimately acquainted with the political and financial institutions
and behaviour which he set out to describe. As one of his biographers
notes, Bagehot "brought the quality of scientific dispassionate description of matters which were hardly thought of previously as subject of
scientific study". Bagehot's *English Constitution* is no dry-as-dust
historico-legal document, but a vivacious piece of social analysis, often
psychological in approach. Bagehot observes that "it is the dull traditional habit of mankind that guides most men's actions".[2] Royalty gets
its pull over republicanism because "royalty is a government in which
the attention of the nation is concentrated on one person doing interesting actions. A republic is a government in which attention is divided
between many who are all doing uninteresting actions."[3] Cabinet government is rare because it depends on certain psychological prerequisites –
not only confidence, calmness, and rationality but a 'deferential community' in which the masses respect their betters. These psychological
*aperçus* Bagehot developed more systematically in *Physics and Politics*
which he described as "thoughts on the application of the principles of
natural selection and inheritance to political society". Again Bagehot
insisted that civilized society depended on habit, on an inherited drill,
a laboriously acquired "cake of custom". This was transmitted and
extended by reason of "the copying propensity of man", which Bagehot
regarded as one of the strongest forces of human nature, and which he
conceived of as acting largely unconsciously. "At first a sort of 'chance
predominance' made a model, and then invincible attraction, the necessity which rules all but the strongest men to imitate what is before their
eyes, and to be what they are expected to be, moulded men by that

[1] l.c., III. 1.                    [2] *English Constitution*, 9.
[3] ibid., 39.

model."[1] It is much harder to break customs once formed than to form them in the first place. In the 'unfixing' of custom discussion had an important part to play. But even so "one of the greatest pains to human nature is the pain of a new idea".[2] The slow acceptance of Bagehot's own ideas could be regarded as an illustration of his own apophthegm. A generation passed before Graham Wallas provided us with psychological analyses of social problems equally concrete and incisive.

## 2. Socialism and Sociology

The individualistic social philosophy in which theories of social instincts had their birth found its ripest expression in Mill's essay *On Liberty* in 1859. Thereafter it gradually receded, as Dicey pointed out in his *Law and Opinion in England* (1905), before the advance of collectivist ideas. Socialism and sociology brought new frames of reference and new conceptions of the relations between the individual and society, and prepared the way for social psychological theories less closely tied to instinct.

We can see the beginnings of new conceptions in the writings of the revolutionists, Tom Paine and William Godwin, at the end of the eighteenth century. Godwin, for example, denied the existence of innate principles and instincts in man. Man's character was made by education and environment. "Compared with the empire of impression the mere differences of animal structure are inexpressibly unimportant and powerless."[3] The matter was stated even more forcibly by the pioneer industrialist, Robert Owen (1771–1858), who not only preached new doctrines but showed at his New Lanark Mills that, at any rate in a paternalistic context, they could be implemented. His later experiments on ideal communities were not so successful! Owen was the originator of the term 'socialist', and set forth his views in numerous writings of which *A New View of Society: Essays on the Formation of Character* (1813–14) may be taken as an example. "Any general character," states Owen, "from the best to the worst, from the most ignorant to the most enlightened, may be given to any community, even to the world at large, by the application of proper means. . . . The character of man is, without a single exception, always formed for him . . . nor is it possible he ever can form his own character." The important period in character formation is infancy, particularly the first two years of life. Human

---

[1] *Physics and Politics*, 36.          [2] l.c., 163.
[3] Godwin *Political Justice*, I. 40.

nature is 'universally plastic', and is in fact moulded by the influence of social training and education.

The socialistic ideas of which Owen was a protagonist made gradual headway in spite of the failure of the Chartist movement in the 1840's and of the Christian Socialists' co-operative experiments between 1848 and 1854. England did not become socialistic, but the prevailing attitudes to the problems of man's relations to society subtly changed. Partly this was the result of the general collapse of the utilitarian concepts with which individualism had become identified, and partly the growing body of factual evidence that all was not well with society. Descriptive accounts like Mayhew's *London Labour and the London Poor* (1861); official reports like the inquiries of the Sweating Commission; and finally comprehensive social surveys like Booth's *Survey of London Life and Labour* (1889-1903) provided factual data in plenty for social reformers and social theorists alike, and pointed at any rate to some problems which it needed a social psychology to solve. The Fabian Society, founded in 1884, did much to advance collectivist ideas in Great Britain. Through Graham Wallas, an original member of the society, there was a direct link between the Fabians and social psychology.

Much less prominent in nineteenth-century England was sociology proper. Indeed this country has been conspicuously backward in the development of sociology, and even to this day many of our universities have no chairs in the subject. The term 'sociology' and the conception of a unified science of society are usually attributed to the French philosopher, Comte, whose principal writings were published in the 1830's. Comtian ideas became disseminated in England in the 1840's and 1850's and had some following right up to the First World War.[1] J. S. Mill, Herbert Spencer, and G. H. Lewes were all influenced by Comte. J. S. Mill in his *System of Logic* (1843) devoted several chapters to the science of society and held that Comte's historical approach was the sound foundation for an empirical social science. But neither Mill nor Spencer could agree with Comte's view that "a society can no more be decomposed into individuals than a geometrical surface can be resolved into lines or lines into points".

The first systematic British sociologist was Herbert Spencer, though H. T. Buckle (1821-61) some years earlier in his *History of Civilisation in England* (Vol. I, 1857) produced the first native attempt at a science of history – a work which it has been said "stimulated sociological

[1] See J. E. McGee *A Crusade for Humanity: the history of organized positivism in England*, 1911.

thought more vigorously than any other in nineteenth-century England", and which certainly adumbrated the possibility of a social psychology of human behaviour on a scientific, statistical basis. Buckle, however, was unfortunate both in the date of the publication of his book and in his early death. He just missed the evolutionary era, and it was left to Spencer and others to apply evolutionary ideas to the study of society. Spencer himself with groaning and toil produced a vast three-volume *Principles of Sociology* between 1876 and 1896, and supplemented this with numerous volumes of *Descriptive Sociology* and by other books and essays with a sociological purport. Sociology was one storey in the edifice of human knowledge, but unfortunately it was not in Spencer's building plan closely connected with the adjoining storey, psychology. So though Spencer was a pioneer both in psychology and in sociology he did comparatively little towards the creation of social psychology. Perhaps Spencer's mind was too tidy to be able to conceive such an untidy subject as social psychology! Spencer's sociology was built in accordance with his customary evolutionary plan. Societies grow: their structure and functions become differentiated and more internally complex. This evolutionary growth of societies he conceived as closely similar to the growth of organisms. Indeed Spencer pressed the comparison between societies and organisms to extravagant lengths; blood corpuscles being likened to money, nerves to telegraph wires, and the cerebral masses to the House of Commons! In his stress on the importance of common principles of organization, of channels of communication and regulating systems applied both to organisms and societies there is a certain likeness between the views of Spencer and those of certain modern cyberneticians. But perhaps the part of Spencer's sociology of most interest to the social psychologist is that dealing with ceremonial institutions, where he interprets, often ingeniously, modern ceremonial observances as vestiges of earlier socially useful practices. Thus the tattooing of sailors, the branding of deserters, and the cropping of the heads of felons he saw as the relics of the primitive custom of mutilation; while badges he regarded as derivations from trophies.

Spencer, however, was so wedded to the idea that the nature of the aggregate, of society, depended on the nature of the units, of the individuals, of which it was composed that he failed to study in any detail the reverse influences of society on the individual, which constitutes the main task of social psychology. Instead he launched into a detailed analysis of the mentality of primitive man, which, being wholly insular, he was not particularly well-equipped to do. However, Spencer held that complex society had evolved from primitive society, and that primitive society was shaped by the mentality of its individual components. Hence it was necessary for him to describe primitive mentality. The dominating fact for primitive man was the duality of nature and the supernatural, and the ever-present reality of a spirit world. All the superstitious practices found in primitive society followed quite logically and rationally from this belief, which was derived ultimately from experiences such as dreaming. Primitive man was perfectly logical; the laws of thought were the same everywhere, and restricted to the data available to primitive man and given his mental powers we ourselves should come to similar conclusions. The work of the social anthropologists was destined somewhat to shake Spencer's neat theorizing about primitive man and primitive society, and undermine the foundations of his sociology.

Spencer, however, was not alone in showing an interest in social development. It was a natural consequence of evolutionary theory. Sir John Lubbock in *Prehistoric Times* (1865) (in which the terms 'palaeolithic' and 'neolithic' were first introduced) and *The Origin of Civilization* (1870) applied evolutionary ideas to technology, beliefs, and institutions, in particular the institution of the family. Sir Henry Maine (1822–88), a distinguished jurist, studied the evolution of legal ideas and customs in *Ancient Law* (1861) and other works. "Few writers", it has been said, "throw so much light on the development of the human mind in its social relations." Maine clearly saw that the past could not be rightly interpreted by a mere backward projection of the present. In primitive times society dominated the individual, the growth of whose independence and individuality was extremely gradual and bound up with the growth of legal conceptions of contract, property and inheritance. In primitive times the family was the unit of society, and, according to Maine, the basic form of the family was the patriarchal one.

Sociology made no substantial progress in Great Britain until the turn of the century. By 1903, however, enough interest had been shown to justify the formation of 'The Institute of Sociology'. Patrick Geddes and Victor Branford were the moving spirits, and among its members were Shand and Sully, psychologists; Haddon, Marrett and Westermarck, anthropologists; Hobhouse, Carr-Saunders, and Ginsberg, sociologists; and Graham Wallas, political philosopher and social psychologist. Geddes (1854–1932) was perhaps the most brilliant and remarkable of the group. Trained as a biologist under Huxley, and for most of his working life holding what in effect was a part-time chair of botany at Dundee, he won his major reputation in the field of town planning. But his mind was synthetic and universal, and inspired by the French sociologists Comte and Le Play he saw all man's social activities in their geographic and economic context. Regional planning was the practical outcome. Geddes was not himself in any specialized sense a social psychologist (though towards the end of his life he became president of the Adler Society), but his conceptual scheme of bio-psychosis (the influence of biological and environmental facts on mental life) and psycho-biosis (the effect of emotion, ideas and imagination upon man's life and deeds) was comprehensive enough, and human enough, to embrace most of the subject matter of social psychology.

## 3. The Beginnings of Social Anthropology

Sociology, however, in spite of this initiative, failed to prosper in Great Britain. Social anthropology was more fortunate. Though the term itself was not used until 1907 when Sir James Frazer gave his Liverpool inaugural on 'The Tasks of Social Anthropology', the study was in fact born in the later nineteenth century, and indeed the last three decades of the century may be regarded as the heroic age of British social anthropology. Tylor's *Primitive Culture* appeared in 1871, Robertson Smith's *Religion of the Semites* in 1889, the first edition of Frazer's *Golden Bough* in 1890, and Westermarck's *History of Human Marriage* in 1891. These were famous works of momentous import, and before the end of the century they were supplemented by the first anthropological field studies deliberately planned as such. Baldwin Spencer accompanied the Horn expedition to Central Australia in 1894 and in *The Native Tribes of Central Australia* (1899) described in detail one of the most primitive of surviving cultures, a Stone Age people without metals, clothes, houses, domestic animals, or the conception of paternity. In 1898 the Torres Straits expedition brought anthropologists and psychologists together in a joint enterprise. In these three decades a new dimension had been added to the study of man and his society.

The systematic study of primitive peoples began in Great Britain in the 1840's. In 1843, less than ten years after the abolition of slavery in the empire, the Ethnological Society[1] was founded, and in the same year J. C. Prichard, to whose psychiatric work we have already referred, published his book *The Natural History of Man*, which marks the beginning of ethnology in this country. New light on the social institu-

---

[1] The Ethnological Society later merged into the Anthropological Institute of Great Britain.

tions of primitive peoples was thrown by J. F. McLennan (1827–81), a Scottish lawyer and parliamentary draughtsman who wrote on *Primitive Marriage* (1865) and introduced to anthropology the concept of 'totemism'. The real founder however of social anthropology in this country was E. B. Tylor (1832–1917), who was also the first holder, at Oxford, of an anthropological chair. Tylor got interested in anthropology when, for reasons of health, he abandoned his position in the family firm of brassfounders which he joined on leaving school, and went on a trip to Mexico. From studies of material culture and language he passed on to the study of myth and belief, and began to conceive the possibility of a universal science of human culture based on evolutionary principles. He argued in support of the view that primitive people were not degenerate backsliders, but exemplars of earlier stages of human development. In the vast maze of primitive myth and practice he saw order and pattern: "legend", he wrote, "when classified in a sufficient scale displays a regularity of development which the notion of motiveless fancy quite fails to account for".[1] Myths and beliefs display not only regularity but also "universal qualities of the human mind". Among these qualities was primitive animism, "the belief in the animation of all nature rising at its highest pitch to personification",[2] the basis of the belief in spiritual beings, of the religious practices of prayer, sacrifice, and purification, and of a general philosophy of nature and man. This animistic mode of thinking, the origins of which Tylor attributed mainly to the experiences of dreams and visions, was a mode in which subjective and objective, imagination and reality were at least partially fused, and was for Tylor the key to the primitive mind and an explanation of many surviving peculiarities of the contemporary mind, since "heirlooms of primitive ages may be claimed in the existing psychology of the civilized world".[3]

No doubt Tylor in his theory of animism hit on an extremely fruitful explanatory concept, of which psychologists have made use in studies both of the primitive and of the child mind. In broad outlines the theory of animism was accepted by Tylor's immediate predecessors, but it was modified in two ways: first, animistic ideas were traced by Andrew Lang and A. E. Crawley to waking hallucinations and imagery rather than to dreams; and secondly a pre-animistic stage of development was postulated in which the projected life force was not personified. Thus Codrington in *The Melanesians* (1891) (peoples among whom he worked for many years as a missionary) noted that anything out of the ordinary,

[1] *Primitive Culture*, I. 415.     [2] l.c., I. 285.     [3] l.c., I. 429.

whether specially powerful or effective or uncanny, was regarded as possessing 'mana', a sort of impersonal force. R. R. Marrett (1866–1943), who followed Tylor at Oxford, coined the term 'animatism' to describe the 'pre-animistic' phase of religion, which was "not so much thought out as danced out",[1] and was insufficiently intellectualized to involve any clear conception of spiritual beings.

The greatest of Tylor's successors in the early development of social anthropology was assuredly J. G. Frazer (1854–1941), a Glasgow classical scholar whose interest in anthropology was roused by reading Tylor and stimulated in Cambridge by contact with Robertson Smith, then professor of Arabic, and editor of the *Encyclopaedia Britannica*. Though Frazer never visited any of the primitive peoples about whose beliefs and practices he wrote, he had indefatigable industry in collecting data, the highest standards in sifting it, and great literary skill in presenting it. The vast corpus of his publications – *The Golden Bough* alone running into thirteen volumes – constitutes a mine of facts not unduly distorted by theory, bearing on "the gradual evolution of human thought from savagery to civilization". In this evolution Frazer distinguished three main stages, magic, religion and science. Frazer believed that among very primitive peoples, such as the aborigines described by Baldwin Spencer, magic existed without religion, and constituted "a sort of spurious system of natural law" based on misapplications of the association of ideas. In *The Golden Bough* (1890–1936) Frazer set out to explain in the first place the particular rituals and magic practices which regulated the succession to the priesthood of Diana at Aricia in the Alban Hills near Rome, and which included the plucking of the sacred branch, or 'golden bough', before the ritual slaying of the priest. In the course of his commentary Frazer wandered over the whole field of primitive cult and belief – magic and kingship, primitive religion, the worship of trees and vegetation, totemism and the sacrificial feast, taboo and the perils of the soul, fire festivals, scapegoats, the cult of the dead and the belief in immortality all found a place in Frazer's matchless volumes. It is customary today to criticise Frazer, partly because his explanations tended to be in psychological rather than sociological terms (and his psychology besides was over-intellectualistic) and partly because he tore his examples from the social contexts which alone could give meaning. No doubt there is a point to these criticisms; nevertheless there is in Frazer, and in Tylor as well, a synoptic vision which the modern anthropologist often lacks, and perhaps we can still regard Frazer, in

[1] Marrett *The Threshold of Religion*, 1914.

the words of a contemporary anthropologist,[1] as "the supreme interpreter on the literary side of man's hopes, fears, and beliefs, his relations with his gods, his fellows, and with his own soul".

The work of the early social anthropologists was in several ways of significance to psychology, and particularly to social psychology. It documented modes of behaviour and belief markedly different from those prevailing in the civilized societies of the western world. Even if, with Frazer, these primitive practices were to be regarded as "a melancholy record of human error and folly" they still needed explaining. The behaviour of civilized man did not seem to be innate, but the result of a special, slowly evolved, social tradition. How was this tradition transmitted to the individual? How did he acquire not merely the techniques and habits but the attitudes and values that characterized his way of life? This was a question largely for the social psychologist to answer.

The considerable measure of uniformity among primitive peoples also raised problems. Both Tylor and Frazer noted this uniformity. Tylor commented, for example, on the uniformity of primitive myths, which he described as "well marked and consistent structures of the human mind" and on the basic similarity of gesture language in all places and ages. Frazer noted "the essential similarity with which under many superficial differences the human mind has elaborated its first crude philosophy of life". How did this uniformity come about? Was it as a result of diffusion from single sources of origin, or as an outcome of common psychological forces working to the same end-products in varying contexts? Tylor and his contemporaries were much exercised by this question and provided conflicting answers. Tylor himself was judicious. "The principle that man does the same thing in the same circumstances will acount for much, but it is very doubtful whether it can be stretched far enough to account for even the greater proportion of the facts in question. The other side of the argument is, of course, that the resemblance is due to connection, and the truth is made up of the two, though in what proportions, we do not know." All but the extreme diffusionists (such as W. B. Perry and Elliot Smith) allowed that primitive beliefs and cults were to some extent an expression of psychological factors common to primitive man all over the world.

Whether this primitive mentality was different in kind from the mentality of civilized man, or merely the result of quantitative differences, to lack of information, and environmental constriction, was a further question. Both Tylor and Frazer tended to hold that there was only a

[1] C. G. Seligman.

quantitative difference between the primitive and the developed mind. Tylor held that the religion of the savage was 'essentially rational', and Frazer in his inaugural lecture also came down in favour of quantitative difference. Psychoanalytic theory was later to make the postulation of qualitative differences of levels more plausible, and to provide a more convincing explanation both of the persistence of survivals and of the revivals of primitive beliefs and practices in advanced societies than Tylor and Frazer were able to provide. Of the facts, however, of survivals and revivals both were well aware. Tylor devoted two chapters of *Primitive Culture* to survivals, and a great deal of *The Golden Bough* is devoted to their documentation. The study of these survivals became the particular province of the folklore movement which followed the institution in London in 1878 of the Folk Lore Society. Thus, the study of social anthropology merged into the study of advanced societies and posed problems for the psychologist. "The psychological study of primitive culture forms the best introduction to the psychology of contemporary social life", wrote F. C. Bartlett a generation later. At least in the light of the data of social anthropology a purely individual psychology was no longer viable.

## 4. Graham Wallas (1858–1932)

While the social anthropologists were concerning themselves primarily with the simpler societies the problems of the contemporary 'great society' were beginning to be analysed from a psychological standpoint. In 1908 appeared two books which marked perhaps not the birth but rather the adolescence of British social psychology, McDougall's *Introduction to Social Psychology* and Graham Wallas's *Human Nature in Politics*. The two books have something in common. Both were protests against the earlier intellectualistic psychologies of social behaviour: both broke new ground. But whereas McDougall was essentially theoretical and attempted to embrace the whole range of social behaviour within the confines of the instinct hypothesis, Graham Wallas was more flexible, more sensitively observant of social behaviour, and more keenly alive to "the infinite complexity of the actual world". Far rather than McDougall, Graham Wallas deserves to be regarded as the first considerable British social psychologist.

Wallas was by training an Oxford classical scholar who throughout his life gained inspiration from Plato, Aristotle and the great classical authors. While still in his twenties he became interested in social questions, and was a very early member of the Fabian Society. For many years he took an active part in London's local politics, and eventually became Professor of Political Science at the London School of Economics. His mind was remarkably far-ranging and free from watertight compartments. In his thinking he fused together classical philosophy, English social history, experience of local government, and wide reading in psychology. From the resulting amalgam sprung a unique and seminal contribution to social and political psychology.

Essentially Wallas was interested in the new problems of human adjustment and control brought about by the change of scale in social organization in what he termed 'The Great Society'. The old habits, the old impulses, the old images and modes of thought often failed when confronted by wholly novel situations, and human beings consequently suffered from 'baulked dispositions'. The task of the social psychologist was in part to understand the primitive and unconscious forces in human nature, which nineteenth-century thinkers had tended to overlook. But it was also equally necessary, as Graham Wallas stressed particularly in his later writings, for human beings to think consciously and creatively about the problems of society. Wallas had a high conception of the task of social engineering which confronted the social scientist and the politician. "If the life of men", he wrote, "is not to lose its savour, their powers must be exercised and the secrets of their natures searched by a way of living more varied, more coloured, more exhilarating than that which most of the present English governing class seems to contemplate in its legislative plans for improving the condition of the governed."[1]

In his analysis of social problems Wallas had a remarkable gift for penetrating to the operative realities. He was not content with verbal labels, or vague concepts such as 'crowd', 'race', 'instinct'. He tended to think in stimulus-response terms and to break down complex situations into their component stimuli. Thus he saw the problem of crowd behaviour in terms of questions such as, "how far reactions, conscious or unconscious, to the stimulus of our fellow-men are different in character when those who affect us are numerous", and "how far can verbal stimuli induce crowd emotion?" Wallas grasped the fact that the diversity of human behaviour could hardly be explained primarily in terms of instinct, but only in terms of 'social heritage'. How the social heritage impinged upon the individual could be studied empirically, often indeed quantitatively with a systematic control of the variables involved. It was the meaning of a situation for the individual psychologically that mattered in the last resort, and Wallas devoted much space

[1] *The Great Society*, 175.

to an analysis of meaning. "The first requisite in anything which is to stimulate us towards impulse or action is that it should be recognizable . . . that it should be like itself when we met it before."[1] Secondly it must have significance, that is have some reference directly or indirectly to feelings. Unconsciously politicians in the past had made use of these psychological principles. The tensions within 'The Great Society' now demanded their conscious application.

In this task of enquiry and enlightenment Wallas believed that thinking could go forward from its own drive. "Thought is a true natural disposition", he held, "not, as McDougall says, a merely subordinate mechanism."[2] Under appropriate conditions the tendency to think was as natural to man as, under other conditions, was the tendency to run away. The problem was largely to provide the conditions. These were partly institutional, and partly psychological. The former Graham Wallas discussed in the last section of *The Great Society*, the latter in more detail in a subsequent work specially devoted to *The Art of Thought* (1926).

Graham Wallas's writings have a perennial and inspiring freshness. In them he married thought and observation. He discussed behaviour with which he himself was directly familiar, "the sordid details of English electioneering" for example, or the municipal councillors who were "entirely unaware that any conscious mental effort on their part was called for" in their committee work. He had a broad but unsentimental humanity which understood and sympathized with the often lonely and frustrated individuals of the urban community. He had a flair for diagnosing the path along which society was moving, so that his remarks were often uncannily prescient. He foresaw the 'organization man' – "we are all of us officials now bound during our waking days by restrictions in our personal freedom in the interest of a larger organization"[3] – he foresaw the possibility of 'wholly fraudulent' movements succeeding by electioneering methods, the shortcomings and embarrassments of competitive examinations, and a world in which there were "two remaining powers after centuries of war". His writing moreover is immensely suggestive; he threw out a rich variety of topics for research, and though he himself never carried out systematic research of a social psychological kind, he wholeheartedly advocated such research, and signposted many roads. The science of social psychology which "aims at discovering and arranging the knowledge which will enable

[1] *Human Nature in Politics.*    [2] *The Great Society*, 176.
[3] *Human Nature in Politics*, 267.

us to forecast and therefore to influence the conduct of large numbers of human beings organized into societies"[1] had with Graham Wallas definitely taken root in this country.

[1] *The Great Society*, 20.

# CHAPTER VIII

## Changes in Philosophical Climate

### 1. Scientific Materialism

In 1870 when Ribot published the first French edition of *La Psychologie Anglaise Contemporaine* Great Britain was still in the van of psychological progress. Bain, Darwin, Spencer, Galton, Maudsley and Carpenter were all alive and near the height of their powers. The laboratories of Germany and America had not yet been established, and, although German work in the physiology and psychology of the senses was already impressive, it was specialized and restricted in scope. To psychology generally Ribot could not unjustifiably claim that Britain had contributed most. And indeed the prospects for the growth of a biologically orientated psychology, founded on the theory of evolution and the physiology of the nervous system, and assimilating all that was of value in the native associationist tradition, seemed not unpromising. It was not to be. British psychology had been for too long too closely identified with a particular philosophical tradition, anti-religious in general tone, and this tradition was about to suffer an eclipse. No science is so self-sufficient as to be wholly immune to changes in philosophic climate. Nineteenth-century psychology, barely emerged from infancy, was especially susceptible to them. When in the third quarter of the nineteenth century British philosophers, renouncing their native philosophic tradition, flocked to the idealistic banner, the development of psychology was necessarily affected. In German and American universities a rapid growth of psychological departments took place in the last two decades of the century. British universities antagonistically held aloof, and for at least two generations the academic development of psychology was retarded, until another change of philosophic climate and a second world war eventually provided more favourable circumstances. It is almost certainly no accident that the oldest and strongest university schools of psychology in Great Britain are precisely in those centres – Cambridge, London and Manchester – where idealism was weakest; while in Oxford, where for two generations the idealists were all-powerful, psychology was not fully accepted into the academic fold until 1947, and in Glasgow, the home of the Cairds, there was no chair of psychology until 1955.

"The idealistic reaction against science", as it has been termed, was not confined to Great Britain. It was a general movement in Western culture in the last third of the nineteenth century, and the early years of the twentieth. But the form which this reaction took differed from one country to another, and its effects on psychology differed correspondingly. The neo-Hegelian form of idealism was much stronger in Great Britain than elsewhere; it tuned in with and lent support to the evangelical conscience which was strong in Victorian England, and which scientific materialism seemed to threaten. And its retarding effect on psychology was the greater simply because the earlier forms of British philosophy were so largely psychological.

Materialism had, of course, been endemic in Britain at least since the time of Hobbes, and the eighteenth century had produced more than one elegant sceptic. But these philosophic doubts had barely affected the deep stream of religious feeling and tradition. As late as 1844 J. S. Mill in a letter to the French philosopher Comte judged that "the time has not yet come when it is possible without prejudice to our cause to make open attacks upon theology". The progress of the sciences in the nineteenth century and the theory of evolution in particular brought about a change. By 1870 "the flood gates were opened and a torrent of books and articles openly attacking Christianity appeared".[1] Thoughtful men like Leslie Stephen, Henry Sidgwick and James Ward felt obliged to resign posts which involved subscribing to the dogmas of Christianity. In his famous Presidential Address to the British Association for the Advancement of Science in Belfast (1874) Professor Tyndall proclaimed "the impregnable position of science" and the intention of science to "wrest from theology the entire domain of cosmological theory". At the same meeting of the British Association T. H. Huxley (1825–95), who had some years earlier scored points over the redoubtable Bishop Wilberforce, restated Descartes' doctrine of animal automatism. Consciousness was merely an 'epiphenomenon', a collateral product of the working of bodily mechanisms and "as completely without any power of modifying their working as the steam-whistle which accompanies the work of a locomotive engine is without influence upon its machinery". Complex behaviour, even speech, could always be reduced to muscular contractions. "The roots of psychology lie in the physiology of the nervous system, and what we call the operations of the mind are functions of the brain."[2] The spiritualistic way of describing mental phenomena was "utterly barren, and leads to nothing but

[1] N. Annan *Leslie Stephen*, 160.    [2] Huxley *Collected Essays*, vol. VI. 94.

obscurity and confusion of ideas". Nevertheless Huxley cannot be
called, and he did not call himself, a materialist. Neither matter nor
mind were ultimately knowable, only "co-existences and sequences of
phenomena". Using the term he himself coined Huxley claimed to be
an 'agnostic'. The burden of his teaching, however, was unmistakable:
it was anti-religious. "Christianity is doomed to fall." The achievements
of the sciences and Huxley's gifts as a propagandist converted many
to this view. The triumph of agnosticism seemed at least possible, if not
inevitable. No wonder the faithful were alarmed!

## 2. Religious Reactions

For sensitive and religiously minded thinkers the diet of empirical philosophy was unsatisfying even before evolution added its taint. Reid and
his Scottish followers had rejected Hume, and their intuitionist views
had survived, though with decreasing vigour, until J. S. Mill's *Examination of Sir William Hamilton's Philosophy* (1865) finished them off.
Coleridge had abandoned Hartley and turned to German metaphysics.
Carlyle railed against the stupidity of the utilitarians and their ilk, and
looked to "learned, indefatigable, deep-thinking Germany" for salva-
tion. Even poor J. S. Mill broke away from the rigidly applied precepts
of a Benthamite education, read Wordsworth's poems as "a medicine"
for the troubled mind, and became concerned for "the internal culture
of the individual".

Meanwhile a more far-reaching reaction against 'liberalism' and
'rationalism' of every description took place among the theologians of the
Oxford movement. The movement began in 1833 when the first of the
*Tracts for the Times* was published. Its author was J. H. Newman
(1801–90), the ablest and most prominent member of the movement,
who later was to direct a powerful critique against the intellectualism of
the dominant psychology in his *Grammar of Assent* (1870), a subtle
analysis of the nature of belief. Assent, as he termed it, was much more
emotional than rational. "The heart is commonly reached, not through
the reason, but through the imagination, by means of direct impression,
by the testimony of facts and events, by history, by description. Persons
influence us, voices melt us, looks subdue us, deeds influence us. Many
a man will live and die upon a dogma; no man will be a martyr for a
conclusion."[1] Life is for action; not logic and 'notions', but concrete
facts and images that mirror concrete facts move men and convince
them. The whole personality, not merely the intellect, finds expression

[1] *Grammar of Assent*, 89.

in assent, working through what Newman called 'the illative sense'. For Newman, of course, 'the illative sense', his practical judgement, had led him as far back as 1843 into the bosom of Rome.

In taking the path to Rome Newman was by no means alone. The Catholic Emancipation Bill of 1829 had removed most of the civil disabilities of Catholics, and it has been estimated that the rate of conversion thereafter was in the neighbourhood of 8,000 persons annually. The Catholic Church began to play a significant part not only in the religious but also in the intellectual life of the country, and its voice, of course, came down against all the main currents of British philosophy and psychology. In W. G. Ward (1812–82), editor of *The Dublin Review*, Catholics found a most effective philosophical controversialist, who forced even J. S. Mill to concede vital points in debate. Ward directed his attack on one of the weakest spots in empiricist theory, memory. How do we know that memory gives knowledge of the past? Ward argued that the empiricist cannot make any inductive generalizations from experience unless he has already intuitively accepted memory as providing veridical data about past events. In the fourth edition of the *Examination* J. S. Mill conceded that Ward had made his point. But once intuition was admitted, why, asked Ward, should it stop with memory? Why not agree that mathematical, moral, and metaphysical truths might also be intuitive? The important point was that Ward's argument on memory made it impossible to accept a too simple-minded empiricism and weakened the whole edifice of traditional British philosophy.

Towards the close of the century the importation of neoscholasticism paved the way for a more systematic psychology based on the Thomistic model. Cardinal Manning, the leader of English Catholics, had maintained in 1873 that in the scholastic philosophy alone were the true answers to psychological problems to be found. In 1879 this philosophy, revived by the Jesuits after a suspended animation of some centuries, was recognized in the papal encyclical *Aeterni Patris* as the official philosophy of the Roman Church. Manuals of scholastic psychology began to appear on the Continent and schools of psychology based on scholasticism were founded, for example at Louvain and Milan. In this country Father Michael Maher (1860–1917), an Irish Jesuit who spent the greater part of his life at Stonyhurst, wrote a textbook of *Psychology* (1st ed. 1890, 9th ed. 1918) for the Stonyhurst Philosophical series. This extremely scholarly and useful text is at once an exposition of the classical Thomistic psychology, and a thoroughgoing critique of the theories and presuppositions of empiricist and naturalistic psychologies. Three main points stand out: first, no psychology can avoid metaphysical preconceptions. The study of these preconceptions by rational psychology is a necessary complement to the study of mental phenomena themselves by empirical psychology. And according to the scholastics rational psychology leads to the conception of the human mind, or soul, as a real, immaterial, unitary being upon which all mental phenomena are dependent. Secondly, scholastic psychology holds firmly that the higher aspects of mind cannot be reduced to the lower. The higher rational level cannot be accounted for in terms of the lower sensuous level. Finally, scholastic psychology is basically a faculty psychology. "The method of grouping like mental activities under some scheme of faculties is abundantly justified", wrote Maher,[1] returning to the two primary faculties, cognition and appetency, of his scholastic predecessors. Within this framework scholasticism was prepared to recognize many of the detailed findings of modern experimental and clinical psychology, but not the atomistic, naturalistic or deterministic presuppositions which were often associated with it. Largely because scholastic psychology gave more room to, and a more adequate consideration of, the higher intellectual and volitional aspects of the human mind it came to exert a considerable influence on Spearman and other psychologists of the London school.

While these developments were taking place among Catholics, a somewhat different but equally decisive reaction from empirical and utilitarian views found expression in the dissenting camp in the work of James Martineau (1805–1900), the distinguished unitarian philosopher who anticipated many of the views of the idealistic movement. Brought up on Locke, Hartley, Bentham and Mill he felt gradually forced "to concede to the self-conscious mind itself, both as knowing and as willing, an autonomous function distinct from each and all the phenomena known and changes willed – a self-identity as unlike as possible to any growing aggregate of miscellaneous and dissimilar experiences".[2] A sojourn in Germany and the study of Greek thought convinced him more deeply that the empiricists' attempt to explain personality from below was mistaken and that it was necessary to postulate a self-conscious, free, reflecting subject. This as Martineau pointed out in his critique of Bain[3] really ruled out the inclusion of psychology among the

---

[1] Michael Maher *Psychology*, 39.
[2] Martineau *Types of Ethical Theory*, Preface.
[3] Martineau 'Bain's Psychology', *National Review*, 1960, Essays, vol. III.

natural sciences. Psychology and the natural sciences were totally disparate, the one dealing with the subjective, the other with the objective.
Bain's account of the physiology of the nervous system in a work on the
mind was therefore "altogether foreign and intrusive"; and the analytic
method practised by Bain had "a peculiar character of ingenious un-
reality". "Experience proceeds and intellect is trained, not by association but by disassociation, not by reduction of pluralities of impressions
to one, but by the opening out of one into many", maintained Martineau
in terms later to be echoed by James Ward. And like Newman, Martineau, as a pastor of many years' experience, felt the inadequacy of a too
intellectualistic psychology to account for "the experiences and faiths
of tempted and struggling men".

In the 1860's and 1870's the conflict between religion and science
was at its height. It exercised the minds of men in many walks of life.
It was waged in the reviews, then at the summit of their influence; it
was waged among the great; and perhaps one of the most extraordinary
phenomena of the time was the foundation in 1869 of the Metaphysical
Society, at the monthly meetings of which many of the most eminent
men in the intellectual and public life of the day tried to thrash out the
ultimate problems of existence in polite debate. The society was started
by J. Knowles, the editor of the *Nineteenth Century*, and Tennyson,
the Poet Laureate. It aimed to bring together the leaders among the
scientists, philosophers and theologians, and if possible to work out an
agreed solution of their differences. Among those who were members
of the society during the twelve years of its existence were an archbishop, three bishops, Dean Stanley, Dean Church and F. D. Maurice
from the Church of England; several Catholics, including Cardinal
Manning and W. G. Ward; Martineau, the Unitarian; W. E. Gladstone
and Lord Selbourne; from among the scientists, Huxley, Tyndall,
Clifford, Sylvester (the mathematician), W. B. Carpenter, and Bucknill
(the psychiatrist); men of letters such as Ruskin, Tennyson, Bagehot,
Froude; and from the ranks of philosophers and psychologists, Leslie
Stephen, Henry Sidgwick, Croom Robertson, A. C. Fraser, A. J.
Balfour (later prime minister, but also a philosopher) and J. Sully. The
society may not have removed any of the differences it set out to
examine, but it was at least a symptom of the immense concern which
the conflict between science and religion then aroused, and it certainly
led to an increased respect and tolerance between the viewpoints and
personalities of divergent sections of the intellectual world.

Certainly by the mid-1870's a distinct change came over the climate of British opinion, affecting politics, religion, philosophy and art alike. In 1874 for the first time for a generation a Conservative Government was returned to power with an assured majority, and the tide of liberalism, which had dominated the country since the Reform Bill, turned. In the same year the first translation of Hegel appeared in English (*Hegel's Logic*, tr. W. Wallace) and the Oxford philosopher T. H. Green issued his summons: "Close your Mill and your Spencer, and turn to Kant and Hegel." Two years later (1876) another Oxford philosopher F. H. Bradley in his *Ethical Studies* destroyed the individualistic foundations of British moral philosophy. The scientists had claimed too much, and had shocked and alarmed the public. In the July 1872 issue of the *Contemporary Review* Tyndall communicated a letter proposing to estimate the value of prayer for the sick by a controlled experiment in a selected hospital! After the Belfast address of 1874 there could no longer be any doubt that science threatened the traditional values and dogmas. Many people were ready for a change.

## 3. German Idealism

It was at this point that German idealism came to the rescue. As Metz points out in his *A Hundred Years of British Philosophy* "the opening of the door to the German invasion was not prompted by purely philosophical interests, but rather by the desire to confirm orthodox theology and revivify the imperilled faith against Angosticism, Naturalism, religious indifference and open unbelief".[1] Among professional philosophers new winds were beginning to blow and the supremacy of Mill was beginning to be challenged soon after the middle of the century. The older traditions of Platonism and Idealism were re-discovered. A. Campbell Fraser (1819–1914), who in 1856 succeeded Hamilton in Edinburgh, resuscitated Berkeley. B. Jowett (1817–93), the famous Master of Balliol, translated and revived the study of Plato. J. F. Ferrier (1808–64) of St Andrews in his *Institute of Metaphysics* (1854) propounded a systematic theory in which the errors of 'the psychologists' were castigated. "The best way of attaining to correct opinions on most metaphysical subjects is by finding out what has been said by the psychologists, and then by saying the very opposite. In such cases we are sure to be right in at least ninety-nine cases out of a hundred."[2] The psychologists confined their observations to 'states of mind' and ignored consciousness itself, which was the distinctive feature of man. Consciousness itself was the unanalysable ground of knowledge and being. In the

[1] l.c., 249.      [2] l.c., 315.

same vein was Carlyle's downright proclamation: "when will there arise a man who will do for the science of mind what Newton did for that of matter—establish the fundamental laws on the firm basis of induction and discard for ever the absurd theories that so many dreamers have devised? . . . I believe it is a foolish question, for its answer is – Never!"[1]

In spite of these premonitory rumblings the dominance of empiricism was not seriously threatened until the 1870's. Professor Sidgwick, writing in 1876 on philosophy at Cambridge, states that no Cambridge thinker for 150 years had had an influence at all equal to that recently exercised by J. S. Mill from a distance. The writings of the great German philosophers, particularly Kant and Hegel, had been very slow in penetrating the barriers of British insularity. Kant's *Critique of Pure Reason* (1781) was not translated until 1838, fifty-seven years after its original publication, and Hegel's *Logic* (1812–16), the first of Hegel's works to be translated, not until 1874, fifty-eight years after the completion of the first German edition. Early accounts of Kant's work, by T. Brown and Dugald Stewart for example, had been based on a French translation and were wrong in important respects. Coleridge, though permeated with Kantian thought, in his *Aids to Reflection* for instance, was too eclectic and confused a thinker to reflect Kant at all accurately. To many of his hard-boiled countrymen it seemed that he had "plunged into the central opacity of Kantian metaphysics and lay perdue for several years in transcendental darkness till the common daylight of common sense became intolerable to his eyes" (Peacock *Nightmare Abbey*, 1818). Sir William Hamilton was the first academic philosopher in this country to show some sort of understanding of Kant and to incorporate Kantian teachings into the corpus of his own thought, A. C. Fraser dates British Kantianism from Hamilton's inaugural address in 1836. Nevertheless even Hamilton's understanding was limited and one-sided, and a reasonably adequate grasp of Kant had to await the publication of Caird's volumes in 1877.

Hegel was for almost as long a closed book to nearly everyone in Britain. His influence had been on the wane for a generation in his native land before J. H. Stirling's *The Secret of Hegel* (1865) awakened the first British interest. This perfervid work is often regarded as the real beginning of the idealist revolution in British philosophy. The religious motive behind the movement is apparent in Stirling's book. "What we all long for is the Christian simplicity, the Christian happiness

---

[1] Quoted by D. A. Wilson *Carlyle till Marriage*, 110 and 117.

of our forefathers – the simple pious soul, on the green earth, in the bright fresh air, patiently industrious, patiently loving. . . . Hegel indeed has no object but – reconciling and neutralizing atomism – once again to restore to us – and in the new light of new thought – immortality and freewill, Christianity and God."[1]

The work of T. H. Green (1836–82) was more important. He had a mind of undoubted philosophic power, and his position as Fellow of Balliol, and later Professor of Moral Philosophy at Oxford, enabled him to exert his influence before his early death at a focal point in British life. Two generations of Oxford students were nurtured on his *Prolegomena to Ethics* (1883) and inoculated against the deceptions of empirical psychology. The corner-stone of Green's position was his doctrine of relation. There are no relations without a relating consciousness. It is consciousness which integrates the discrete particular terms. The system and order of the world imply relationships, imply, therefore, consciousness, or in other words, the activity of a divine mind of which our minds are particular and limited manifestations. Consciousness is the presupposition not merely of knowledge about, but of the very existence of the world. To explain consciousness, as the empiricists attempted to do, genetically and as a derivate, and to suppose "an evolution of the unifying agent from that which it renders one", was preposterous. The method of empirical psychology was in principle mistaken since "self-consciousness is not reducible to a series of events; being already at its beginning formally, or potentially, or implicitly all that it becomes actually or explicitly in developed knowledge".[2] An attempt to explain mind physiologically must fail because it takes for granted what it seeks to explain—there would be no such thing as a relation between mind and brain without the prior existence of a relating consciousness.

Green not only examined the foundations of empirical philosophy in his lengthy introductions to Hume's *Treatise*, but in a series of articles on Spencer and G. H. Lewes directly attacked the teachings of contemporary psychology. To this attack he returned in his post-humously published *Prolegomena to Ethics*. Man as an intelligence was a free, self-determining agent, and such an agent could not be explained in psycho-biological terms. "The man who knows, so far from being an animal altogether, is not an animal at all or even in part."[3] Even at the perceptual level knowledge involved a 'neutralization of time', and

---

[1] op. cit., 750.          [2] *Introduction to Hume*, 200.
[3] *Prolegomena*, 79.

this required an agent not itself subject to time, an intelligence related to the eternal divine consciousness upon which the whole order of the world depends. Thus man "in respect of that principle through which he at once is a self and distinguishes himself as such exerts a free activity—an activity which is not in time, not a link in the chain of natural becoming, which has no antecedents other than itself but is self-originated".[1] Only in this way did Green conceive it possible to safeguard morality and religion against the corroding effects of natural science. In so doing he excluded from the outset any possibility of a science of psychology. "The consciousness through which alone nature exists for us is neither natural nor a result of nature."

The Oxford attack on the empirical tradition, or at least on certain aspects of it, was continued by F. H. Bradley (1846–1924), commonly regarded as the greatest of the British idealists of the late nineteenth century. Bradley, though more discriminating in his targets than Green, was as bitter as Green in his hostility to empiricism. To psychological enquiry in its proper place and by what he regarded as proper methods Bradley was not averse. But 'psychologism' and associationism received from him no mercy.

It is indeed strange that Bradley should ever have claimed, as he did, that he was "endeavouring to work in the spirit of the best English tradition". British philosophy, both in its English and Scottish branches, had been from the time of Locke onwards essentially 'psychologistic'. It held that the investigation of the human mind or understanding was the royal road towards solving such philosophical problems as could be solved, and banishing those that could not. As Hume put it, "there is no question of importance whose decision is not compris'd in the science of man . . . the science of man is the only solid foundation for the other sciences".[2] In line with this tradition, logic and mathematical reasoning were regarded as mental derivatives, and J. S. Mill defined logic as "the analysis of the mental process which takes place when we reason".[3]

It was this psychological interpretation of logic and epistemology that Bradley contested. "In England we have lived too long in the psycho-logic attitude", he asserted. Logic and psychology, he held, were perfectly distinct disciplines—logic was concerned with the contents or meanings of ideas, the reference to a reality beyond themselves: psychology with ideas as mental facts and the laws of their manifestation. Both logic and psychology abstracted from the totality of thought,

[1] op. cit., 82.     [2] Hume *A Treatise of Human Nature*, (1739) Introduction.
[3] J. S. Mill *A System of Logic*.

and nothing but confusion could result if their diverse modes of abstraction were not kept distinct. How far Bradley's attack on 'psychologism' would have been in itself effective it is impossible to say. It was reinforced by the more stringent arguments of the mathematical logicians who followed Frege, and it was their reformulation of logic rather than Bradley's that gained acceptance. We must, however, allow Bradley some part in the demise of 'psychologism', and it is worth noting that he did not regard this demise as invalidating all psychological study of logical processes.[1] In the history of the establishment of psychology as a science the eradication of 'psychologism' marks an important stage.

Bradley's attack on associationism was particularly directed against its atomism. Bradley was the arch-exponent of monism, of the one all-embracing 'absolute' in which all distinctions and appearances merged and found their resting place. Atomism must go wholly. "We must get rid of the idea that our mind is a train of perishing existences." It is rather "a continuous mass of presentation in which the separation of a single element from all context is never observed".[2] Discrete events, whether regarded psychologically as sensations or ideas, or physiologically as 'neural shocks', could never become bonded together as a result of prior experience. "No particular ideas are ever associated or ever could be. What is associated is and must be always universals"[3] he wrote in his *Principles of Logic* which appeared in the same year (1883) as Green's *Prolegomena*. Ideas are not ideas unless they are symbols, and as symbols it is not their existence as psychical facts but their meaning that counts. Association is a matter of meanings, and meanings even at the beginnings of soul-life are universal. "When I talk of an idea which is the same amid change, I do not speak of that psychical event which is in ceaseless flux, but of the portion of the content which the mind has fixed, and which is not in any sense an event in time."

How this affected psychology in detail Bradley did not say. It might almost seem that association in being excluded from the stream of time was being excluded from psychology. Bradley's own psychological theories unfortunately, for he was potentially a talented psychologist, were only very tentatively sketched. Psychology was for him phenomenalistic, that is to say concerned with the coexistence and sequence of immediately experienced events together with the dispositions legiti-

---

[1] See *Princ. Log.*, 2nd ed. II. 613, note.    [2] *Mind*, o.s. XII (1887).
[3] *Princ. Log.*, I. 304.

mately postulated to explain the occurrence of such phenomena. It had nothing to do with physiology, nor at the other pole with 'a self'. "The idea of a self or ego joining together from the outside the atomic elements and fastening them together in some miraculous way not involved in their own nature is quite indefensible."[1] Nor could Bradley accept a special activity of attention. Hence he disagreed with some of the fundamental doctrines of Ward, with whom he waged a prolonged controversy.[2] There was for Bradley within thought itself a natural movement, starting from immediate feeling in which knowing and being were united, subject and object indistinguishable (again a point of conflict with Ward), proceeding through the stage of relational thinking, always unstable and imperfect, to the transcendent state of supra-relational thought in which all relations and the separation of thought from reality are once more abolished. In a sense Bradley was sketching in ideal terms a sort of developmental psychology. But any constructive suggestions which his writings contained were less influential than his destructive attacks on associationistic psychology, and he must mainly be remembered in the history of British psychology for the part he played in the collapse of this older tradition.

The teachings of Green and Bradley were taken up by a numerous band of idealistic followers who dominated the philosophical scene at the end of the nineteenth century. The most notable of these followers was perhaps Bernard Bosanquet (1848–1923) whose *Psychology of the Moral Self* (1897) summarizes many of the main doctrines of the idealistic psychology.

[1] *Mind*, IX (1900).      [2] *Mind*, o.s. XI (1886).

# CHAPTER IX

# Systematic Psychology at the Turn of the Century

## 1. James Sully (1843–1923)

James Sully and James Ward, the leading luminaries of London and of Cambridge psychology at the end of the century, were almost exact contemporaries, and their careers, so far as externals were concerned, were remarkably similar. Both were the sons of ephemerally prosperous business men whose businesses ultimately failed; both were haphazardly schooled and after a spell of office work were trained for the nonconformist ministry; both turned to psychology and studied at Göttingen and Berlin after their faith had lost its assurance; though neither was himself an experimentalist, both were instrumental in establishing psychological laboratories at their respective universities; both made major contributions to systematic psychology; and finally both died in the mid-1920's. In point of view, however, there was a marked difference between them. Sully in spite of his sojourns in Germany remained broadly faithful to the empirical analytic tradition of British psychology which he endeavoured to systematize on developmental foundations. Ward abandoned this tradition and reconstructed psychology on the basis of a spiritualistic monism which gave the central position in the scheme of things to mind.

It was while a student at the Regent's Park Baptist College studying for a London degree that Sully first became seriously interested in psychology. Mill, Spencer and Bain were the diet provided, and though he did not find it 'very soul-satisfying' it gave him a sufficient love of clear thinking to arm him against the seductions of German philosophizing. Sully could never abide Hegel; and reacted critically not only to the British Hegelians, Green and Bradley, but also to the watered-down idealism of Ward. His knowledge of German philosophy and psychology was, however, extensive. It was the new fashion to study at German universities, and Sully, after abandoning his plans to enter the ministry, migrated to Göttingen to sit at the feet of Lotze, the eminent German thinker. On a second visit a few years later to Berlin he concentrated mainly on physiology under the guidance of Helmholtz and Du Bois Reymond. Sully's musical gifts and his interest in aesthetics made him especially interested in Helmholtz's researches on sensation, and one of his early articles contains an account of them. Of German philosophical trends he was far more critical. In a large work entitled *Pessimism* (1877) he examined the methods and conclusions of Schopenhauer and E. von Hartmann and maintained that they were psychologically unacceptable. (This book incidentally lost Sully the Chair of Philosophy at Liverpool; the selection committee considered that the author of a tome on pessimism must be to some extent pessimistically inclined; which would hardly do for a then infant university college!) Sully in fact was prepared to absorb all that was empirical in German psychology; he was not prepared to accept its philosophic framework. Instead it was the theory of evolution, in its first heyday in the 1860's, which exerted the major pull on his mind. Sully studied evolution intensively; he was asked to write the article on 'Evolution' in the ninth edition of the *Encyclopaedia Britannica*; and he opened his first book *Sensation and Intuition* (1874) with a chapter on 'The relation of the evolution hypothesis to human psychology'. Evolution remained the cornerstone of his thinking up to the end of his productive life; in his last book on *Laughter* (1902) the basis of his theory is evolutionary, and his well-known *Studies of Childhood* (1895) were cast in an evolutionary mould.

Academically Sully was long in establishing himself. For many years after his return from Germany he survived on writing and odd teaching jobs, helped out by an allowance from his father until the business failed. It was not until 1892, on Croom Robertson's death, that he was appointed to the Grote chair at University College, London, and he held this post for only eleven years, retiring at the age of 60 in 1903. Although never one of its most influential figures Sully was in the centre of the intellectual life of London for at least a quarter of a century. He was a sociable person and friendly not only with leading scientific and philosophical figures, Darwin, Huxley, Tylor, Hughlings Jackson, Bain, Sidgwick, Lewes, Ward, but with many literary men, Meredith, R. L. Stevenson, and Leslie Stephen, as well as with foreign scholars from Europe and America. He was a member of the select Metaphysical Society, and a founder member of the British Academy. When the Second International Congress of Psychology met in London in 1892, Sully was joint secretary with F. W. H. Myers. A long absence in Italy after his retirement and declining health prevented him from playing a large part in the British Psychological Society which he helped to found.

Sully deserves to be remembered mainly for four things:

(i) He was the author of the most scholarly, comprehensive and well-balanced factual textbook of psychology ever produced by a British psychologist. Originally entitled *Outlines of Psychology* (1884), it was revised and resissued in two volumes as *The Human Mind* (1892). A modified version specially prepared for training colleges appeared as *The Teacher's Handbook of Psychology* (1886). Though *The Human Mind* does not compare with William James's *Principles of Psychology* (1890) for verve and originality – James himself thought it far too impartial, and told Sully so! – its more sober merits gave it a wide vogue on both sides of the Atlantic.

(ii) Sully was a pioneer in scientific child psychology. His *Studies of Childhood* (1895), though not a complete or systematic treatise on child psychology, was the first adequate work produced in this country, and preceded only by those of Preyer in Germany and Stanley Hall in America. Two years previously Sully had associated himself with the British Association for Child Study which played an important role in the psychological study of the child. We shall return to this aspect of Sully's work in the chapter on applied psychology.

(iii) Sully was responsible for the establishment of the laboratory at University College, London, in October 1897 – an important landmark in the history of British psychology. The following notice appeared in *Mind* in July of that year. "A laboratory for experimental psychology will be opened in University College, London, in October next. The committee have secured a considerable part of the apparatus collected by Prof. Hugo Münsterberg of Freiburg, who is about to migrate permanently to Harvard College. Among those who have contributed to the movement are Mr F. Galton, Prof. H. Sidgwick, Mr A. J. Balfour, Mr R. B. Haldane, Sir John Lubbock, Mr Shadworth Hodgson, and Dr Savage. It is hoped that the name of George Croom Robertson may in some way be connected with the laboratory. It is further hoped that Dr W. H. R. Rivers whose work as a teacher in Cambridge and elsewhere is well known will be able to start the work of the laboratory and superintend it during the October term." It was in the same year that Michael Foster, the Cambridge professor of physiology, secured a room for experimental psychology in Cambridge. Rivers, who had been working in Cambridge on the special senses for several years, was also in charge of this laboratory. So

1897 can be regarded as the year of the formal establishment of experimental psychology in Great Britain, and Rivers as our first experimentalist.

(iv) Sully wrote the first full-scale work on laughter in English – *An Essay on Laughter* (1902) – and made a number of contributions to the psychology of aesthetics – a field which had been little developed in this country.

The framework of Sully's psychology was essentially of an orthodox British type. Psychology was the study of consciousness and its method primarily introspective. This did not render it any the less a science; but its status was a peculiar one, and psychology was at the same time the keystone of all the philosophic disciplines, including logic, and of the theory of politics, education and the other activities of man. Mind and body were disparate, but somehow related, so that physiology was of relevance to the psychologist. The job of the psychologist was by analysis to disentangle and reduce to simplicity the web of consciousness, and the main analytic classification was into the threefold functions, feeling, knowing, and willing. The more complex phenomena of the human mind were elaborated chiefly through experience, but in the process not only passive association was involved, but also active construction. Sully did not believe in a transcendental self – or at least he relegated it to philosophy – but he had absorbed something from his German contacts, and was by no means a pure associationist. Attention had a role to play, though not so large a role as Ward had accorded it; and even in dreams directive factors were involved besides association. In perception "we attend in the first place to the form of objects", and particularly when the object of perception was vague there was an opening for the capricious play of fancy. Sully was especially interested in the borderland between the normal and abnormal, in the imaginative and the fanciful, and in his book on *Illusions* (1881) he made a detailed study not only of perceptual illusions, but of dreams, hallucinations and delusions. His work on dreams was commended by Freud, and his *Studies in Childhood* excel in the chapters on imagination, play and art.

There is an attractive combination in Sully's work of scholarly thoroughness and an almost playful sensitivity to the nuances and mysteriousness of the human mind. Though not a great original investigator it is unfair to dismiss him, as Boring does, as a mere writer of textbooks. In his outlook Sully was essentially scientific: he was undogmatic and brought a critical, balanced judgement to his task. He got things moving institutionally, and his pioneer contributions to the study of childhood and to the psychology of laughter are by no means negligible.

## 2. James Ward (1843-1925)

Sully's contemporary Ward is, no doubt, both a more significant and at the same time a more controversial figure. However out-dated Ward's philosophical psychology may seem to the contemporary psychologist, there can be no question of the important influence he had upon the development of psychology in Great Britain. His imposing article in the *Encyclopaedia Britannica* (ninth ed. 1885) was from the outset recognized even by his opponents as "among the masterpieces of the philosophy of the human mind" (Bain, 1886). Its impact on British psychology can be clearly traced for two generations. McDougall regarded his own *Outline of Psychology* (1923) as "an endeavour to carry to its logical conclusion that critical rejection of the mosaic psychology which had been a main theme of the psychological writing of James Ward" and others. C. S. Myers in his presidential address on 'The Nature of Mind' at the British Association in 1931 put forward an almost wholly Wardian point of view. R. J. Bartlett presiding at the British Psychological Society in 1947 made numerous references to Ward. From 1885 to 1947 – a span of over 60 years – Ward's ideas were a power to be reckoned with in shaping the outlook of British psychologists. If British psychologists were for long almost wholly unsympathetic to behaviourism in any of its forms, if they showed little enthusiasm for physiological psychology, and were tardy experimentalists, and if the educated British public came to regard psychology – as they mostly did till Freud and World War I changed the tune – as merely a rather odd sub-species of philosophy, the responsibility lies to a considerable extent with Ward.

What Ward essentially did was to replace the traditional British analytical approach to the study of mind, an approach which has been termed 'Lockean' after John Locke, by a 'Leibnitzian' point of view. "The Leibnitzian tradition", writes Gordon Allport, "maintains that the person is not a collection of acts, nor simple the locus of acts; the person is the source of acts."[1] The active, unitary self, or subject, was the keystone of Ward's psychology. He maintained that Hume, and all who followed Hume in the main features of his teaching, were wholly mistaken in supposing that mind could be analysed into a string of successive perceptions. The associationism which attempted

[1] G. W. Allport *Becoming*, 12.

to derive complex states, including the self, from simpler components was just 'a soulless blunder'. The proper job of the psychologist was to study the modes of experience of the active, individual subject as this experience develops and unfolds. In this task the psychologist could learn little from the physiologist. Mental life and experience was a realm of its own, governed by its own principles and to be studied by its own methods.

This point of view was largely derived from German sources, from Leibnitz, Kant, Lotze and Brentano, and it shows affinities with later developments in German psychology inspired by the same tradition. An underlying personal motivation in Ward's revulsion from British empiricism was no doubt, as with many others of his contemporaries, religious. Ward's early training had been for the congregational ministry. But agnostic doubts grew during his sojourn in Germany in 1870. Largely through contact with the German philosopher, Lotze, these were temporarily allayed. He returned to England and accepted a call to the Cambridge Congregational Church in Downing Street. Fifteen months later in 1872 he tendered his resignation; and though then 30 years of age entered Trinity College to read moral sciences. This was followed by a further visit to Germany, studies in physiology and natural science (Ward had from his boyhood in Liverpool been a keen student of natural history and retained this interest throughout his life), and eventually a lectureship in moral sciences at Cambridge in 1881 and a chair in 1897. Ward's life's work culminated in the two series of Gifford Lectures, *Naturalism and Agnosticism* (1899) and *The Realm of Ends: Pluralism and Theism* (1911), in which he attempted to answer the question which he had set himself at the outset of his Cambridge career in 1873, "how is a disciple of modern thought to be religious?" Physiology, psychology and philosophy were in a sense but stepping stones towards an answer to this question.

Ward's final statement of his psychological position is contained in *Psychological Principles* (1918), a re-statement with additions and some minor modifications of his Encyclopaedia article of 1885. The main features of Ward's psychological teaching may be summarized as follows, though no summary can do justice to Ward's careful analysis of particular topics.

(i) Psychology is the science of individual experience. The term 'experience' (unlike the term 'soul' or 'mind') always implies both subjective and objective components, and thus transcends the dualism of mind and matter. There is no special subject matter of psychology. All sciences are based on 'experience'. Psychology deals not with some part of experience, but with the whole of experience from the special point of view of the individual experiencer.

(ii)   Psychology as a science is totally distinct from the biological sciences which study living organisms objectively. Physiology can, therefore, never be a substitute for psychological analysis even in the study of simple sensations. Psychology is an independent science in its own right.

(iii)  There is always a self or subject of experience, which can never be explained in terms of experience, but is itself the explanation of the unity and continuity of experience. The self can never be left out of any psychological analysis.

(iv)   The self cannot be broken down into a congeries of faculties. There is a single subjective activity which may be termed 'attention' (a term Ward prefers to 'consciousness'). Attention may be variously distributed cognitively and conatively. It is, therefore, more basic than awareness or than conation. It is the ultimate, unanalysable subjective activity.

(v)    Mental contents or 'presentations' may be either sensory or motor. They are never isolated units but part of a continuum. Differentiation within the presentational continuum is the main form of psychological development, but by a sort of epigenesis 'higher' continua, a 'memory continuum' and an 'ideational continuum', are formed. The continuity of attention is a more important explanatory factor in the development of the presentational continuum than laws of contiguity and association.

(vi)   There is also continuity from generation to generation in the inheritance of a 'psychoplasm' which explains the *a priori* features of the presentational continuum.

(vii)  Feeling is not a presentation any more than is the ultimate activity of attention. It is a wholly subjective and unique factor in experience ranging between the opposite extremes of pleasure and pain. It cannot exist on its own, but only in company with presentations and attention.

(viii) There is no special 'inner sense' revealing the self and its activity. The 'I' is known reflectively in the 'me'; the self as one presentation among others.

(ix)   General psychology studies the individual experiencer in general terms. Individual psychology studies the concrete individuals, "the innumerable unique personalities" we encounter in real life. These unique personalities cannot be psychometrically sized up, but there can be "a living interpretation from within of the thoughts and contents of the heart". Personality is shown not merely in what a man is, but in what he is striving to be.

Ward's exposition, in spite of its age, remains one of the most important statements in the English language of a point of view not characteristically British. It has close affinities with the phenomenalistic, 'Gestalt' and personalistic trends in twentieth-century German psychology and with some recent developments in the United States. On the whole it is a point of view that is unfriendly to scientific progress in psychology. In its attempt to keep psychology unspotted by physiological impurities and psychometric methods; in its postulation of an unanalysable and ultimate self activity; in its constant stress on continua and on the inappropriateness of analysis it turned psychology away from empirical investigations and towards philosophical abstractions. The one link which Ward always retained with scientific thought was his emphasis on genetic development, and for this philosophers even purer than himself heavily criticized him.

## 3. G. F. Stout (1860–1944)

At the beginning of the century the biblical form and bulk of Stout's *Manual*, at that time and for nearly a quarter of a century the textbook of psychology most used in British universities, was familiar to all psychologists in this country. Certainly it was "a mighty difficult book", as one reviewer put it, but it was "by far the best textbook provided students were intelligent enough to make use of it". Though revised and re-issued as recently as 1938 the modern student rarely consults it; perhaps this is a pity, for Stout had a penetrating mind and an exceptional conceptual clarity.

As an undergraduate at Cambridge Stout came under the influence of Ward. After a double first in classics, he read for the moral science tripos, and then became a Fellow of St John's College. Here he remained from 1884 to 1896. Then two years at Aberdeen were followed by five years in the psychological wilderness of Oxford, where Stout became the first 'Wilde Reader'. From 1903 to 1936 Stout held the Chair of Logic and Metaphysics at St Andrews. He retired to Sydney, Australia, and died there in 1944. Stout's psychological work was mostly done before he migrated to St Andrews in 1903: thereafter his primary interests were epistemological and metaphysical. As editor of *Mind* from 1891 to 1920 he exerted a considerable influence upon British philosophy during an important phase of its development; and he was recognized as one of the most acute philosophical discussants of his day.

As a psychologist Stout was even more essentially philosophical in his approach than Ward. He lacked Ward's training in the biological sciences and was, if anything, less interested than Ward in the experimental developments of his time. He was essentially an 'arm-chair' psychologist, and predominantly concerned with theoretical concepts in psychology. Moreover he was a very academic person. His interests, if we may judge from the *Manual*, were chess-playing, cigar-smoking, botanizing and the classics of English literature. He could be academically trivial, as when he cites the fossil-hunter baffled by an unfamiliar fossil as an important example of psychological conflict! He often niggled; and oddly enough at times he was quite uncritical as when he projected himself imaginatively into animals – "the hungry lion deprived of the opportunity of satisfying its hunger, may attend to the hunger itself instead of its prey"; or "when one dog is fighting with another it is not aware of its opponent merely as a changing complex of colours, pressures, sounds, etc.; it is aware of its opponent as initiating active movement and feeling emotion". Yet in spite of his limitations and occasional sillinesses of this sort Stout was in many ways a great psychologist whose contributions to theoretical psychology remain even today as powerful as those of any modern British psychologist.

For Stout possessed, as his pupil G. E. Moore the philosopher observed, "a quite exceptional gift for seizing on some particular point of importance and putting that point in the simplest and most conversational language". He had a strong vein of common sense and indeed believed that "we are incomparably more assured of the general truth of the system of beliefs implied in our daily dealings with our fellow men than we can be by any metaphysical theory which conflicts with it".[1] He had an acute power of analysing psychological phenomena and of extracting information which others had overlooked. This capacity, together with his power of assimilating the strong points of divers schools of thought, gave his psychology a remarkably firm and catholic basis.

Though Stout is frequently coupled with Ward and though in certain respects their views were similar, Stout was far less of a renegade from

[1] G. F. Stout *Mind and Matter*, 115.

the main British tradition of psychology than was Ward. He could not follow Ward into the empyrean of the pure ego, and in his method of approach, if not always in his conclusions, he remained faithful to empiricism. Among German thinkers he was mainly influenced by Herbert and Brentano, much less by Kant and the idealists. To Spinoza he more than once acknowledged his debt.

The mind which it was the psychologist's job to study was in Stout's view tied in two ways to the objectively observable material world. It was on the one hand always 'embodied mind', so that "awareness of external objects is inseparable from the percipient's awareness of his own bodily action in relation to them"; while on the other hand the individual mind was always inseparable from "what it minds, what it is cognizant of and interested in". Thus, though Stout held experiencing to be essentially discontinuous from and incommensurate with material happenings, and theories of the emergent evolution of mind from matter nonsensical, he regarded mind in its functioning and development as firmly anchored to the physical world. Nevertheless Stout always insisted that it was the psychologist's job to study mental not bodily processes, and that the primary method of psychology was introspection. "When muscular contraction begins", wrote Stout in 1896, "the psychological series breaks off. The analytical psychologist is concerned with psychical activity, not with the physical changes it initiates." [1] Perhaps it is the abiding faith which he retained in the sufficiency of introspective analysis that above all dates Stout's psychological writings; for in many points of doctrine he was in advance of his time.

Like Ward Stout was in revolt against associationism. Associationism failed to do justice to the unity and continuity of psychic life, and it ignored the creative and active aspects of mind. These failings Stout, while still adhering to the method of empirical analysis and eschewing the *a priori*, endeavoured to rectify. He postulated a process of noetic synthesis involving the apprehension of "wholes" around the "central idea of a topic". The apprehension of the whole "determines the order and connexion of the apprehension of the parts". [2] Broadly speaking the power of noetic synthesis corresponds to the everyday concept of intelligence. "The more conspicuous it is the less conspicuous by comparison is the part played by mere association." [3] Noetic synthesis brings order and consistency to the mind on the plane of meaning. There was, however, nothing transcendental in Stout's doctrine of noetic synthesis.

---

[1] *Analytic Psychology*, I. 126.         [2] ibid., II. 41.
[3] l.c., 34.

He believed it had a neural basis, and that in Hughlings Jackson's doctrine of levels there was "a physiological counterpart of the systematic organization of the mind".

In his terminology Stout was often conspicuously old-fashioned. 'Noetic synthesis' smacked of Kant; 'relative suggestion' which he borrowed from Thomas Brown, and which he used to describe the creative processes of mind, effectively obscured his meaning; and the term 'apperception', of Leibnizian origin, has never commended itself to British taste. Yet the doctrines which Stout was expounding under these rubrics are psychologically important. 'Relative suggestion' covered all the phenomena of generalization and transfer and those constructive intellectual processes that Spearman, who acknowledged his debt in this matter to Stout, was later to include under his principle of the eduction of correlates. 'Apperception' embraced all the assimilative processes "by which a mental system appropriates a new element or otherwise receives a fresh determination".

Even more important than these cognitive reformulations was Stout's doctrine of conation. Fundamentally the unity of mind was a unity of interest, a conative rather than a merely cognitive unity. All cognitive achievements even at the perceptual level were held together by conation, and were "merely modes in which conscious strivings seeks satisfaction". Mind in other words was active. In the first volume of the *Analytic Psychology* Stout considered in some detail the meaning of mental activity. "The stream of consciousness," he wrote, "though its course is perpetually controlled and restricted by extraneous conditions, has nevertheless a current of its own. . . . This is an indispensable part of the connotation of all such words as activity, conation, effort, striving, will, attention." [1] Activity existed at all levels of mind, according to Stout, who, unlike Bradley, did not equate it with voluntary behaviour. Consciousness was never merely passive even in its less developed forms. Thus not only were associative and noetic processes linked and guided conatively, but perception also was to a large extent shaped by conative forces, by instincts, interests and so on. The philosopher S. Alexander, who borrowed from Stout the foundations of his own conative theory of knowledge, held that Stout's conative treatment of perception was "one of the greatest contributions that have been made to Psychology".[2] A characteristic feature of all conation was its expectant or prospective nature. This applied equally to perceptual activity and to the more

---

[1] *Analytic Psychology*, I. 147.
[2] S. Alexander *Space, Time and Deity*, II. 119.

complex forms of voluntary attention. Stout, unlike Ward, did not hypostatize attention. The separation of activity from content seemed to him a most serious error. There were no special centres for attention; rather attention had nervous correlates in "the tendency of neural systems towards virtual equilibrium – towards a stationary condition, which is only liable to change from without, and not from within".[1] Thus "every specific process of attention tends to bring about its own cessation".[2]

Another important feature of Stout's psychology was its emphasis on development. Strictly this was the theme of the *Manual of Psychology* (1st ed. 1898), while the *Analytic Psychology* (1896) was concerned with the general analysis of consciousness. In particular the *Manual* analysed in detail the development of our perception of the external world. Stout held that we mainly have to learn by a gradual process to discern the shape, situation and distance of objects, and that the perceptual processes generally were the result of a complex process of development in which experiences of movement played a prominent part. "Our power of freely controlling, detaining, modifying and repeating mental images depends in a large measure on our power of controlling their motor constituents or accompaniments." [3] The external world as we finally experience it is an ideal construction, as indeed is the self. And in this constructive process social factors play an important part.

This brief survey of some of Stout's main psychological teachings perhaps provides some evidence to support Passmore's judgement that "far from being antiquated Stout is much more revolutionary than exponents of such 'modern' doctrines as the conditioned reflex".[4] There are no doubt dangers in interpreting the past anachronistically; but Stout's theories often seem to anticipate views current one or two generations later. In his emphasis on 'wholes'; in his doctrines of conative activity and the spontaneity of the mind; in his references to the striving for equilibrium (which has since become known as homeostasis); in his doctrine of 'relative suggestion'; and in his frequent allusions to the role of the social factor in the development of human mentality; in all these ways Stout tunes in with a good deal that contemporary psychologists have become interested in after long wanderings. We can now see, if we care to look, that in spite of its old-fashioned dress, a new mode of psychological thinking was emerging in Stout's psychology.

---

[1] l.c., I. 199.    [2] l.c., I. 190.    [3] *Manual*, 2nd ed., 483.
[4] J. A. Passmore, in G. F. Stout *God and Nature* (1952).

# CHAPTER X

# Abnormal Psychology from 1875 to 1914

## 1. The Management of the Insane

If we were to seek the reasons for the striking contrast which has long obtained between the eminence of British neurology and neurophysiology and the comparative mediocrity of our contribution to abnormal psychology and psychiatry, we should probably fasten at least in part on the administrative system in which psychiatry in this country developed. The lunacy legislation and the asylum building of the Victorian era had four main aims in view: first, to remove the public scandal and nuisance of the lunatic at large; secondly, to salve the Victorian humanitarian conscience by doing away with physical restraint and squalor in the management of the insane; thirdly, by the medico-legal procedure of certification to safeguard the sane individual from being wrongly locked up; and fourthly to do all this as cheaply as possible by establishing large asylums capable of being economically administered. These aims were largely achieved by the Lunacy Commissioners presided over from 1834 to 1885 by the 7th Earl of Shaftesbury. A growing number of lunatics were accommodated as the century progressed. In 1859 the lunatic population numbered 36,762 (18·67 per 10,000 of the population of England and Wales); by 1899 it had risen to 105,086 (31·11 per 10,000); by 1907 to 123,988 (35·48 per 10,000). The Lunacy Act of 1890, which consolidated earlier legislation, and remained in force, with modifications, until 1959, laid down the routines for certification and asylum administration.

To the complacent administrator looking through rosy spectacles all seemed well on the lunacy front. "The modern hospital for the insane does credit to latter-day civilization. Physical restraint is no longer practised . . . neat dormitories, cosy single rooms, and sitting- and dining-rooms please the eye. In the place of bare walls and floors and curtainless windows are pictures, plants, rugs, birds, curtains, and in many asylums even the barred windows have been abolished. Some of the wards for milder patients have unlocked doors. Many patients are trusted alone about the grounds and on visits to neighbouring towns. An air of busy occupations is observed in sewing-rooms, shops, in the fields and gardens. . . ." [1] By the commencement of the twentieth century, however, the medical profession was beginning to have serious doubts. German psychiatry, led by Kraepelin, was forging ahead; research was being vigorously prosecuted; and psychiatric clinics had been established in most German university towns. In America, too, new developments were afoot. By comparison in Great Britain the picture was a stagnant one, and the status of psychiatry low. The management of the insane had indeed become an administrative backwater largely divorced from medicine. The authority of the asylum superintendent within his own domain was so absolute that he necessarily became almost wholly an administrator. By contrast the status of his assistant medical officers was pathetic, and highly discouraging to the recruitment of men of quality. The assistant medical officers were compelled to live on the asylum premises, were forbidden to marry, had no independent sphere of authority, and few prospects of promotion. They came to their posts with no special qualifications, and, as asylums were mostly remote, had no opportunities for further education. Duties were largely routine and included a great deal of clerical work, while opportunities for research were few and far between. The researches of Ferrier at Wakefield, of Campbell at Rainhill, and of Mott at the central pathological laboratory established by the London County Council at Claybury, were exceptional.

Equally restrictive was the lack of provision for the voluntary treatment of the mentally disordered and the legal necessity of certification. Voluntary admission to public lunatic asylums was prohibited by law until the London County Council obtained special powers in 1915 to establish the Maudsley Hospital for the treatment of "any person suffering from incipient insanity or mental infirmity who is desirous of voluntarily submitting himself to treatment". Not until the passing of the Mental Treatment Act of 1930 did the admission of voluntary patients become general. Prior to this it was impossible to obtain treatment even in private institutions without legal formalities. An individual was either mad, in which case he was certified and compulsorily shut up, or sane, when nothing need or could be done about him. No half-way stages were officially recognized, and the early treatment of incipient breakdown was thus actively discouraged. Facilities for such treatment were indeed non-existent, except in Scotland where the legal barriers were fewer. In its origin the provision for lunatics had been closely linked with the problem of pauperism. Wynn's Act in 1808

[1] *Ency. Brit.*, XIth ed., 'Insanity'.

set up County Asylums "for the better care and maintenance of lunatics, being paupers or criminals in England". As late as the middle 1920's 90 per cent of admissions to asylums came through poor-law channels. The usual procedure was under Section 20 of the Lunacy Act 1890 whereby the lunatic was committed to a poor law institution on a three-day order by the 'relieving officer', as he was called, and subsequently removed after medical certification to an asylum. No wonder there was a certain stigma attached to mental illness!

Yet some progress was made. The Criminal Lunatics Acts of 1860 and 1884 and the establishment of Broadmoor in 1863 led to the segregation of insane persons with criminal records. The training of nursing staffs was an important development. Classes had been given in some individual asylums since 1854 when Dr Browne started classes at the Crichton Royal, Dumfries. The Medico-Psychological Association took the matter up and in 1890 promoted a scheme for the systematic training of male and female nurses, awarded certificates of proficiency in mental nursing, and sponsored a *Handbook for Attendants on the Insane* which, in a revised form, is still prescribed for examination purposes. The Medico-Psychological Association was indeed an important agent of progress. In 1903 a joint committee of the Association and the British Medical Association presented a deputation to the Lord Chancellor urging the importance of early treatment and the need to remove legal obstacles. In 1913 a special committee issued a first report on the means needed "to remedy the grave defects in the present position of psychiatry in Great Britain and Ireland".[1] And throughout this period the Association provided a forum for information and discussion in the *Journal of Mental Science*. The way was being prepared for post-war developments.

## 2. Psychiatric Thought

Apart from some changes in nomenclature and systems of classification, some swings of therapeutic fashion, and a few substantial advances in isolated areas, there was no great dissimilarity between the general psychiatric outlook in this country in 1880 and in 1914. In 1880 Bucknill and Tuke's *Manual of Psychological Medicine*, which originally appeared in 1858, was still the standard textbook, a fourth edition having been published in 1879. For purposes of comparison we may look at T. S. Clouston's *Clinical Lectures on Mental Diseases* (1st ed. 1883, 6th ed. 1904), Maurice Craig's *Psychological Medicine* (1905) and Mercier's

---

[1] *Journal of Mental Science*, LX (1914).

*Textbook of Insanity* (2nd ed. 1914). Clouston was for thirty-five years superintendent of the Royal Asylum, Morningside, Edinburgh, and the first lecturer in mental diseases in the University of Edinburgh, and a very influential psychiatric figure during this period. Both Craig and Mercier had served as asylum medical officers in the London area, and both lectured in mental diseases at London hospital medical schools. Mercier, who was something of a doctrinaire, wrote several books including a large *Psychology, Normal and Morbid* (1901) and works on criminal behaviour. On the strength of a book on logic he had the temerity to apply for the Waynflete Chair of Metaphysical Philosophy at Oxford in 1910.

As a result of advances in, and the popularity of, genetics in the early years of the century there is perhaps in the writers of this period a stronger emphasis on heredity, an inherited 'insane diathesis' or 'weakness of the brain', than in the earlier writers. But the stress on physical causative agents is the same. "Mental health", wrote Bucknill and Tuke, "is dependent upon the due nutrition, stimulation and repose of the brain, that is upon the conditions of the exhaustion and reposation of its nerve substance being maintained in a healthy and regular state." Irregularities of circulation might be one cause of insanity, but any pathological condition might disturb brain functioning, and exclusive theories were to be rejected. Bucknill and Tuke might be vague, but within the physical frame of reference they were not unduly dogmatic. The later writers were if anything more dogmatic, without having much additional scientific evidence for being so. In 1905 Craig, though recognizing the part played indirectly by anxiety and worry, regarded the condition of the blood as a major direct causative factor. "Every year brings more and more convincing evidence of the importance of recognizing that autotoxins derived from the alimentary tract play no small role in the production of insanity. Blood changes, including poisons circulating in the blood, have for some time past been placed in a prominent position among the various factors to be considered when studying physical disease. The case is no different in insanity, and it may fairly be said that the advantages to be gained by a careful study of the blood in cases of mental disorder cannot be over-estimated. Constipation is not only a common symptom in the insane, but it is the rule rather than the exception to find a history of prolonged constipation before the mental disorder supervened."[1] Mercier similarly emphasized the condition of the blood: "by far the most important of the direct

[1] M. Craig op. cit., 28–9.

stresses, perhaps the most important of all the stresses which contribute to the production of insanity is alteration in the composition of the blood by which the highest nerve regions are nourished. Simple deficiency of nutriment reduces the efficiency of the functions of the nerve tissue, which exhibits itself in deficiency of sanity. . . . In a large proportion of the cases of acute insanity that we have to treat a greater or less degree of starvation has been one of the factors in its production."[1]

In general any process that was exhausting could contribute to the production of insanity, and a most important cause of exhaustion was the reproductive instinct. Clouston, Craig and Mercier all shared the commonly held view that insanity was frequently a result of sexual excess. According to Mercier "the reproductive act is a great exhauster of energy. It is always and of necessity inimical to life. In many of the lower animals it is *ipso facto* destructive of life. In man, while it is not thus necessarily fatal, it is yet detrimental. It is exhaustive; it renders the organism less fit and less capable of resisting adverse circumstances; and, if it is repeated with undue frequency, its ill-effects become conspicuous."[2] Craig, while recognizing that "excess in one person may not be so in another", still holds it to be "an important factor in the production of mental disorder", in extreme cases producing symptoms not unlike those of general paralysis. Particularly deleterious was masturbation. "Masturbation in both sexes", wrote Craig, "is closely connected with insanity." [3] And Mercier, while disputing that it was "the prime and sole cause of insanity" (a belief he says which was once universal), held that it was often a contributory cause. Clouston recognized a 'masturbatory insanity', the chief cause of which was masturbation.

Exhaustion and strain might also result from unwise stimulation during the period of growth and development. It was commonly believed that mental development and physical development in children alternated with each other, and that to force mental development during the bodily phase could lead to nervous breakdowns and insanity. Precocity was a particularly dangerous sign. "Brilliancy", wrote Craig, "ought to be a warning note to the parent and the teacher." The intellect should not be forced: "a child should be treated as a child; regular hours of rest should be insisted on; the modern tendency to permit young girls to stay up late at night, attending dances and theatres, is a grievous error; all too frequently it sows the seeds of future years of ill health and disappointment".[4] Clouston was particularly concerned with

[1] C. Mercier op. cit., 9–10.    [2] C. Mercier op. cit., 16.
[3] Craig op. cit., 33.    [4] ibid., 265.

the ill effects of higher education on the tender organism of the female. "Why should we spoil a good mother by making an ordinary grammarian?" he asked.[1]

If exhaustion due to excess and unwise modes of living was a basic cause of insanity, treatment naturally must be aimed at the correction of these errors. Most important of all was rest. "The first and all-important point is to secure rest for the patient. . . . Absolute rest in bed is undoubtedly the best, and it may almost be said, the only way in which acute cases may be treated." [2] Mercier, who regarded starvation as one of the common precipitating causes of insanity, not unnaturally also stressed the value of food. "Our first cure must be to administer abundance of food. The patient must not merely be fed, he must be over-fed. He must have food in super-abundance and excess; he must have twice or three times as much as would suffice for a healthy man of his age and weight." If he refuses food he must be "dealt with promptly and vigorously. The patient must be forcibly fed."[3] Clouston on the other hand was strongly opposed to a flesh diet. According to him "an undue proportion of the adolescent insane had been flesh-eaters". Milk and porridge were one of his principal remedies. Another treatment advocated was the 'prolonged bath', where the patient was left for up to six or seven hours with his head projecting through a hole in the lid. Craig regarded such mechanical restraints (permitted with safeguards under the Lunacy Act, 1890) as more valuable than hypnotic drugs, which even then were quite widely employed.

This folk-lore was perhaps inevitable in the absence of precise knowledge, and precise knowledge of the nature of mental disorder, when it has been achieved, has been achieved slowly. Research findings did gradually modify exaggerated views, however, and even led to the solution of some obstinate problems. Thus research at Claybury, Hanwell and other asylums led to a more moderate estimate of the role of alcohol in the production of mental disorder. And about the turn of the century the most striking advance was the elucidation of the cause of general paralysis. Largely as a result of the researches of Sir Frederick Mott, F.R.S. (1853–1926), director of the pathological laboratories established by the London County Council at Claybury Asylum, Essex, in 1895, it became gradually established beyond doubt that general paralysis of the insane was invariably the result of syphilis. This had been regarded as a possibility for some time, and particularly on the

[1] T. S. Clouston *Mental Diseases*, 583.   [2] Craig op. cit., 287.
[3] Mercier op. cit., 200–1.

Continent many were prepared to accept the dictum of Krafft-Ebing that "general paralysis is a product of civilization and syphilization". But there was much controversy and doubt about the matter right up to 1913. Maudsley had noted the connexion between general paralysis and sexual excess, but sexual excess was often held to be in some way directly responsible. Savage, for instance, was struck "by the frequency of the occurrence of general paralysis in the husbands of some women of voluptuous physique".[1] Mott's researches published in the Archives of *Neurology and Psychiatry*, which he founded and edited, in 1899, together with various advances in the understanding and diagnosis of syphilis, resolved the mystery. Particularly convincing was Mott's investigation of juvenile cases of paralysis, and his demonstration that congenital syphilis was involved as the causative agent.

In addition to the work on general paralysis, Mott and his co-workers published reports on the relationship between dementia praecox and endocrine disorders, on the connexion between alcohol and insanity, on the hereditary aspects of mental diseases, and, during the First World War, on 'shell shock'. Mott also greatly reduced the mortality of mental patients by demonstrating that 'asylum dysentry' was not due to a 'nerve lesion' but was a preventable infection. As we have already noted it was largely due to Mott's advocacy that the Maudsley Hospital was established. Thither Mott transferred, taking the Claybury Laboratory with him. He retired in 1923, but before doing so had commenced lecturing for the Diploma in Psychological Medicine, and had been instrumental in persuading other universities and the Royal Colleges to institute similar diplomas. Mott also deserves to be remembered by psychologists for his assistance to the British Psychological Society in its early days, and for his contributions to musical psychophysiology, in particular *Brain and Voice in Speech and Song*.

Mott's work at Claybury constituted the most important stream of psychiatric research in the country prior to the First World War. Elsewhere development was slow, though the need for research was increasingly recognized. From 1907 the annual reports of the Lunacy Commissioners (later the Board of Control) contained a section on research. In 1914 the Treasury made its first grant – a sum of £1,500 – for research into the causes and treatment of mental disease and mental defect.

In spite of these beginnings the period under review was not only one of relative stagnation in British psychiatry, but one in which there

[1] G. Savage *Insanity and Allied Neuroses*, (1856) 282.

was considerable resistance to the importation of ideas from abroad. This applied both to psychoanalytic concepts and to Kraepelin's classificatory scheme, the most important feature of which was a distinction between a group of disorders he termed 'dementia praecox' [1] (later renamed by Bleuler, in 1911, schizophrenia), and cyclical 'manic-depressive' insanity. This scheme and its sub-divisions was not generally accepted by British psychiatrists, or alienists, as they were then generally called, until after the First World War, and they continued to devise their own indigenous systems. Thus Tuke (1892) based his classification on the divisions of sensory, motor, and ideational centres, with correspondingly disordered manifestations of hallucination, paralysis and dementia. Sir George Savage (1884) proposed a developmental classification based on the stages of life. In 1905 a committee of the Medico-Psychological Association drew up a classification which was adopted by the Lunacy Commission. Among the clinical groups listed were insanity with gross brain disease, acute delirium, confusional insanity, stupor, primary dementia (dementia praecox), mania, melancholia, alternating insanity, delusional insanity, volitional insanity, moral insanity and senile dementia. No wonder that this strangely mixed list did not satisfy everyone! Mercier in despair spoke of "the utter failure of every classification of insanity hitherto proposed", and went on to advocate an even more obscure distinction between 'forms of insanity' and 'varieties of insanity'. The First World War at least blew away some of these cobwebs.

### 3. Mental Defect

A number of causes led, towards the close of the nineteenth century, to a growing interest in the problem of mental defect. Compulsory education was finally introduced in 1876, and dull and feeble-minded children became an inescapable educational problem. Studies of town life and of poverty had brought forcibly to notice the degraded condition of the 'submerged tenth', and these social problems were attributed in no small measure to mental defect. Finally new knowledge of heredity and the eugenic movement associated with Galton gave rise to acute and, it may seem now, exaggerated fears of racial degeneration resulting from the frightening fertility of the feeble-minded. The appointment of a Royal Commission on the Care and Control of the Feeble-Minded in 1904, the publication of its report in 1908, and the passage of the Mental

---

[1] Clouston's clear description of 'adolescent insanity' considerably influenced Kraepelin in arriving at the concept of 'dementia praecox'.

Deficiency Act in 1913, were landmarks in the history of the treatment of mental defectives in this country.

Except on a limited or local scale and on a voluntary basis no special provision was made for mental defectives until the passage of the Mental Deficiency Act. The Lunacy Act of 1890 applied to all lunatics including 'idiots'. But in fact large numbers of defectives, estimated by the Royal Commission to amount to nearly 150,000, were not certified. Of these just over a third were under poor law supervision, and workhouses were full of defectives of all grades and ages indiscriminately housed with the destitute but normal poor. Another third were receiving no care or supervision at all; and the remainder were either children at school or inmates in prisons, inebriate reformatories and similar institutions.

Voluntary efforts to provide care for mental defectives were made from the 1840's onwards, but were necessarily on a relatively small scale. Park House, Highgate, founded by Andrew Reed, a philanthropist, in 1847, was soon full, and an annexe was opened in Colchester in 1849, becoming the Eastern Counties Asylum in 1859. Meanwhile Earlswood, near Redhill, had been opened in 1855 to take the original Park House patients, and the Royal Albert Asylum at Lancaster was opened in 1864. In 1875 the Charity Organization Society took up the cause of 'improvable idiots' and it was partly as a result of their advocacy that the Royal Commission on the feeble-minded was eventually set up. A number of voluntary institutions for epileptics were also founded towards the end of the century starting with the Maghull Home near Liverpool in 1888. In 1890 a National Association for promoting the welfare of the feeble-minded was formed, followed in 1902 by a Lancashire and Cheshire Society for the permanent care of the feeble-minded. These societies were instrumental in establishing a number of small voluntary homes for mental defectives. In 1886 the Idiots Act empowered local authorities to build institutions specifically for mental defectives, but in the following twenty years only eight such institutions were opened. Only in the London area had a serious attempt been made to care for defectives. In 1867 a Metropolitan Asylums Board was set up to provide for physical and mental sickness among the London poor. The Board continued to function until 1930 when its duties were transferred to the London County Council, and, among institutions of various kinds, it established a number of large asylums for mental defectives at Leavesden, Caterham and later at Tooting Bec. In 1878 a training colony for defective children was opened at Darenth, and in

1911 the Fountain Hospital at Tooting was detached from the fever service and allocated to the use of low grade mentally defective children.

It was an untidy pattern that confronted the Royal Commission when they began their labours in 1904. After reviewing the evidence and carrying out inquiries into the incidence of mental defect the Commission was impressed with the gravity of the situation. "There are numbers of mentally defective persons whose training is neglected, over whom no sufficient control is exercised, and whose wayward and irresponsible lives are productive of crime and misery, of much injury and mischief to themselves and to others, and of much continuous expenditure wasteful to the community and to individual families." [1] Their main recommendations were that special protection should be extended to all mentally defective persons, that it should be the duty of local authorities to 'ascertain', certify and detain mental defectives in their areas. Defectives were to be classified into four main groups – idiots, imbeciles, the feeble-minded and moral imbeciles. (The first three of these grades had been suggested by Dr Duncan of the Eastern Counties Asylum in 1860. The term 'moral imbecile', derived from J. C. Prichard's 'moral insanity', was used to describe persons with strong vicious or criminal propensities on which punishment had little or no deterrent effect and which had existed from an early age – it included but did not entirely correspond with the current 'psychopath'.) The Commission also recommended that a central body, the 'Board of Control', should be established to take over the central supervision of arrangements for both the insane and mental defectives. The Commission's main recommendations were accepted by the government of the day and embodied in the Mental Deficiency Act, 1913. This act remained in force, like the Lunacy Act, 1890, until 1959, when it was repealed by the Mental Health Act, which not only abolished the Board of Control, but abandoned the fourfold classification of defectives, did away with the rigid distinction between mental illness and mental deficiency and, though retaining a limited measure of compulsion, discarded the formal procedure of certification. In spite of this reversal of many of the Royal Commission's main recommendations the Commission's report did lead, at the time, to a substantial advance in the provision for mental defectives, and an appreciation of the magnitude of the problem they presented. It was the rigidity of the classification and of the arrangements they proposed that was most open to criticism.

[1] *Reports of the Royal Commission*, 1908.

To some extent this rigidity was an outcome of the prevailing ideas of the time. Both the report of the Royal Commission and the standard textbook on *Mental Deficiency* by A. F. Tredgold (1870–1952), the first edition of which appeared in 1908,[1] were strongly hereditarian in outlook. Tredgold giving evidence before the Commission maintained that "In 90 per cent of patients suffering from mental deficiency the condition is the result of a morbid state of the ancestors". Environmental factors were discounted or regarded as of very secondary importance. In his textbook Tredgold states, "my own enquiries have convinced me that in the great majority of these slum cases there is a pronounced morbid inheritance, and that their environment is not the cause but the result of that heredity".[2] The Commission thus came to the conclusion that the prevention of mentally defective persons from becoming parents by segregating them was an important way of dealing with the problem of deficiency. It would, however, be wrong to suppose that the value of training was discounted. This is not, as is sometimes believed, a modern discovery. It goes back at least to the Frenchman, Seguin, who in 1846 demonstrated the value of training idiots, and Tredgold, though fully appreciative of the difficulties and limitations of training, was insistent on its importance. "The training of the mentally defective child should begin", he said, "at birth or as soon as the condition is diagnosed." And he goes on to discuss training of the senses, of movement, of the intelligence, industrial training and moral training. The atmosphere is by no means one of stagnant and hopeless institutionalization.

One consequence of the segregation and institutionalization of defectives was a gradual improvement in the clinical description of various types of mental defect. In 1866 Dr J. Langdon-Down first described the condition of mongolism.[3] Dr W. W. Ireland in his work *Idiocy and Imbecility* (1877) distinguished ten main types. Further clinical types were added during the next few decades. Tredgold in 1908 simplified the classification by recognizing two main divisions Primary Amentia and Secondary Amentia, primary being due to a defective developmental potentiality in the germ cell, and secondary due to arrest of cerebral development after fertilization. This dichotomy was widely accepted, though as Penrose was to show a quarter of a century later, it is in fact impossible to class more than half the cases of mental defect with certainty as either primary or secondary.

[1] 9th ed., revised 1956.
[2] A. F. Tredgold op cit., 4th ed., 39.
[3] J. Langdon-Down *Clinical Lectures and Reports, London Hospital*, III (1866).

## 4. Crime and Delinquency

The backward state of British psychiatry at the close of the century was matched by the backward state of British criminology. There was in fact almost no systematic or scientific study of crime and delinquency in this country when Havelock Ellis in 1890 compiled his work on *The Criminal*; and at the second international Congress of Criminal Anthropology held in Paris in 1889 there was not a single British representative, though delegates were drawn from most civilized parts of the world. The enthusiasm of early penal reformers, such as John Howard (1726–90) and Elizabeth Fry (1780–1845), had largely petered out, and Mary Carpenter (see Chapter II) had no immediate successors in the field of juvenile delinquency. Apart from a few incidental observations in Maudsley's writings, an occasional article from prison doctors in the *Journal of Mental Science* and the descriptive accounts in Mayhew's *London Labour and the London Poor* (1861), there was an almost total absence of criminological literature in this country, in striking contrast to the Continent and in particular Italy, where flourishing schools of criminology and criminal anthropology had grown up, and where the scientific study of crime was a fashionable intellectual pursuit.

The last third of the nineteenth century was in fact a period of repression in British penology. Throughout the eighteenth century transportation was the penalty for most dangerous criminals who had not been sentenced to death and for many perpetrators of even quite trivial offences. Transportation diminished in volume and finally petered out in 1867 when the last British convicts were sent to Western Australia. Confronted with the task of dealing with all criminals within the confines of the country the House of Lords Committee which was set up in 1863 recommended severity and repression – "hard labour, hard fare, and a hard bed" – and advocated the efficacy of solitary confinement and silence. These recommendations were incorporated in the Prison Act, 1865, and coloured prison administration for the rest of the century and beyond. Under this stark system there was no place for consideration for the criminal as an individual and little occasion for the psychological study of crime.

The period of deterrence by severity of punishment failed to achieve its object. Crime did not diminish in volume, and recidivism was as frequent as ever. Conditions in the prisons led to increasing disquiet and protest, and eventually in 1895 a Departmental Committee on Prisons was set up under the chairmanship of Lord Gladstone. Although many of the recommendations of this committee were slow in being effectively implemented, its report marks the beginning of a new era in the British penal system. The committee started from the principle that prison treatment should have as its primary objects deterrence and reformation equally and concurrently. In their view "prison treatment should be effectually designed to maintain, stimulate or awake the higher susceptibilities of prisoners, and turn them out of prison better men and women, both physically and morally, than when they came in". The report of the Gladstone Committee was followed by the Prison Act of 1898, by the establishment of the probation system in 1907 and by the Borstal system for young offenders in 1908. The Children Act of 1908 made the imprisonment of boys and girls under sixteen illegal, ordered the setting up of Juvenile Courts, and encouraged the establishment of remand homes. In 1913 the report of a departmental committee on reformatory and industrial schools led to much-needed improvements in the management of these establishments. These changes all prepared the ground for a psychological approach to crime and delinquency. As soon as serious attempts were made not merely to punish but to reform the offender some understanding of his psychological make-up, his motives, and the background of his criminality, became urgently necessary. The more enlightened magistrates at the newly established juvenile courts made some attempts themselves to grapple with the problems with which they were confronted. Sir William Clarke Hall, for example, analysed the records of the juvenile cases appearing before him at Old Street, London. But psychological studies of a systematic kind, inspired by the work of Healy and others in the U.S.A., had to await the end of the First World War.

Meanwhile two pieces of work stand out. Havelock Ellis's *The Criminal* (1890), though largely second-hand, was an admirable survey of the field. Based largely on continental research Ellis's book was much influenced by the evolutionary and anthropological ideas of the time. Summing up the evidence of the continental criminal anthropologists Ellis writes, "By some accident of development, by some defect of heredity or birth or training, he (the criminal) belongs as it were to a lower and older social state than that in which he is actually living. It thus happens that our own criminals frequently resemble in physical and psychical characters the normal individuals of a lower race . . . they constantly reproduce the features of savage character – want of forethought, inaptitude for sustained labour, love of orgy etc." There is in other words either an arrest of development or a regression. Even if these interpretations seem inadequate Ellis's work awakened interest in the individuality of the criminal, in his psychology, and in more enlightened methods of treatment, and introduced to British readers the results of continental criminology.

The other piece of work by Charles Goring was more original. In 1913 Goring, who was a prison medical officer, published *The English Convict*, in which he reported the results of an investigation carried out with 3,000 convicts. He was particularly concerned to test the theories of the Italian criminologist, Lombroso, who held that there was a distinct 'criminal type', almost a sub-species of humanity. Goring's anthropometric measurements showed that there was no significant difference between groups of convicts and groups of university students. In a chapter on the psychology of the convict Goring also maintained, though his evidence was less conclusive, that "there is no such thing as a mental criminal type". As a refutation of Lombroso's theories Goring's work had an international importance at the time. As a contribution to the psychology of crime it was, however, relatively slight.

## 5. Psychical Research

The relation between psychical research and abnormal psychology is a problematical one. 'Psychical' phenomena are abnormal in a statistical sense in that they are comparatively rare occurrences. But if, as F. W. H. Myers believed, both pathological and psychical phenomena frequently have a common origin in the subliminal mechanisms of the mind, then a more substantial affinity than the statistical may be held to relate them. Psychical research as an ostensibly scientific activity was born towards the end of the nineteenth century. It was a cross between the spiritualism, which we have already seen re-emerged after the hibernation of the age of reason in a new guise amid the table-turnings, rappings, and mediumistic trances of the 1850's, and the religious starvation of the scientific agnostic. For some highly intellectual members of the upper and upper-middle classes, to whom the worldly utopias of the socialists for the most part made no appeal, it restored the hope of immortality and alleviated the fear of 'spiritual extinction' and 'spiritual solitude', which withered sensitive souls like Myers.

The movement began in a small way in the older universities. The Cambridge 'Ghost Society' was founded by E. W. Benson, later Archbishop of Canterbury, in 1851–2. It is important as the parent of the Society for Psychical Research founded in 1882, with Henry Sidgwick, the Cambridge philosopher, who had been a member of the 'Ghost

Society', as first president. The Oxford 'Phasmatological Society' was later in time and less influential. Both societies collected records of spontaneous psychical phenomena, hauntings, apparitions, and hallucinations. Much more sensational was the career of the American medium, D. D. Home, who came to Europe in 1855 and remained until his death in 1886. His physical manifestations, often of the most astonishing kind (on one famous occasion he floated out of one window 70 feet above ground and in at another!), were produced in most of the capitals of Europe, and no trickery was ever discovered. The distinguished physicist, Sir William Crookes, who examined Home in the laboratory, was completely convinced of the genuineness of the phenomena in spite of their extraordinary character. Another scientist, Sir William Barrett, Professor of Physics in Dublin, also conducted experiments on psychical phenomena and gave an account of them to the British Association in 1876. It was on Barrett's suggestion that a conference was convened in 1882 at which the formation of a Society for Psychical Research was proposed.

The leading figures in the new society (the S.P.R.) were the three Cambridge classical scholars, Henry Sidgwick (1838–1900), F. W. H. Myers (1843–1901) and Edmund Gurney (1847–1888). An impressive list of members including such names as Lord Rayleigh, Sir Oliver Lodge, A. J. Balfour, Andrew Lang, and William James of Harvard, was before long gathered together. Six main fields of enquiry were mapped out for investigation:

(i) telepathy,
(ii) hypnotism and allied phenomena,
(iii) Reichenbach phenomena (see Chapter II),
(iv) hauntings and apparitions,
(v) physical phenomena (poltergeists, etc.),
(vi) the history of psychical phenomena.

The aim of the society was to approach these various problems without prejudice or prepossession of any kind, and in a strictly scientific way. The society still continues to flourish, and its *Journal* and *Proceedings* constitute a rich mine of information on psychical phenomena.

Particularly significant in the early work of the society was the study of apparitions and spontaneous telepathic phenomena which was published in *Phantasms of the Living* (1886) by Gurney, Myers and Podmore; the *Census of Hallucinations* based on a questionnaire to which 17,000 replies were received (the veridical nature of some death-coincidental hallucinations was considered established); and an extended set of experiments on automatic writing in which a group of correspondents, some of them unknown to each other, produced a set of interlocking messages purporting to come from Sidgwick, Gurney and Myers, after their deaths. The society adhered to its principle of impartial scientific scrutiny to the extent of exposing a great many fraudulent mediumistic tricks and of providing, wherever possible, explanations of a naturalistic kind. Thus Myers went so far as to say that "by far the larger proportion (of phenomena) are due to the action of the still embodied spirit of the agent or percipient himself and not to external spirit agents". To the psychologist, Myers's attempt in his classic work *Human Personality and its Survival of Bodily Death* (1903) to explain a whole range of normal and abnormal phenomena in terms of the working of the subliminal self is the most permanently interesting outcome of the society's early activity.

F. W. H. Myers (1843–1901) was a very talented scholar who wrote on classical and modern literature and also occasional verse before turning his whole time and attention to psychic matters, in which he had been given an interest by Sidgwick as early as 1869. Though not a scientist by training he became learned in neurology and scientific method, and he steeped himself in the writings of psychologists, particularly the abnormal psychologists of the French school. He has the distinction of being the first Englishman to give an account of the work of Freud in this country. Only three months after Breuer and Freud published their first paper on hysteria in 1893, Myers reported it to a meeting of the S.P.R.[1] Four years later he reviewed the famous *Studien über Hysterie*, and a summary was included in the society's *Journal*. Before this in 1891 Myers himself had described hysteria as a disease of the hypnotic stratum. His services to psychology were rated very highly by William James. "I expect that Myers will ere long distinctly figure in mental science as the radical leader in what I have called the romantic movement. Through him for the first time, psychologists are in possession of their full material and mental phenomena are set down in an adequate inventory." What James could not at that time foresee was that Myers was shortly to be eclipsed by a much tougher and more ruthless thinker, Freud.

The theories which Myers put forward are not uninteresting as in some respects a foretaste of the analytic psychology of Freud, or perhaps rather of Jung. Myers held that personality was composite in character,

[1] Ernest Jones *Freud*, vol. II. 30.

and that large areas of it were 'subliminal', i.e. below the threshold of consciousness. These subliminal regions in which symbolism was the natural language not only accounted for many abnormal phenomena, hysteria, dreams, fixed ideas, automatisms and so on, but also for 'supernormal' phenomena. The subliminal was the possessor of remarkable powers which brought man into contact with a wider spiritual environment. It was capable not only of telepathy, but of 'ecstasy' or 'psychic excursions'. For parts of the personality, since personality was a 'colonial' organization, could become dissociated and temporarily break away altogether and leave the organism. Psychical 'invasion', possession by alien personalities, was equally possible. For all this Myers believed he had empirical evidence obtained by scientifically conducted psychical research.

The truth perhaps rather is, that both in Myers and the other early psychical researchers, scientific method was never pushed to its final limits. Their theories were ultimately shaped by the wishes and yearnings which decided them to undertake the task. Myers himself in his address *In Memory of Henry Sidgwick* tells us of his own psychical dedication. "In a star-light walk which I shall not forget (3 December 1869) I asked him (Sidgwick), almost with trembling, whether he thought that when Tradition, Intuition, Metaphysic, had failed to solve the riddle of the Universe, there was still a chance that from any actual observable phenomena – ghosts, spirits, whatsoever there might be – some valid knowledge might be drawn as to a World Unseen. Already, it seemed, he had thought that this was possible; steadily, though in no sanguine fashions, he indicated some last grounds of hope; and from that night onwards I resolved to pursue this quest, if might be, at his side." [1] This starry-eyed attitude, more marked in Myers than in Sidgwick, but present even in the circumspect Sidgwick and his brilliant wife, for many years Principal of Newnham College, Cambridge, persisted and biased the interpretation of data. Thus Myers believed himself to be "within sight of a religious synthesis which, although provisional and rudimentary, may in the end meet more adequately than any previous synthesis the reasonable needs of men"; and he ventured to predict that "in consequence of the new evidence, all reasonable men, a century hence, will believe the resurrection of Christ". [2] William James was no doubt right in claiming that Myers "staked out a vast track of the mental wilderness", but his preconceptions were such that his conclusions can hardly be regarded as 'genuine science' and nothing else.

[1] *Proc. S.P.R.*, XV.    [2] *Human Personality*, 351.

## 6. Havelock Ellis (1859–1939)

Among psychologists Havelock Ellis is certain to be remembered primarily for his *Studies in the Psychology of Sex*, the enormous master-piece which appeared in seven volumes between 1897 and 1928. But this was not his only contribution to psychology, for he wrote books on crime and on dreams and articles and reviews on various psychological topics, as well as a number of works on literature, life, social problems, and philosophy. The width of Ellis's interests was extraordinary. He has been described as "the most civilized Englishman of his generation", and indeed he showed a rare combination of scientific, artistic, literary and philosophical gifts, and possessed a profound acquaintance with the culture of Western Europe, particularly of France and Spain.

Yet Ellis came from a humdrum background in the southern suburbs of London, and his undistinguished schooling terminated at the age of sixteen without his having acquired any qualifications or formed any vocational ambitions. His father was a sea captain, an essentially well-adjusted man with no intellectual interests, plying sailing ships between England and Australia. It was suggested that a spell in Australia might benefit the shy, and not very robust, Havelock, and accordingly to Australia he sailed on his father's ship in 1875. In Australia he remained four years, landing up eventually at a one-teacher school in the bush, remote from towns. Here as a result of reading and a sort of mystical experience he found himself and determined that his main life's work would be to unravel the mysteries of sex. "In Australia I gained health of body; I attained peace of soul; my life task was revealed to me; I was able to decide on a professional vocation; I became an artist in literature",[1] he states in his autobiography. He returned to London and embarked on a medical course at St Thomas's Hospital. He was enabled to do this partly by a small legacy left to his mother, partly by a gift from the Hinton family (he had become interested in the writings of James Hinton, the strange medical philosopher who died in 1875) and partly by editorial work on the 'Mermaid' series of Elizabethan dramatists in unexpurgated form. After qualifying Ellis never practised medicine, except in a few temporary locums. He supported himself for many years in a very modest way by writing and editorial work, 'The Contemporary Science Series' being for long his main source of income. He never held any position; he belonged to no organizations; never

[1] *My Life*, 139.

appeared in public, and was essentially a lone wolf, dividing his time between a flat in London and a cottage in Cornwall, and devoting himself wholly to literary and scientific work, apart from a series of unusual love affairs with a series of unusual women. His capacity for work was tremendous, and his power of synthesizing, arranging, and presenting huge masses of facts quite phenomenal.

The importance of the *Studies in the Psychology of Sex* is still far more than historical. Though scientifically parts of it are dated, and new knowledge has been obtained on such matters as the endocrinology and genetics of sex, and on the sexual behaviour of animals, Havelock Ellis's work is still an unrivalled mine of information on many aspects of sex, culled from medical, historical, literary and anthropological sources, as well as from studies carried out by Ellis himself. His aim was "to get at the real facts of sex apart from all would-be moralistic or sentimental notions". Ellis was, as Lord Brain points out, "a new type of man, one of the first in our era to view sex without the emotion of guilt". Apart from its general significance as marking a new approach to the whole topic of sex, the *Psychology of Sex* was important in three particular ways. Primarily it was the first work on sex to include careful studies of normal sexuality and case studies of normal development, earlier works such as Krafft-Ebing's *Psychopathia Sexualis* (1893) having dealt solely with pathology. Secondly Ellis made the first comprehensive study of auto-erotic phenomena, and coined the term 'auto-erotic'. Freud more than once expresses his debt to Ellis in this area. Thirdly, Ellis's work contained the first full and scientific account of sexual inversion in the English language, earlier studies of homosexuality being mainly German.

For a variety of reasons Havelock Ellis decided to finish the volume on sexual inversion first. Though intended for restricted circulation among medical practitioners, the work was turned down by various medical publishers. Dr Hack Tuke, editor of the *Journal of Mental Science*, thought it impossible to keep it to medical readers, and "there are always the compositors, whose susceptibilities ought to be respected". In the end it was published by a quack publisher and led to a famous law case in which the publisher was prosecuted for selling "a wicked, bawdy, scandalous and obscene book called *Studies in the Psychology of Sex*, vol. I, intending to vitiate and corrupt the morals of the liege subjects of our Lady the Queen, to debauch and poison the minds of divers of the liege subjects of our said Lady the Queen, and to raise and create in them lustful desires, and to bring the liege subjects into a state of wickedness, lewdness and debauchery". As a result Havelock Ellis published the remaining volumes of the *Studies* in America, where they were available until 1935 only to medical readers. On inversion Havelock Ellis's conclusions largely anticipated subsequent enlightened opinion. On the basis of the evidence and case studies he collected he urged the need for a modification of the law, and for the removal of inversion from the category of penal offences, provided public decency were preserved and the young protected. It was, of course, entirely erroneous to accuse Havelock Ellis of advocating libertinism and the abandonment of modesty. In fact in the collected edition of the *Studies* the first volume became his lengthy account of 'The Evolution of Modesty'. This was the first comprehensive treatment of the subject ever made, marshalling as it did biological, anthropological, and historical data; and it stressed the important role played by modesty in the psychology of love. Later, in his final volume 'Sex in Relation to Society', and again in his *Essays of Love and Virtue*, he discusses the role of chastity, the aesthetic element in sex, and the nature of sexual morality. "I have always instinctively desired to spiritualize the things that have been counted low and material" he asserted in *My Life*.[1] The difference between Ellis's ideals and the conventional ones is that Ellis had faced every relevant fact he could lay his hand on, however unpleasant. Ellis's volume on 'Sexual Selection' is of special psychological interest in that it examines the sexual involvement of the main sensory channels, touch, smell, hearing and vision, as well as containing interesting observations on such diverse topics as ticklishness, kissing, bathing, and perfumes. Other volumes include treatments of sadism and masochism, and the relation between love and pain; of erotic symbolism and fetishism; of the psychic state in pregnancy; of eonism (or transvestitism) and other sexual deviations; and of sexual periodicity. But this bald summary can give little idea of the rich texture and fascinating by-ways of Ellis's *Studies*. There is, for example, a long chapter entitled 'The Synthesis of Dreams' in which Ellis records a series of one hundred dreams from the same person, and insists that the broad comprehensive picture of dream territory obtained by synthesizing data from many dreams is complementary to the Freudian method of dream analysis. This topic Ellis returned to in a separate book *The World of Dreams* (1911) based largely on a twenty-year study of his own dreams. Though influenced by Freud and recognizing the sexual element in many dreams, Ellis did not accept the exclusiveness of

[1] op. cit., 363.

Freudian theory, and adopted a more flexible approach to what he described as "an archaic world of vast emotions and imperfect thoughts".

Among other works of psychological interest by Ellis may be mentioned his early study *Man and Woman* (1894), an account of what was then known of the anatomical, physiological and psychological differences between the sexes; *A Study of British Genius* (1904), an analysis of the parentage, heredity, social background and other characteristics of representative eminent men and women from the sixteenth to the nineteenth centuries, inspired by Galton's work; a series of articles in the *Lancet* and elsewhere on the psychological effects of the drug mescalin, with which Ellis was the first to experiment in England; and his early book *The Criminal* (1890) discussed in the previous section.

It is difficult even now to evaluate the place which Ellis is likely to occupy in the history of psychology. To some extent he has been eclipsed by his almost exact contemporary, Freud, a more robust and masterful personality who both subdued himself and imposed his views on the world more effectively than did Ellis. But Ellis perhaps had a greater sensitivity, and a greater awareness of the richness and complexity of life, was more of an artist and a better 'natural historian' of the soul, though less powerful a theorist. Perhaps the two men are in some senses complementary.

### 7. The First Incursions of Psychoanalysis

In more ways than one, therefore, abnormal psychology was extending its boundaries as the twentieth century commenced, with Myers into the psychic realm, with Ellis into the forbidden territory of sex, and then with the incursions of psychoanalysis into the unconscious regions of the mind. Myers and Ellis themselves sowed the first psychoanalytic seeds in this country in the 1890's. By 1914, however much denigrated by the medical profession, psychoanalysis had taken root in Great Britain. The London Society of Psycho-analysts was founded by Ernest Jones in 1913. In the same year papers on the Freudian theories of dreams and of the unconscious were read to the British Association in Birmingham by T. H. Pear and William Brown, and in 1914 a symposium on the Freudian theory of forgetting was held at a joint meeting of psychologists and philosophers in Durham.[1] Occasional papers on psychoanalytic themes had begun to appear in the medical press and in journals such as *Brain*. The publication of Ernest Jones's *Papers on Psychoanalysis* and of Bernard Hart's *The Psychology of Insanity* both

[1] Published in *B. J. Psych.*, VII.

in 1912 presented British readers with the first systematic expositions of many of the main psychoanalytic concepts. Without any conspicuous publicity such as the famous Clark University Conference with which psychoanalysis came to America in 1909—a conference graced not only by Stanley Hall, William James and other leading figures in American psychology, but by Freud himself and several of his principal psychoanalytic lieutenants—without any signal event of this kind, psychoanalysis silently percolated into the ken of British psychologists, medical men and philosophers in the years immediately preceding the outbreak of the First World War.

The first clinic for psychotherapeutic treatment, partly inspired by psychoanalytic ideas, the Medico-Psychological Clinic of London, was opened in 1913 by Dr Jessie Murray, who had attended lectures by Janet in Paris. Sessions were held on three afternoons a week at premises in Brunswick Square under the direction of Dr James Glover, a brother of Dr Edward Glover, who later became a well-known analyst. Spearman was a founder member of the clinic, and Aveling was associated with it and employed hypnosis in the treatment of patients. The clinic eventually wound up in 1923, after James Glover and his brother had become orthodox analysts following their visit to Abraham, one of Freud's leading followers, in Berlin. A related organization, the Society for the Study of Orthopsychics, was founded in 1915, with first Percy Nunn and then L. T. Hobhouse as president, and was concerned with training courses in psychology, the programme of study including a personal analysis.[1]

The key figure in the psychoanalytic movement in Great Britain was certainly Ernest Jones (1879-1958); indeed he was one of the key figures in the international development of psychoanalysis and a devoted member of the 'inner six' most intimate associates of Freud. Born, brought up and educated in South Wales, Ernest Jones after qualifying in medicine became a house surgeon at University College Hospital, London, and worked for a time with Victor Horsley in the neurological field. Here he became closely associated with Wilfred Trotter, who though primarily a surgeon was profoundly interested in psychology. Trotter married Jones's sister, and the two men set up together for a time in Harley Street. It was Trotter who first mentioned Freud to Jones. Jones, who was a voracious reader, soon became steeped in

---

[1] For details of the clinic and the society see Theophilus E. M. Boll 'May Sinclair and the Medico-Psychological Clinic of London', *Proceedings of the American Philosophical Society*, vol. CVI, (1962) 310-26.

psychoanalytic literature, and in 1906 had begun experimenting with the analysis of patients. He first met Freud personally at a psycho-analytic congress at Salzburg in 1908, and it was at this congress that he delivered his first psychoanalytic paper, on rationalization, a concept which he was responsible for introducing. Jones's attachment to Freud – disturbed only temporarily by the First World War – became closer and more intimate as time progressed, and he was finally instrumental in securing asylum for Freud in this country and wrote his official biography. Meanwhile, however, in 1908 Jones's medical career in London, in spite of a brilliant academic record, had miscarried and he had failed to secure any satisfactory hospital posts. As a result he decided to emigrate temporarily to Canada, where he remained from 1908 to 1913 as director of a psychiatric clinic in Toronto. These were years of great significance and productivity for Jones. He underwent a training analysis with Ferenczi in Budapest, the first analysis of the kind, made many contacts in America, and produced a large number of expository and clinical papers which were collected together in *Papers on Psychoanalysis* (1st ed. 1912). On his return to England in 1913 he set up as a consultant in Great Portland Street, London, and established the London Society of Psycho-analysts with a membership of fifteen. Owing to disagreements the society was dissolved after the war and re-placed by the present British Psychoanalytic Society. In the considerable expansion and recognition which psychoanalysis enjoyed after the First World War, Jones was intellectually and personally the dominant figure. His collected papers, written without compromising the essential fea-tures of Freudian theory, but in a scholarly and lucid style, did more than anything to make psychoanalysis scientifically acceptable in this country. Indeed until the publication of the English translation of Freud's own *Introductory Lectures on Psychoanalysis* in 1922 they con-stituted the best general account of psychoanalysis in English.

On a more popular level the effect of Bernard Hart's little book on *The Psychology of Insanity* (1st ed. 1912) was probably almost as im-portant. In the following forty years the book was reprinted twenty times without substantial alteration in its contents. Hart (born in 1879), who lectured on psychiatry at University College Hospital and later at the Maudsley Hospital, and also served as a consultant at the National Hospital, Queen Square, early became interested in psychoanalytic problems, and published important papers in *Brain* on hysteria and on the unconscious. *The Psychology of Insanity* was designed to introduce to British readers some of the ideas of Freud, "probably the most original and fertile thinker who has yet entered the field of abnormal psychology". Hart, however, unlike Jones, was by no means a pure Freudian. He borrowed from various sources – from Janet, for example the concept of dissociation – and in his book he deliberately omitted any consideration of the sex instincts. It was, in fact, an early example of the 'watered-down' depth psychology which later became popular with many British psychotherapists. Nevertheless Hart's book had many merits, including brevity, clarity and balance, and it effectively introduced many of the key mechanisms and dynamic concepts of the Freudian system, such as conflict, repression, projection and identification, to medical students, psychologists and the general public.

How long these pioneer studies would have taken to make an impact but for the First World War it is impossible to say. The war stimulated the development of psychoanalysis in two ways: first, it produced a large crop of psychological disorders among combat troops, so-called 'shell shock' cases; and secondly it profoundly stirred up and discredited conventional beliefs on human nature, society and conduct. The resistances to the acceptance of psychoanalytic doctrines, though not removed, were markedly lowered, and psychoanalysis was to become in the post-war period of the 1920's and 1930's a major intellectual movement, by no means confined to medical circles.

# CHAPTER XI

# Experimental and Institutional Beginnings

## 1. Individual Pioneers

When the First World War broke out in 1914 experimental psychology was exiguously established in Great Britain. The small laboratories at Cambridge, London, Manchester, Edinburgh, and Glasgow could not be compared in size or importance with those existing in most German and many American universities, or even with those of other continental countries. The slow development of experimental psychology in this country can be attributed to a number of reasons – the conservatism of British universities; the philosophical resistance to the human sciences, which has shown itself in various ways, for example in the opposition to the study of sociology, besides a dislike of psychology; and our general backwardness in the organization of science and the establishment of laboratories. Great Britain has produced so many illustrious scientists that it is not always realized that in the organization and public support of science we have, until well into the present century, lagged far behind other Western countries. For many years the Royal Institution in London was the only public research laboratory. The Cavendish Laboratory at Cambridge and the Clarendon Laboratory at Oxford were not founded until the 1870's. Karl Pearson could proclaim with justification just before the close of the century that there did not exist in London a physical laboratory worthy of the capital. The Royal Commission on scientific instruction and the advancement of science under the chairmanship of the Duke of Devonshire, which reported between 1872 and 1875, revealed the parlous state of our scientific facilities. It is hardly surprising that universities which had only just become seriously aware of the need to provide laboratories for teaching and research in the physical and biological sciences, should have not regarded the establishment of psychological laboratories as a very urgent requirement, particularly as they would have had to provide the funds from their own resources. It took a good deal of persuasion on William Thomson's (Lord Kelvin's) part to extract even £100 for physical apparatus from the University of Glasgow, and the university set up a special committee to see that he did not misapply the money. The state of affairs in Germany was very different. There were many more universities; they were much better supported; and from 1825 onwards when Liebig the chemist established the first university teaching laboratory at Giessen, there had been a rapid growth of university laboratories, particularly in chemistry and biology. Wundt's establishment of the first psychological laboratory at Leipzig in 1879 was, therefore, quite a natural development in the German scene, and the growth and proliferation of similar laboratories in Germany was equally natural.

The achievements of British science from the seventeenth until the late nineteenth centuries were mainly the result of individuals working without public support and as the spirit moved them. Untroubled by interdisciplinary boundaries men whose primary claim to fame was as physicists or chemists at times made important pioneering contributions to the foundations of experimental psychology. Newton's *Opticks* (1704) established the basic mode of operation of the eye, and laid the groundwork of colour theory. A hundred years later Thomas Young elucidated the mechanism of the accommodation of the eye to different distances, and propounded a three-colour theory of colour vision, suggesting that there were three types of nerve fibres responding to the three primary colours. The chemist John Dalton in 1798 reported to the Literary and Philosophical Society of Manchester some "extraordinary facts relating to the vision of colours". He both described his own defects of colour vision (red-green blindness) and made some attempt to assess the number of colour-blind in the population. "It is remarkable that out of 25 pupils I once had, two were found to agree with me; and on another similar occasion one." [1] Defective colour vision, first termed colour-blindness by Sir David Brewster, was further studied by Sir John Herschel, Professor George Wilson of Edinburgh, and the famous Clerk Maxwell. Herschel in 1845 was the first to attempt an explanation of colour-blindness in terms of 'dichromism', i.e. the ability to see only two instead of three primary colours. George Wilson's *Researches on Colour Blindness* (1855), the first comprehensive review of the subject in English, contained a number of careful case studies, reviewed the various theories that had been put forward, and discussed methods of testing (including the wool test later improved by Holmgren) and the importance of testing the colour vision of railway servants. Wilson estimated colour-blindness to occur in about five per cent of the male population, and to be largely hereditary. He also recognized that it occasionally occurred in females, and described the case of a flower girl who made

[1] *Mem. Lit. and Phil. Soc.*, M/C 1798.

frequent mistakes in the flower shop. Unlike Herschel who held that the colour-blind saw as long a spectrum as the normal, Wilson held that it was often truncated at the red end. Clerk Maxwell, adopting Young's three-colour theory, devoted himself chiefly to the devising of methods for combining and recording mixtures of colours. His colour top (later improved as the colour wheel) and his colour equations for evaluating any colour in terms of the three fundamental colours became basic tools of the psychological laboratory. Interestingly enough it was Clerk Maxwell, the physicist, who clearly recognized the psychological nature of colour vision. "If the sensation which we call colour has any laws, it must be something in our own nature which determines the form of these laws." "The science of colour must, therefore, be regarded as essentially a mental science." But mere introspection was not enough. "It is impossible by a mere act of introspection to make a true analysis of our sensations. Consciousness is our only authority; but consciousness must be methodically examined in order to obtain any trustworthy results." [1] Maxwell's successor in the Cavendish Chair at Cambridge, Lord Rayleigh, also interested himself among numerous other topics in colour. His 'colour box' (later to be known as the 'anomaloscope'), described in *Nature* in 1881, was able to reveal colour weakness in persons not classifiable as 'colour-blind'. Among his experimental subjects were the Balfour brothers to whom he was related by marriage. Other writers on colour vision during this period were W. Abney[2] and Edridge-Green.[3] The latter is now mainly remembered for his lantern test which was used for some time as a test for colour defect.

Another psychological problem which interested British scientists, perhaps because of Berkeley's theories, was the problem of space perception. Sir Charles Wheatstone, Professor of Physics at King's College, London, was the first person to record[4] the different perspectives of the two eyes when viewing not too distant objects. Wheatstone went on to ask what would be the visual effect of simultaneously presenting to each eye its projection on a plane surface. To answer this question he devised his mirror stereoscope, and devised a number of demonstrations with outline figures. He noted the singular effect produced when the figures were reversed and the right-hand figure was seen with the left eye.[5] In a later article he observed "it is necessary to endeavour not

---

[1] *Proc. Roy. Inst. G. S.*, vol. vi, 'Sci. Papers', vol. I, 267–79.
[2] W. Abney *Colour Vision*, 1895.
[3] Edridge-Green *Colour Blindness and Colour Perception*, 1891.
[4] *Phil. Trans.*, 1838.      [5] ibid., 1852.

only to analyse the elements of vision, but also to recombine them in unusual manners". His 'pseudoscope' enabled the magnitude of retinal images to be dissociated from binocular convergence: larger pictures on the retinae could be associated with less convergence. Objects could be made to approach or recede without changing distance, and the relief of objects inverted. "Distance", stated Wheatstone, "instead of being a simple perception is a judgement arising from a comparison of retinal and perceived magnitudes." Wheatstone's mirror stereoscope was a clumsy instrument, and was largely superseded by Sir David Brewster's prismatic instrument,[1] which became, particularly as a result of the development of photography, quite a popular toy.

Important contributions to the solution of the problems of the perception of sound direction were made by Professor S. P. Thompson. Professor of Physics at Bristol, and Lord Rayleigh, whose *Theory of Sound* (1st ed. 1877–8) long remained a classic. In 1877 Thompson demonstrated the existence of an interference in the perception of sounds by leading separately to the two ears with india-rubber pipes the sounds of two tuning forks struck in separate apartments. The effects he particularly noted were 'beats' rather than directional effects, Rayleigh repeated the experiment with Thompson's 'pseudophone', as it was termed, and reported directional effects which he demonstrated were due to phase differences. Localization by phase differences particularly applied to lower notes; with high notes directional indications could be explained by intensity differences at the two ears.[2]

This is by no means a complete list of the contributions by British scientists to the early development of experimental psychology. Michael Faraday, Wheatstone and others were interested in optical illusions; and physiologists such as Sherrington studied muscular, cutaneous and visual sensations. But it suffices to show that some experimental work in the psychological field had been done in this country before the opening of specialized laboratories.

## 2. The Cambridge Laboratory

The first moves to establish experimental psychology as a distinct discipline were made by James Ward and Dr Venn, the logician, in Cambridge, as early as 1877. But the Cambridge Senate rejected their proposed laboratory of psychophysics on the grounds that it would "insult religion by putting the human soul in a pair of scales". It was

[1] D. Brewster *The Stereoscope*, 1856.
[2] Rayleigh *Phil. Mag.*, 1907, 'Sci. Papers', vols. I, II, IV, V.

fourteen years later before Ward managed to obtain a small grant of £50 for psychophysical apparatus. In 1893 W. H. R. Rivers was invited to come to Cambridge as a lecturer on the physiology of the special senses, and in 1897 he was made lecturer in experimental psychology and the physiology of the senses, and given a room in the physiology department. The laboratory was transferred to a house (16 Mill Lane) in 1903.

W. H. R. Rivers (1864–1922) was not by training a Cambridge man. He qualified in medicine at St Bartholomew's Hospital, and after various jobs as ship's doctor, house physician, etc., obtained an appointment at the National Hospital, Queen Square. Here he came under the influence of Hughlings Jackson, Victor Horsley and Henry Head. Partly as a result of these influences and partly as a result of a visit to Jena, he determined to devote his life to psychology. On his return he was for a time clinical assistant at Bethlem Hospital, and gave occasional lectures on experimental psychology at University College, London, before being appointed at Cambridge. Rivers's early interest was primarily in vision. Between 1893 and 1901 he published a number of papers on colour vision and in a chapter on vision in the second edition of Sharpey-Schafer's *Textbook of Physiology* (1900) he produced what has been described as "the most accurate and careful account of the whole subject in the English language". Another of Rivers's interests was fatigue. He had carried out a brief investigation into mental fatigue and recovery with Kraepelin in Germany. In his Croonian lectures (1908) he reported on 'The influence of alcohol and other drugs on fatigue'. Rivers believed that the most fruitful results could be obtained from experimental techniques when abnormal states, whether produced by pathological conditions or artificially by drugs, were subjected to testing. Rivers ceased teaching experimental psychology in 1907 and between 1907 and 1913 published nothing of psychological interest. Until the First World War he was preoccupied mainly with ethnology, and during and after the war with psychotherapy. An important factor in turning his mind to ethnological studies was his participation in the Torres Straits expedition in 1898 under the leadership of A. C. Haddon, the zoologist and ethnologist, an expedition which has been described as "epoch making for the science of man", and which certainly had an important impact on Cambridge psychology.

Haddon had been out to the Torres Straits as a zoologist in 1888, and it was while on this expedition that his interest turned decisively to ethnology. "Zoology could wait; man's life history was changing more rapidly", explains why. He determined to organize another expedition, this time anthropological, but equipped to carry out thorough psychological investigations of native people. Naturally, he approached Rivers, who at first turned down the invitation to accompany the expedition. Instead his pupil C. S. Myers was appointed; and at Myers's suggestion McDougall joined them. When Rivers found that his two best students were going he changed his mind, and was put in charge of the psychological work. "I put the direction of psychological department entirely into the hands of Rivers", states Haddon, "and for the first time psychological observations were made on a backward people in their own country by trained psychologists with adequate equipment." [1] A portable psychological laboratory was taken to Murray Island and experiments were carried out on the principal senses, on reaction times, the estimation of time intervals, memory, mental fatigue and muscular power. The results obtained were compared with those gathered from control groups in the British Isles. The differences observed were comparatively small, and supported neither the idea of the sensory superiority of native peoples, nor the belief that natives were incapable of concentrating on a laboratory type task. The importance of the Torres Straits expedition to Cambridge psychology was not, however, in any particular findings but in the fact that it shaped the outlook of Rivers and Myers, the two principal figures in Cambridge psychology before the First World War, and through their influence coloured the thinking of F. C. Bartlett who followed Myers as director of the Cambridge laboratory after the war. Bartlett's *Psychology and Primitive Culture* (1923) and the later *Study of Society* (1939) which he assisted in editing are testimonies to this influence.

Shortly after the return of the Torres Straits expedition C. S. Myers (1873–1947) who had attended Rivers's classes on the special senses while reading for the Natural Sciences tripos at Cambridge, and afterwards qualified in medicine at St Bartholomew's Hospital, was appointed to assist Rivers as University Demonstrator in Experimental Psychology, becoming a lecturer in 1909, and director of the laboratory in 1912. Myers, who was a competent musician, was particularly interested in auditory problems, and carried out research on auditory localization, synaesthesia, individual differences in attitudes to music, and into primitive music. But he was a broadly competent experimentalist, and his *Textbook of Experimental Psychology* (1st ed. 1909) was a thorough and scholarly treatment of the classical fields of experimentation. Myers

[1] A. H. Quiggin *Haddon the Head-Hunter*, 97.

always laid great stress on the importance of the psychophysical methods. As he affirmed in his presidential address to the psychology section of the British Association in 1931 "more than 30 years experience has convinced me that a thorough familiarity with the practice and theory of the psychophysical methods is essential for reliable systematic psychological investigations of any kind". But he also believed that psychology properly deals with experience, not conduct, and that "introspection should never be omitted in a psychological experiment".[1] During his Cambridge period Myers had a number of able pupils who formed the backbone of British psychology between the wars – F. C. Bartlett, Eric Farmer, C. A. Mace, W. H. J. Sprott, R. H. Thouless, and C. W. Valentine among others. Bartlett comments on "the scientific temper, the sanity, the breadth, the clarity, the insight possessed to the same degree by no other living English psychologist",[2] which characterized Myers. At a time when psychology was beginning to break up into 'schools' Myers held steadily to an empirical 'middle-of-the-road' position, seeking for steady advances both in experimental and applied psychology, never over-theoretical, though, as his later papers showed, his work was founded on a deeply thought out position. He was one of the ablest and most balanced minds that have contributed to the development of psychology in Great Britain, and his international reputation was recognized by his election as President of the International Congress of Psychology held in Oxford in 1923. His career at Cambridge virtually terminated with the First World War. During the war he became psychological consultant to the British armies in France, and after his return to England in 1917 was appointed to supervise and co-ordinate the psychological teaching and training of special medical officers in neurological centres. Shortly after the war Myers resigned his Cambridge post to undertake the organization of the National Institute of Industrial Psychology. But before his connexion with Cambridge had terminated he had seen the Cambridge laboratory established in new premises, based on his own plans, and indeed largely financed by his own money, for he was a man of some wealth.

### 3. London Developments

The year 1897 which saw the foundation of the Cambridge laboratories also saw the beginnings of experimental psychology in London. For it was in that year that Sully persuaded University College to start a small laboratory, and also that Miss Beatrice Edgell, who had been trained in

---

[1] *Textbook*, 2nd ed., 4.    [2] F. C. Bartlett *Am. J. Psych.*, 1 (1937).

Spearman's reign heralded the beginning of a characteristic 'London School' of psychology which is so important in the history of British psychology that a separate chapter must be devoted to it.[1] The London departments, however, were never wholly 'London', and the staff which Spearman, and later Burt, appointed represented a range of interests. J. C. Flugel (1884–1955) for instance, whose appointment in 1909 followed closely on Spearman's, and who spent his whole working life at University College, was primarily interested in psychoanalysis and the application of psychoanalytic ideas to the understanding of family life, to moral and social problems, and to world issues like warfare and population pressures. But he was also an experimentalist and helped Spearman with his work on oscillation, and, as his *One Hundred Years of Psychology* (1933) shows, there were few aspects of the subject with which he was unacquainted. S. F. J. Philpott (1888–1952), who taught in the department for over thirty years, was trained originally as a physicist, and was for long the buttress of its laboratory classes. His own main research work was summed up in his monograph on *Fluctuations in Human Output* (1932).

The Bedford College department has always been a smaller department. Beatrice Edgell (1871–1948), who became Professor in Psychology in 1927, deserves to be remembered as the first woman professor of psychology in Great Britain, and the first woman president of the British Psychological Society. Her *Theories of Memory* (1924) was a scholarly account of the philosophical and psychological problems of memory. She was assisted in the department by Victoria Hazlitt (1887–1932) who wrote a stimulating book on *Ability* (1926) in which she discussed her pioneering experiments in the selection of university students in this country. Before her untimely death she had turned her attention to children's thinking and the psychology of infancy, and her lectures on this subject were posthumously published.

The third main London department was originally established at King's College and transferred to Birkbeck College after the Second World War. C. S. Myers of Cambridge held a part-time chair in psychology, and started a small laboratory in 1903. He was after a time first assisted, and then succeeded, by William Brown (1881–1952), fresh from multiple Oxford courses in classics, mathematics, philosophy cum psychology and physiology. While at King's Brown qualified in medicine, and later turned to psychotherapy and the rich pastures of Harley Street. Also at King's he wrote his influential book *Essentials of Mental*

[1] See below, chap. XIII.

*Measurement* (1st ed. 1911)[1] in which he criticized Spearman's two-factor theory. After the war F. A. P. Aveling (1875–1941) moved from University College to take charge of the department at King's. A Canadian by birth, Aveling was trained in philosophy, theology and psychology at McGill, Oxford, Rome and Louvain. At Louvain he was a pupil of the distinguished Belgian psychologist, Michotte, and there commenced a series of researches on the higher thought processes. His investigations into conceptual thinking, published in his book *On the Consciousness of the Universal and the Individual* (1912), although making extensive use of introspective data, broke new ground experimentally, and deserve to be better remembered than they are. His work on the psychology of conation, choice and volition, which he also endeavoured to tackle experimentally, was summarized in *Personality and Will* (1931). The more mundane experimental work of the department was meanwhile carried out by R. J. Bartlett (born in 1879), who will be remembered by a generation of students for his qualities as a teacher, and by British psychologists generally for his many services to the British Psychological Society.

Psychology teaching elsewhere in London was of a more specialized character. The London Day Training College (founded 1902, and renamed the Institute of Education in 1932) naturally concentrated on educational and child psychology. Since Susan Isaacs' appointment in 1933 to take charge of the department of child development the Institute has been one of the main centres of child psychology in the country. At the London School of Economics where D. W. Harding was appointed lecturer in 1933 the focus has been on social and industrial psychology, and industrial psychology (under Dr May Smith and Dr H. G. Maule) has also been taught in the London School of Hygiene.

### 4. Psychology in Other Universities

Outside Cambridge and London the Scottish universities can perhaps claim priority in the academic teaching of psychology. At Aberdeen psychology from the time of Bain onwards had been prominent in the school of philosophy. In 1896 the Anderson lectureship in comparative psychology was established and Stout became the first holder. The lectureship was administratively attached to the department of moral philosophy, but practical work was carried out on topics such as sensation, memory, and association, and consideration was given to child and abnormal psychology as well as the psychology of primitive peoples.

[1] In later editions Godfrey Thomson collaborated with Brown.

There has been a continuous development at Aberdeen from 1896 culminating in the establishment of the Anderson chair exactly half a century later. Stout was succeeded in 1899 by Dr J. L. McIntyre who held the lectureship until 1929, when Rex Knight, the first holder of the chair, was appointed.

At Edinburgh development was more rapid. The George Combe laboratory was established in 1906 and Dr W. G. Smith (1866–1918) was appointed to take charge. Smith came with an extremely valuable background of experience, first in philosophy at Edinburgh, and then in psychology at various German universities, including Leipzig under Wundt. After five years in the U.S.A. he was appointed in 1901 to take charge of the department of experimental psychology at Claybury Asylum. He also lectured in the physiology department at King's College, London, before proceeding to Liverpool to work under Sherrington in 1905. A year later he moved to Edinburgh. In spite of the fact that from 1906–18 Dr Smith ran the Edinburgh laboratory alone, for most of the time without even the help of a laboratory boy, he managed very quickly to equip it on a scale second only to Cambridge. When shortly afterwards in 1912 Moray House Training College was opened in Edinburgh and a laboratory of experimental education established, the Scottish capital became one of the main centres for psychological work in the country. On Smith's death James Drever snr. (1873–1950), who had taken an external London degree in psychology after graduating at Edinburgh, took over the George Combe laboratory, the directorship being raised to a chair in 1931. In association with Dr Mary Collins, one of Smith's pupils, Drever built up a vigorous department with a sound balance between laboratory work and practical applications, and a thorough coverage of theory. Drever was succeeded in the chair by his son, James Drever jnr., in 1944.

In Glasgow, which followed Edinburgh in establishing a lectureship in 1907, there has also been a continuous though not so rapid development of psychology under a distinguished series of psychologists – Dr H. J. Watt (1907–25), Dr R. H. Thouless (1926–38), Dr P. E. Vernon (1938–47), and Professor R. W. Pickford (1947–   ), the first holder of the chair created in 1955. H. J. Watt (1879–1925) was one of our most eminent academic psychologists of the first part of the century. After graduating in philosophy at Aberdeen he went to Germany and was interested in experimental psychology by Stumpf in Berlin. From 1902 to 1906 he studied and worked in Würzburg and made an important contribution to the Würzburg investigations into the psychology of the thought processes. On his return to England he held a lectureship under Sherrington in Liverpool for a year, and his interest switched to the problem of sensory integration. This led to the publication towards the end of his life of a systematic introduction to the psychology of cognition, *The Sensory Basis and Structure of Knowledge* (1925), in which he endeavoured to show how sense develops smoothly and continuously into intellect through a regular process of integration. The book followed a series of papers published in the *British Journal of Psychology*, and prolonged researches on the psychology of sound, also published in book form in 1917. Watt's early death was hastened by his internment in Germany in 1914.

In St Andrews, where Stout held the chair of logic and metaphysics from 1903 onwards, psychology was slower to take root. Wasn't Stout enough to satisfy any demand for psychology? Hadn't St Andrews the prince of theoretical psychologists? It was not till 1924 that St Andrews appointed a lecturer in experimental psychology, C. A. Mace, a Cambridge graduate, migrating from Nottingham, and even today there is no chair of psychology at St Andrews.

The development of psychology in Scotland has been both promoted and shaped by the institution of the Bachelor of Education degree (B.Ed.) in the Scottish universities after the First World War. (In St Andrews, however, the full degree was not awarded until 1950.) The syllabus of this degree contained a large amount of both general and educational psychology, and the holder of a B.Ed. has been generally regarded as qualified to carry out psychological work, at least in the educational field.

In English universities the progress of psychology was slower, more curious, and more patchy than in Scotland. Manchester soon took the lead by establishing a chair of psychology in 1919, our first full-time chair properly and exclusively psychological – the London professorship at University College being technically 'of Mind and Logic' until 1928. The young T. H. Pear (born in 1886) who had switched from physics to psychology at King's College, London, was the first holder (from 1919–51), having been invited by Professor Alexander, the philosopher, to go to Manchester in 1909 as a lecturer. After spending a session at Würzburg he returned to Manchester and started a course in experimental psychology for B.Sc., a full honours course in the Faculty of Science being run from 1913. Courses in psychology were also included in the Diploma of Psychological Medicine inaugurated in 1910. The First World War naturally interrupted the development of psychology in Manchester, and Pear was involved both in psychotherapy at Maghull Military Hospital and research on submarine location in H.M.S. *Crystal Palace*[1] – early wartime ventures in applied psychology. Between the wars the department attracted a flow of research students, many from overseas, the bias of interest more and more veering to the social psychology of everyday life to which Pear himself contributed a number of lively studies.

Liverpool, though earlier in the field, was less fortunate. Sherrington introduced a general course on 'elementary psychophysiology' in 1899, and a practical class in 1900. In 1903 psychology became one of the subjects which could be taken for the final B.Sc. and education and philosophy students were recommended to attend some of the lectures. In 1905 Dr W. G. Smith was appointed to Sherrington's department to run the classes in psychology: he was followed by Dr H. J. Watt in 1906, and Mr Cyril Burt in 1907. Burt remained five years in Liverpool. His adventurous courses included probably the first lectures on psychoanalysis in any university precinct in Great Britain, demonstrations of hypnotized subjects, and the testing of criminals. It is even said that he made some innocent and wholly scientific studies of prostitutes. And while in Liverpool he laid the foundations of his reputation as an indefatigable research worker, producing a number of important papers on the testing of higher mental processes and on the mental differences between the sexes. This promising plant, however, failed to grow on Merseyside. Sherrington's departure for Oxford, Burt's appointment to the London County Council, and the outbreak of the First World War which closely followed, put an end to psychology in Liverpool for a quarter of a century.

At Reading psychology, an offspring of philosophy and education, became an independent department just after the First World War in 1920. The department will always be identified with A. W. Wolters (1883–1961) who after graduating at Reading returned in 1908 to assist in the training of teachers. Though himself "an entirely self-taught psychologist" he soon began to teach psychology to his charges, and even introduced them to experiments with home-made apparatus and packets of postcards. In 1910 he was accorded "a very foul attic", £25 for initial expenses, and a £10 annual grant. From these beginnings he eventually built up one of the finest laboratories in the country. Wolters became professor in 1943, and retired in 1948, having spent nearly all his working life in Reading. To Wolters's engaging

[1] See chap. XV, 1.

qualities Reading, and indeed British psychology, owes a great deal.

In other English universities psychology was a later development, though philosophical smatterings might be given to metaphysicians and educationists. Even at Bristol, where Lloyd Morgan retained a chair of Psychology and Ethics, after he ceased to be Principal, this was all that happened. For the most part the Universities of England remained unreceptive to psychology until after the Second World War. The strangest case, and the best example of cold shouldering, was Oxford. A readership in Mental Philosophy was established in 1898 by a wealthy electrical engineer, Dr Henry Wilde (1833–1919), who made a fortune from lightning conductors, among other electrical gadgets. Wilde had distinct ideas of what he wanted; a lover of Locke, he desired Locke's university to follow in the footsteps of the master, and to study the human mind non-experimentally, though there was no harm in examining the "illusions and delusions" of the human mind or contemplating "the fetish objects in the Anthropological Museum" as a key to the minds of primitive man. The first holder of the Readership, G. F. Stout (1898–1903), kicked over no traces. His successor, the young and forthright William McDougall (1904–20), was less amenable. He dared to experiment, and in doing so caused the elderly Wilde some headaches. Wilde actually tried, unsuccessfully, to eject him. McDougall held on and even got a few pupils, among them William Brown, Cyril Burt, J. C. Flugel, and May Smith, though the only recognition accorded to psychology was that it could be taken as an elective subject in the Final Honours School of Literae Humaniores (Ancient History and Philosophy). After the war, space for experimenting could no longer be accorded to psychology in the department of physiology, and McDougall packed up for what seemed the more friendly terrain of Harvard. His pupil William Brown, by then a psychotherapist, succeeded to the Wilde Readership and held it from 1921–46. It was the result of his efforts and a second benefaction that the Institute of Experimental Psychology was founded in 1936. But not till 1946 was a chair of Psychology created and an honours school established. And even then the first holder, George Humphrey (born in 1889), an Oxford man brought back from Canada, had to battle against hostile philosophers and narrow suspicions.

## 5. The British Psychological Society

The learned society in its present form is largely a nineteenth-century creation. Older and more venerable institutions, like the Royal Society (founded 1660) and the Linnaean Society (founded 1788), had originally a strongly amateur flavour and the earliest of the more specialized societies were in those observational branches of science, such as astronomy, geology and meteorology, to which amateurs could make effective contributions. By the end of the century, however, the continents of knowledge had been pretty extensively colonized by learned societies, and these societies had tended to become more and more professional in character. The establishment of a psychological society at the beginning of the twentieth century was a natural development, therefore, arising from the emancipation of psychology from philosophy and the birth of a new breed of psychological specialists working in laboratories, which, however small, possessed an identity of their own.

The British Psychological Society was born in University College, London, 24 October 1901. In addition to Professor Sully, who summoned the first meeting, there were present nine other persons, including Rivers, McDougall, W. G. Smith, Mott and Shand.[1] Hitherto psychologists had been able to meet and discuss their problems only under other auspices, medical, philosophical, or educational, at meetings of the Medico-Psychological Association (1841), the Aristotelian Society (1880) or the Child Study Association (1894). Now they had an organization of their own, and were falling into line with the U.S.A. and France, whose psychological societies had already been founded.

Until the end of the First World War the society remained small and select. Its membership in 1918 was still under one hundred, and its meetings, organized by its secretary-treasurer, Dr A. F. Shand, were followed by informal dinners, in which the male members only of the society participated. Five years after its foundation the society began its library of psychological journals which now forms one of its most valuable assets, and in 1914 it took over the responsibility for the *British Journal of Psychology* which Ward and Rivers first brought out independently in 1904.

In 1919 the character of the society was markedly altered by the opening of its doors not merely to those working in and teaching psychology but to all those interested in the subject. Its membership increased rapidly, and much needed finance was provided to meet postwar costs. Sections devoted to the medical, industrial and educational

---

[1] The complete list and fuller details of the early years of the society is given in Beatrice Edgell's article, *B. J. Psych.*, XXXVII (1947).

fields of psychology were formed,[1] and local branches shortly afterwards began to spring up in Scotland and the provinces.

This somewhat indiscriminate expansive phase of the society's development reflected the greatly increased popular interest in psychology after the First World War. Mental tests, industrial psychology, and above all psychoanalysis had put psychology 'on the map' and a good many persons whose training in psychology was slight or non-existent joined the society. By 1941 the membership stood at over 800. In that year the society was incorporated, and by the institution of fellows and associates a move was made to re-establish its professional functions, a process taken a stage further in the new Articles and Bye-Laws approved in 1958. The rapid growth of psychology after the Second World War led, however, to a continued increase in membership, the total (excluding overseas branches) exceeding two thousand by 1958.

Though now supplemented by a number of more specialized societies and groups, the British Psychological Society is the nuclear organization in psychology in this country, performing a variety of functions, scientific, professional, and administrative. Apart from a few psychologists located mainly in Oxford or Cambridge, the vast majority of British psychologists are members of the society, which shows every sign of continued growth in size and in the scope of its activities.

## 6. The British Association (*Section J*)

Another forum for psychologists in this country for the last half-century has been the British Association for the Advancement of Science. The parent body was founded in 1831, and was at first concerned with the promotion of the physical and biological sciences. In 1884, however, an anthropology section (H) was established, in 1893 a special section for physiology (I), and in 1901 an education section (L). Papers on psychological topics were from time to time given in these sections. At Sheffield, for example, in 1910, an important symposium on mental testing and factor theories was held, at which Spearman, Burt, William Brown, and C. S. Myers spoke, Myers characteristically warning against the pitfalls of mental tests and the dangers of a plethora of statistics. In 1913 a special sub-section of Section I (Physiology) was set up for psychology, and meetings were held in that year and in 1915, 1916, 1919 and 1920. At the Birmingham meeting in 1913 papers were given by McDougall, H. J. Watt, C. S. Myers, May Smith, Godfrey

---

[1] An aesthetics section also functioned from 1922–37, and a social psychology section was formed in 1940.

Thomson, Shephard Dawson, W. H. Winch, William Brown, Pear, Valentine and W. G. Smith – an impressive list. In 1921 a separate section (Section J) for Psychology was established and from that time on, apart from the years of the Second World War, a series of papers and symposia on psychological topics, usually of a slightly more general and popular character than those of the British Psychological Society, have been held during the summer meetings of the Association.

But the British Association has not merely provided a forum. Before the First World War and the establishment of government research departments (Medical Research Committee 1913, Department of Scientific and Industrial Research 1916) the Association played a considerable role in the promotion and co-ordination of research. Anthropometric investigations, inspired by Galton, commenced in 1875 and continued for many years, embracing the assessment of mental as well as physical characters. The proposals for the rating of personality traits prepared by the anthropometric committee during the years 1902–8 were among the earliest enterprises in personality rating, a number of leading psychologists, McDougall, Rivers, C. S. Myers, Shand, etc., participating in the work. Another committee was concerned with the "mental and physical factors involved in education", and reported from 1909 onwards on such matters as the testing of mental deficiency and psychological factors involved in reading, writing and spelling. In 1932 a joint committee of the physics and psychology sections was appointed to examine the problem of quantitative estimates of sensory events. The final report, which discussed some of the fundamental problems and difficulties of psychophysical measurement, was issued in 1939.

Above all, perhaps, the meetings of the Association helped to put psychology on the general scientific map and bring it to the notice both of the public and of other scientists. Notable was the pronouncement of the President, Sir Ray Lankester, then Director of the Natural History Museum, at the York meeting in 1906: "I have given a special heading to this subject (Psychology) because its emergence as a definite line of experimental research seems to me one of the most important features in the progress of science in the past quarter of a century." Perhaps not very many of Lankester's scientific hearers would have been prepared to agree with him; but attitudes to psychology were beginning to change. It was no longer universally regarded as a mere branch of philosophy; it was beginning to be recognized by scientists themselves as a science in its own right.

CHAPTER XII

# William McDougall (1871–1938)

William McDougall was born in June 1871 at Chadderton in Lancashire, a grim industrial suburb of Oldham, where his father was a manufacturing chemist. His education was unusual, and William himself abnormally precocious. After schooling in Germany he entered Manchester University at the age of 15 and graduated four years later with first-class honours in science. He then proceeded to St John's College, Cambridge, where he studied physiology, anatomy and anthropology, again obtaining first-class honours in 1894. He qualified in medicine at St Thomas's Hospital, London, in 1897. A year later he was fortunate enough to be included in the Cambridge Anthropological Expedition to Torres Strait under A. C. Haddon, and spent some time not only in the Torres Strait area, but in the nearby island of Borneo. In addition to his contributions to the expedition's reports he collaborated with Dr C. Hose of the Sarawak political service in a full-length study of *The Pagan Tribes of Borneo* (1912). On his return to Europe, McDougall spent one further year (1900) completing his apprenticeship under one of Germany's most distinguished experimental psychologists, G. E. Müller of Göttingen. On his appointment in 1900 to a part-time readership in the Department of Psychology at University College, London, McDougall came with fourteen years' training for the job – probably no psychologist anywhere at any time has ever been more magnificently equipped. The tragedy was that British universities were unready to provide the scope and facilities he needed. McDougall spent an uneasy ten years at Oxford from 1904 till the First World War, surrounded by hostile critics, prevented by the terms of his appointment from experimenting, and with a mere handful of voluntary pupils. In 1920 he left for America and the remainder of his teaching life was spent first at Harvard then at Duke University, North Carolina. In America he came into conflict with the dominant behaviourism of the day, and got involved in acrimonious controversy. Partly because of these frustrations, and partly because of flaws in his own character, McDougall's immense promise was never fully realized. He became less and less a scientist, more and more a psychological journalist, pouring out pontifical and prejudiced writings on human affairs in the large.

In spite of this his influence on British psychology and educational thought in the generation prior to the Second World War was immense, and he was unquestionably one of the most striking and forceful figures in the psychology of his day.

His early work, and perhaps his best work, was done in the field of physiological psychology. If the knowledge and techniques of the time made it impossible for McDougall to provide the right answers, his genius prompted him to ask significant questions, on the physiological basis of consciousness and attention, on the nature of inhibitory processes, on the *modus operandi* of drugs, fatigue, hypnosis etc. His brief *Physiological Psychology* (1905) did for its generation what Hebb's *Organization of Behaviour* (1949) did nearly half a century later – it brought perspective into the field of physiological psychology – and though speculative in its proposed solutions, it had at least one foot planted in empirical research. At the time of its publication, moreover, when the influence of Ward and Stout was predominant, it was important that someone should insist on the necessity of a physiological foundation for psychology. "If the psychologist wishes to advance his science, he must descend into the dark places of physiology, and become himself a neurologist", stated McDougall in 1902.[1]

What McDougall did was to take certain new discoveries in neurophysiology and apply these speculatively to the interpretation of more complex psychological phenomena. He was influenced by the work of Sherrington, under whom he briefly studied at St Thomas's Hospital, in particular by the theories of synapses and of reciprocal innervation (both dating from 1897), and by the Jacksonian doctrine of levels of functioning. McDougall postulated that the same basic principles of nervous interaction and co-ordination must apply at the highest cortical level as at the spinal reflex level, and that the various phenomena of consciousness and attention as well as differences in temperamental characteristics between individuals could be thereby explained. The seat of the psychophysical processes was the cortical synapses themselves. Each neurone in the nervous system possessed a charge of energy, which McDougall conceived of as in the nature of a fluid which he termed 'neurin'. All neurones continuously produced 'neurin', in small quantities, but sensory neurones being played upon by outside stimuli were excited more than others. The 'neurin' thus secreted flowed from places of high potential to places of lower potential, eventually escaping into the muscles and producing either a gentle tonic contraction or, at times,

[1] *Mind*, XI. 320.

a sudden phasic contraction. The quantity of available 'neurin' was, however, a strictly limited one, and its canalization in one channel caused it to drain away from other channels. This 'drainage hypothesis', as McDougall termed it, explained the phenomena of inhibition, and made it clear why we could only attend to one main thing at a time. The course of the flow of 'neurin' was largely determined by the state of synaptic resistance, and this was affected by fatigue products, drugs and so on. Moreover, individual differences of temperament were probably bound up with differences in synaptic resistance. In his postulation of 'neurin' McDougall, we can see now, was as mistaken as the physicists who postulated an 'ether'; but his theories were an attempt to explain an important set of problems, and in some respects his 'drainage hypothesis' is akin to Pavlovian theories of induction, which have received some support. The hypothesis did also inspire in McDougall and some of his early pupils some quite interesting experimental work.

McDougall was not by temperament or inclination primarily a laboratory psychologist. He spoke towards the end of his life of "the failure of the experimental method to bring us, during 50 years, appreciably nearer to a socially useful psychology", and apart from his protracted experiment on Lamarckian transmission his own experimental work almost ceased after he had crossed the Atlantic. It was indeed always subordinated to the vein of polemical theorizing, which was one of McDougall's most marked characteristics. None the less he experimented vigorously during his Oxford period, working, since he was debarred from having his own laboratory, in Gotch's department of physiology, and devising several useful pieces of apparatus, of which his 'dotting machine' for the study of attention and fatigue is perhaps the best known.

His first field of research was visual sensation. He believed this to be a royal route for the understanding of the general functioning of the nervous system and its dynamics. In particular he was interested in phenomena such as the fading and fusion of visual sensations, their competition as seen in reversible perspectives and in the effects of simultaneously applied stimulation, and in the reinforcement of one channel of stimulation by another; above all, in colour vision and the phenomena of successive and simultaneous colour contrast. The widely accepted colour theories of the German physiologist, Hering, he came to regard as radically vicious, and advocated a return with some modifications to the three-colour theory of Young and Helmholtz. He believed that the difficulties involved in Helmholtz's explanation of simultaneous contrast could be overcome by postulating the inhibition of one colour mechanism by the other two in accordance with the 'drainage' hypothesis. His theorizing, though it went beyond the evidence, led to a good many experiments of considerable interest, for example, his experiments on the sensations excited by a single momentary stimulation of the eye,[1] and those on the effects of muscular activity on the fading of visual images and after images.[2] Inspired by similar theoretical considerations was McDougall's work on fatigue and the effect of drugs, for the study of which his 'dotting machine' was devised.[3] The results were finally published in a Medical Research Council report on "The effects of alcohol and some other drugs during normal and fatigued conditions",[4] in the preparation of which his former pupil Dr May Smith collaborated – a report which marks the close of McDougall's contribution to experimental physiological psychology.

His interests, indeed, had already shifted to wider fields, and he was bent on refashioning psychology as a whole. His *Introduction to Social Psychology* (1st ed. 1908) marked not only an epoch in McDougall's own development but an epoch in the history of psychology. "Psychologists must cease to be content with the sterile and narrow conception of their science as the science of consciousness, and must boldly assert its claim to be the positive science of the mind in all its aspects and modes of functioning, or, as I would prefer to say, the positive science of conduct or behaviour." So wrote McDougall in 1908. His message fell on receptive ground. Within twenty years the *Social Psychology* had passed through twenty-one editions, and unquestionably it prepared the way for the still more far-reaching theories of Freud. It was a major influence in replacing the static, descriptive, purely analytical psychology of the nineteenth century with a psychology that was functional and dynamic. McDougall, whose utterances particularly in later life were not exactly characterized by modesty, summed up its influence a quarter of a century after its first publication as follows: "that semi-popular little book made a considerable step of advance. It gave more definite form and substance to the teleological, hormic, Dionysian view of man (adumbrated by Aristotle, Schopenhauer, von Hartmann, Nietzsche); it formulated for the first time an adequate theory of action, of conduct and of character; it provided a first sketch of the much needed psychological foundation for ethics and all the social sciences; a foundation which,

---

[1] *B. J. Psych.*, I (1904); III (1909).
[2] *Mind*, XII (1903).          [3] *B. J. Psych.*, I (1905).
[4] *M.R.C. Report 56* (1920).

though it will be improved in detail, will stand good in its general principles." [1]

The first objective of the *Social Psychology* was, then, to put forward a 'hormic' theory of behaviour. The term, which refers to the purposive striving that is the characteristic mark of behaviour, McDougall later adopted from Sir Percy Nunn's book on education, and McDougall's special brand of psychology is generally known as 'hormic psychology'. A second objective was to establish instincts as the sole ultimate sources of hormic energy; a third, to erect a theory of character on these foundations. The whole was intended as a prolegomenon to social psychology proper. In putting forward this position McDougall claimed for himself a considerable degree of originality – indeed he did not tire in pointing out both the originality and the importance of his contributions to psychology. "The only author who, to my knowledge, has anticipated me in proposing a purely and consistently hormic psychology (but without working it out in detail) was the late E. von Hartmann." [2] This claim can hardly be sustained. James Drever snr. in his *Instinct in Man* (1917) showed that the doctrine of instincts had various roots in philosophy and biology, and R. Fletcher in his work on instinct[3] points out that many of McDougall's views can be found in the writings of William James, Lloyd Morgan, and Hobhouse. Nevertheless McDougall propounded hormic theory with striking simplicity and force, and he is rightly regarded as its most important exponent.

On the negative side hormic psychology was strenuously anti-intellectualistic and anti-materialistic. It rejected both the older associationist psychology so largely devoted to cognitive contents and the teachings of the newer mechanistic biologies with their attempts to explain behaviour in terms of reflexes. Positively the essential mark of behaviour, by virtue of which we recognized it as behaviour, was purposive striving; and psychological explanation must, therefore, be in teleological, not in mechanical, terms. "The essential nature of mind is to govern present action by anticipation of the future in the light of past experience; to make, in short, effects precede and determine their causes." [4] Purposive action is always a total reaction of the organism, and it always implies some sort of foresight.

To the generality of the hormic principle McDougall allowed no exceptions; not only was all the behaviour of the lower animals determined by instinctive drives, but at the human level "the instinctive

---

[1] *Character and Personality*, vol. I. 206 (1933).    [2] *Energies of Men*, XIII.
[3] R. Fletcher *Instinct in Man* (1957).    [4] *Outline of Psychology*, 195.

impulses determine the ends of all activities and supply the driving power
by which all mental activities are sustained; and all the complex intellectual apparatus of the most highly developed mind is but a means
towards these ends, is but the instrument by which these impulses seek
their satisfactions".[1] Neither habits, nor intellectual interests, nor
pleasure and pain could sustain action without the support of the instincts. They were the sole motors of both animal and human behaviour,
and ultimately every aspect of mind was geared to and could only be
explained in terms of instinct. Perception was an active process instinctively determined; the emotions closely tied to corresponding
instinctive drives; intellectual functions performed in the service of the
instincts; and behaviour itself, however flexible and capable of modification through experience, always directed to instinctive goals.
McDougall's well-known definition of instinct was intended to give expression to its all-embracing psychological relevance. "We may, then,
define an instinct as an inherited or innate psycho-physical disposition
which determines its possessor to perceive, and to pay attention to,
objects of a certain class, to experience an emotional excitement of a
particular quality upon perceiving such an object, and to act in regard
to it in a particular manner, or, at least, to experience an impulse
to such action." [2]

McDougall followed up this general statement in his *Social Psychology*
with a classification of the principal instincts and primary emotions of
man, and with an account of how character is built upon these foundations. For hormic psychologists of the McDougall type the classification
of the major instincts has always been a troublesome problem. Not only
did other writers disagree with McDougall, but McDougall could not
agree with himself, and each new book contained a somewhat different
list. The hormic principle, however, even when McDougall abandoned
the term 'instinct' for 'propensity' remained basically unaffected by this
difficulty. In fact McDougall stated on one occasion that he regarded all
instincts as "essentially differentiations of the will to live that animates
all organisms", and seen in this light classification becomes of secondary
importance.

The formation of character, the account of which McDougall regarded
as his most significant contribution to psychology, was described primarily in terms of 'sentiments', a concept used by Dr A. F. Shand to
refer to an organized system of emotional tendencies centred around an
object. The typical sentiments were love and hate, which McDougall,

---

[1] *Social Psychology*, 38.        [2] ibid., 25.

following Shand, regarded not as emotions but as enduring tendencies to experience emotions whenever the loved or hated object came to mind. The stability and integration of character was dependent on the gradual building up of an organized, harmonious, integrated system of sentiments, both concrete and abstract. Crowning the system McDougall placed the sentiment of self-regard, a largely social product, which was closely linked with the development of self-consciousness and the genesis of the idea of the empirical self. It was the intervention of this self-regarding sentiment that explained the phenomenon of volition. Volition involved no new principle of activity, but only a more complex organization of basic impulses.

This account of the organization of character structure was supplemented in McDougall's later books with what he called "a natural history classification of the main factors of personality". The principal 'factors', as he called them,[1] were disposition, temper, temperament and mood. Disposition he defined as "the sum total of instinctive tendencies"; temper as "the way in which conative impulses work" (their strength, urgency, etc.); temperament as the effect of metabolic or chemical changes (which he linked with his theory of inhibition by drainage), and mood as the result of the tendency of emotions to persist. Character as a whole was differentiated from intellect, the two together constituting the complete personality.

In spite of the criticisms which McDougall's hormic psychology met with, a great deal of it has in fact become part of contemporary psychology. As McDougall was not slow to point out, the concept of 'drive' is essentially a hormic concept, and even behaviourists speak of drives. Ethology has resurrected instincts, and the psychology of personality, which emerged in America between the wars, incorporated and developed McDougall's account of character. Even teleology has become respectable under the rubric of programmes and plans. Were McDougall alive today he would regard many of his views as having been vindicated. Yet in the way he put them forth there was something fatally wrong, which justified much of the sniping against him. In spite of his prolonged scientific education McDougall was never at heart a scientist. His writings were not the carefully tested bricks of a gradually constructed edifice; they were vast speculative plans, based it is true on a many-sided erudition, a wide vision and a powerful systematic propensity, and not, therefore, without their value, but in the development of psychology proving as much an irritant as an inspiration. For what

[1] *Outline of Psychology*, ch. XIII.

McDougall was constantly trying to do was to provide the answers to problems before the factual data needed even for provisional answers were available, and to steal a march on the empirical enquiries of ethologists, and social and clinical psychologists. Even when he turned out to be right his methodology in arriving at his conclusions was often unscientific.

Moreover, some of the causes he espoused stuck in the throats of scientifically minded psychologists. This was particularly the case with animism which McDougall defended, eloquently and ably, in two books *Body and Mind* (1911) and *Modern Materialism and Emergent Evolution* (1929). After reviewing the history of the psycho-physical problem from the days of primitive animism up to the beginning of the twentieth century McDougall in *Body and Mind* presented arguments both against the adequacy of mechanistic explanations of the facts of physiology, organic evolution, and behaviour, and positively in favour of the animistic solution. The strongest pro-animistic argument rested on the observed unity of consciousness, "a unity of a unique kind which has no analogue in the physical realm, and that cannot properly be regarded as consisting of elements, units, or atoms of consciousness, put together or compounded in any way; consciousness cannot, therefore, parallel anything in the nervous system which is composed of discrete units; it must be something *sui generis*".[1] It implies in other words 'the soul'. Supplementary arguments McDougall derived from the nature of meaning, which he held cannot have any immediate physical correlate; from the facts of 'true' memory, which following Bergson he sharply distinguished from habit; and from the role of pleasure and pain, as psychical not physiological states, in directing behaviour. Neither pure materialism, nor parallelism, nor emergent evolution could account for these facts, urged McDougall; only animism.

The animism, however, which postulated a unitary, immaterial and goal-directed soul began to get into difficulties when it came to the data of abnormal psychology. In 1915 after the outbreak of the First World War McDougall joined the Royal Army Medical Corps, and quite naturally gravitated to the treatment of 'shell shock' casualties. First at Netley and then at Littlemore Hospitals, a good many cases of war neurosis passed through his care, providing him with much of the data for his *Outline of Abnormal Psychology* (1926). There was nothing specially distinctive about McDougall's approach to psychopathology: he belonged to the eclectic school of thought to which many British

[1] *Body and Mind*, 282.

psychopathologists after the First World War, Rivers, William Brown, Culpin, Hadfield, Crichton Miller, tended to gravitate. Though much influenced by psychoanalytic teachings none was narrowly Freudian. McDougall's own attitude to Freud was strongly ambivalent. He recognized the value of Freud's work, but he was never tired of castigating Freudian errors or asserting the superiority of his own system. Clearly it was not difficult for McDougall to graft the dynamic sides of Freudian teachings on to his own hormic psychology; and he was naturally disposed to allow functional as well as organic interpretations of mental disorders. But he made no use of the unconscious as an explanatory principle, preferring his own theory of inhibition, and Janet's theory of dissociation; and he 'maintained the most obstinate scepticism' in face of the libido doctrine. The difficulties for McDougall and his animistic viewpoint arose from the recognition which pathological conditions forced him to accord to the disintegration of personality. What then happened to the unity of the soul? To save the case for animism McDougall had to postulate that "the normal human personality is an integrated system of monads" – each monad being in its own sphere a 'unitary soul', and the whole a hierarchical system in which subordinate monads were controlled by a supreme monad, 'myself'. The postulation of monads has always raised the problem of interaction between monads. McDougall evaded this by proposing that the communication between monads could be telepathic. He even went so far as to regard dreams as "the telepathic reflection by the chief monad of bits of the mental life of many subordinate members of the hierarchy of monads".[1] If this is what animism involves one wonders whether it has substantial advantages over other systems!

Notwithstanding these speculations *An Outline of Abnormal Psychology* was a valuable book, firmly based on clinical observation even if the cases were restricted in type, and it did something to bring together the academic and medical branches of psychology. Another book published just after the First World War, *The Group Mind* (1920), McDougall's sequel to the *Introduction to Social Psychology*, has dated far more. In concepts and methods it is quite alien to contemporary social psychology. It postulated in society "a mental life which is not the mere sum of the mental lives of its units", not, McDougall was careful to point out, a 'super-individual consciousness', but nevertheless a mental structure of a higher order possessing its own 'group spirit'. It was the job of the social psychologist to study these super-individual 'minds', in particular

[1] *Outline of Abnormal Psychology*, 551.

the 'national minds' of the highly evolved nation states. This McDougall regarded as "the crowning task of psychology". Unfortunately Mc-Dougall proceeded to have a shot at this 'crowning task' and to write about national mind and character before any of the essential spade-work had been accomplished – the observation of group behaviour in simple situations, the social measurements, and devising of experimental techniques, upon all of which an empirical social psychology necessarily must rest. In the absence of proper data McDougall had recourse to incidental observations, to illustrations from history and anthropology, and to the views of political theorists and writers on affairs. He was often guided in his selection of material by his own marked prejudices, which led him to most dubious conclusions. "The best observers assure us", he writes, "that were the reins of representative government (in India) in native hands it would be but a few years before the whole country would be reduced to a chaotic anarchic condition." [1] For "innate mental constitution, and therefore race, is of fundamental importance in determining national character". Racial differences abundantly justified the refusal of white populations to mix with coloured peoples.[2] National greatness depended on the maintenance of an "intellectual aristocracy",[3] and socialism, which sacrificed the future to the present, would be "decidedly bad".[4] Whether or not one agrees with these opinions, the work which contained them certainly ought not to have masqueraded as "a strictly scientific work".[5]

This unfortunately was the tenor of a great deal of McDougall's writing in his American period. A succession of semi-popular books flowed from his pen, on eugenics, democracy, war, ethics, religion, world chaos, etc. His psychology was popularized in *The Character and Conduct of Life* (1927), a somewhat humourless lay sermon on how to behave. Even his more technical works, such as the *Energies of Men* (1932) and *Psychoanalysis and Social Psychology* (1936), added little that was new to his system of psychology. The results of his one piece of extended experimental work in America, "An experiment for the testing of the hypothesis of Lamarck",[6] have not been replicated by other workers (e.g. Crew)[7] and must be regarded as of dubious validity. McDougall admitted his strong desire to find support for Lamarck's hypothesis of the inheritance of acquired characters, and thereby to undermine the theory of natural selection, and he believed that his

[1] op. cit., 118.    [2] op. cit., 244.    [3] op. cit., 256.    [4] op. cit., 173.
[5] op. cit., xi.    [6] *B. J. Psych.*, XVII (1927).
[7] F. A. E. Crew *J. Genet.*, XXXIII (1936).

successive generations of rats had learned a water-tank task with increasing facility. No one doubted the honesty of McDougall's conviction, but considerable doubt has been cast on his techniques. To psychology as a science McDougall contributed comparatively little, therefore, during the later period of his life.

McDougall had nearly all the ingredients for the making of a scientific psychologist except the scientific attitude. For the cultivation of this he had not the patience, nor it would seem the humility. He had, however, compensating qualities, a vigorous and well-stored mind and a gift for writing. His psychology had breadth and sweep, though it lacked scientific precision. In British psychology he was a dominating influence for at least a quarter of a century. His views fitted in with the mood of the times and the trend towards irrationalism; and in a country where behaviouristic concepts have never been popular, and where experimental psychology has been slow to get going, McDougall's hormic theory provided just what was required. It elevated the irrational, saved 'the soul', and being non-experimental, was cheap enough to flourish when money for psychology was hard to come by. Together with mental testing and psychoanalysis it constituted the working capital for a generation of psychologists between the wars.

psychology by Külpe in Würzburg, was appointed to teach philosophy and psychology at Bedford College. Fresh from Germany she, too, soon introduced experimental work.

University College was, of course, favourable soil for psychology, and psychology of a philosophic type in the British empirical tradition had been effectively taught since Croom Robertson's appointment to the Grote Chair of Mind and Logic in 1866. Croom Robertson (1842–92) had been a pupil, and doctrinally was a close follower, of Bain. He adhered to the traditional British view that "psychology is the most fundamental and representative part of philosophy".[1] His advance on Bain was mainly the result of his much better knowledge of Continental work, particularly in physiology and physiological psychology. For he had followed his Aberdeen training with study in Berlin under du Bois Reymond, the physiologist, in Göttingen under Lotze, and in Paris under Broca. He expressed the view that "our psychology should be as physiological as we can make it".[2] But for his early illness, the onset of which dated from 1880, he might have made a considerable impact upon British psychology, for he was highly regarded by his contemporaries. As it was, his lecture notes on psychology, which were posthumously published as *Elements of Psychology* (1896), did not add a great deal to Bain.

It was his successor, Sully, who first introduced experimental work in psychology at University College. Sully was fortunate both in obtaining apparatus from Münsterberg's laboratory in Freiburg (Münsterberg having migrated to Harvard some years previously to succeed James), and in securing the services first of W. H. R. Rivers and then of William McDougall to take charge of experimental work. Sully's retirement in 1903 and Carveth Read's appointment did not hinder the new development, for although Read (1848–1931) was by training primarily a philosopher, he was sympathetic to experimental psychology, and in fact his own interests became increasingly focused on psychology – it is true of a rather theoretical comparative kind. After handing the chair over to Spearman he remained in the department for ten years as a lecturer in comparative psychology, and wrote an entertaining book, *The Origin of Man and His Superstitions* (1920), in which he attributed many of the quirks of human mentality to man's ancient conversion to carnivorous habits.

[1] Inaugural lecture, University College, 1866, reprinted in *Philosophical Remains*.
[2] *Elements of Psychology*, 33.

# CHAPTER XIII

# The London School

## 1. Charles Spearman (1863–1945)

We have already noted in a previous chapter the beginnings of psychology in London. In 1907 Charles Spearman was appointed Reader in Psychology and given charge of the small laboratory which Sully had founded ten years previously at University College. On Carveth Read's retirement from the Grote Chair of Mind and Logic in 1911, Spearman was appointed professor in his place, a position he held until 1931, though the title of the chair was changed to the Chair of Psychology in 1928. Spearman very soon began to place his stamp upon the department, and London psychology to acquire the features, methodological and theoretical, which characterized it for a generation – a focus of interest on the problems of human ability and personality, a reliance on statistical and psychometric rather than experimental methods, and a relative indifference both to the data of, and the theories derived from, laboratory research as such. The first decade of the twentieth century saw the birth of most of the major schools of recent psychology – psychoanalysis, hormic psychology, Gestalt psychology, behaviourism – all of which were in revolt in their various ways from the artificiality and narrowness of the psychology of the early Wundtian laboratories. The London School was a facet of this general revolt, an attempt to bring psychology face to face with the problems of mind as met with in daily life, while retaining a scientifically tough methodology, quantitative rather than qualitative, analytical rather than wholistic. Its basic inspiration was Galtonian.

Spearman's entry into psychology was late and unusual. In spite of "an excessive but secret devotion to philosophy" during his schooldays, Spearman became a regular officer in the Royal Engineers, and saw active campaigning in some of the colonial wars of the late nineteenth century. It was not until 1897 that he extricated himself from the army (to be entangled again for short periods during the Boer and First World Wars), and not until 1907 at the age of forty-four that Spearman obtained his first academic appointment. By 1897 he had realized that his military adventure was the mistake of his life, and hastened to repair it as best he could by recourse to German universities. He had kept alive his philosophical interests while serving abroad, carrying around philosophical classics in his kit, and had gradually come to the view that psychology, particularly experimental psychology, was likely to hold the answers to his questions. So in 1897 he proceeded to Leipzig and attached himself to Wundt, for whom personally and professionally he always held the highest of respect. Eventually he obtained a Ph.D. for research on spatial perception. This was followed by a further five years at various German universities, Würzburg, Göttingen and Berlin, and further studies in physiology, psychiatry, experimental psychology and philosophy.

It was during his sojourn in Germany that Spearman's interest became increasingly focused on intelligence and its measurement, in spite of the fact that few German psychologists apart from Ebbinghaus were prepared to give him much encouragement. It was from Germany in 1904 that he sent to the *American Journal of Psychology* his epoch-making article "General Intelligence objectively determined and measured",[1] which first clearly enunciated the idea of factor analysis. Inspired by Galton's work Spearman had obtained various psychological measures on groups of schoolchildren and correlated the scores. This, of course, had been done before, particularly in America, but Spearman laid a new emphasis on methodological rigour and the importance of avoiding, where possible, and correcting for, when not possible, unwanted variables and sources of error. All earlier investigations he regarded as methodologically weak and their results as open to question. In an earlier article in the same journal Spearman had provided mathematical formulae for correcting correlation coefficients for errors of 'attenuation', and these he now applied to the correlations obtained from his school populations. The resulting table showed large positive correlations arranged in a neat hierarchical order, and Spearman showed that this could be explained on the assumption that each psychological capacity measured, either by test or by academic performance, was variously saturated with a common intellective function, of a unique and universal character. In addition each capacity contained a distinctive specific factor wholly distinct from the common factor. These two factors were later termed 'g', the general factor, and 's', the specifics, and an improved method of ascertaining hierarchical arrangement was introduced by means of 'tetrad equations'.[2] For practical purposes Spearman showed that 'g' could be assessed by measuring promiscuously

[1] *Am. J. Psych.*, XV.     [2] C. Spearman *Abilities of Man*, Appendix.

any large number of different abilities and pooling the results together, thus cancelling out the effect of the 's's. According to Spearman 'g' was unique and universal, and accounted for the whole of the overlap between the abilities measured. Additional broad, or 'group', factors were conspicuously absent. Later Spearman was to admit the existence of certain 'group' factors in verbal, mechanical, and a few other close related tasks. But he believed to the end in the predominant role played by 'g', the general intellective factor, and his last, posthumous article[1] was devoted to a review in its support.[2]

Though Spearman's own 'two-factor' theory has been drastically modified, if not abandoned, by subsequent workers, and his methods of computation wholly superseded, the birth of factor analysis was a momentous development in psychology, destined to have a wide impact on theories of ability and of personality, and to lead to voluminous research. His claim to priority has been questioned recently by Burt, and no doubt there were adumbrations of factorial concepts particularly in Pearson's work. But the clear and explicit formulation would seem to have been Spearman's, as Burt himself unequivocally recognized at least up to 1940. As one of Spearman's principal critics, Godfrey Thomson, put it, "only Professor Spearman's enthusiasm and originality could have given to psychological correlation research the life and activity which it has shown during the last fifteen years",[3] a sentiment he reiterated a quarter of a century later in his obituary notice on Spearman.[4] The theory itself, however, soon ran into difficulties. William Brown and Pearson criticized his correction formulae; some investigators found hierarchy, others did not, in their correlation matrices; Thomson denied the necessity of the two-factor theory as a deduction from the hierarchical order of coefficients, and proposed an alternative 'sampling' theory of ability, whereby hierarchy could be produced by the random sampling of mental bonds. Moreover he demonstrated by generating a number of artificial correlation matrices from card sorting and dice throwing that chance could give rise to hierarchical order. Burt, using a 'summation' method of computation derived from Pearson's method of 'principle axes', came down in favour of 'group' factors. To all these criticisms Spearman counter-attacked, conceding a little ground but very little, and, to support his claims, carried out larger and more exacting

---

[1] *B. J. Psych.*, XXXVI (1948).
[2] See also *Human Ability* (1950), by Spearman and Wynn Jones.
[3] W. Brown and G. Thomson *Essentials of Mental Measurement*, 154.
[4] *Obit. Notices, F.R.S.*, no. 15.

investigations, culminating in the Chicago experiment in which, in collaboration with Holzinger in the late 1930's, more than a thousand children were tested with nearly one hundred tests – the outcome being the emergence of a stable, consistent 'g' from the data. The dust of this controversy has hardly settled yet. The usefulness of 'group' factors is now commonly conceded, however, and in this sense Spearman may be said to have got the worst of the fray; but 'g' is also commonly admitted, even by some American investigators, though it is not given quite the special status that Spearman gave it. Perhaps, as Thomson always claimed, 'factors' are only 'mathematical entities', not real components of the mind, and what factors we choose is largely a matter of convenience. Neither the factors nor the test measurements from which they are derived would now be accorded quite the exalted place that Spearman was disposed to accord them.

Factor analysis, however, was only one-half of Spearman's psychology, though it has turned out to be the most influential half. Spearman was concerned not merely with demonstrating the existence of 'g', but also in elucidating its nature and laws of functioning. He would have agreed that 'g' is roughly equivalent to the loose everyday term 'intelligence'. But 'intelligence' is a vague concept and Spearman came to prefer 'mental energy' as a designation, partly because it lent itself better to analysis in terms of qualitative and quantitative principles. It is to Spearman's credit that he saw the need for a systematic psychology of cognition to supplement his statistical findings. Too many factorists have neglected this complementary theoretical task. But the claims Spearman made for his scheme, first propounded in *The Nature of Intelligence and the Principles of Cognition* (1923), were fantastically exaggerated. "The entire range of all cognition whatsoever, as regards both form and material, would appear to receive its definite and final boundaries." [1] Psychologists quite naturally have ignored these pretensions, and indeed it is doubtful whether Spearman's principles can be regarded as more than a historical curiosity. His belief, and no doubt he regarded the matter most momentously, was that all cognitive content could be explained in terms of the three laws he termed "laws of noe-genesis" (= creative mind); first, the law of the apprehension of experience; second, the law of the eduction or relations; third, the law of the eduction of correlates. In other words the mind tends to become aware of its experience, to grasp relations between items of experience, and to create new items which are based on, but go beyond, its experience.

[1] *Nature of Intelligence,* 354.

In a sense this scheme was a derivative of the old law of the association of ideas, but by postulating the eduction both of relations not
necessarily given in experience in the first place, and of correlates which
by definition extended the bounds of experience, it allowed the mind to
transcend the raw initial data. 'Noegenesis' accepted the atomism of
associationism, but not its empirical limitations.

Spearman's noegenetic scheme was not without its points. It recognized the creative potential of mind, which had often been neglected; at
a time when 'Gestalt' ideas were becoming fashionable, it kept alive the
analytical approach; it proved of some value in the practical task of intelligence test construction. But as anything like a definitive and final
account of cognition it was hopelessly jejune, as indeed any scheme
which professes to explain the whole range of cognition from the simplest
sensory awareness to the most complex intellectual processes in one
simple set of formulae must necessarily be. For it is the variety and
differences of level among cognitive structures, and the actual complexity of their mechanics, that are among the most important facts to be
explained. A highly abstract, 'one-level' formula for the whole range of
cognition ignores too many major problems, and becomes, as noegenesis
did, merely trite.

Spearman's quantitative laws of cognition were not more satisfactory.
They were indeed only empirical generalizations, and too vague to be
either significant or productive. Cognitive output tends to remain constant in quantity, though varying in kind; mental events tend to recur
more easily than when they first occurred; there is an inertia or lag in the
beginning and ending of mental events (perseveration); fatigue tends to
diminish mental processes; there is a tendency to fluctuate (oscillation);
cognition may be controlled by conation and volition; all mental occurrences depend on bodily conditions, or primordial potencies. Not that
these so-called laws did not lead to some research. Several of Spearman's associates and pupils, Wynn Jones, Bernstein, etc., studied, for
example, perseveration, and came to the conclusion that there was a
second universal factor 'p', alongside 'g'. Philpott (1888–1952) spent a
large part of his time as a lecturer at University College studying
oscillation, without, however, convincing the world that it was as fundamental a characteristic of mind as Spearman made out. Perhaps the truth
of the matter was, as Spearman himself hinted, that these quantitative
principles were at bottom physiological; and perhaps the upshot of the
researches derived from Spearman's ideas was to demonstrate that
physiological issues cannot be much elucidated by psychometric and

statistical means, at least without a great deal more basic physiological research.

It would be unfair, however, to minimize the work done in Spearman's department. Spearman established the first really live and important school of psychological research in this country. Research students eventually came to him from many parts of the world, and Spearman steered them into a co-ordinated scheme of research, thus ensuring that his students added something to a planned edifice instead of dissipating their energies on diverse trivialities. The result was in many ways impressive. Seven out of the first ten, twelve out of the first twenty, of the *Monograph Supplements* of the *British Journal of Psychology* were written by those who had worked with Spearman, and Spearman's own book *The Abilities of Man* (1927) is largely documented with the researches of his pupils.

Spearman's other activities were essentially subordinate to his two major projects – the two-factor theory, and the laws of cognition. He made certain contributions to statistical methodology, the best known being his rank correlation method, and the Spearman–Brown prophecy formula for estimating the gain in reliability resulting from lengthening a mental test. He also wrote a two-volume historical work *Psychology down the Ages* (1937), designed essentially to show that his own system was properly the culmination of psychological speculation since the dawn of history. The book is full both of curious erudition (for Spearman was with Sir William Hamilton one of the most learned of British thinkers) and of stubborn obtuseness, and it showed surprisingly little awareness of many vigorous growing points of contemporary psychology. His contributions to experimental psychology proper were comparatively few, being either outcomes of his German period, or the result of some researches on visual and auditory problems carried out during the First World War.

In spite of the shortcomings of his system Spearman was a great pioneer in British psychology – remarkable for his singleness of purpose, the immense synthetic power and range of his mind, the originality of his vision, and his capacity to inspire a varied and devoted following.

## 2. Sir Cyril Burt (b. 1883)

Spearman was succeeded in the London chair by Cyril Burt who, in spite of his disagreement with Spearman on many points both of doctrine and of detail, carried on the same broad tradition of interest. Writing of his work at University College, Burt stated "my aim has been to preserve its original traditions, and to make it a focus for that branch of psychology which was founded and developed there by Galton, 'individual' or 'differential' psychology. No other psychology department in Britain has specialized in this particular sphere, whether for training or research."[1] It was not unnatural that Burt should have shown an early interest in Galton, for Burt's father was a rural doctor with a practice in Warwickshire three miles only from the Galton home at Claverdon, and members of the family were among his patients. The young Cyril was early steeped in Galtonian lore, and with remarkable consistency he has devoted his life to 'individual' psychology, its framework, techniques and data. At Oxford, where he became one of McDougall's first pupils, his special topic was the standardization of psychological tests. The investigations he carried out at McDougall's suggestion, and with Flugel's assistance, were some years later published in his first and famous article 'Experimental Tests of General Intelligence' in the *British Journal of Psychology*.[2] After a brief interval at Würzburg, this line of work continued and developed, first at Liverpool, where for five years (1907–12) Burt was a lecturer in experimental psychology in Sherrington's department, then in London as psychologist to the London County Council and our first professional psychologist, and finally in the chairs of educational psychology at the London Day Training College (now the Institute of Education) and of psychology at University College (1926–31, 1931–51 respectively). Since his retirement Burt has remained vigorously active both in writing and as editor of the *British Journal of Statistical Psychology*.

"The experimental determination of the mental characters of individuals is admittedly a problem of wide theoretical interest and of vast practical importance. The particular mental character which in importance is perhaps above all supreme, is that traditionally termed 'General Intelligence'." [3] Such were the opening words of Burt's first published article. No one could accuse Burt of beating around the bush. Far from it, he went straight to the central problem which was to occupy him for the remainder of his professional life. Though not first in the field Burt's contribution to the techniques of intelligence testing was of cardinal importance, and is often underestimated, particularly in America. The written group test of intelligence is in fact due primarily to Burt, rather than to Yerkes and the American army psychologists of the First World War. For the essential aim of Burt's early investigations was "to deter-

[1] *History of Psychology in Autobiography*, IV (1952).
[2] *B. J. Psych.*, III (1909).      [3] *B. J. Psych.*, l.c.

mine whether higher mental functions would not show a closer connexion with general intelligence than was shown by simpler mental functions, such as sensory discrimination and motor reaction, with which
previous investigators had been so largely engrossed".[1] His results
showed that this was so, and he went on to devise tests such as analogies,
sentence formation, syllogisms, reasoning, and so on which were
"capable of application to large numbers of children at once" and "capable of application by teachers untrained to any considerable degree in a
psychological laboratory". Herein lies the germ of the group intelligence
test, and indeed many of Burt's ideas have become standard features of
intelligence tests. The group test he himself devised for the National
Institute of Industrial Psychology (Group Test 33) in 1923 has been in
continuous use ever since. In his test construction Burt was helped by
his training in logic under Cook Wilson and other Oxford philosophers,
and he still believes that philosophy is the most useful introduction to
psychology.

During the immensely productive years that Burt held the London
County Council post some of his time and of his prodigious energies
were devoted to the adaptation and construction of tests. The results
were published in *Mental and Scholastic Tests* (1921), a classic work
which contained Burt's 'London' revision of the Binet-Simon Scale, and
his tests of educational attainment (reading, spelling, composition,
arithmetic, drawing etc.). Interest in the Binet tests was being shown
before the war both among educationists and school medical officers.
Professor J. A. Green of Sheffield sent Miss K. L. Johnston to Paris to
study Binet's methods and she published an English translation of the
1908 scale in the *Journal of Experimental Pedagogy*.[2] Dr F. C. Shrub-
sall, the mental deficiency expert, published a critical account of the tests
in the same year, and various other medical officers had made use of it.
But Burt's 'London' revision involved a more thorough study of the test,
and some of the techniques of analysis that Burt employed broke new
ground in the field of mental testing. His revision was widely used
prior to the standardization of the Terman and Merrill version in 1937;
his factor analysis and his general critical assessment of the test still
remain of value. His scholastic attainment tests have also been extensively used. Here again he was preceded by others, by P. B. Ballard, for
example, and J. A. Green; but the more advanced techniques of construction and standardization used by Burt have given his tests an
exceptionally long life.

[1] *B. J. Psych.*, l.c.         [2] *J. Exp. Ped.*, I (1911).

Great as have been his contributions to testing, Burt has never been a mere tester. He has always regarded tests as but one facet in the examination and assessment of the individual, and he has always been more interested in the results of testing, practical and theoretical, than in the tests themselves. Burt's first major report to the L.C.C. on *The Distribution and Relations of Educational Abilities* (1917) exemplified these interests. The report contained a survey of the educational abilities of the entire elementary school population of a representative London borough with a view (i) to finding the most suitable lines of demarcation between children in ordinary school and special schools for defectives; (ii) to estimating the number of backward children in ordinary schools; and (iii) to verifying the hypothesis of a 'general educational ability' underlying all school work. Burt was also concerned in other reports with the selection of the exceptional child for the award of scholarships. Burt returned to all these matters in later publications, the first two in *The Backward Child* (1937), an intensive study of schoolchildren with mental ratios in the 70 to 85 range, numbering perhaps some ten per cent of the school population; the third, with greatly increased sophistication, in *The Factors of the Mind* (1940).

Factor analysis, and the mathematical and logical foundations of factor analysis, has indeed been one of Burt's major interests throughout his long career. Galton and Pearson, whom he met while still a student at Oxford, had introduced him to correlations. Spearman's work provoked and inspired his own early investigations, though his methods and conclusions were soon to diverge from those of Spearman. For Burt early came to the conclusion that it was necessary to postulate 'group' factors, and he finally formulated not a two-factor but a 'four-factor' theory. The four kinds of factor (general, group, specific, and error) he equated with the fourfold classification of Aristotelian logic: *genus, species, proprium, accidens.* All other factor theories he regarded as simplifications and reductions of this basic four-factor theorem.

Burt came to differ from Spearman, too, both in the philosophy and methodology of factor analysis. Spearman in equating his general and specific factors with 'energy' and 'engines' had clearly postulated their causal agency and substantial reality. For Burt on the other hand factors are 'principles of classification', a convenient aid to exact and systematic description. Thus negative saturations of a factor, which to Spearman were meaningless, are for Burt perfectly possible. We have left the world of simple physical reality for the world of mathematical relationships. In this world anything is possible and what we choose is a matter to be decided on other grounds than the mathematical. Thus Burt has constantly emphasized "the absurdity of divorcing the mathematical or statistical evidence from evidence procured by other means", and the scheme which Burt believes the other evidence favours is the hierarchical scheme of levels derived from Spencer, Hughlings Jackson, Sherrington and McDougall. Human ability functions at four main levels, the sensori-motor level, the perceptual level, the associative level, and the highest relational level. From the days of his very early investigations Burt's choice of tests has been guided by this hierarchical scheme, and the factors he finds are correspondingly hierarchical.

Methodologically Burt also believes that all factor methods are transformations of the same set of basic values, and that the apparent differences between factorists are superficial. The problems of factor analysis can be treated basically by means of matrix algebra, and it is in these terms that he has expounded and justified his own methodological procedures.

Partly as a result of his factorial studies, and partly as a result of his general psychological standpoint, Burt early came to define intelligence as "innate, general cognitive efficiency". This definition is given in *Mental and Scholastic Tests*.[1] It was foreshadowed in the 1909 article in *Child Study* Vol. IV on 'The experimental study of general intelligence'. 'General' signalized Burt's acceptance of a common intellective factor penetrating all cognitive activities: 'innate' signalized his conviction, derived from Galton but supported by evidence of his own and of others, that the level of cognitive efficiency or 'intelligence' was primarily dependent on heredity. To this view he has remained consistently faithful from the beginning of his psychological career right up to the present. His first article on intelligence contained evidence of the superiority of the children of upper professional groups, and arguments to suggest that this was due to superior innate ability. The evidence was set out more fully in a contribution to the *Eugenics Review*[2] in 1912, and re-stated with additions in a number of subsequent articles and pamphlets, culminating in his address to the British Psychological Society in December, 1958. Never, in any of his studies, has Burt denied the influence and importance of social and environmental forces – he has frequently been misrepresented in this connexion – but he has firmly maintained that with regard to the level of intelligence innate influences are the more weighty of the two.

Like Spearman Burt has always recognized that cognition is only one

[1] Memo I. App. III (1921).        [2] Vol. IV.

side of mental functioning and that in real life the 'orectic' or emotional side is equally important. The statistical and factorial methods, however, which were the backbone of the London school's methodology, have not lent themselves so readily to the orectic field. True Spearman's pupil, Webb, did a factorial study of character in which he extracted a general factor 'W' (consistency of action resulting from deliberate volition); and Burt in 1915 reported to the British Association in Manchester an investigation into the 'General and specific factors underlying the primary emotions'. It was in this investigation, of which an abstract only was published, that Burt first put forward his hypothesis of a factor of 'general emotionality'. But it was not until the late 1930's that psychologists anywhere, including Burt, seriously took up this problem. Burt's own contributions were contained in his articles on 'The analysis of temperament' and 'The factorial analysis of emotional traits',[1] and in the concluding part of *The Factors of the Mind*.[2] In these publications Burt reaffirmed his belief in a factor of 'general emotionality', and also postulated a bipolar factor distinguishing extraverted from introverted temperamental types, though the distribution Burt found to be normal and not bimodal. In other words a mixed or relatively well-balanced type was the most frequent, and extraverts and introverts the opposite tail-ends of the distribution curve. An interesting off-shoot of Burt's work on emotionality was his interest in aesthetic taste. Quite early – in 1919 – he carried out some preliminary work on artistic preferences, and this was followed up by a number of his pupils, including H. J. Eysenck some twenty years later.[3]

As befits Great Britain's first professional psychologist Burt has never been an academic recluse. He has plunged into the stream of life (residing, for example, in social settlements in Liverpool and London), applied his findings to practical problems, and been influential on committees and behind the scenes. His contribution to a series of Government committees and reports has been exceptionally important, and has helped to mould the development of the educational system of the country.[4] He played a notable part in the movement which led to the establishment of the Child Guidance Clinics in 1927. He was the first head (part-time) of the vocational guidance department of the National

---

[1] *B. J. Med. Psych.*, XVII (1938).     [2] *Char. and Pers.*, VII (1939).

[3] See H. J. Eysenck *B. J. Psych.*, XXX (1940).

[4] See for example: Board of Education *Report on Psychological Tests of Educable Capacity*, 1924; Board of Education and Board of Control *Report on Mental Defect*, 1929; Board of Education *Report on the Primary School*, 1931; Board of Education *Report on the Infant and Nursery Schools*, 1934.

Institute of Industrial Psychology, and helped to formulate the theory and the practice of vocational guidance in this country. His *Study in Vocational Guidance* (1926), produced with May Smith and others, outlined the methods of guidance used at the N.I.I.P. and contained an early follow-up study of the results. During the Second World War Burt played an important part in initiating the application of psychological methods to military problems.

This many-sidedness of Burt, and his rare combination of the highest academic gifts with an appreciation of practical problems and clinical insight, have nowhere found better expression than in his famous and classic volume *The Young Delinquent* (1925). In this study of some two hundred delinquent cases examined during his L.C.C. days Burt brings to bear all his psychological armoury, psychometric and conceptual; but beneath this massive scholarship the young delinquents live as real people, illuminated by Burt's humanity and balanced wisdom. Even if some of its conclusions are modified and added to by subsequent research *The Young Delinquent* is likely to remain a classic, and perhaps the best introduction to the work of Burt and the London school of psychologists.

# CHAPTER XIV

# British Psychology between the Wars

## 1. The Academic and Philosophical Background

The academic development of psychology in Great Britain between the wars was a slow one, lagging far behind that in the United States. When the Second World War broke out in 1939 there were still only six chairs of psychology in all the universities of Britain, and three of these were in London, at University College (Spearman, Burt), King's College (Aveling), and Bedford College (Edgell). The Manchester chair was held by T. H. Pear from 1919 to 1951, the first provincial chair to be established; Edinburgh promoted James Drever snr. in 1931, and in the same year a chair of experimental psychology was created for F. C. Bartlett at Cambridge. The total lecturing staff in departments of psychology at the outbreak of Second World War numbered only about thirty. This academic starvation and emaciation of psychology must be kept in mind in any critical evaluation of British psychology between the wars.

In part this starvation was due to the general conservatism of British universities and their dislike of new disciplines and technologies, in part to the scepticism, amounting sometimes to hostility, towards psychology on the part of many philosophers. The revolution in British philosophy which dated from G. E. Moore's famous article in *Mind*, 'The Refutation of Idealism',[1] though it undermined the stranglehold of neo-Hegelianism, confronted psychology with new difficulties. Though Moore himself was not overtly unfriendly to psychology – indeed from 1911 to 1918 he taught a philosophical brand of psychology for the Moral Sciences tripos in Cambridge – the consequences of his teaching were equivocal. Accepting the distinction between acts and contents of consciousness Moore made it clear in a subsequent paper "On the Subject Matter of Psychology"[2] that in his view psychology must study acts, not contents. The status of 'sense-data' was a vexed problem, but at any rate 'sense-data' were not simply mental. It was not, therefore, the psychologist's job to describe the contents of consciousness in the way that the older introspective schools of psychology believed it could be

[1] *Mind*, n.s. XII (1903).      [2] *Proc. Amt. Soc.*, X (1909–10).

described. Was, then, the psychologist to study 'acts'? The difficulty here was that Moore soon became convinced that 'acts' were transparent or 'diaphanous'. "The moment we try to fix our attention upon consciousness and to see *what* distinctly it is, it seems to vanish." It was not at all clear, therefore, what the psychologist should study, or how he should study it.

The extremist view was to conclude that there was nothing for psychology to study – that psychology could not, therefore, be a branch of science. This was the conclusion reached, for example, by H. A. Prichard and some other Oxford philosophers, who held that because knowing always implied a subject-object relation, knowledge itself, and consequently the knowing mind, could not be an object of study. Thus there could be no science of psychology. At most psychology was a branch of philosophy, and a not very important branch at that. Between these realist and the older idealist fires psychology made little headway at Oxford, until as a result of a private benefaction a small Institute of Experimental Psychology was established in 1936 as an extra-curricular ornament.

A second course was to accept the contention that psychology was concerned with acts not contents, and to refashion psychology accordingly. Samuel Alexander (1859–1938), for example, Professor of Philosophy at Manchester, proposed his "Foundations and Sketch Plan of a Conational Psychology".[1] While non-mental objects, which on his theory included even images, were 'contemplated', the corresponding acts were 'enjoyed', and it was the task of the psychologist to analyse 'enjoyments'. All 'enjoyments' were conations, and conations, to which feelings were attached, could be 'speculative' as well as 'practical'. The outcome of Alexander's 'sketch plan' was to exclude cognitions as such entirely from the subject matter of psychology. Though few psychologists accepted Alexander's theory as it stood, the emphasis on conation, propounded in less extreme forms by Ward and Stout, became a marked feature of psychology between the wars, tuning in with McDougall's hormic theory and with psychoanalytic doctrines. Perhaps C. S. Myers's re-formulation of the acts-contents dichotomy was one of the most ingenious.[2] He held that presentations *to* consciousness were originally modifications *of* consciousness, and that these modifications which resulted from lower level activities of the nervous system could be contemplated cognitively at higher levels. Thus while the foundations of mind were conational, in its most highly evolved forms cognitive

[1] *B. J. Psych.*, IV (1911).     [2] C. S. Myers *B. J. Psych.*, XXIII (1933).

content, as commonly understood, emerged, though never wholly disentangled from its conative basis. Myers's attractive suggestions, according presciently with a number of later proposals, deserve to be remembered.

A third standpoint, held mainly by philosophers, was to accept a truncated psychology; to rule out the higher levels of conscious mind from the field of study of psychology, but to allow to the psychologist certain inferior functions. Thus John Macmurray in *The Boundaries of Science: a Study in the Philosophy of Psychology* (1939) argued that the psychologist could study unconscious mental processes but not conscious ones, as the methods of natural science were inapplicable to the study of consciousness as such. R. G. Collingwood, Oxford historian and philosopher, argued in his *Essay on Metaphysics* (1940) that the psychologist could study feelings but not thought. The claim of the psychologist to study thought was, he maintained, not only false, but corrosive of the foundations of Western civilization, and, in so far as they made this claim, psychologists had become merely the fashionable frauds of the age.[1]

The one road which no British psychologist of standing took was the road of behaviourism. Bertrand Russell, indeed, in his *Analysis of Mind* (1921) professed to have been influenced by behaviourism, and he questioned the existence both of conscious acts and of consciousness itself. But the view he put forward was very unlike behaviourism, and far more like a revived Humian atomism of sensations and images. Bertrand Russell's radical suggestions recruited no followers, and did not for long recruit even Russell himself. Most British philosophers and psychologists between the wars would have agreed with C. D. Broad's judgement that behaviourism was simply a 'silly' theory with no claim to be taken seriously.[2] There was general agreement among both philosophers and psychologists about this at least, that consciousness or experience in some form or other was the supposed subject matter of psychology; it was as to the methods and limits of this study that they disagreed. C. S. Myers expressed the conservative standpoint of British psychologists when he asserted that "the fundamental subject matter of psychology is conscious experience, not conduct".[3] It was the entanglements and disillusionments of this belief that finally after the Second World War led Gilbert Ryle in *The Concept of Mind* (1949) to aban-

---

[1] R. G. Collingwood *Autobiography*.
[2] C. D. Broad *The Mind and its Place in Nature* (1923).
[3] C. S. Myers *The Nature of Mind* (1930).

don 'the two worlds legend' and to propound a sort of philosophical behaviourism.

It was, we may surmise, the doubts and inhibitions engendered by this long philosophical debate during the first half of the twentieth century which retarded the development of British psychology and blocked its academic growth. For unenthusiastic philosophers were in a key position to advise on matters still generally regarded as falling within their province. And undergraduates who heard philosophers musing about "the barrenness of psychology" (Wittgenstein), castigating its "conceptual confusion" (Wittgenstein), deriding "the modern claim of psychology to be a science of mind" (Collingwood), and describing it as "an empty dream" (Ryle), had to show an obstinate independence before taking up psychology. Only a few psychologists, C. A. Mace and W. J. H. Sprott, for example, were sufficiently versed in the new philosophical disciplines to serve as mediators between what in effect were becoming divergent professions.

Such was the academic and intellectual soil in which British psychology had to grow between the wars. Had it rested with the philosophers alone the growth of psychology would have been even slower than it was. Psychology was saved by its applications, educational, industrial and medical. Here indubitably, and beyond the boundaries of philosophic controversy, progress was being made, new disciplines were being forged, new professions created. The academic world could not indefinitely refuse to recognize these developments. Psychologists were needed, and the universities had to train them. It was this more than anything else that surmounted the obstructiveness of philosophic sceptics. There was, too, a body of psychological theory, psychoanalytic theory, which became soon after the First World War of general intellectual interest, and was taken up not only by medical psychologists, but by the literary world, theologians, educators, art critics, and even physical scientists. Indeed in the popular mind psychology became almost identified with psychoanalysis. Though academic psychologists themselves had rather more reservations towards 'the new psychology', there is no doubt that psychoanalytic theory exerted a powerful influence on British psychology between the wars, and was one of the factors that led to psychological recognition.

## 2. Theoretical Trends

The one essentially native school of theory that had been founded and fostered by British psychologists was associationism. In the twentieth century it provided one of the main sources of inspiration both for the reflexology of the Russians and the learning theories of the Americans. In its native land it was despised and rejected, except perhaps as a contributory stream to the noegenetic theory of Spearman. The theoretical ferment of the period of the 'schools' (roughly the years 1900–40 when psychologists were divided into dissentient groups, structuralists and functionalists, Gestalt psychologists, behaviourists, hormic and personalistic psychologists, and various brands of depth psychologists) largely passed by British psychology, partly because British psychologists have always tended to distrust theoretical systems, and partly because they were slow to abandon older ways of thought.

Indeed the slowness of the rate of change in the basic positions of British psychology was a noticeable feature of the inter-war years. Ward's *Psychological Principles*, an expanded but not fundamentally altered version of his *Encyclopedia Britannica* (IXth ed.) article of 1885, was published in book form in 1918, and continued to exert a powerful influence on British psychologists for many years. R. J. Bartlett, presiding at the British Psychological Society in 1947, still urged psychologists to remain faithful to Ward. Stout's *Manual of Psychology*, which first appeared in 1898, was brought out in a new edition in 1938 and reprinted in 1945. But above all British psychology was largely shaped by McDougall's *Social Psychology* which was reprinted twenty-four times between its first appearance in 1908, and McDougall's death in 1938. A number of primary instinctive drives, developed, organized and canalized into 'sentiments', integrated into character and a directing self – such was what C. K. Ogden in his *A.B.C. of Psychology* (1929) would have described as "the nucleus of accredited opinion". Drever in *Instinct in Man* (1917), Thouless in *Social Psychology* (1925), Edgell in *Mental Life* (1927), Aveling in *Personality and Will* (1931), Burt in *The Subnormal Mind* (1935), Sprott in *General Psychology* (1937) – all propounded a psychology which in fundamentals adhered to the hormic system. C. S. Myers's concluding words to the symposium "Is the doctrine of instincts dead?"[1] were to the effect that properly conceived the doctrine of instincts was 'immortal'. Paired with a factor analytic theory of intelligence and cognition this psychology provided the framework of a comprehensive theory of personality in its dual aspects of conduct and ability, and a working basis for applications, particularly in the field of education – witness Godfrey Thomson's *Instinct, Intelligence and*

[1] *B. J. Ed. Psych.*, XI–XII (1941–3).

*Character*[1] (1924) and Percy Nunn's *Education, its Data and First Principles* (1920).

From among contemporary foreign schools of thought a good deal was borrowed from psychoanalysis and something from Gestalt psychology, for which Ward and Stout had paved the way. The more extreme movements, American behaviourism on the one hand and German phenomenological schools on the other, made little headway in Great Britain. British psychologists remained like the Conservative Governments which dominated political life, respectable, moderate, unadventurous. Even in the fields of comparative and social psychology, upon which on the face of it they had the closest bearing, their theories stimulated little, if any, research. Indeed on the whole they tended to divert psychologists from experimental and, in particular, physiological investigations.

Psychology, "the science of mental life", as Edgell defined it, was concerned fundamentally with consciousness or experience, and introspection was still regarded as a basic method of investigation. This was by no means merely lip service, as a glance at the researches reported in the *Monograph Supplements* of the *British Journal of Psychology* will show. Well into the 1930's many of the researches there reported relied extensively on introspections of the kind fashionable in the first decade of the century. Thus Honoria Wells enquired into *The Phenomenology of Acts of Choice* (1927), R. B. Cattell into *The Subjective Character of Cognition* (1930), H. L. Philip into *The Frustration of Will-Acts and Conation* (1936). C. K. Ogden listed[2] the principle questions raised when 'looking inwards' as (1) What is the self? (2) What kind of thing is an experience? (3) What are the essential aspects of experience? No respectable British psychologist questioned the existence of a conscious subject or self. This was a primary fact of experience. It was as Aveling put it "a centre or focus of all that is felt, known, or actively performed".[3] Moreover, "the self is in some way very intimately experienced in volitional processes".

Between 'the self', whether experienced or conceived as a directing agent, and the instincts which men shared with other animals, there was something of a gap which, however, could be bridged in theory by an hierarchical system of organizational levels. The key concept of

---

[1] Though Thomson's instincts were derived from Thorndike rather than McDougall.
[2] C. K. Ogden *A.B.C. of Psychology*, 144.
[3] F. A. P. Aveling *Personality and Will*, 16.

'sentiment' was introduced by A. F. Shand in an article in 1896,[1] and borrowed by McDougall in his *Social Psychology*. When Shand's own *Foundations of Character* appeared in 1914 there proved to be some differences of emphasis between the Shand and McDougall doctrines, but in general they agreed that a sentiment was an organized system of emotional dispositions centred round the idea of an object; that the characteristic sentiments were love and hate; and that these sentiments were the functional units from which character was organized. In McDougall's scheme the master sentiment was the sentiment of self-regard centred round the idea of the self, and it was in terms of this sentiment that volitional action was to be explained.

There was something about this system both solid and re-assuring. It avoided most of what Drever termed "the vagaries of an emancipated psychology".[2] It seemed to safeguard the higher moral levels of character, and the freedom and integrity of the self; to transmute and put into their proper place the disquieting revelations of psychoanalysis; and to be sufficiently biological to pass for scientific. The main objection, and a very serious objection, was that it was basically a speculative system, rather tenuously linked with empirical data – Shand, for example, drew most of his material from literature – not easily invalidated by crucial tests, nor issuing in operational methods of investigation. It is, we may suspect, for this reason above all others, that hormic psychology has lost ground to less comprehensive but more operationally secure systems, and if recently the concept of instinct has come back into favour this has been the result of the detailed spade-work of the ethologists.

The other main theoretical concept, which has had a long life in British psychology, is the concept of 'the schema', described by Oldfield and Zangwill as "a truly novel approach to some of the fundamental problems of psychology".[3] Like the hormic system it has been almost wholly a British concept which has gained little recognition or support from abroad. Originally propounded by the neurologist, Head,[4] in 1920 the schema was taken up by F. C. Bartlett and A. W. Wolters among others, and as recently as 1961 was still held by G. P. Meredith[5] to be "the basic unit of explanation" in psychology. According to Head schemata were physiological dispositions and they were introduced to explain how movements were controlled. The function of the schemata

[1] A. F. Shand 'Character and the Emotions', *Mind*, n.s. V (1896).
[2] J. Drever B. J. Psych., XXVII (1937).
[3] R. C. Oldfield and O. L. Zangwill B. J. Psych., XXXII (1942).
[4] See ch. V, 4.
[5] G. P. Meredith *Learning, Remembering and Knowing* (1961).

neglected, and such investigations as there were concerned either complex skills and memory or applied problems. In America the importance of the conditioned reflex was widely appreciated, and it became one of the main planks of behaviourism; in Britain it was not regarded as much more than a minor curiosity. Finally, in America there were attempts to push experimental methods into the study of personality and social psychology, which in Britain still remained largely observational and verbal. If, since the Second World War, this gulf has been bridged it is mainly because British psychology has moved nearer to American methods and ways of thinking.

## 3. Sir Frederic Bartlett (b. 1886)

F. C. Bartlett (born in 1886) has, of course, played a very dominant role in British psychology from 1920 onwards, and both the direction of his interests and his method of approach have had a considerable influence, particularly on Cambridge psychology, where Bartlett was in turn lecturer, reader and professor. "If I am to say what sort of psychologist I am", writes Bartlett,[1] "I think I can say only that I am a Cambridge psychologist. . . . Cambridge psychology of the laboratory type has never committed itself to any hard and fast and settled scheme of psychological explanation . . . complete systems and schemes of psychological explanation are the biggest stumbling block to progress in psychology." Bartlett's earlier training in philosophy at London, before he moved to Cambridge, had a remarkably slight corrupting influence on his psychology, which has from the first been essentially concrete and empirical in its approach. The problems that have interested Bartlett have been real life problems, and his aim has been to study these problems with as few artificial simplifications as the laboratory situation permitted. The ideal of rigour must not be pushed too far in psychology, for "subjective attitudes and orientations are an important part of every response at the psychological level". So as Bartlett pointed out in *Remembering* the simplification of stimulus situations does not in itself lead to simplification of responses. Nor has Bartlett held any truck with quantification. His writings are free of statistics. Statistical methods he regards as scientific make-shifts; a stricture which spreads to the whole field of testing and psychometrics; and which is shared by most Cambridge psychologists, apart from Thouless. Thus E. G. Chambers describes statistical computations in psychology as "elegant and dizzy numerical exercises", and holds that "it is at least very doubtful

[1] C. Murchison *History of Psychology in Autobiography*, vol. III.

whether the concept of measurable quantity may be applied at all to psychological qualities".[1] In his book on *Thinking* (1958) Sir Frederic Bartlett gave his account of how the experimental scientist went to work, of how, in fact, he himself has worked and the generation of Cambridge psychologists he has trained. "The scientific experimenter is by bent and practice an opportunist . . . [he] must be able to use specific methods rigorously, but he need not be in the least concerned with methodology as a body of general principles." No theory, no statistics, no methodology! There may seem to be, and indeed there is, something engagingly amateur about all this. It has, however, no doubt at a price, saved Cambridge psychology, and to some extent British psychology, from a good deal of pretentiousness.

Bartlett's personal contribution to experimental psychology has been primarily in the fields of perceiving, imaging, remembering, and thinking, and is contained in his two principal books, *Remembering* (1932) and *Thinking* (1958). In the preface to the first of these books Bartlett relates how the problems first presented themselves to him in May 1913, at the opening of the new Cambridge laboratory, when by way of demonstration geometrical forms and pictures were exposed to a string of visitors, and he was fascinated by the great variety of interpretations given. This led him to ask what were the factors determining different ways of perceiving. The experiments he went on to undertake led him to the conclusion "that a great amount of what goes under the name of perception is, in the wide sense of the word, recall".[2] In a psychological sense perceiving proved to be an exceedingly complex reaction, active and constructive in its essential nature, and involving imaging, valuing, the beginnings of judgement, an 'effort after meaning', and an inferential element. These conclusions led on to Bartlett's famous experiments on remembering. Abandoning the use of nonsense syllables Bartlett employed pictures, pictorial symbols and prose passages. His subjects were asked to give repeated reproductions after varying intervals of time, sometimes a series of subjects being involved in the transmission of the material. In this way Bartlett was able to study the changes that took place in remembering. His interpretation of the experimental results was both stimulating and suggestive. Perceiving, recognizing and recalling were regarded as psychological functions belonging to a common series. All were determined not merely by sensorial data, but by 'schemata' and by attitudes. In a sense, too, each act of recall involved novelty; it was reconstructive, not merely reproductive, just as skilled acts were not

[1] E. G. Chambers *B. J. Psych.*, XXXIII (1943).      [2] *Remembering*, 14.

mechanical motor habits but built up afresh each time to meet the demands of each situation as it arose.

The strength of Bartlett's work was its capacity to embrace relatively
complex functions such as are met with in real life, images and consciousness, for example, and the social factors involved in behaviour.
Indeed the second part of *Remembering* was devoted to the social factors,
"the passing fashion of the group, the social catchword, the prevailing
approved general interest, the persistent social custom and institution"
which set the stage for all human experience and behaviour. This
emphasis on, and awareness of, social forces has been a constant feature
of Bartlett's psychology and found earlier expression in his *Psychology
and Primitive Culture* (1923), and no doubt reflects the influence of
W. H. R. Rivers.

It was a natural transition from the constructive processes involved in
remembering to the study of thinking. In his book on the subject,[1]
published six years after his retirement in 1952 from the Cambridge
chair, Bartlett aimed to put thinking into its place as a development
from earlier and simpler forms of skilled behaviour. Thinking "within
closed systems" was concerned largely with "filling in gaps in information"; "adventurous thinking", such as that of the experimental scientist or the artist, was concerned more with "going beyond the evidence".
Bartlett made some tentative suggestions for an experimental investigation of these ideas, and included some 'case studies' of thinking, but the
book is a much slighter contribution to its subject than was *Remembering*,
and paid little regard to the considerable volume of work on thinking
being carried on outside Cambridge. The book is valuable, however, for
the light it throws on Bartlett's approach to psychology, and for its
stimulating qualities.

Bartlett's other contributions to psychology have been mainly in the
applied field. He has written books on *Psychology and the Soldier* (1927),
*The Problem of Noise* (1934) and *Political Propaganda* (1941), and articles
on fatigue, skills, incentives, subjective judgements and so on. In the
First World War he carried out research on the auditory problems connected with submarine detection;[2] between the wars he became interested in the industrial applications of psychology; and in the Second
World War he became involved in problems of display and control and
their relation to skills. An important paper on fatigue following highly

[1] F. C. Bartlett *Thinking* (1958).
[2] F. C. Bartlett and E. M. Smith 'Listening to Sounds of Weak Intensity',
*B. J. Psych.*, X (1919).

skilled work[1] laid the foundations for the subsequent Cambridge work on skill. Skills were described as complex, co-ordinated and accurately timed activities; under stress conditions standards of performance deteriorated, patterns altered, and perceptual stimuli tended to be ignored.

Bartlett's influence on British psychology both scientifically and administratively has been far-reaching. Since the deaths of Myers and Spearman he has been the only psychologist among the Fellows of the Royal Society, to which he was elected in 1932. He has had a guiding hand in the sponsoring of psychological research by Government research organizations. For many years (1924–48) he edited the *British Journal of Psychology*. Above all his influence has made itself felt through his pupils. More than half the chairs of psychology in the country were in 1960 held by Cambridge graduates trained by Bartlett, including the important chairs at Cambridge itself (Zangwill), Oxford (Oldfield), University College, London (Drew), and Edinburgh (Drever jnr.). Though not by any means the whole of British psychology, Cambridge psychology is its most vigorous living component. To a remarkable extent, over a period of nearly forty years, Bartlett has kept abreast with and influentially shaped what he has referred to as 'the changing scene', retaining a youthfulness of spirit and an infectious zest, together with firm ideas of what is scientifically and ethically respectable in psychology.

## 4. Experimental Psychology

British contributions to experimental psychology between the wars' with the exception of Bartlett's work on memory, were mostly modest in scale and sporadic in their coverage. No body of work comparable in value to that of the Gestalt School in Germany, the learning psychologists in America, or the Pavlovians in Russia emanated from British laboratories – which was hardly surprising, since these laboratories were poorly staffed and financed and generally inadequately housed.

The main fields in which research was carried out between the wars in British laboratories were (a) visual perception, (b) audition, (c) memory, (d) the psycho-galvanic response, (e) perseveration and oscillation, and (f) higher cognitive and voluntary processes. Cambridge was the main centre for the first three topics, London for the last three; and the *British Journal of Psychology* (General Section) was the usual locus of publication for experimental reports.[2]

[1] *Proc. Roy. Soc.*, B.131 (1943).
[2] Detailed references are not given. See *B. J. Psych.*, X–XXX (1919–39).

a) *Visual perception*

A good deal of the British work on vision and visual perception was the outcome of practical problems – problems of war-time leading to studies such as Flugel's and Wynn Jones's on night vision, or Banister's investigation of eye dominance in relation to marksmanship; problems raised by technological change, such as glare and flicker resulting from new sources of light; and problems of educational origin, for example, reading. In this connexion M. D. Vernon's work on visual perception, the most substantial British contribution to the subject, originated from her *Experimental Study of Reading* (1931), and led on to a comprehensive survey of the facts relating to visual perception, published in two books,[1] and to experimental work on the perception of movement and distance. Her work was characteristic of British experimentation in that it not merely aimed to present facts as far as possible without theoretical bias, but even suggested that comprehensive theories are likely to prove chimerical. Nevertheless something of a standpoint did begin to emerge, particularly in the second of Miss Vernon's books; a conviction, derived from Bartlett's original perceptual experiments, that perception was largely a constructional process, determined as much, or more, by the needs and the pre-existing schemata of the individual perceiver, as by the stimulus situation. Thus the end product, the percept, was highly unlike the original stimulus field, and showed wide individual variation – a conclusion not dissimilar to that of Wolters' short popular survey *The Evidence of our Senses* (1933). R. H. Thouless (born in 1894) in some penetrating but isolated studies of constancy phenomena stressed rather the opposite, what he termed "phenomenal regression to the real object".

Very little fundamental work on vision was carried out in Britain between the wars; colour vision continued to interest some psychologists (for example, Mary Collins of Edinburgh, who published a book on *Colour Blindness* (1925) and a number of experimental studies) as well as some physiologists (H. Hartridge), physicists (W. D. Wright), and ophthalmologists (Sir John Parsons). Just before the Second World War K. Craik began to reveal his calibre in some brilliant work on visual adaptation.

b) *Audition*

The contribution of British psychologists to the study of hearing was rather more considerable, partly because at least three of our lead-

---

[1] M. D. Vernon *Visual Perception* (1937). *A Further Study of Visual Perception* (1952).

ing experimentalists, C. S. Myers, H. J. Watt, and H. Banister, were musically gifted. Watt's book, *The Psychology of Sound* (1917), was perhaps less influential than it might have been because his approach was somewhat doctrinaire. He set out to demonstrate that sensory psychology could be carried out in purely psychological terms "without our having recourse to the discoveries of physics or physiology". His work, nevertheless, was very scholarly and contained many suggestive ideas, even if some of them have been shown to be unsound (e.g. his views on the elementary nature of the experience of volume). Myers's work was partly anthropological and concerned with primitive music, and partly an experimental investigation into the role of binaural phase differences in the localization of sound. He also collaborated with C. W. Valentine in a study of individual differences in attitudes towards tones. Rayleigh had shown in 1877 that localization of sound in the front-back plane was often confused. Myers in an important paper[1] demonstrated that effective localization was the result of phase and intensity differences at the two ears. The problem was taken up at Cambridge by Banister in the 1920's using greatly superior equipment and more stringent controls. Banister showed[2] that pure tones could be localized by phase differences alone, without bringing in intensity differences resulting from bone conduction. He also emphasized the importance of binaural time differences.

Another auditory problem which interested several British psychologists after the First World War was that of auditory 'fatigue'. It arose from war-time experiments on listening and submarine detection. Flugel noted displacement effects in localization following previous stimulation of one ear, and explained these effects in terms of fatigue. F. C. Bartlett preferred an explanation in terms of 'adaptation'. More generally Ewing and Littler showed that auditory acuity could be diminished by intense stimulation of the ear, even when pain and discomfort were not caused. Rawdon Smith with much improved apparatus demonstrated that the effect of fatigue was largely confined to frequencies above 1,000 cycles per second. A rather different line of enquiry was P. E. Vernon's work on the Gestalt approach to auditory perception.

The value of British work on audition during this period received recognition in that the principal contributors on hearing in Murchison's *Handbook of General Experimental Psychology* (1934) were H. Banister and H. Hartridge – the only British contributors to this standard work.

[1] *Proc. Roy. Soc.*, A.1908.  [2] H. Banister *Phil. mag.*, II (1926).

c) *Memory*

Not unnaturally Bartlett's *Remembering*, to which reference has already been made, constituted a starting point for further work, particularly by Bartlett's pupils. O. Zangwill and R. C. Oldfield working in Cambridge extended and, with some modifications, confirmed Bartlett's views. Zangwill in a neat experiment demonstrated the role of attitude in recognition. Broadly speaking he confirmed Bartlett's general standpoint, but not all his data fitted into Bartlett's theory, nor for that matter into the Gestalt theory of dynamic traces. However, in a study on verbal recognition habits Oldfield and Zangwill came to the conclusion that Bartlett's schemata provided a better explanation of the changes in reproduced material than the older trace theories of memory.

Apart from the Cambridge work investigation on memory and related processes was sporadic. Pear popularized some of the psychoanalytic findings on forgetting, and wrote on skill. The educationalists were concerned in the problem of transfer of training, and just before the war P. B. Ballard was the first to call attention to the phenomenon of 'reminiscence', the slight superiority of the delayed over the immediate recall of some types of material.[1] In general, however, there was a conspicuous absence among British psychologists during the inter-war period of a sustained attack on the question of learning, either animal or human, or on the problems of skills. The one exception, G. Humphrey's *Nature of Learning* (1933), was written during Humphrey's Canadian period, before he returned to Oxford, and though by a British psychologist it can hardly be claimed for British psychology.

d) *The psycho-galvanic response*

The psycho-galvanic response (P.G.R.), the change in the electrical resistance of the skin, was discovered by the French psychologist, Féré, in 1888. A good deal of experimental work on the P.G.R. was done on the Continent prior to the First World War. In Great Britain it became a popular topic of study in the 1920's. It was used first by Whateley Smith in his work on *The Measurement of Emotion* (1922), carried out in the Cambridge laboratory. P.G.R. was employed by him as an index of emotional responses in word association and other tests. It was taken up by Pear and Thouless in Manchester in the study of dream

[1] P. B. Ballard *B. J. Psych.*, Mon. Supp. II (1913).

material, and later by a group of workers at King's College, London, under Aveling's general direction. Aveling himself, working with the physiologist R. J. McDowell and employing anaesthetized cats subjected to nocive stimuli, came to the conclusion that P.G.R. was related not to emotion but to organic sets of a conative character. This finding was broadly confirmed in a careful introspective study by R. J. Bartlett who linked P.G.R. generally to complex 'orectic' processes though it could sometimes occur with 'passive enjoyment' and 'task relaxation'. R. B. Cattell, however, failed to find the response in states of 'passive enjoyment' and in the main associated it with emotion.

Outside the King's College group the use of P.G.R. soon came under critical fire. In a scholarly survey of the literature and techniques E. Farmer and E. G. Chambers of Cambridge came to the conclusion that P.G.R. was "not a reliable means for measuring differences between individuals. The factors of error are so many and our present knowledge of the field of their operation so limited that it would be impossible to assign differences in the P.G.R. to their specific cause with any degree of certainty."[1] They stressed the need for more research, both psychological and physiological. Thouless, when studying some years later the related Tarchanoff phenomenon – a change in the potential difference between two points on the skin when no external source of current was used – also stressed the need for more knowledge. Since 1930 comparatively little work has been done on the P.G.R. in Great Britain.

### e) *Perseveration and oscillation*

The concentration of effort by British, mainly London, psychologists on these two topics in the inter-war period was a direct result of their erection by Spearman to the status of important general 'factors' – after intelligence ('g') the most important 'factors' of the mind.

The tendency of perceptual and motor phenomena to persist had been noted in Continental laboratories, and speculatively linked with individual differences in temperament and personality. A succession of Spearman's pupils, Wynn Jones and others, set out to test first, whether perseveration ('p') was a unitary, general trait, and came to the conclusion that it was; and secondly whether it was linked with character qualities. Pinard (1932) found that both high and low perseverators were prone to be unreliable and difficult. W. Stephenson (1932) related 'p' to psychiatric types, and R. B. Cattell (1933, 1936) advocated

[1] E. Farmer and E. G. Chambers *B. J. Psych.*, XV (1925).

perseveration tests as important diagnostic tools. These conclusions have proved over-optimistic. Perseveration would seem to be neither theoretically so simple, nor practically so important as Spearman and his school made out.[1]

It is equally doubtful whether oscillation deserved the high place that Spearman accorded it as the third great 'general factor' of the mind, though unquestionably it is an interesting phenomenon. Fluctuation in attention and performance had once again been noted by early experimenters. Flugel (1928) applying several measures of oscillation to a group of schoolchildren concluded that oscillation ('o') was a unitary general factor distinct from 'g' and 'p'. Philpott extended the mathematical analysis of oscillations of output curves much further, and came to the conclusion that there were certain constants which obtained for all persons under all experimental conditions.[2] He even suggested that there was a close relation between these psychological constants and certain basic physical constants – a conclusion both abstruse and enigmatic. R. B. Cattell after his migration to America in 1938 continued to include oscillation, together with fluctuation, as component factors of personality and to link it with behavioural traits.[3] But in general the conceptual framework within which these investigations were set, and the techniques with which they were investigated, have changed, and the older work now has a dated look.

f) *Higher cognitive and voluntary processes*

The leading figure in the experimental investigation of higher cognitive and voluntary processes during the inter-war period was F. Aveling (1875–1941). Aveling first investigated problems of perceptual generalization under Michotte in Louvain, and then, at University College, London, turned to the experimental investigation of conceptual thought. His work *The Consciousness of the Universal* (1912), though heavily relying on introspective reports in the Würzburg manner and confirming the Würzburg doctrine of 'imageless' thought, was forward-looking in its experimental technique and use of artificial 'nonsense' concepts. After the war this work was followed up by some of Aveling's pupils at King's College, London, in particular by Stevanovic[4] who

---

[1] For a review of the evidence see H. J. Eysenck *The Structure of Human Personality*, (1953) ch. IX.

[2] S. J. F. Philpott *B. J. Psych.*, XL (1950).

[3] R. B. Cattell *Description and Measurement of Personality* (1946).

[4] B. P. Stevanovic, 'An Experimental Study of the Mental Processes involved in Judgement', *B. J. Psych.*, Mon. Supp. XII (1927).

studied the development of meaning, and the employment of concepts in judgements or propositions, again using 'nonsense' material.

Aveling's work on conation and volition was also derived from Continental sources, in this case from the German psychologist, Ach, as well as from Michotte. It was similarly both experimental and introspective in the classical manner. The conclusion of a long series of investigations by Aveling himself and his pupils was not perhaps very fruitful or encouraging. Will-acts, such as resolutions and decisions, must be 'lived' in order to be understood. They involve 'self-actuality' and can be distinguished from striving or mere feelings of strain and effort. It is hard not to feel that there was, in fact, a good deal of philosophy still intermixed with this work, and that neither conceptual analysis nor experimental techniques were ripe for investigations of the kind that Aveling undertook.

## 5. Experimental Design and Statistics

As important for psychology as any progress made by experimental psychologists themselves between the wars were the advances in statistical methodology and in the design of experiments associated particularly with the name of R. A. Fisher. Fisher (1890–1962) was a Cambridge mathematician whose main work was carried out between 1919 and 1933 at the Rothamsted Agricultural Station. Though building on the work of Pearson and others, Fisher was highly critical both of Pearson's pretensions and of his workmanship. "The traditional machinery of statistical processes is wholly unsuited to the needs of practical research. Not only does it take a cannon to shoot a sparrow, but it misses the sparrow!" At Rothamsted Fisher was closely concerned with agricultural experiments and most of his statistical work was illustrated with agricultural examples. But Fisher was not content until he had got down to the rock bottom of fundamental principles, and consequently his methods have proved to be universally applicable. From a practical point of view Fisher grasped that the research worker in the field or the laboratory is necessarily concerned with small, not infinitely large, samples. Methods of statistical inference, therefore, needed tailoring to the small sample situation. The problem then was to exclude, at an assigned level of significance, hypotheses which could only by a more or less implausible coincidence have led to what had been observed. This led to the calculation of exact sample distributions. The first of these sampling distributions – that for $\chi^2$ – had been worked out by Pearson in 1900. Fisher in 1922 showed that there was a serious error in the assumptions underlying Pearson's tables, which could be straightened out by introducing the concept of 'degrees of freedom'.[1] In 1908 a research chemist at Guinness's brewery in Dublin, W. S. Gossett, writing under the name of 'Student', introduced the 't' statistic for the distribution of sample variance. Fisher gave a rigorous proof of 't', and went on both to provide a more generalized sampling distribution, known as the 'z' statistic (now usually used in a revised form, 'f', devised by Snedecor, an American statistician), and to give a unified treatment of practically all the important distributions involved in testing 'null hypotheses'. Fisher's 'z' found an important application in the method termed 'analysis of variance', first set out in *Statistical Methods for Research Workers* (1st ed. 1925). This led on naturally to the whole question of the design of experiments. Fisher always insisted that "statistical procedure and experimental design are only two different aspects of the same whole", that if experiments are to provide clear-cut answers, they must be properly designed in the first place. Fisher's prescriptions, based as they were on a fundamental analysis of the logical foundations of inductive inference, were of revolutionary importance, particularly for 'vague' sciences like psychology. They introduced into experimental practice concepts such as randomization, replication, null hypothesis (any *exact* hypothesis which the investigator is concerned to disprove), level of significance, 'Latin square', and the factorial design of experiments, described in Fisher's second statistical book, *The Design of Experiments* (1935). Fisher's other major achievement was the application of statistical mathematics to the problems of genetics and evolution. In *The Genetical Theory of Natural Selection* (1930) he did much to reconcile Darwinian natural selection and Mendelian genetical concepts. After ten years (1933–43) in the Galton chair at University College, London, Fisher, who became Sir Ronald in 1952, held the Chair of Genetics in Cambridge until his retirement in 1957.

Fisher's methods were slow to percolate into psychology both in this country and in America. His mathematics were difficult, and the language of the farm somewhat strange to psychologists. Nevertheless his simple illustration of experimental procedure in *The Design of Experiments* (the famous test of whether the lady really can discriminate if milk or tea was first put into her cup of tea) was a psychophysical one. R. H. Thouless was the first British psychologist to refer to Fisher's work in an article on phenomenal regression in 1932,[2] and he was also

---

[1] *J. Roy Stat. Soc.*, LXXXV (1922).     [2] *B. J. Psych.*, XXII.

one of the first to use analysis of variance in his "Review of Mr Whatley Carington's Work on Trance Personalities".[1] Shepherd Dawson's *Introduction to the Computation of Statistics* (1933) referred to Fisher's 'z' but not to analysis of variance. E. C. Chamber's *Statistical Calculation for Beginners* (1940) did not include a chapter on analysis of variance until the second edition (1952). So for practical purposes the application of Fisherian methods to psychology in Great Britain was a phenomena of the post Second World War period.

## 6. Aesthetics

For fifteen years between the wars, from 1922 to 1937, a special section of the British Psychological Society was devoted to the study of aesthetics. During this period the rather faint flame of British aesthetics, a subject which has only fitfully interested philosophers and psychologists in this country, burned with a brighter radiance. Herbert Spencer, of course, though doubtfully gifted with much aesthetic sense himself, had theorized a bit on the topic of aesthetic sentiments. Sully was more knowledgeable, and his article in the *Encyclopaedia Britannica* was a valuable survey of aesthetic theories; he also contributed a number of specialized papers, which being musically and artistically gifted he was well qualified to do. But neither German philosophical aesthetics, nor Fechner's experimental approach, made much impact in Great Britain until after the First World War. The disturbing effects of the war, and the new movements in art and literature which it encouraged, brought aesthetic problems to the fore. Clive Bell, Roger Fry and the Bloomsbury group propounded new aesthetic doctrines, and cultivated aesthetic attitudes. The astringent writings of Lawrence, Eliot, Joyce – to name only a few – compelled a re-thinking of the whole problem of aesthetic appreciation and the nature of criticism, and led to the work of I. A. Richards and others. G. E. Moore in his influential *Principia Ethica* (1903) had not only provided new analytic tools, but had himself set up beauty as a supreme good. From the Continent Croce and his aesthetic theories began to percolate. Several British philosophers, such as Alexander and Collingwood, began to think and write on beauty and art. It was against this background that a sufficient number of British psychologists between the wars became interested in aesthetics to justify the establishment of a special section of the British Psychological Society.

The proceedings of the section were partly concerned with reports

[1] *Proc. S.P.R.*, XLIV (1937).

of experimental work and partly with theoretical, even philosophical, discussions on the nature of aesthetic experience. How far was art a matter of expression, how far a matter of communication to others? How important was imagery in the process of artistic creation and in artistic appreciation? How intrinsically was the medium of an art involved in the creative processes of the artist? The yield of these discussions may have been somewhat problematical. But some ideas of importance emerged from the experimental work, particularly from that of E. Bullough of Gonville and Caius College, Cambridge;[1] for example, the concept of 'psychical distance', which implied that one of the essential characteristics of the aesthetic consciousness was a certain emotional standing back, so that the spectator was able to appreciate a tragedy without being overwhelmed by pity or horror. Bullough also distinguished four types of aesthetic attitude, the objective, the physiological, the associative, and the character type. These four attitudes Bullough held to be fundamental and stable modes of apprehension. Individuals in whom the objective attitude predominated based their aesthetic judgements on objective qualities of colour, tone and so on; those with a predominantly physiological attitude upon the stimulating or depressing effects on their bodily functions; the associative type upon the associated memory and other images evoked; and the character type on suggested or projected character qualities. The value of this typology was confirmed by various investigators, C. W. Valentine and C. S. Myers among others, working with a variety of artistic media.

These, and other, early experimental investigations in aesthetics were summarized in a small book by C. W. Valentine, *The Experimental Psychology of Beauty* (1919).[2] The experiments described, some of them carried out by Valentine himself, were mainly concerned with the judgement of the relative aesthetic value of pairs or groups of objects. For the most part the stimuli or stimulus objects were kept very simple, simple colours and colour combinations, simple tones and tone combinations, though pictures were employed in some experiments.[3] Not surprisingly Valentine showed a special interest in the development of aesthetic preferences in young children. He commenced experiments in his own children in the first four months of life; and also noted that the appreciation of the excellence of a picture apart from the pleasing-

---

[1] See articles of Bullough in *B. J. Psych.*, II, III and V.

[2] An earlier and shorter version of this book was published in 1913. A much revised and enlarged version appeared in 1962, and readers are referred to this for a much fuller account of aesthetics.

[3] See C. W. Valentine *B. J. Psych.*, VI.

ness of the things represented does not often occur in children before the ages of twelve to fourteen – an age which accords rather well with Piaget's later findings, of which Valentine was to show himself critical.

In spite of the value of this early experimental work it was rather widely felt that it failed to reach the heart of the aesthetic experience. Thus I. A. Richards in his *Principles of Literary Criticism* (1924), although basing his book on "the desire to link even the commonplaces of criticism to a systematic exposition of psychology", held that only the simplest human activities were amenable to laboratory methods. His own approach was theoretical and analytical. As one of the few attempts in English to work out a systematic aesthetic theory and to link it to psychology Richards' work was important, stimulating, and at the same time essentially forward-looking. He recognized the vital role of communication in shaping the nature of experience; propounded a psychological theory of value – "that organization which is least wasteful of human possibilities is the best" – and rejected "the scientifically desperate belief in the soul", for a sort of subjective behaviourism in which attitudes and expectations played a central part. Art was essentially concerned with 'the incitement of attitudes' rather than with 'a statement of the facts', with the emotive rather than with the referent aspect of mind. This duality of emotive and referent, already expounded in *The Meaning of Meaning* (1923) jointly written by Richards and C. K. Ogden, was to exercise an important influence both on criticism and psychology between the wars, according well with the increasing popularity of psychoanalytic doctrines.

Psychoanalysis, indeed, appeared to hold the clue to many of the mysteries of art. There seemed to be an obvious and illuminating parallel between the dream symbols and phantasies discussed by the analysts, and the symbols and images employed by modern poets, writers and painters, between the creative upsurges of the artist, and the spontaneous fecundity of the unconcious mind. Only in the light of unconscious forces could some of the stranger and more macabre productions of the moderns be interpreted. The analysts themselves had not hesitated to apply their finding to the arts – Freud, for example, discussing the paintings of Leonardo, and Jones the psychology of Hamlet. Soon art critics like Herbert Read in *The Meaning of Art* (1931), and still more in *Education Through Art* (1943), were applying psychoanalytic, particularly Jungian, ideas to aesthetic interpretation and theory. Maud Bodkin discussed *Archetypal Patterns in Poetry* (1934), and before long psychologists were following suit. Thus R. W. Pickford held[1] that "every picture is a sublimation", and W. R. D. Fairbairn likened art to play activity, at the same time holding that an element of repression and restraint was necessary before any high achievement in art was possible.

Just at the time when Fairbairn was maintaining that psychoanalysis could rescue the psychology of art from the doldrums into which the older aesthetics had fallen, and just at the time when Burt and Eysenck had launched a new statistical, factor-analytic attack on the problem of aesthetic types, the aesthetic section of the British Psychological Society regrettably came to an end, and has not yet been revived.[2]

## 7. Physiological and Comparative Psychology

To the fields of physiological and comparative psychology British psychologists made few contributions between the wars. If, as Stout had maintained, "mental processes cannot be explained as special complications of processes which are not mental", why waste time with physiology? According to Spearman "the renunciation of physiology" was as important an ingredient in the development of psychology as "the renunciation of philosophy". Hence arose what MacCurdy described in 1928 as the 'the bulkhead' between psychology and physiology – a separation which excited the alarm of Russell Brain and E. B. Strauss who in their *Recent Advances in Neurology* (1929) wrote, "the study of psychological problems without an adequate knowledge of the physiology and pathology of the central nervous system can be likened to the exploration of uncharted seas without the aid of a compass; and yet there are many psychologists who undertake the rash venture".

The important advances were made on the physiological side of the boundary between physiology and psychology. The work of Sherrington, Head and the early work of Adrian has already been reviewed. Adrian's investigations on the nature of the nerve impulse continued in the 1920's, and were first made available in book form in *The Basis of Sensation* (1928). These investigations led Adrian to the conclusion that there were no radical differences in the nature of the nerve impulses from different kinds of sense organs or from different parts of the brain. "The nerve fibres carry out their work on a simple and uniform plan." [3] This conclu-

[1] R. W. Pickford *B.J. Psych.*, XXVIII (1938).
[2] The British Society of Aesthetics has, however, recently been formed to fill the gap. Its journal *The British Journal of Aesthetics* commenced publication in 1961.
[3] E. D. Adrian *The Physical Background of Perception*, (1947) 15.

sion seemed at first to result in a discontinuity between the physiological and the psychological facts – on the physiological side uniformity, on the psychological side the diversity of sensory quality and modes of experience. As Adrian suggested, however, it was probably in patterns of excitation that the resolution of the discontinuity was to be sought.

The injuries of the First World War were a considerable stimulus to the growth of neurological knowledge and to an understanding of brain functioning. Gordon Holmes, for example, studied the effect of cortical injuries on spatial perception and of cerebellar lesions on muscular control; another neurologist, Kinnier Wilson, elucidated some of the extra-pyramidal mechanisms involved in movement. Subsequently Le Gros Clark and others threw light on the important functions of the hypothalamus, and Sir Geoffrey Jefferson, the Manchester neuro-surgeon, worked on the role of the frontal areas of the cortex. Also in Manchester Sir John Stopford provided additional evidence in support of Head's two-level theory of sensation. Again borrowing largely from Head, Sir John Parsons, ophthalmic surgeon at University College Hospital, reviewed the physiology and psychology of perception and endeavoured to provide a physiological basis for pattern perception. Equally significant for the psychologist were advances made in the field of biochemistry, such as the study of endocrine secretions, particularly those of the thyroid and pituitary glands, and the work of Sir Henry Dale on the chemical factors (e.g. acetylcholine) involved in the transmission of the nerve impulse at neuro-muscular junctions. Finally, and perhaps most momentously of all for the psychologist, was the confirmation in 1934 by Adrian and Matthews of Berger's observations on the electrical rhythms of the cortex, first noted by the Liverpool physiologist R. Caton as early as 1875, but not seriously regarded until Adrian and Matthews's work. This led to the development of the electroencephalogram (E.E.G.) and important work by Golla, Gray Walter and others not only on the nature of epilepsy and the location of intracranial tumours, but on the relation between cortical rhythms and mental activity.

One of the few psychologists in Great Britain between the wars to make a serious attempt to incorporate physiological advances into psychology was J. T. MacCurdy, a Canadian medical psychologist, who came to deliver a course of lectures in Cambridge in 1922 and remained for twenty-five years as lecturer in psychopathology. His book *Common Principles in Psychology and Physiology* (1928) was perhaps unduly dominated by the Gestalt concepts which were prevalent at the time and which he linked to the integrative notions of Sherringtonian neurophysiology and to the organismic philosophy of Whitehead. It was in 'patterns' that MacCurdy saw the bridge between physiology and psychology, 'patterns' being defined as "the immaterial agencies that guide and control the physico-chemical processes involved in all living". But within this scheme MacCurdy found a place for images and consciousness, which he regarded as having a real function to play, and no doubt he would have approved of modern 'subjective behaviourism' with its emphasis on images, attention, meanings and plans. MacCurdy's was, however, an isolated endeavour.

In comparative psychology the situation in Great Britain between the wars was broadly similar to that in physiological psychology – neglect by psychologists, but interesting relevant work in neighbouring disciplines. There was no parallel in this country to the American cult of the white rat. Indeed few British departments of psychology had any dealing with animals, or showed more than a remote theoretical interest in animal psychology.

An exception was the brief but excellent survey, *The Investigation of Mind in Animals* (1915) by Miss E. M. Smith of Cambridge (Mrs F. C., later Lady, Bartlett), whose earlier studies on the colour vision of dogs were published in the *British Journal of Psychology* before the war.[1] Dealing with a variety of animal species from the protozoa to mammals, Miss Smith showed a remarkably sound judgement in her selection of topics for discussion. She was among the first in this country to appreciate Pavlov's work, and in her account of instinct clearly anticipated the ethologists of the next generation. Her account of homing noted the role of experience and the use of visual landmarks, emphasized the complexity of the phenomenon, and dismissed as improbable the telepathic hypothesis which had already been broached.

Almost the only other psychological investigators in comparative psychology between the wars were G. C. Grindley and his pupil G. C. Drew. Grindley commenced his investigations in Bristol under Lloyd Morgan's guidance and then became a lecturer at Cambridge. He investigated the role of rewards of various sorts in the learning of chickens, and by means of rewards taught guinea pigs to make adventitious head movements (later termed by Skinner 'superstitious' behaviour). Drew carried out experiments on the effects of mixed in-

[1] *B. J. Psych.*, V (1912).

centives on the behaviour of rats, and the function of punishment in learning. He was one of the first British psychologists to get interested in Hull's theory of goal gradients. In a brief factual book, characteristic of Cambridge in avoiding the theoretical issues involved, Grindley reviewed American and German work on animal learning.[1]

It was, however, the zoologists and naturalists who carried on the main lines of advance. In the 1920's and 1930's bird watching ceased to be little more than a charming hobby and turned into a serious branch of science, supported by trained biologists and backed by learned societies. Julian Huxley wrote on *Bird Watching and Bird Behaviour* in 1930, and in 1933 the British Trust for Ornithology was founded to co-ordinate the collection of information about British birds. Detailed studies were carried out by E. Howard on *Territory in Bird Life* (1922), by F. B. Kirkman on the behaviour of the black-headed gull (*Bird Behaviour* (1937)), by Landsborough Thomson on *Bird Migration* (1936), and by E. A. Armstrong on *Bird Display* (1942). In the 1930's W. H. Thorpe, later to become one of the leading experts on animal behaviour, commenced his studies on the behaviour of insects, a summary of which was published in a series of articles in *The British Journal of Psychology*.[2] Particularly notable work with mammals was carried out by S. Zuckermann in the London Zoo on *The Social Life of Monkeys and Apes* (1932), and by B. P. Wiesner and N. M. Sheard in Edinburgh on *Maternal Behaviour in the Rat* (1933).

The naturalistic approach to the study of animal behaviour was broadly and systematically reviewed in E. S. Russell's *The Behaviour of Animals* (1934) based on lectures given to zoology and anatomy students at University College, London. Russell's emphasis was on instinctive behaviour, and particularly on the perceptual aspects of instinct. His book included a wealth of observational and experimental material, and was the best British survey of the field prior to Thorpe's *Learning and Instinct in Animals* (1956).

In 1936 largely as a result of the efforts of Julian Huxley and F. B. Kirkman the Institute for the Study of Animal Behaviour was established, to be followed in 1953 by *The British Journal of Animal Behaviour*. Not until after the Second World War, and after Lorenz, Tinbergen and the Continental ethologists had begun to make themselves felt, did the study of animal behaviour once again seriously begin to engage the interest of British psychologists.

[1] G. C. Grindley *The Intelligence of Animals* (1937).
[2] W. H. Thorpe *B. J. Psych.*, vols. XXXIII, XXXIV (1943-4).

## 8. Social Psychology

In the early years of the century, we have already seen, the foundations of social psychology were laid in the writings of sociologists, social anthropologists and social philosophers, and there seemed to be some signs of the rise of a social psychology, not unduly theoretical, and based on a first-hand study of social behaviour. The promise, unfortunately, was not realized. Primarily, no doubt, this was due to the sidetracking of social psychology by McDougall into the discussion of instincts and the group mind. But a secondary and not unimportant contributory cause was the rejection of psychology by the rising British school of social anthropologists led by Radcliffe-Brown.

The enormous vogue of McDougall in the inter-war period was reinforced by psychoanalytic teaching and by the writings of Wilfred Trotter (1872–1939), a distinguished surgeon who early became acquainted with psychoanalysis and was deeply interested in human behaviour. His papers on the gregarious instinct, published in journal form in 1908–9, were collected together with additional chapters as *The Instincts of the Herd in Peace and War* (1914) and reprinted many times.[1] Trotter's writing was extremely readable, based on shrewd observation and considerable reflection, and had a considerable influence in winning acceptance by British psychologists for the concept of "a gregarious system of instincts" consisting in, as Thouless put it, "not merely the innate tendency of men to live in groups, but also all the tendencies which are called out by a social environment".

Criticisms of this viewpoint came first from the sociologists, implicitly from Hobhouse, and explicitly from M. Ginsberg in his *The Psychology of Society* (1921). Though agreeing that "speculations on social and political problems must from the nature of the case have a psychological basis", Ginsberg was critical of McDougall's account. Human behaviour was so moulded and modified by social forces that little remained of pure instinct. "Social life is not a mere balance of instincts but a new product or synthesis on which the original instincts have been greatly transformed." In this synthesis reason and will played their part, not in the hypostatized form of a 'group mind', or a 'general will', but in the interaction of individuals in a community, differentiated into institutions and shaped by custom and tradition. Although Ginsberg expressed himself in abstract terms he possessed a firm insight into the realities of individual action in a social milieu.

---

[1] A new edition appeared as recently as 1954.

Indeed he arrived at a conception not unlike contemporary role theory. "The individual", he stated, "is a unique focus or centre of reference conscious of himself as a single whole, related in very different ways to the different social wholes of which he is a member."

The more radical rejection by the social anthropologists of the Radcliffe-Brown school of any kind of psychological interpretation of social phenomena deprived social psychology of an important source of stimulus and suggestion. Prior to the First World War there had been a growing intimacy between psychologists and anthropologists, and W. H. R. Rivers was eminent in both fields. Rivers's aim, indeed, was to integrate psychology and 'ethnology', as he preferred to call it, into a single discipline – to discover the psychological reasons for social customs, and at the same time the historical and cultural reasons for the beliefs, symbolizations and fantasies of the individual. In his presidential address to the Anthropological Section of the British Association in 1911 Rivers outlined and illustrated his standpoint, which he was to expound at greater length in his *History of Melanesian Society* (1914). Ethnological analysis made it possible to reconstruct the history of social groups and of culture contacts; but it could only do this by using psychological data upon which to base its inferences. "The chief instrument for the study of past history is a knowledge of psychology." Reciprocally, as Rivers's pupil, F. C. Bartlett pointed out in *Psychology and Primitive Culture* (1923) the study of primitive culture was the best method of revealing the underlying mechanisms of all human social groups.

It was this happy marriage that A. R. Radcliffe-Brown (1881–1953) so rudely shattered. Radcliffe-Brown had already been brought into prominence by his detailed field study of *The Andaman Islanders* (1922), a year before the publication of his provocative article 'The Methods of Ethnology and Social Anthropology' (1923).[1] In this article he emphatically repudiated the idea that social anthropology was concerned with the history of society or that it was dependent in any way on psychology. As he reiterated in his presidential address to the British Association in 1931 any attempt to explain sociological phenomena in psychological terms was invalid. The anthropologist was concerned with the functions of social institutions and customs, and his method was to analyse these functions contemporaneously and comparatively on a sociological level. For example, he was interested neither in the speculative historical origins of totemism nor in the psychological mechanisms involved in totemism, but in the part which totemism was actually

[1] Reprinted in A. R. Radcliffe-Brown *Method in Social Anthropology* (1958).

playing in society. Fundamentally this involved an analysis in terms of social structure.

A closely allied 'functional' viewpoint, but less extreme and 'isolationist' in its attitude to psychology, was held by B. Malinowski (1884–1942), a Pole who settled in England in 1910 and, after a series of expeditions to the Trobriand Islands off New Guinea, returned to the London School of Economics where he taught from 1918 to 1938. Malinowski's intensive field studies of the Trobrianders were landmarks in anthropology, making particularly important contributions to primitive economics, linguistics and myth. Like Radcliffe-Brown he insisted on the need to study the use or function of tribal customs, institutions and beliefs. Thus "myth fulfils in primitive culture an indispensable function; it expresses, enhances and codifies belief; it safeguards and enforces morality; it vouches for the efficiency of ritual and contains practical rules for the guidance of men".[1] But behind this emphasis on functional analysis Malinowski held a theory of needs, and he conceived behaviour, both rational and irrational, as rooted in the motivation of individuals. Thus Malinowski's account of the sexual behaviour of primitive peoples was as illuminating to the psychologist as to the anthropologist. *Sex and Repression in Primitive Society* (1927) and *The Sexual Life of Savages* (1929) threw light on, and enforced modification of, psychoanalytic concepts such as infantile sexuality and the Oedipus complex.

Nevertheless as a result of this trend in anthropology, and particularly of Radcliffe-Brown's influence, a much greater aloofness developed between psychologists and anthropologists in Great Britain than between their opposite numbers in America. At least one concerted attempt was made to bridge the gulf. From 1935 onwards a select group of psychologists, sociologists and anthropologists met together in a series of meetings to discuss the co-ordination of their disciplines and their application to the problems of modern society. Their deliberations resulted in the publication of *The Study of Society* (1939),[2] a set of contributions on the problems and methods of the social sciences. It cannot be said, however, that any very clear pattern or noticeable *entente* emerged from this exercise, and more important perhaps in the long run were the tentative beginnings of practical work.

In 1935 the Pilgrim Trust gave funds to the psychology department of St Andrews University for the study of unemployment in Dundee.

---

[1] B. Malinowski *Myth in Primitive Psychology* (1926).
[2] Edited by F. C. Bartlett, M. Ginsberg, E. J. Lindgren and R. H. Thouless.

Under the direction of O. A. Oeser, then in this country, a decisive advance was made in the direct study of social problems by a team of investigators employing 'functional penetration' as a basic method.[1] Shortly afterwards in 1936 the B.B.C. set up a 'Listener Research' department, and a year later in 1937 the British Institute of Public Opinion and on a more popular level 'Mass Observation' were established.

To some extent, no doubt, the awakening interest in social psychology in the late 1930's was due to Hitler. The corruption of a great people by the Nazi movement raised urgent questions of a social psychological kind. And as a secondary consequence, among the refugees from Germany were some able psychologists and sociologists who stimulated, and gave a new turn to, British intellectual life. Among these the most notable influence on the social sciences was that of Karl Mannheim (1893–1947) who became a lecturer at the London School of Economics. In his *Man and Society* (1940) he stressed the need for a psychology which would be socially and historically relevant. The time indeed was ripe. Mounting international tension and finally the outbreak of war threatened the very structure of society. "War today has become a sentence of death for civilization as we know it", wrote Pryns Hopkins in his *The Psychology of Social Movements* (1938), a sentiment to which nearly every thoughtful person would have been prepared to agree. Had psychologists no light to throw on the psychological roots of war? Freud's *Civilization and its Discontents* (Eng. tr. 1930) had put forward some speculations, and was followed by contributions to the psychoanalytic study of war by British analysts; Edward Glover's *War, Sadism, and Pacifism* (1933), for example, and for a more eclectic standpoint, William Brown's *War and Peace* (1939). E. F. M. Durbin and John Bowlby in *Personal Aggressiveness and War* (1939) reviewed both anthropological and psychological evidence, and D. W. Harding in *The Impulse to Dominate* (1941) wrote an immensely sensitive and balanced "personal attempt to make the problem of war intelligible".

In spite of these developments, and in spite of the contributions to social psychology contained in works primarily devoted to other areas, such as Bartlett's work on remembering, and Susan Isaacs' on child development, social psychology remained a backward area in British psychology, inadequately supported by the universities, starved of research funds and relatively neglected by psychologists themselves. It was not until 1940 that a Social Psychology section of the

[1] O. A. Oeser 'Field Work in Social Psychology', *B. J. Psych.*, XXVII (1937).

British Psychological Society was formed, and not until 1962 that a journal partly devoted to Social Psychology, *The British Journal of Social and Clinical Psychology*, commenced publication.

## 9. Psychoanalytic Derivatives

No branch of psychology was so conspicuously before the public eye, nor aroused such strong feelings between the wars, as the various 'depth' psychologies deriving their main inspiration from Freud. Orthodox psychoanalysis, centred round the London Institute of Psychoanalysis and the figure of Ernest Jones, never indeed gained a wide following in Great Britain, though it recruited some able and distinguished followers, J. C. Flugel, John Rickman, the Quaker, and Adrian Stephen, brother of Virginia Woolf the novelist, for instance. The Kleinian variant likewise, though eventually converting a substantial proportion of British analysts, was too esoteric a doctrine to have much general appeal. But a hybrid, eclectic 'depth' psychology, purged of the more bizarre, 'improper' and pessimistic features of Freudian theory, spread prodigiously, and was to be found in many forms, medical, metaphysical and popular.

Bernard Hart set the fashion with his *Psychology of Insanity* (1912), an immensely successful book reprinted fifteen times before 1940. Soon after the First World War a succession of books put 'depth' psychology on the map: *Instinct and the Unconscious* (1920) and *Conflict and Dream* (1923) by W. H. R. Rivers; *Psychology and Psychotherapy* (1921) followed by a series of more popular books by William Brown; *Psychology and Morals* (1923) by J. A. Hadfield; *Personality* (1926) by R. G. Gordon; *An Outline of Abnormal Psychology* (1926) by William McDougall; *Problems of Psychopathology* (1927) by T. W. Mitchell; and the various writings of Crichton Miller, Emanuel Miller and Millais Culpin, to mention but a few of the more noteworthy. Perhaps also deserving special mention is *The New Psychology and its Relation to Life* (1920) written by a distinguished botanist, A. G. Tansley, F.R.S., later Professor of Botany at Oxford, who had been analysed by Freud immediately after the war. His book went through ten impressions in five years and did much to popularize a biologically orientated, somewhat diluted form of psychoanalysis.

Among the group of eclectic 'depth' psychologists there was no uniform body of doctrine nor central organization. They were, however, marked by certain common tendencies, and the Tavistock Clinic and the Medical Section of the British Psychological Society provided them with common fora for discussion. Two main features marked their standpoint: first, their qualified, ambivalent attitude to Freudian teaching; and secondly, their willingness to assimilate concepts and techniques from other sources. McDougall's statements in the Preface of his *Outline of Abnormal Psychology* well exemplify the ambivalence. "I believe that Prof. Freud has done more for the advancement of psychology than any student since Aristotle. . . . I regard much of the current psychoanalytic doctrines as ill-founded and somewhat fantastic." Certain features of Freudian theory – the dynamic unconscious, the principal mental mechanisms (repression, sublimation, etc.), and the stress on conflict – were generally accepted and provided the unifying bonds among the group. Freudian metapsychology, libido theory, and determinism were more often than not rejected, though to varying extents. T. W. Mitchell (1869–1944), a remarkable country G.P., who was editor of the *British Journal of Medical Psychology* from 1922 to 1934, accepted a large part of Freudian teaching, including libido theory and infantile sexuality; while Bernard Hart in his *Psychopathology* (1927) expressed a 'benevolent scepticism' and criticized not only many of the findings but also the methodology of the Freudians. No doubt, as R. G. Gordon pointed out, 'the ultra-sexual veneer' of Freudian theory proved the main stumbling block to the acceptance of full-blooded psychoanalysis. But the criticisms of Rivers, MacCurdy (in his *Problems of Dynamic Psychology*, 1923), Hart and McDougall were more far-reaching than this. The 'pleasure principle' was 'glaringly false' (MacCurdy); the Freudian 'wish' was unacceptable (Rivers); Freud's dream theory was too narrowly conceived (Rivers, Tansley); Freud ignored social purpose and social instincts (Trotter, Suttie).

On to the bowdlerized psychoanalysis which emerged from this critique elements from other sources were generally grafted – instincts from the hormic catalogue, particularly Trotter's 'herd' instinct; 'complexes' from Jung; 'inferiority feelings' from Adler; 'dissociation' from Janet; and the doctrine of 'levels' from Spencer and the neurologists. Above all the whole was diluted with strong doses of conventional 'common sense', and the resulting mixture turned out to be not merely in line with, but a buttress to, idealism and true religion. The final *bouleversement* of Freudian theory is well exemplified in Suttie's *The Origins of Love and Hate* (1935) where love, social not sexual, becomes the central force, while neurosis and aggressive hate are outcomes of 'a tenderness taboo' and separation from maternal affection. Ghost of Pelagius!

This eclectic transmogrification of psychoanalysis was comforting and in its compromises perhaps typically British. The same could not be said of the Kleinian variant to which the label 'British school' has often been attached. Melanie Klein (1882–1960) was born in Vienna and trained in analysis by Ferenczi and Abraham, two of the inner circle of Freudian followers. In 1925, at the invitation of Ernest Jones, she lectured in London on her work as a child analyst. In the following year she settled in London, and remained until the end of her life. In her principal work *The Psychoanalysis of Children* (1932) Mrs Klein described the play techniques by means of which she pushed down the process of analysis to the earliest months of infancy, and the startling results which she obtained. It was precisely the destructive and aggressive impulses which the eclectics tended to explain away upon which Klein laid her principal emphasis. These impulses were predominant in the early months of life, and "an integral part of mental life, even in favourable circumstances". But how they were manifested depended on the dual processes of 'introjection' and 'projection', the 'introjection' of 'objects' into the ego, and the projection of the contents of the ego on to objects. The establishment of these 'object relations' Klein believed to commence 'almost at birth', and the beginnings of super-ego formation, which Freud placed roughly in the fifth year of childhood, to go back to the fifth or sixth month of life. Thus feelings of guilt and the correlated tendency to make reparation have very deep roots in infancy. For Klein the young infant, long before it was weaned, was a dramatic cockpit of warring emotions of the most profound and devastating kind. To the Kleinians this seems a natural development of Freudian theory, an extension not an abnegation of the pristine doctrine. To the orthodox analysts, led after her arrival in this country in 1938 by Anna Freud herself, it appeared of dubious validity. But few British analysts have been unaffected by Kleinian views; Ernest Jones was certainly by no means unfriendly to them, and among child psychologists Susan Isaacs and later Agatha Bowley were close followers. Perhaps Kleinian views derived their greatest general appeal from the fact that, as Guntrip put it, they constituted "a replacement of the outmoded impulse psychology which, once adopted, Freud had never seen fit to abandon, by a new psychology of dynamic structure".[1] It is this tendency that has more recently received further development in the 'object relations' theory of W. R. D. Fairbairn.

The impact of psychoanalytic theory and its derivatives upon general

[1] H. J. S. Guntrip *B. J. Med. Psych.*, XXIX (1956).

psychology, though profound, has been mixed. There has been, and still is, a spectrum of attitudes from the warmly accepting to the implacably hostile. Some academic psychologists have themselves been analysts and made contributions both to psychoanalysis and to normal psychology. Of these J. C. Flugel was the most conspicuous and his writings on the applications of psychoanalysis to family life, social problems, and ethical theory were notable. R. W. Pickford has also done valuable work in both experimental and analytic fields. A considerable and important group of psychologists have accepted some form of modified 'depth' psychology – McDougall, Burt, Pear, Thouless, Sprott and Knight, for example. C. S. Myers, C. W. Valentine and J. Drever snr. were lukewarm and tended to be critical. Finally, there has always been among psychologists, as well as among the ranks of psychiatrists, a small number of the implacably hostile, exemplified a generation ago by the tirade of A. Wohlegemuth, author of *A Critical Examination of Psychoanalysis* (1923), who regarded psychoanalysis as "a confidence trick", an "utter absurdity", devoid of "a shred of proof", and on the contemporary scene by the embittered broadsides of H. J. Eysenck for whom "the answer to the question – what is wrong with psychoanalysis ? – is simple: Psychoanalysis is unscientific". Thus these issues which so deeply influenced the psychological discussions of the inter-war period still remain unsettled!

## 10. Psychical Research

The links between psychical research and academic psychology in Great Britain have been few. Three psychologists have been presidents of the Society for Psychical Research, McDougall in 1920-1, T. W. Mitchell in 1922, and R. H. Thouless in 1942. Burt, Mace, Aveling, William Brown and a few others have shown a polite and more distant interest. The majority have been aloofly sceptical.

None the less some valuable work was carried out by British investigators between the wars. The effect of the First World War was greatly to increase the public interest in psychical phenomena, and in particular in the problem of survival. Membership of the Society for Psychical Research reached a peak in 1920, and books like Sir Oliver Lodge's *Raymond* (1916), in which communications with his son killed in action were reported, were widely read. The aim of the psychical researchers was to check, and if possible test experimentally, the hypothesis that these and other paranormal phenomena were veridical. The medium, Mrs Leonard, through whom young Lodge's communications were believed to be transmitted, later placed them at the disposal of the S.P.R. Not only was a great deal of material obtained under controlled conditions, but experimental studies of considerable psychological interest were undertaken, such as Whately Carington's quantitative studies of trance personalities by means of word association tests. Mrs Leonard and her control, Feda, were one of the subjects of Carington's tests, which revealed what Carington called 'countersimilarity', or a negative correlation, between the medium's personality and the personality of the control.[1] This suggested, though it did not prove, that the control personality might be a repressed part of the medium's own. Another interesting experimental method was the 'book test', in many examples of which Mrs Leonard also played a part. In these tests the medium's control attempted to indicate the contents of a particular page of a particular book unknown to the medium herself. Mr T. Besterman who analysed the results concludes that "all the control experiments in book tests so far devised strongly indicate the presence of some extra-chance factor in the book tests given by Mrs Leonard".[2]

The physical phenomena allegedly produced by some mediums or occurring spontaneously were also a subject of investigation, though with far more dubious results. As Tyrrell notes, all or nearly all physical mediums have been shown to be fraudulent.[3] Even the famous haunted rectory at Borley in Essex, "the most haunted house in England", which Harry Price leased in 1937, and where many observers reported strange sounds, movements and communications, turned out, in spite of all the documentation, to be in the main a hoax.[4]

Less melodramatic, but certainly carrying greater weight among psychologists, were the purely experimental investigations carried out under rigorous conditions and with rigorous statistical checks. Experimental investigations were not, as is sometimes supposed, initiated by Dr Rhine's much publicised *Extra-Sensory Perception* (1934), but go back to the 1880's and the early days of the S.P.R. Sir Oliver Lodge suggested the card guessing method and the mathematical means for assessing the results in 1885 when he was still Professor of Physics in Liverpool.[5] In 1924 Miss Jephson conducted a series of experiments

---

[1] *Proc. S.P.R.*, XLII, XLIII, XLIV.          [2] *Proc. S.P.R.*, XL.
[3] G. N. M. Tyrrell *The Personality of Man*, 218.
[4] For the original account see Harry Price *The Most Haunted House in England* (1940). For the exposure see E. J. Dingwall, K. M. Goldney and T. H. Hall 'The Haunting of Borley Rectory', *Proc. S.P.R.*, LI (1956).
[5] *Proc. S.P.R.*, II.

with playing cards and obtained positive results.[1] In her statistical computation she was advised and assisted by R. A. Fisher. In 1927 a large-scale experiment in paranormal cognition was carried out by the S.P.R. in collaboration with the B.B.C. Objects exposed in the society's rooms and known only to the research officer and agent had to be telepathized by listeners. Neither in this experiment, nor in a subsequent experiment, were any clear positive results obtained. The experiment did, however, lead on to the important work of Soal.

Dr S. G. Soal, a London University mathematician, first became interested in psychical research in 1918 after his younger brother had been killed in action.[2] Influenced by Lodge's *Raymond* he joined the London Spiritualist Alliance and became convinced by a remarkable medium, Mrs Cooper, that paranormal phenomena did take place. Soal, however, became dissatisfied with the credulity of the spiritualists and turned to experimental testing. For many years the results he obtained were consistently negative; nevertheless Soal's conviction in the paranormal never wavered. He took part in the B.B.C. mass experiments; for a time he was associated with Harry Price's so-called 'University of London Council for Psychical Investigation' (set up in 1934 with support from Aveling, Burt, Flugel and Mace among others, but never officially recognized by the University of London); and he carried out card guessing experiments in Burt's laboratory at University College from 1934 to 1939. It was these last experiments, which unlike Rhine's experiments in America seemed to be wholly negative, that ultimately in the case of two subjects, Mrs Stewart and Basil Shackleton, yielded such astonishing results, even though the experiments were carried out under conditions considerably stricter than those of Rhine. It was Carington who suggested to Soal, after the experiments had concluded apparently without results, that he should re-examine his data "in order to ascertain whether any of the percipients had been making significant scores not on the card the agent was looking at, but on the preceding and following cards". Carington had found such 'displacement effects' in a series of picture guessing experiments. Soal, therefore, re-examined his data, and in the cases of Mrs Stewart and Shackleton it was found that significant scores had been obtained on cards one or two places ahead of or behind the card actually focused by the agent. The phenomena of displacement, and in

[1] *Proc. S.P.R.*, XXXVIII.
[2] S. G. Soal 'My 30 Years of Psychical Research', *Proc. S.P.R.*, L (1953).

particular of precognition, were confirmed in later experiments with the same subjects with results significant at astronomical levels.

These findings, of course, raised far-reaching issues of a metaphysical nature. They were not, however, unsupported by other evidence. J. W. Dunne in *An Experiment with Time* (1927) had collected a number of precognitive dreams and to explain them propounded a serial theory of time. And there were a good many spontaneous cases of precognition sifted and recorded by the S.P.R.[1]

In fact the whole of the evidence for psychical or paranormal phenomena, however secure it may be observationally or statistically, is theoretically baffling. No convincing explanations for any of the phenomena have been forthcoming, though Carington, Tyrrell, Broad and others have speculatively attempted to suggest such explanations. Soal with his usual caution would seem to sum the situation up fairly when he said in his F. W. H. Myers Memorial Lecture (1947), "Psychical Research today resembles a number of heaps of material stacked in a builder's yard. Many of the materials for building are there, but no edifice has as yet arisen."

[1] See G. N. M. Tyrrell *The Personality of Man*, chs. 8 and 9.

# CHAPTER XV

## Applied Psychology

### 1. Psychology in World War I

Applied psychology was brought to birth, as far as Great Britain was concerned, in the 1914–18 war. Earlier small-scale ventures in mental testing and in psychotherapy were hardly more than intra-uterine tremors. But the vast and unprecedented convulsion of the Great War confronted the nation within a year with serious psychological problems both at the fronts and in the munitions factories, and it was to meet these problems that applied psychology was born. Three problems, in particular, engaged the attention of psychologists: 'shell-shock', the health of munitions workers, and selection for highly specialized military tasks.

'Shell-shock', as the war neuroses were termed in the First World War, manifested itself almost as soon as the British Army began fighting in France. By December 1914 from seven to ten per cent of officer casualties, and from three to four per cent of other rank casualties, were 'shell-shock' cases. During the whole war the number of such cases was estimated at 80,000. In 1921 some 65,000 ex-servicemen were still receiving disability pensions for 'shell-shock'. The term 'shell-shock' was apparently first used, if not coined, by C. S. Myers, who had proceeded on his own initiative to France in October 1914, to do what he could to help the war effort. In February 1915 he described cases of 'shell-shock' in *The Lancet* and in the following month Myers was appointed to special duties in charge of psychological work with the British Armies in France, a post which he held until November 1917. It was at first believed that 'shell-shock' was a physical result of a nearby shell burst. F. W. Mott, for example, attempted to show that it was caused by minute cerebral haemorrhages, and even though he later came to accept the idea of emotional origin, he devoted a large part of his book to a description of anatomical and cellular charges in the nervous system.[1] Myers was at first influenced by, and partly accepted, this view. It was only later that, in company with most other psychiatrists and psychologists, he became convinced that the symptoms were wholly

---

[1] F. W. Mott *War Neuroses and Shell Shock* (1919).

psychological, though no doubt precipitated by exhaustion and fatigue. This view, which was ably expounded by Professor Elliot Smith (then Dean of the Medical School and Professor of Anatomy at Manchester) and T. H. Pear in *Shell Shock and its Lessons* (1917), had to face the opposition not only of orthodox medicine, but of many of the military. It was indeed not always easy to distinguish 'shell-shock' from 'malingering', or 'anxiety states' from 'cowardice'; and 'cowardice' was a military crime punishable by death. The firing squad, *pour encourager les autres*, was in fact the remedy which some regular officers prescribed. Their views were well represented by Lord Gort, V.C. (later Commander of the British Army in France, 1939–40), in his evidence to the Southborough Committee on 'Shell-shock'.[1] 'Shell-shock' was "a form of disgrace"; it would be "practically non-existent in the face of strong morale and *esprit de corps*"; "officers must be taught man mastership in the same way as horse mastership", and as for "the large number of men who two to three years after the war were still suffering from 'shell-shock' ", most of them "were probably bordering on lunacy before".

There was, of course, an important element of truth in Lord Gort's emphasis on morale. The incidence of 'shell-shock' varied a good deal from unit to unit; it was as the Southborough Committee pointed out "a contagious malady", and firm treatment was quite essential, especially as in the First World War many of the neuroses were of an hysterical nature. Therefore Myers, working in close conjunction with the neurologist Gordon Holmes, recommended that treatment should in the first instance be given in France at army receiving stations fairly near the forward areas. It was found that the majority of cases after spending two to three weeks in these centres could be returned to duty. Only the more serious cases were sent home to England, where a special hospital was established at Maghull, near Liverpool, in December 1914. This famous establishment (later supplemented by hospitals at Netley, Craiglockhart, Denmark Hill, and elsewhere) had an important influence on the development of psychology and psychotherapy, for it was here under the leadership of Lt.-Col. R. G. Rows, that many of our leading psychologists (Rivers, McDougall, Pear, William Brown, etc.) obtained their initiation into the study of functional disorders, and the techniques of psychotherapy. Moreover, it seemed pretty clear that the sexual theory of the psychoanalysts could only be a special theory, not a general theory, of the aetiology of neurosis.

[1] *Report of the War Office Committee of Enquiry into 'Shell-Shock'*, 1922.

Meanwhile on the home front almost equally urgent problems were arising. By 1915 when the battle-fronts had settled down into a nearly stationary position, the war became as much a war of industries as a war of armies. The demand for munitions was almost unlimited. New factories were established; old factories were switched over to war production; new workers, including thousands of women, were recruited, and working hours were drastically increased. British factories before 1914 were working from 48 to 55 hours a week. A year after the war had broken out "the employment of men for 70 to 90 hours a week was common, for over 90 hours not infrequent, and there were even cases in excess of 100". Of 500 boys questioned by one investigator, three-quarters worked between 60 and 70 hours a week, and women were working just as long. The effect of these long hours on the health of the munition workers and consequently on production was so alarming that in September 1915 Mr Lloyd George, then Minister of Munitions, set up a Health of Munitions Workers Committee "to consider and advise on questions of industrial fatigue, hours of labour, and other matters affecting the physical health and physical efficiency of workers in munitions factories and workshops". The committee issued its first report to Mr Winston Churchill, the then Minister, in 1918, having produced in the meantime an interim report, a handbook for circulation to factory managers, and twenty-one memoranda in which the findings of their investigations on hours of work and output, industrial fatigue, the ventilation and lighting of factories, industrial accidents and numerous matters connected with health and welfare were set out. Although the first small beginnings of Industrial Psychology in Germany, France and America date from the decade before the First World War, the thorough field investigations of the Health of Munitions Workers Committee constitute perhaps the most important of all the pioneer studies of the human factor under modern industrial conditions. Their recommendations have even today by no means been fully put into practice. Besides this valuable contribution to the data of industrial psychology and hygiene the work of the committee led to the establishment of three bodies to continue the work instituted in the munitions factories: the Industrial Welfare Society, founded in 1919, the National Institute of Industrial Psychology, established in 1921, and more directly in June 1918 a government body, the Industrial Fatigue Research Board (renamed in 1928, Industrial Health Research Board). To this last body H. M. Vernon (1870–1951), who before the war had been a Fellow of Magdalen College, Oxford, and engaged in teaching and research in physiology, transferred his services. He had been one of the principal investigators of the Health of Munition Workers Committee, and later he summarized many of its findings in his books *Industrial Fatigue and Efficiency* (1921) and *The Health and Efficiency of Munition Workers* (1940). He was to become between the wars one of our leading industrial psychologists.

Finally, and tackled on a much smaller scale – for there was nothing comparable in the British forces to the massive psychological selection procedures adopted by the American Army in 1917 – were certain problems connected with the selection of specialized personnel. For example, the selection of flying personnel began to exercise attention, and Henry Head carried out investigations into the value of tests of ocular muscle balance, vestibular stability, neuro-muscular co-ordination and nervous stability, without, however, arriving at any very positive results. In 1917 when the submarine menace was at its height and new listening devices for submarine detection were invented, the problem of the selection of operators for these listening devices became important. The story of 'H.M.S. *Crystal Palace*' has never been published in full.[1] The original initiative came from Mr A. P. M. (later Sir Arthur) Fleming of Metropolitan-Vickers Ltd, Manchester, who was a member of the 'Lancashire Anti-Submarine Committee'. He approached Pear, who was then at Maghull, asking for information about the psychology of sound localization and the possibility of selecting listeners for manning localization equipment. Pear suggested that Myers be brought back from France for discussions, as Myers had specialized on this problem. Fleming, Pear and Myers next met Commander W. Fisher, who was in charge of Anti-Submarine Measures at the Admiralty, and as a result a laboratory was set up at the Crystal Palace for the selection and training of listeners. Attached to the laboratory were F. C. Bartlett and Miss E. M. Smith of Cambridge, S. Wyatt (a Manchester graduate in psychology, and later investigator to the Industrial Health Research Board) and two musicians (one of whom was Hugh Allen, later Professor of Music at Oxford). Tests of auditory acuity, auditory discrimination and binaural localization were employed as well as tests of intelligence. Some related research work was carried on, mainly in Cambridge, and one paper was published after the war.[2] The problems

---

[1] I am indebted to Sir Frederic and Lady Bartlett and Professor T. H. Pear for this information.

[2] On listening to sounds of weak intensity, see F. C. Bartlett and E. M. Smith *B. J. Psych.*, X (1919).

raised by this war-time work were largely responsible for the auditory researches of H. Banister carried out in Cambridge in the 1920's.[1]

Quite independent of 'H.M.S. *Crystal Palace*' were various laboratory investigations carried out by Spearman. Spearman too became interested in sound localization, and devised an ingenious 'reverser', an arrangement whereby sounds arriving at each ear could be switched to the opposite ear. Although this gadget enormously increased the accuracy of location it does not appear to have been officially adopted. Spearman, assisted by Flugel and Wynn Jones, also carried out investigations on night vision, and on the training of naval gunlayers. Finally, the British Association set up a committee with a grant of £10 for "psychological war research", Burt acting as secretary. Though all this was on a small scale, "the experience so gained", writes Burt, "was useful in 1939".[2]

## 2. Psychological Tests

The psychological test, a standardized measure of human performance, has been an indispensable tool of applied psychology in all its main branches, educational, occupational and clinical, so much so that psychologists working in applied fields have sometimes erroneously been regarded simply as testers. This, of course, is not so; for applied psychology comprises far more than just testing – it is concerned, among other things, with the nature of skills and the processes of learning, with the interaction between man and his environment, both material and social, and with the whole realm of mental hygiene. Nevertheless it remains true that tests are indispensable tools for the psychologist, and that reliable information about the level of human performance is necessary equally in assessing educational progress, vocational potential, and clinical deterioration or rehabilitation.

Though mental tests were born in Great Britain with Galton, and though the marriage of psychological appraisal with statistical methodology is an important British contribution to the whole mental testing movement, the first developments of Galton's initiative were undertaken elsewhere, by J. M. Cattell (who, however, worked for a time in London) in America, by Ebbinghaus, Stern and others in Germany, and by Binet and Simon in France. In Great Britain before the First World War, apart from Spearman's and Burt's major contributions to which reference has already been made, developments were small and haphazard. Some small experiments by schoolteachers; symposia and

---

[1] See Chapter XIV. 4(b).     [2] Personal communication.

reports at the meetings of the British Association; some early experiments with the Binet-Simon Scale; and the construction of some early scholastic scales.[1]

After the First World War there was a moderate blossoming of tests – nothing like that after the Second World War, when few children in the land escaped them – but still fairly considerable. Some education committees experimented with them; the Civil Service in 1920 used a psychological test paper in the examination for women clerks. Among the spate of books and articles mention may be made of P. B. Ballard's *Mental Tests* (1920), C. L. Burt's *Mental and Scholastic Tests* (1921), Ballard's *Group Tests of Intelligence* (1922) (Ballard's books were immensely popular and went through many impressions), and in 1924 the Board of Education's authoritative report, *Psychological Tests of Educable Capacity*, which gave a qualified blessing to the use of intelligence and scholastic tests for educational purposes, and which was followed in 1928 by a comprehensive list[2] of books and articles on psychological tests – an invaluable bibliography of the early material on testing running to over two hundred pages. Meanwhile the National Institute of Industrial Psychology was using tests on a growing scale for vocational guidance and selection. Every aspect of the use of intelligence, educational and vocational tests was reviewed in the contributions edited by H. R. Hamley to the *Year Book of Education* (1935). A rather indiscriminate survey, half of it devoted to personality tests, was contained in R. B. Cattell's *Guide to Mental Testing* (1936); and in 1940 P. E. Vernon with his usual scholarly care reviewed in *The Measurement of Abilities* the techniques of measurement, listed the chief available tests, and critically appraised them.

Only a brief reference to the main types of test in use between the wars can be made here.[3]

### (i) The Binet-Simon Scale

Burt's revision (1921) and the Stanford revision (1916) – after 1929 Burt's unpublished re-standardization was often used – were both extensively used particularly for diagnosing mental deficiency, but also by teachers for scholastic purposes. This applied especially in Scotland, where as a result of the institution of the B.Ed. degree, and the

[1] See *Psychological Tests of Educable Capacity*, (1924) Board of Education, ch. I.

[2] *Board of Education Select List of Books etc., No. 3*, 1928.

[3] For fuller details see P. E. Vernon *The Measurement of Abilities*, 1st. ed., 1940.

requirement (introduced in 1924) of graduation for all male teachers, the teachers were far better trained. The Binet scale was attacked by R. B. Cattell (1936) as being less valid than tests devised according to Spearman principles, but defended by P. E. Vernon (1940) as "a much better measure of everyday intelligence than perfect tests of unadulterated 'g' ".[1] In 1937 an unstandardized English version of the Terman and Merrill revision of Binet was published, and a version of Form L was also produced by Burt. A few years later (1945) the Scottish Council for Educational Research published their revisions in a report edited by Kennedy-Fraser entitled *The Terman-Merrill Intelligence Scale in Scotland*.

(ii) *Performance tests*

Most of the tests used in Great Britain were of American origin, and taken from Pintner and Patterson (1917), Kohs (1923) and Dearborn (1923). Miss Gaws reviewed these tests for the Industrial Fatigue Research Board in 1925 and provided tentative norms.[2] Drever and Collins produced a scale of performance tests (1928) with the testing of deaf children largely in mind. Most of the tests were American, and adequate norms were not available until 1935. Even then P. E. Vernon complained that performance test norms were often unsatisfactory.[3] Further data, however, for several tests was provided by the Scottish Intelligence Survey and published in *An Analysis of Performance Test Scores of a Representative Group of Children* (Godfrey Thomson, 1940).[4]

A second performance scale was devised by W. P. Alexander for his research *Intelligence, Concrete and Abstract* (1935).[5] In addition to the Kohs Block Design and Cube Construction Tests he devised a new test of his own, the 'Passalong'. The battery was held to measure a practical factor, 'F', as well as 'g'.

(iii) *Group tests*

Owing to their use for educational purposes group verbal test of intelligence were relatively numerous and generally well standardized. The most important were Northumberland Tests (G. Thomson,

[1] *I.F.R.B. Report*, 31.
[2] See also P. Vernon 'The Stanford-Binet Test as a Psychometric Method', *Character and Personality*, VI (1937).
[3] P. E. Vernon *B. J. Ed. Psych.*, VII (1937).
[4] Published by the Scottish Council for Educational Research.
[5] *B. J. Psych.*, Mon. Supp. XIX.

1922; Burt, 1925), Simplex Tests (C. A. Richardson, 1922), N.I.I.P.
Group Test 33 (Burt, 1925), Moray House Tests (G. Thomson), and
Cattell Tests (Cattell, 1933–4).

A useful non-verbal test for younger children (six to ten years) and
backward juniors was that compiled by W. G. Sleight.

Just before the war J. C. Raven published his 'Progressive Matrices'
(1938),[1] a perceptual test based on Spearman's noegenetic principles.
This test was adopted on a large scale by the British Armed Services
in 1941 and has proved one of the most valuable of all intelligence tests.

### (iv) *Scholastic tests*

After the initial impetus given by the Ballard and the Burt tests, and
the group tests for attainments in English and Arithmetic contained
in the Northumberland and Moray House batteries, the most important development was the construction by F. J. Schonell and Eleanor
Schonell of a whole range of attainment and diagnostic tests for
spelling, reading, arithmetic and English.[2]

### (v) *Vocational tests*

The most valuable vocational tests were the mechanical aptitude
tests designed and described in his book *Mechanical Aptitude* (1928)
by J. W. Cox. The N.I.I.P. produced a modified version of some of
these tests, designed by D. F. Vincent. Manual Dexterity tests
proved in general disappointing.[3]

### (vi) *Personality tests*

In the field of personality testing British psychologists have shown
nothing like the energy or the optimism of their American colleagues.
P. E. Vernon (born in 1905), who after a Cambridge training spent two
years at Harvard with Gordon Allport, was the principal British
worker. In a joint book with Allport, *Studies in Expressive Movement*
(1931), he reported on the use that could be made of gestures, voice,
handwriting,'etc. in the assessment of personality. Also with Allport he
devised the well-known 'Study of Values' test,[4] designed to measure

---

[1] See L. S. Penrose and J. C. Raven 'A New Series of Perceptual Tests',
*B. J. Med. Psych.*, XVI (1936); and J. C. Raven 'The R.E.C.I. Series of Perceptual Tests', *B. J. Med. Psych.*, XVIII (1939).

[2] F. J. Schonell *Backwardness in the Basic Subjects* (1942); and Schonell's
specialized books on spelling, reading and arithmetic.

[3] See reports 64 and 74 of the Ind. Health Res. Board.

[4] G. Allport and P. E. Vernon *J. Abn. Soc. Psych.*, XXVI (1931).

an individual's main types of value or interest, theoretical, economic, artistic, social, political and religious. Vernon has always been much concerned with the clash between the quantitative and qualitative approaches to personality (see for example his article 'The American *v.* the German approach to the study of personality') [1] and has refused to come down decisively on one side or the other. Thus in his pioneer study of the Rorschach test in Great Britain his principal conclusions were as follows: "The deficiencies of the Rorschach ink-blot method as a psychometric test have been amply demonstrated, in particular the uncertainties and subjectivity of its scoring, the lack of adequate norms, poor reliability, and almost complete lack of scientifically controlled validation. Yet I cannot agree that these deficiencies should lead to its rejection by investigators in the field of personality . . . and I am unable to call to mind any other test of personality or temperamental traits which will tell me as much about my subjects in so short a time as does the Rorschach test. There is no reason why the quantitative and qualitative viewpoints should be irreconcilable." [2] In his later review for the Industrial Health Research Board, *The Assessment of Psychological Qualities by Verbal Methods* (1938), a survey of attitude tests, rating scales and personality questionnaires,[3] Vernon stresses the relative unreliability of these methods compared to tests of abilities, but holds that they are potentially capable of being improved. He expressed doubt, however, of the factor-analytic attempt to describe personality in terms of unitary traits.

Psychological testing between the wars suffered from a number of handicaps. No central organization existed for the control or co-ordination of work on tests, which remained a matter mainly for individual initiative. Means for adequate standardization and validation were often lacking, and techniques of test construction were sometimes primitive. There were, of course, exceptions, and in particular the Moray House Tests which were models both of construction and standardization. There was, moreover, as we now know, a rather naïve faith that tests could measure basic aptitudes more or less uncontaminated by environmental pressures and opportunities. H. Gordon's results based on his experiences in testing canal boat children and gipsy children were

---

[1] P. E. Vernon *B. J. Psych.*, XXIV (1933).
[2] *B. J. Med. Psych.*, XIII (1933).
[3] *I.H.R.B. Report 83*. A good deal of this material was included in his *Personality Tests and Assessments* (1953).

attributed to his use of the Binet tests, and his warning that "mental tests do not measure native ability apart from schooling, except in the case of children under 6 or 7" [1] was little heeded. Similarly A. E. Chapman's conclusions on "The effect of school training and special coaching on intelligence tests" [2] made little impact. Though P. E. Vernon in his important article "Intelligence Test Sophistication" [3] urged that practice effects might be quite large, amounting to 8 points of I.Q. at least, the problem was not squarely faced until the mass eleven-plus testing programmes of the 1950's. Nevertheless in spite of these handicaps the experiences in the construction and use of psychological tests acquired by British psychologists between the wars were of the utmost value and equipped them for the large-scale programmes of the Second World War and after.

## 3. Educational Psychology and Child Study

### (a) *Educational development*

The years 1870 to 1944 were years of revolutionary development in British education, and in some of these developments psychology was to play no small part. There was indeed from the beginning of the twentieth century a growing interaction between education and psychology, so much so that Sir John Adams, speaking no doubt with some slight exaggeration to the Education section of the British Association in 1912, proclaimed that "education has captured psychology" and was providing the major field of activity for psychologists and the principal source of their problems.

In 1870 British education was in a dismal state. The Newcastle Commission which reported in 1861 had revealed the inefficiency of many of the small private schools, which, in default of any comprehensive public system of elementary education, were trying to fill in the gap. Secondary education only existed for the privileged few; technical education was rudimentary; and outside Scotland university education was a luxury. Between 1870, when schools boards were set up to provide elementary education where it was needed, and 1944, when Mr R. A. Butler's Education Act required that all children should receive the type of education, primary and secondary, best suited to their aptitudes, the structure of the education system was gradually worked out. The Board of Education was established in 1899; local education

---

[1] *Board of Educ. Pamphlet 44* (1923).     [2] *Forum of Education*, II (1924).
[3] *B. J. Ed. Psych.*, VIII (1938).

authorities in 1902, by an Act which also provided for local authority grammar schools, new developments in technical education and new teacher training colleges. Equally important was the initiation of the school health service – London taking the lead in 1890, followed by Bradford in 1894, and regulations making medical inspection mandatory in 1907. The first beginnings of public provision for handicapped children also dates from the 1890's. In most of these educational developments Scotland, which has its own system of education, has been a jump ahead of England. In particular from 1906 onwards Scotland has required all teachers to be trained for their job. Scotland, too, long preceded England in establishing university chairs of education, the Edinburgh chair dating from 1876, while the first English chair, at Manchester, dates only from 1899. These facts have a bearing on the development of educational psychology in the two countries.

The heroic nature of the educational advances of this period should never be underestimated. Ballard's picture of the east-end school in London, where in 1887 he taught a class of 75 boys, gives an idea of the obstacles which had to be overcome. "Schooling in those days was a grim business. The annual examination was the big controlling factor which kept the children's bodies within the four walls of the school and their minds within the confines of books and lessons. There was no medical inspection, no handicraft, no domestic science, no organized game, no educational visit, no school journey, no segregation of the mentally and physically unfit – nothing but a dismal grind for the great annual event. Here were children who were dirty and needed washing, sickly and needed sunshine and open air, inarticulate and needed human speech, unmannerly and needed human graces, unhappy and needed the joy of childhood." [1] In 1938 the Board of Education's report, *The Primary School*, could state with some justification, "few features in the history of the last thirty years are more striking or more inspiring than the improvements in the health, the manners, the level of intellectual attainment, the vitality and the happiness of the rising generation".[2]

These developments were the necessary foundation for the rise of educational psychology, which was indeed in many respects their logical fulfilment. Fortunately the men to take advantage of the opportunities were forthcoming at several centres. First there was the remarkable

---

[1] Quoted in the tribute to Ballard by A. G. Hughes *B. J. Ed. Psych.*, XVI (1951).

[2] See *The Health of the School Child* (1958) for a detailed account of the progress over 50 years.

was "to provide permanent yet continuously modified physiological dispositions which, acting in co-operation with the immediate clues, can endow perception with the determinativeness of which we are in fact aware". The schemata were in fact in Head's theory a sort of postural model built up largely by experience and serving as a frame of reference for skilled movement. There was a good deal that was vague in Head's concept, but it made room for two things that were needed and which reflex theory did not provide, firstly, organizational patterning, and secondly, central control. It was F. C. Bartlett in his book on *Remembering* (1932) who translated the schema to psychology and to the data of consciousness. Past experiences were organized in schemata; in this way the past could act as a whole and could be matched with the present. Moreover, at the conscious level, the level of images and words, the subject could 'turn round' on his schemata, could single out items from the temporal matrix and free intelligence from its bondage to the passing of time. Wolters[1] employed the schema to explain the phenomena of concept formation in terms more biological, and less philosophically abstract, than 'ideas'. As Northway has pointed out[2] the concept of the schema is a complex one, involving the storing of experience, organization, and executive functions. It bears some resemblance to the older concept of 'apperceptive mass'; and obviously links with newer concepts such as 'phase sequences' (Hebb) and 'plans' (G. A. Miller). It has also some affinity with Gestalt, though derived from the study of movements rather than of perceptions.

By 1940 these theoretical trends had led to a wide divergence between British and American psychology. In an American textbook such as Woodworth's *Psychology* (1935) only some five per cent of the bibliographical references were to British work; in a British textbook, such as Thouless's *General and Social Psychology* (1937), only about fifteen per cent of the references were to American work. Outside the field of psychometrics there were few close links between the psychologists of the two countries. While American psychology showed an increasing concern with problems of methodology and with operational definitions, and traditional concepts were subjected to a fierce criticism, British psychologists remained mainly faithful to the older ways of thought. In America there was a growing concentration of research on the topic of learning, and serious attempts to tackle the problem fundamentally in its simplest forms using animals as subjects. In Britain learning was largely

[1] A. W. Wolters *B. J. Psych*, XXIV (1933).
[2] M. L. Northway *B. J. Psych.*, XXX (1940).

groups of inspectors attached to the London County Council, who were not only instrumental in the appointment of Burt in 1913 as the first educational psychologist, but who in their own right made important contributions to the subject: C. W. Kimmins (1856–1948), chief inspector at the L.C.C. from 1904 to 1923 and author of several psychological works; P. B. Ballard (1865–1950), popularizer of testing and discoverer of the 'reminiscence' effect;[1] W. H. Winch (1864–1935) who made pioneer contributions to educational research; and A. G. Hughes, part author of one of the most successful British textbooks of educational psychology, *Learning and Teaching* (1st ed. 1937, 21st impression 1959).

Secondly, there was the staff of the London Day Training College, founded in 1902 and reconstituted as the University of London, Institute of Education in 1932; Sir John Adams (1857–1934), a Scotsman who through his *Herbartian Psychology applied to Education* (1897) did much to undermine the old theories of formal discipline; Sir Percy Nunn (1870–1944) who succeeded Adams in 1922 and whose *Education, its Data and First Principles* (1920) was perhaps the most influential educational treatise of its day; Burt; H. R. Hamley (1883–1949); and Susan Isaacs (1885–1948) who joined the Institute in 1933 to take charge of a new department of child development.

Thirdly, in Scotland, where the Scottish tradition of education provided favourable ground for psychological developments, strong centres developed both in Edinburgh and Glasgow. In Edinburgh Godfrey Thomson (1881–1955) took up his chair at the Moray House Training College in 1925 and, supported by J. Drever snr. at the University, created a centre influential far beyond Scotland. In Glasgow were William Boyd (1874–1962), head of the department of education in the University from 1907 to 1946, who did much to introduce psychological tests to teachers and pioneered child guidance; R. R. Rusk (born 1879), one of the first post-graduate students at the Cambridge laboratory, lecturer at Jordanhill Training College, and Director of the Scottish Council of Educational Research from its inception in 1928 to 1958; and D. Kennedy-Fraser (1886–1962), who initiated the local authority psychological service in 1923.

Finally, some departments of education in the English provincial universities showed more than a polite and academic acknowledgement of psychology. Outstanding among these was Birmingham where C. W. Valentine (born in 1879), a Cambridge graduate in psychology, was

[1] See Chapter XIV, sect. 4.c.

Professor of Education from 1919 to 1946, becoming one of the leading figures in educational and child psychology, and editing from 1923 to 1930 *The Forum of Education* and from 1931 to 1956 its successor, *The British Journal of Educational Psychology*. When Valentine retired in 1946 the psychological tradition of the department was maintained first by F. J. Schonell and then by E. A. Peel.

(b) *New ideals in education*

In the history of educational thought there has been a natural alliance between psychology and progressive trends in education. For these progressive trends have usually been 'child-centred', and regarded education not as an enforced imposition, but as a natural process of growth and development; and this point of view is almost by definition psychological. As far back as 1693 John Locke, though Spartan in some of his prescriptions, deplored "the usual lazy and short way by chastisement and the rod, which is the only instrument of government that tutors generally know, or ever think of",[1] and held that "children must be tenderly used and must play and have playthings". Herbert Spencer, in one of his best books, *Education, Intellectual, Moral, and Physical* (1861), likewise advocated freedom and play, and urged that education should be based on the laws of child development. Several nineteenth-century psychologists grasped the potential value of psychology in its applications to education and wrote psychological textbooks for teachers – Bain, Ward,[2] Lloyd Morgan and Sully, for example – and in the first decade of the twentieth century several works aimed at the new training colleges and university schools of education made their appearance. Unfortunately, the psychology that they endeavoured to impart was the largely philosophical psychology current at the time, and psychology, as Sir John Adams observed, acquired a reputation for "everything that is dull and unreadable".

Sir John Adams himself broke the barriers with his *Herbartian Psychology applied to Education*[3] (1897) – in spite of its title a most lively book containing, as Rusk has said, "more of Adams than of Herbart".[4] By placing 'interest' in the centre of the educational picture,

---

[1] *Some Thoughts concerning Education.*

[2] Ward's *Psychology Applied to Education*, though not published until 1926, was based on lectures delivered in 1880.

[3] The German philosopher and psychologist J. F. Herbart (1776–1841) had a considerable influence on both Ward and Stout and through them on British psychology at the turn of the century. See Stout's articles in *Mind*, XIII and XIV (1888–9).

[4] R. R. Rusk *B. J. Educ. Stud.*, X (1961).

and by questioning the generally accepted notions of formal training, it had a stimulating effect on educational thought. It did not shock educational feelings by disparaging the intellect, and it made teachers realize the importance of a clearly worked out psychology as the basis of educational theory.

Even more influential were the new ideals of infant teaching, largely continental in origin, and partly psychologically inspired, which spread to England in the later part of the nineteenth and early years of the twentieth centuries. The first kindergarten in England based on Froebel's ideas indeed goes back as far as 1854. The Froebel Society was founded in 1874 and their journal *Child Life* commenced publication in 1899. The Froebelians had a considerable part to play in awakening interest in the natural development and activity of the child. Just before the First World War a new impetus came with the teachings of Maria Montessori, the Italian psychiatrist, who as a result of her experiences in teaching mentally defective children, devised a new scheme of 'didactic material' to train sensory discrimination and motor activity. A Montessori Society was established in this country, and Montessori schools opened. A Board of Education pamphlet described the system as early as 1912 and educational conferences were devoted to discussing it. Perhaps Montessori's condemnation of classroom teaching did more than anything to break down the regimentation of traditional schooling. Less doctrinaire, and probably sounder in its belief in the value of the child's imaginative activities, was the nursery school movement started by Margaret Macmillan (1860–1931). Her first open-air nursery school at Deptford and her book *Education through the Imagination* both date from 1913. "Margaret Macmillan", wrote Cyril Burt after her death, "somehow managed to integrate in a kind of synoptic vision a practical synthesis of child psychology, child medicine, and child training in an inspired educational plan."[1] Her methods and aims had a profound effect on nursery education in this country.

Gradually these ideals spread from the nursery world to the higher regions of education. After the First World War came the Dalton Plan from the U.S.A. – which broke down for older age groups, as Montessori did for the younger, the regimentation of the classroom – as well as a growing number of experimental schools: Homer Lane's 'Little Commonwealth' for delinquents; Summerhill, started in Germany in 1921 by A. S. Neill, and later transferred to England; Beacon Hill, run by Bertrand and Dora Russell; the Malting House School, Cambridge,

[1] In G. A. N. Lowndes *Margaret Macmillan* (1960).

under Susan Isaacs, to mention only some of the better known. A good many of these schools were short lived; some of them depended as much, or more, on the personalities of their founders as on any principles involved. The principles indeed were often slight or iconoclastic. Homer Lane's prescription for Utopia in the nursery was to "abolish three adjectives – naughty, nasty, dirty". According to Russell what was required was "a reversal of much of the practice of nurses and ignorant mothers" – "the driving force in education should be the pupil's wish to learn, not the master's authority".[1] A. S. Neill, who won some notoriety with his books *The Problem Child* (1928) and *The Problem Parent* (1932), held it was necessary to "renounce all discipline, all direction, all suggestion, all moral training, all religious instruction". Neill's school, however, though always a small one, was still flourishing forty years later, and even if based on a highly questionable interpretation of the early versions of psychonanalysis, has undoubtedly achieved successes.[2]

In a modified and diluted form these progressive ideas came increasingly to dominate educational thinking between the wars, and even obtained the blessing of the Board of Education. Nunn's influential book, *Education, its Data and First Principles* (1920), paved the way. Nunn was a man of intellectual power and eminence. He had been President of the Mathematical Association in 1915, and was to become President of that highbrow and select philosophical body, the Aristotelian Society, in 1923. He had made important contributions to the teaching of mathematics. His views could not lightly be disregarded. When, therefore, he proclaimed that 'individuality' was the ideal of life, and maintained that "in the understanding of play lies the key of most of the problems of education", people, even teachers, began to listen. In spite of counter-attacks from the disciplinarians and the traditionalists C. W. Kimmins could proclaim, perhaps somewhat prematurely, just before the Second World War, *The Triumph of the Dalton Plan*, and state that its principles "justify themselves as being a psychologically sound approach to the education of a child"; and the Board of Education report on *The Primary School* (1935) came down in favour of the new trends. "A good school is not a place of compulsory instruction, but a community of old and young, engaged in learning by co-operative experiments." There should be provision of ample opportunities for healthful activity as part of its normal work, and "liberal opportunities for individual work under the guidance of the teacher",

[1] B. Russell *On Education* (1926).       [2] See A. S. Neill *Summerhill* (1962).

while "the experience, the curiosity, and the awakening powers and interests of the children themselves" must be the starting point of the educative process.

There is no doubt that these new ideals in education were partly inspired by, and came in the public mind to be closely identified with psychology. This identification, though not unjustified, had its dangers. For psychology in its essence is neither a creed, nor a body of ideals, but a tested, ever developing, corpus of knowledge. Susan Isaacs sounded a salutary warning. Influenced in part by her experience from 1924 to 1927 at the Malting House School, and in part by her conversion to the newer psychoanalytic doctrines of Melanie Klein with their emphasis on the aggressive and destructive components of the child's mind, she criticized the exaggerated notions of freedom and the garbled psychoanalytic teaching which ignored the burden of guilt in the child's mind accruing from unrestricted activity. What the child wanted was "a settled framework of control and routine, and definite help along personal paths, yet with ample personal freedom". Some repression was "essential to a balanced conscious life and adaptation to reality".[1] In spite of these warnings, however, Susan Isaacs remained a progressive force: "The educator cannot teach the child, nor can he learn for him. All he can do is to create such situations as will give the child opportunities to learn for himself." The ultimate emphasis is on the spontaneity of the child.

In the controversy between the older notion of regimented classroom discipline and the newer ideals of a freer, child-centred education, clearly what was wanted was an experimental test, and here D. E. M. Gardner's *Testing Results in the Infant School* (1942) pointed the way. Applying a variety of scholastic and social measures in eighteen schools (six experimental 'child-centred' and twelve conventional) she came to the conclusion that the children from the experimental schools were clearly superior in creative activities and social behaviour, and, in spite of the fact that the amount of time devoted to formal instruction was less, their performance in the basic scholastic subjects was not significantly different from that of the children in the conventional schools. These later showed no evidence of superiority in any direction, except in minor ways such as handwriting at the age of six, a superiority, however, not maintained a year later. The new ideals in education seemed, in short, to be justifying themselves, not only psychologically, but also academically.

[1] Isaacs *Social Development in the Young*.

c) *Experimental pedagogy and educational research*

The first beginnings of 'experimental pedagogy' in England were, like so much else, inspired by Galton. C. H. Lake, headmaster of a school in Chelsea, applied psychological tests to his pupils in 1881. A few years later Sophie Bryant, headmistress of Campden High School and a founder member of the British Psychological Society, reported her 'Experiments in Testing Schoolchildren'.[1] Galton himself in 1888 invited members of the teachers' guild to contribute to a study of mental fatigue. The big developments, however, took place abroad, in particular in America and in Germany. In the U.S.A. Stanley Hall founded his *Pedagogical Seminary* in 1891 – "seminary and laboratory are now perhaps the noblest words in the vocabulary of higher education", he asserted in its first volume; and in Germany E. Meumann started the *Zeitschrift für experimentelle Pädagogik* in 1905. There followed Meumann's two-volume treatise in 1907, and in the U.S.A. Thorndike's huge *Educational Psychology* (3 vols. 1913–14).

In this field Great Britain soon lagged distinctly behind. The first issue of *The Journal of Experimental Pedagogy* (which was the direct ancestor of our present *British Journal of Educational Psychology*) appeared in 1911, edited by Professor J. A. Green of Sheffield. A certain amount of preliminary work had been done by the Child Study Associations; there were departments of education (springing from the Day Training Colleges established in the 1890's) in most of the provincial universities; and a nucleus of psychologically trained educationalists to provide the necessary stiffening. The early numbers of the *Journal* contain articles by Spearman, Burt, Ballard, Winch, William Brown, Sleight, Drever, Rusk and others. Experimental pedagogy, as Rusk pointed out in his comprehensive and scholarly work, *Experimental Education* (1919), was not simply experimental psychology. It had a special subject matter of its own in the school situation. But its scientific standing depended upon the adaptation of techniques evolved in the psychological laboratory; upon the application of statistical methods; and upon the development of mental tests. Its links with psychology have, therefore, always been intimate.

The progress of educational research – as it has generally been termed, rather than experimental pedagogy, since the First World War – in Great Britain has been sketched more than once, by Winch, by Rusk, and by Schonell, and its haphazard and unco-ordinated nature

[1] *J. Anthrop. Inst.*, XV (1886).

noted. It was in fact mostly carried out by postgraduate students and by part-timers, and carried out on a shoestring. Rusk urged that "the research movement must have a local habitation and a name, and must employ permanent officials devoting themselves exclusively to its administration. This implies the establishment of a Bureau or Institute of Educational Research."[1] Scotland got this, largely owing to Rusk's efforts, in 1928; England not until the establishment of the National Foundation for Educational Research in 1945. Before these bodies were set up, attempts to co-ordinate research devolved upon various committees – the British Association Committee on "mental and physical factors involved in education" (1909), the research committee of the Educational Institute of Scotland (1919), and the British Psychological Society Committee of Research in Education, set up in 1923 with Mrs S. Brierley (Susan Isaacs) as secretary. But without full-time personnel and with negligible or no funds at their disposal these committees could not do a great deal, and Winch could write in 1927 that "with the possible exception of France there is less provision for educational research (in Great Britain) than in any of the leading countries in the world".[2]

The establishment of the Scottish Council for Educational Research in 1928 was certainly a landmark, not only because it was a recognition of the need for a permanent co-ordinating body, but also for the first-class job of work it did from its inception. Its achievements, indeed, before the Second World War considering its limited budget (its annual income averaged about £1,500) was truly remarkable. It published in a space of twenty years, under Rusk's direction, no less than thirty reports, many of them of the highest value and technical excellence.

It is impossible in a brief space adequately to describe the educational research work of the inter-war period,[3] largely because of its fragmentary nature. Certain main topics only of special interest to psychologists can be selected for brief mention.

(i) *Formal training*

The problem of formal training very early began to interest educationalists, and indeed was a continuing interest throughout the inter-war period; particularly as it had a bearing on the place of some of

[1] Rusk *Research in Education*, (1932) 79.
[2] Winch op. cit., 13.
[3] See Schonell's articles in the *B. J. Ed. Psych.*, XVIII–XXII, for a fairly full account, and C. M. Fleming *Research and the Basic Curriculum* (1946). Also *A List of Researches in Education and Educational Psychology*, A. M. Blackwell (National Foundation for Educational Research, 1950).

the traditional subjects, like Latin,[1] in the school curriculum. The whole topic, however, was early bedevilled by conflicting results and dubious conclusions. Formal training was, of course, the traditional theory springing originally from faculty psychology – the idea that memory, powers of observation, imagination, and so on, could be trained by formal exercises devoid in themselves of any other intrinsic value. It was the theory which served to justify the dullest of scholastic disciplines – they were good for the training of the mind. Psychologists of the newer schools began, however, to question this doctrine. Bain cast doubt on it – "most definitions of training are obscured through the mode of describing mind by faculties".[2] In America first William James, then Thorndike and Woodworth carried out experiments which seemed to show that memory and learning were highly specific, and that training led to no general improvement. Meumann in Germany, however, got contradictory results, and British investigators soon began to play a part in the controversy.

W. H. Winch obtained results which supported Meumann.[3] He set out to discover whether training in rote memory for nonsense material had any effect on substance memory for meaningful material. He found a considerable transfer effect: similarly, some years later, with reasoning processes. W. G. Sleight, a pupil of Spearman's and lecturer in education under the L.C.C., reinvestigated the matter with methodological improvements and came to the reverse conclusion,[4] that there appeared to be no general memory improvement as a result of practice, and that any transfer that took place was dependent on 'useable common elements', in material, method of presentation, method of learning or attendant circumstances. This was broadly the conclusion reached by the British Association Committee, which included Burt, Nunn, Pear, and Godfrey Thomson among its members in their report on 'Formal Training' in 1930. Research, however, continued. G. P. Meredith of Leeds carried out an important experiment in which groups of pupils were required to define terms.[5] One group got mechanical practice in defining; a second group were trained in the basic principles involved in definition; a third group

---

[1] In this connexion see C. W. Valentine *Latin: its Place and Value in Education* (1935).
[2] A. Bain *Education as Science*, 139.
[3] W. H. Winch *B. J. Psych.*, II (1908), III (1910), XVII (1923).
[4] W. G. Sleight 'Memory and Formal Training', *B. J. Psych.*, IV (1931); *Education, its Value and Methods* (1915).
[5] G. P. Meredith *Forum of Educ.*, V (1927).

acted as a control. The group which got mechanical practice showed no improvement in general; the group given training in principles showed large and significant improvement. A similar conclusion was reached by J. W. Cox in the experiments reported in *Manual Skill* (1934). Skill developed by mechanical practice failed to transfer to other operations. But "a specially devised scheme of training which aimed at giving the subject insight into the best way to use his fingers" brought about marked transfer effects.

In spite of this experimental work – and in America its volume was many times as great as in this country – Hamley, writing in 1936,[1] concluded that there was a "dearth of well-planned and executed research", and Meredith commented in 1941 on the "difficult and elusive" nature of the problem.[2] There were indeed lessons in all this: first, the importance of experimental design; and secondly, quite as essential but even more often neglected, the importance of conceptual clarity. No doubt Meredith in his 1941 article laid his fingers on at least one of the troubles – that "at least seven different problems have been investigated under the heading 'transfer of training' . . . the phrase has shifted, often unnoticed, among its seven or more meanings".

## (ii) *Surveys of intelligence*

Though Burt had carried out surveys on a considerable scale in London, and Godfrey Thomson in Northumberland, the first large scale survey of the distribution of intelligence in the population, covering more than a single locality, was that carried out on behalf of the Joint Mental Deficiency Committee (Wood Committee) of the Boards of Education and Control by Dr E. O. Lewis between 1925 and 1927.[3] Lewis was one of the early Cambridge graduates in psychology and had lectured in the subject at St. Andrews before becoming medically qualified and being appointed a medical inspector of the Board of Control. The aim of his investigation was, of course, primarily to determine the number of mental defectives in the community. To this end six sample areas, three urban and three rural, each with a population of about 100,000, were selected. Otis group intelligence tests were given in the schools, and Burt's version of the Binet-Simon test to suspected defectives. In all some 66,000 persons were tested;

---

[1] H. R. Hamley *B. J. Ed. Psych.*, VI (1936).
[2] G. P. Meredith *Occ. Psych.*, XV (1941).
[3] *Report of the Mental Deficiency Committee*, (1928) pt. IV.

and the number of defectives estimated at 8·57 per 1,000 of the population, about three times the number actually ascertained by the authorities.

The survey of *The Intelligence of Scottish Children* (1933) carried out by the Scottish Council for Research in Education followed on from Lewis's work, but the Council wisely decided to get a complete cross-section of the Scottish school population. Therefore, in the first week of June 1932 every child born in 1921 and attending school in Scotland was tested with a modified Moray House Intelligence Test. In all 87,498 children took the test (91·12 per cent of the children on the registers). In addition at Shepherd Dawson's insistence a sample of 1,000 children were tested on the Stanford Binet. The whole survey was repeated using the same group test, but with the Terman and Merrill (Form L) version of the Binet, in 1947 and reported in *The Trend of Scottish Intelligence* (1949). The investigation was in many ways a model of experimental design, and its data on the distribution of intelligence of unique value. The second report did much to lay to rest the fears and predictions of a rapid decline in national intelligence.

### (iii) *The examination of examinations*

It was not unnatural that psychologists who had become versed in the processes of standardizing and validating psychological tests, and accustomed to statistical concepts like norm and reliability, should turn a critical eye on the conventional type of scholastic examination. As Ballard put it, "the mental tester is a reformer of examinations".[1] F. Y. Edgworth, the statistician, had produced evidence as far back as 1888 of the unreliability of the results of competitive examinations. There were enough data by 1918 for Hartog to write a book, and for Ballard to advocate the merits of new style examinations of the objectively scorable type. Experimental work followed. Boyd in 1924 got 271 teachers in Glasgow to grade a set of essays on 'A day at the seaside' written by 26 eleven-year-old children.[2] The grading was a seven-point one: nearly every essay was placed in six of the seven possible grades, although the essays had been chosen originally as differing markedly in merit. A more extensive enquiry was reported by Valentine and Emmett in a book which, as Valentine himself later agreed, should have been entitled 'the validity', not *The Reliability*

[1] P. B. Ballard *The New Examiner* (1923).
[2] W. Boyd *Measuring Devices in Composition, Spelling and Arithmetic* (1924).

*of Examinations* (1932). For Valentine and Emmett asked how far the results of grammar school and university scholarship examinations were validated by subsequent performance. The results were disquieting. For example, at the university level roughly two-fifths failed to justify their promise, obtaining only third class honours or pass degrees.

A larger enquiry on an international scale followed. In May 1931 an international conference on examinations was held at Eastbourne under the auspices of the Carnegie Corporation. Delegates from England, Scotland, France, Germany, Switzerland and U.S.A. attended. As a result of the conference committees were set up in the participating countries to carry out investigations in their respective territories. The Scottish committee, working through the Scottish Council for Research in Education, undertook and published a study of *The Prognostic Value of University Entrance Examinations* (1937), and a study of *Selection for Secondary Education* (1942). The English committee, under Sir Michael Sadler's chairmanship, included Ballard, Burt, Hamley, Hartog, Nunn, Spearman, Thomson and Valentine, and was responsible for initiating a number of experimental and statistical enquiries into both written examinations and interviews. The results reported in *An Examination of Examinations* (1935) and *The Marks of Examiners* (1936)[1] showed again disquieting evidence of unreliability. Thus in 'special place' examinations in English and Arithmetic in which 150 candidates were competing for 50 grammar school places, there was agreement among the 10 examiners on only 33 of the awards. Vernon has suggested that "Hartog and Rhodes doubtless desired to shock the public conscience . . . and so did their best to emphasize the disagreements". Nevertheless disagreements there certainly were, and in the problem which became urgent after the passing of the Education Act of 1944 – the problem of the allocation of pupils to different types of secondary education – this evidence no doubt was one of the factors that led to the widespread adoption by local education authorities of standardized tests after the Second World War.

(iv) *Selection for secondary education*

The problem of selection for secondary education was already beginning to exercise the attention of psychologists between the wars. In 1907 the Board of Education passed a regulation requiring all

[1] P. Hartog, and E. C. Rhodes.

secondary schools in which fees were charged to offer a proportion of 'free' or 'special' places to pupils from elementary schools, as a condition of their continuing to receive public funds. Some authorities had in fact made such provision on a limited scale from 1889 onwards. To ensure the maintenance of academic standards applicants for free places had to pass an entrance test. By 1918 thirty per cent of the places in grant-aided grammar schools were 'free'. Normally these 'free place' examinations were held at the age of elevenplus. In Scotland the corresponding 'qualifying examination' was usually a year later. The selection of the top 5 per cent or so of elementary school pupils for 'free places' was obviously a delicate operation, and it was soon apparent that the usual scholastic examinations could be extremely unjust to pupils handicapped by poor teaching or an uncultured home background. The use of intelligence tests, which were widely held to test innate, general ability, seemed to offer a much fairer method of selection. The city of Bradford adopted a group test of intelligence for this purpose in 1919. In 1921 Godfrey Thomson, at that time Professor of Education in Newcastle-on-Tyne, became concerned at the apparent inequalities of selection among Northumbrian children. Nearly one-third of the elementary schools, Thomson noted, sent no children forward for a grammar school education, and these schools were mainly those in remote country districts. It seemed possible that the scholastic examinations which were then employed for 'free place' selection were biased against rural children. Thomson's Northumberland Intelligence Tests showed that this was so;[1] that there were many intelligent children in rural areas who were failing to obtain places, and that a better selection could be obtained by the use of intelligence tests. Later Thomson moved to Moray House Training College in Edinburgh, and the Moray House Tests which he and his assistants devised became used for selection purposes in many parts of the country.

Meanwhile further experiments had been carried out by various investigators and again by Thomson himself in Yorkshire tending to show that the intelligence test was the best single prognostic test,[2] and that combined with standardized tests for English and Arithmetic it materially improved upon the conventional type of examination.

[1] Thomson *B. J. Psych.*, XII (1922).
[2] See P. B. Ballard 'The Use of Intelligence Tests in selecting Children for Secondary Schools', *Human Factor*, XI. 3 (1937).

The matter was taken up further by the Scottish Council for Research in Education on behalf of the International Examinations Enquiry. Professor McClelland of St Andrews University was in charge of the investigation,[1] which involved following up all those leaving the junior primary schools in Dundee during 1935–6, and comparing intelligence tests, teachers' estimates, and scholastic qualifying examination marks with subsequent performance in the secondary school. The analysis showed that the best predictor was I.Q. plus qualifying examination plus teachers' estimate. The best single predictor, however, was not the intelligence test, but a 'carefully set and corrected examination'.

Concurrently with these investigations discussions were being held by Committees of the Board of Education into the whole structure of secondary education. A series of notable reports, to which psychologists, particularly Burt, contributed much evidence, were issued. The Hadow report (1927), the Spens report (1938) and the Norwood report (1943) prepared the ground for the Education Act of 1944, which required that all children should receive secondary education suited to their abilities, and proposed three main types of school, grammar, technical and modern, to which children should be allocated at eleven-plus. It was hoped that these schools would have 'parity of esteem'. With the selection and allocation problems this scheme gave rise to, we are not here concerned. But it should be noted that psychologists, who are in the public mind sometimes held responsible for 'the eleven-plus', were uneasy from the start at the way the evidence had been interpreted and with the tripartite scheme that emerged.[2]

### d) *Child study and child guidance*

In the 1890's following the pioneering work of Darwin, Galton and Sully, there was a quickening of interest in the problems of child development. A contributory factor in this awakening was no doubt the shocking condition of many of the children herded into the new 'Board Schools' of the 1880's. In 1888 the British Medical Association set up a committee to enquire into the "average development and condition of brain power among schoolchildren". The Charity Organization Society

[1] W. McClelland 'Selection for Secondary Education', *S.C.R.E. Report*, XIX (1942).
[2] See Olive Wheeler 'Modern Psychology and the Spens Report', *B. J. Ed. Psych.*, IX (1939); C. Burt 'The Psychological Implications of the Norwood Report', *B. J. Ed. Psych.*, XIII (1943).

in 1891 issued a report of an inspection of 50,000 London schoolchildren which so appalled the members of the International Congress
of Hygiene and Demography that a more extensive enquiry under the
chairmanship of Sir Douglas Galton (cousin of Francis Galton) was
initiated. The resulting report published in 1894 revealed once again
the large volume of physical and mental retardation and a lack of adequate provision for handicapped children of all sorts. In 1896 the Childhood Society was formed to continue investigations into physical and
mental development.[1]

Meanwhile in 1894 a rival body, The British Child Study Association, had been founded as a direct result of contact between a group of
British lady teachers and Stanley Hall, the American psychologist,
during the World Fair held in Chicago in the year 1893.[2] A meeting was
called in Edinburgh in August 1894 and the Association founded with
branches in Edinburgh, London, Cheltenham and later in several other
British cities. Miss Louch of Cheltenham Ladies' College, who had been
one of the British representatives at the World Fair, was one of the
moving spirits, and Sully,[3] Dr Langdon and T. S. Clouston, the
Edinburgh psychiatrist, became early supporters. A central council was
established in 1898, and a journal founded in 1899, *The Paidologist*
(renamed in 1908 *Child Study*). In 1907 the Childhood Society and the
Child Study Association amalgamated to form the Child Study Society
which continued in being until January 1948, though the journal *Child
Study* ceased publication in 1921.

There is no doubt that the child study movement did some useful
educational work, and the early numbers of the journal contain some
important articles by persons of standing – Sully, Burt, W. Boyd,
W. H. Winch, for example. But it was also responsible for much
amateur work, and its methods were at times undiscriminating. There
was a somewhat naïve belief that records kept and questionnaires an-
swered by mothers could provide scientifically reliable material. C. S.
Myers[4] in 1910 lodged a protest against the "collecting of masses of
psychological data with the help of an army of untrained observers",

[1] I am indebted to Dr Caw's article for these facts, 'Child Study Fifty
Years Ago', *Bulletin of the B.P.S.*, 3 (1949).
[2] K. Stevens 'Child Study in Great Britain', *Ped. Sem.*, XIII (1906).
[3] I can find no evidence for the commonly stated view that Sully himself
'founded the Child Study Association'. He was, however, the first president of
the London Branch of the Association and played a prominent part in its early
days.
[4] Brit. Ass., Sheffield, 1910.

and W. H. Winch expressed the view[1] that the "extravagances and inutilities" of the child study movement had raised a prejudice against educational research.

For a contemporary account of the aims and achievements of the movement we may refer to W. B. Drummond's *An Introduction to Child Study* (1907). Drummond was a physician at the Edinburgh Hospital for Sick Children and he himself was scientifically trained. But he wrote at length about 'the framing of a syllabus' (by which he means a plan of investigation) for use by relatively untrained persons, and included a thirteen-page syllabus 'how to study a baby' in his book. His general observation is revealing: "if we are to study children to any purpose at all, we must be prepared to take a little trouble about it. . . . I sincerely trust that nothing I say will seem to warn off intending enquirers. I am not one of those who thinks that child study is for specialists only".[2] There was, in fact, an amateur flavour, not unlike that of the early bird watchers, about the child study movement; and after the establishment of academic departments of psychology, and the evolution of research tools and techniques, it inevitably became outmoded.

Particularly important landmarks in the psychological study of children in this country were the setting up of a department of child development under Susan Isaacs at the University of London Institute of Education in 1933, and the creation of a Diploma in the Psychology of Childhood by the University of Birmingham in 1937. Prior to this child psychology tended to be the part-time concern of interested individuals in departments of education or psychology. Some of the individual studies so carried out were notable – in particular, of course, those of Burt on delinquent and backward children, of Susan Isaacs on the intellectual and social development of young children, and of Valentine on early childhood – but they were necessarily on a comparatively small scale and lacked the scope of the developmental surveys carried out in America, or at the Institute J. J. Rousseau in Geneva, where Piaget started his momentous researches in 1921. The translation of Piaget's early works into English from 1926 onwards provided, however, an enormous stimulus to British child psychologists, if only because some of his major conclusions seemed to them to be questionable. Victoria Hazlitt, indeed, held that Piaget's conclusions about the egocentricity of the thinking of young children were "entirely counter to

[1] W. H. Winch in H. B. Chapman *Organised Research in Education* (1927).
[2] W. B. Drummond op. cit., 9.

commonsense".[1] She carried out a number of experimental tests which seemed to show that children could grasp logical relationships at quite an early age. Susan Isaacs, though much more sympathetic to Piaget, questioned the dating of Piaget's stages of development. She found, for example, quite clear cases of mechanical understanding in five-year-olds (the bright five-year-olds of the Malting House School); and as for Piaget's view that children's discourse was in the form of monologue she observes, "The talk of our children almost always seemed to be definitely directed. They talked to each other, and quite rarely to themselves in the presence of others. . . . I thus find myself quite unable to accept the view that there is any stage of development corresponding to the concept of monologuism." [2] Valentine, who carried out very detailed observations on the development of his own five children, casts similar doubts on Piaget's findings and notes many examples of the early group of logical relationships. He came to the conclusion that development was in fact intermittent, and that only intensive observation in the natural environment of the home was capable of arriving at the truth.[3] He found the amount of egocentrism and animism much less than that recorded by Piaget, and the stages of development much less sharply distinguished than Piaget had made them out to be.

The contributions both of Susan Isaacs and of Valentine to child psychology were, however, of much greater importance than merely negatively as criticisms of Piaget. Both were positive contributions in their own right. Susan Isaacs, it is true, became increasingly influenced by psychoanalysis and the teachings of Melanie Klein, but nevertheless her second major book, *Social Development in Young Children* (1933), contained rich and penetrating observations of children's aggressiveness and children's play, of value quite apart from their ideological setting. Valentine, as a corrective, was markedly anti-psychoanalytic and much more interested in the intellectual and motor development of young children than in their emotional and phantasy life. His *Psychology of Early Childhood* (1942) included original material on the development of reflexes, on early fears (some of which he suggested were innate) and on imitation in children, besides a wealth of observational records on intellectual and linguistic growth.

Two special topics to which British child psychologists made contributions of some importance were those of speech and play. The

[1] V. Hazlitt 'Children's Thinking', *B. J. Psych.*, XX (1930).
[2] S. Isaacs *Intellectual Growth in Young Children* (1930).
[3] C. W. Valentine *The Psychology of Early Childhood* (1942).

treatment of speech disorders in children is a twentieth-century development. Classes for stammerers were opened in Manchester and in Glasgow in 1906. Speech clinics were set up at St Bartholomew's Hospital, London in 1911 and St. Thomas's Hospital, London in 1913. Under the L.C.C. both Ballard and Burt became concerned with speech problems. Ballard in 1912 was one of the first to suggest that there was a connexion between sinistrality and speech[1] (a finding which has led to a good deal of controversy) while Burt made a survey of the frequency of speech defect among London schoolchildren, estimating that about five per cent of the total school population suffered from speech defects.[2] In 1927 William Boyd of Glasgow University, who was particularly interested in the development of language and speech in children, opened the first speech clinic in Scotland. From this time onwards speech therapy became a recognized profession with training courses organized by the College of Speech Therapists, and before the outbreak of the Second World War both education and hospital authorities were appointing speech therapists in increasing numbers.

This interest led to a number of special studies, in particular to G. Seth and D. Guthrie's *Speech in Childhood* (1935), M. M. Lewis's *Infant Speech* (1936) and Anne M'Allister's *Clinical Studies in Speech Therapy* (1937). M. M. Lewis's study was a detailed account of the vocalization of his own son from shortly after birth until the age of two. Written from a behaviouristic standpoint it contained a valuable discussion of the characteristics of language, as well as a detailed case record.

About this same time two important works on children's play were published, *Play in Childhood* (1935) by Margaret Lowenfeld, and *Imagination in Early Childhood* (1935) by Ruth Griffiths. Lowenfeld's book was based on observations carried out at the child guidance clinic and training centre (The Institute of Child Psychology) which she founded in London in 1928. Rejecting any narrow views of the functions of play (such as the Kleinian view which saw all play as exclusively symbolic) she held that "play in children is the expression of the child's relation to the whole of life"; that for children play fulfilled all the functions which in the adult are fulfilled by work, thought, art, and relaxation. The importance of play was immense since "forces unrealized in childhood remain in adult life as obsessive inner drives demanding an outlet". For the purposes of her work Lowenfeld devised a num-

---

[1] P. B. Ballard *J. Expt. Ped.*, I (1912).
[2] C. Burt *The Backward Child* (1937).

ber of new techniques, the 'world game', and her Mosaics Test (where the child arranges coloured counters of various shapes to make designs). Similar conclusions as to the importance of phantasy were reached by Ruth Griffiths. Working under Flugel's direction at University College, London, she collected a variety of phantasy material – drawings, stories, dreams, interpretations of ink blots – from five-year-old children. She brought together a great deal of evidence to show that phantasy was not merely a way of escaping from reality or discharging tensions, but was the child's way of coping with reality and solving its difficulties.

These investigations take us into the field of child guidance, and by the 1930's the child guidance movement had got well under way. In Britain as in America the beginnings of child guidance were psychological rather than medical, but the full-scale development which came later involved an inter-disciplinary collaboration between psychiatrist, psychologists and social workers, usually though not always under psychiatric direction. In England Burt's appointment to the London County Council in 1913 was the first official appointment; Scotland followed in 1923 when Kennedy-Fraser was appointed psychological adviser to the Glasgow Education Committee with special reference to mentally handicapped children. Until special clinics were established with full-time staff, however, developments were necessarily on a small scale. A. C. Cameron, a children's specialist at Guy's Hospital, London, was among the first physicians to treat children's behaviour problems. The observations based on his common-sense clinical approach were published in *The Nervous Child* (1919), one of the pioneer works in the field. The concept of the psychological clinic, and an outline of its organization and methods, were first formulated in this country by Burt, and published as an appendix to his *Young Delinquent* (1925). It was this appendix which inspired the early moves towards the establishment of child guidance clinics in Great Britain. The first such clinic in England was that established by Dr E. Miller in East London in 1927 under the auspices of the Jewish Health Organization. In 1928 a Child Guidance Council was set up by the National Committee for Mental Hygiene and the Central Association for Mental Welfare, and in 1929 with support from the Commonwealth Fund of America the London Child Guidance Clinic was opened in Islington under Dr William Moodie. This clinic was intended as a training clinic where psychiatrists, psychologists and social workers could be trained in child guidance methods. From 1932 onwards local authorities in Birmingham, Leicester, Liverpool, Manchester and elsewhere began to establish clinics, and by 1939 there were seventeen clinics wholly maintained by local education authorities and five partly maintained, as well as a number of other clinics attached to hospitals and university departments or run independently. Among these last were the Lowenfeld Institute of Child Psychology mentioned above, and the children's department of the Tavistock Clinic, which was separately constituted in 1926. In Scotland a notable feature were the clinics attached to the university departments of education or psychology (in Dundee attached to the Teachers' Training College), and the Catholic Notre Dame Clinic established through the efforts of Sister Marie Hilda in Glasgow in 1931.[1] Scotland has shown a stronger tendency than England to favour "the teacher psychologists as the dominant person in child guidance".[2]

Although it is only ten years since the publication in the *British Journal of Educational Psychology* of a somewhat acrimonious discussion on psychologists and psychiatrists in the child guidance service,[3] there would today be widespread agreement with Agatha Bowley's essentially sane observation, "These three sciences – medicine, education and psychology – must develop side by side . . . they are all equally concerned with the satisfactory growth and development of the child."[4] The difficulties that confront the child may be of physical origin; they may, on the other hand, be educational or social. Only a team approach can cover the ground adequately; and the Commonwealth Fund wisely insisted that the Child Guidance Clinics established here should follow the tried American pattern of staffing with psychiatrist, psychologist, and social worker. Case material on the psychiatric disorders of childhood was soon forthcoming in plenty and within ten years the Child Guidance Council had commissioned Dr R. G. Gordon, its Medical Director, to edit a *Survey of Child Psychiatry*, which was published in 1939. The Survey contained material on the psychiatric accompaniments of physical illness (encephalitis, juvenile rheumatism, biochemical and metabolic disturbances), and on the usual neurotic and psychotic disorders, as well as discussions of problems such as enuresis, tics, sleep disorders and sexual difficulties. The special problems of partially sighted children and children with defective hearing had been the sub-

[1] The Liverpool Notre Dame Clinic, an offshoot of the Glasgow clinic, was not established until 1942. It has been directed from the beginning by Sister Beatrice.

[2] C. McCallum 'Child Guidance in Scotland', *B. J. Ed. Psych.*, XXII (1952).

[3] *B. J. Ed. Psych.*, XXI–XXII (1951–53).

[4] A. Bowley *Natural Development of the Child*, (1942) 179.

ject of special committees of enquiry by the Board of Education, committees to which J. Lumsden, a member of the inspectorate and a trained psychologist, had largely contributed.

At the same time equally cogent evidence was forthcoming to indicate that many childhood maladjustments were of educational origin and resulted from difficulties in adjustment to educational demands. The work of F. J. Schonell was particularly important in this connexion. In the course of his meteoric career, originating in Perth, West Australia, and culminating in the Vice-Chancellorship of the University of Brisbane, Schonell spent twenty years in this country, first at Goldsmith's College, and then as Professor of Education in succession at Swansea and Birmingham. It was during his period in Great Britain from 1932 to 1952 that Schonell, assisted by his wife Eleanor Schonell, carried out his work on backwardness. First Schonell clarified the problem of backwardness conceptually by drawing distinctions between (a) dullness or intellectual deficiency; (b) backwardness or scholastical deficiency, which might either be general (characterizing all school work) or specific (characterizing some subjects only), and (c) retardation or "a condition of unrealized intellectual ability which characterizes bright, normal, or dull pupils alike".[1] Secondly, Schonell devised a set of diagnostic tools for spotting the source of a child's difficulties in basic subjects, such as reading, spelling and arithmetic. Thirdly, he was a pioneer in the development of techniques of remedial teaching. This work of Schonell has not only shown beyond question that a great many childish difficulties are of educational origin, it has also demonstrated that the educational psychologist has quite as important a task to perform in remedial teaching as in diagnosis and assessment. The ground had been prepared for the large scale development of child guidance and educational psychology after the Second World War.

## 4. Industrial Psychology

Just before the First World War the main ingredients of industrial psychology mingled together both in America and in Germany, and produced a new and clearly demarcated field of applied psychology. The first systematic exposition of this new field was that of Münsterberg, the German psychologist who followed William James at Harvard. *Psychology and Industrial Efficiency* appeared in English in 1913, a year later than a similar work in German. The new doctrines were translated

---

[1] F. J. Schonell *Backwardness in the Basic Subjects* (1942).

to Great Britain during the First World War. The problems of war-time munitions production, in particular the problem of fatigue, had made men's minds receptive. The Government set up the Health of Munition Workers Committee in 1915, to the work of which reference has already been made; and the British Association promoted a special committee on fatigue which carried out some first-hand studies, as well as collating information from various sources, and reported in 1915 and 1916. The study of fatigue, however, was an interdisciplinary study engaging the attention of physiologists and economists as well as psychologists, and the introduction to Great Britain of industrial psychology as such, Münsterberg's conception of a systematic branch of applied psychology, was due to the advocacy of an Australian psychologist, Bernard Muscio (1887–1926). From 1914 to 1916 Muscio served as a demonstrator in experimental psychology at Cambridge and from 1919 to 1922 he was employed as one of their first investigators by the Industrial Fatigue Research Board. He returned to Sydney from 1916 to 1919 as a lecturer, and finally as Professor of Philosophy from 1922 until his death. It was in 1916 that he delivered in Sydney the series of *Lectures on Industrial Psychology*, later published in book form (1917), which first awakened British psychologists to the possibilities of the subject. "It was through his pioneer lectures", wrote C. S. Myers, "that I first got to know anything about Industrial Psychology. Professor Pear drew my attention to the book. Hence Bernard Muscio was responsible for the development of the subject throughout the British Empire." [1] Myers' own lectures on *Present Day Applications of Psychology with special reference to Industry, Education and Nervous Breakdown*, inspired in their references to Industrial Psychology by Muscio, were delivered at the Royal Institution, London, on 11 and 18 April 1918, and proposed the establishment of "institutes of applied psychology in each of our largest cities". These lectures roused some interest in some members of the business community, and later in the year Mr H. J. Welch, director of the importing firm of Harrisons and Crosfield Ltd, approached Dr Myers with a view to the establishment of such an institute. The National Institute of Industrial Psychology, formally incorporated on 11 February 1921, was the direct result, and in June 1922 Dr C. S. Myers resigned from his Cambridge post to take on the full-time direction of the Institute. The N.I.I.P. soon secured influential support, academic, industrial and financial. The first meeting of the scientific committee brought together a strong contingent of the most

[1] *Aust. J. Psych. & Phil.*, IV (1926).

eminent psychologists in the country and several leading physiologists.[1] Promises of support came from firms such as Rowntree, Cadbury, Tootal Broadhurst Lee, Cammell Laird, etc., and the Carnegie Trustees donated £1,000 per annum for five years in support of the Institute's vocational guidance work, followed by further donations and considerable sums from the Rockefeller Trustees and from the proceeds of appeals. By 1924 C. S. Myers had been joined by Dr G. H. Miles as assistant director and secretary (later Director), by Cyril Burt as senior investigator in charge of vocational guidance, assisted by Winifred Spielman (later Raphael), by Eric Farmer of Cambridge and May Smith of the Industrial Fatigue Research Board (both part-time), by six full-time investigators and several research students. A Scottish branch office of the N.I.I.P. was opened in 1930 under the direction of C. A. Oakley. The technical staff of the Institute grew rapidly, and by the mid-1930's numbered about forty. The N.I.I.P. indeed, in the years between the wars, when university departments were small and posts in educational and clinical psychology few and far between, was the most considerable avenue of employment for psychologists. Its service to British psychology was of incalculable importance, without which the expansion of psychology in the Second World War and after would have been virtually impossible.

The work of the National Institute of Industrial Psychology was of three main types: service, research and education. Myers more than once likened the set-up to that of a teaching hospital. During the inter-war years the balance fell rather heavily on service, for the simple reason that the Institute, though a non-profit-making corporation and though partially supported by members' subscriptions and research grants, had nevertheless for the most part to pay its way by its own earnings. To do this it had to carry out fee-paying work for industry, other organizations, and individuals. A steady stream of such work continued throughout the inter-war period for an increasing number of firms into problems of staff selection and training, environmental conditions in the factory, motion study and methods of work, production planning, the management of personnel, workers' grievances, and marketing. Some of the results were published in the Institute's journal,

---

[1] The first meeting was held on 11 December 1921 at 329 High Holborn. Present at the meeting were F. C. Bartlett, Mrs Brierly (Susan Isaacs), William Brown, Cyril Burt, Professor Collis, J. Drever, Beatrice Edgell, E. Farmer, Professor A. V. Hill, Mr Hardy, L. Wynn Jones, Dr Kent, B. Musico, Mr McSwiney, C. S. Myers, P. Nunn, T. H. Pear, C. Spearman, Godfrey Thomson, C. W. Valentine. Dr Myers took the chair.

but many remained the private property of the firms paying for the investigations. Locked away in these confidential reports is a good deal of pioneering work in fields which became known after the Second World War as human engineering, ergonomics, and human relations. In addition to work for firms the N.I.I.P. also provided services for various government departments (the Civil Service Commission, the Post Office, the Ministry of Agriculture, the War Office, etc.), for education authorities and other public bodies. And to the Institute's premises came an ever-growing number of individuals, mainly adolescents, seeking vocational guidance. This, indeed, has been from the beginning one of the N.I.I.P.'s main activities. Along lines laid down by its first head, Cyril Burt, and developed by his successors, F. M. Earle, Angus Macrae, G. E. T. Whiting and A. Rodger, the vocational guidance section of the Institute has provided a service, which, judged by follow-up investigations, has proved remarkably successful.[1]

The Institute's major research effort also went into the vocational guidance field; a number of large-scale experiments into psychological methods of choosing careers were conducted in London, Fife, Birmingham and a Borstal Institution. The Borstal experiment, carried out by A. Rodger, compared the allocation of Borstal boys to working parties by psychological methods and by housemasters' judgements, and showed the clear superiority of the former. Equally convincing results in favour of psychological methods were obtained in the other investigations.[2] An important aspect, though by no means the only aspect, of psychological vocational guidance is, of course, the use of tests. The N.I.I.P. has largely employed its own tests, and for this purpose has devised and carried out research into tests of various sorts – tests of intelligence (Group tests 33 and 34), of clerical aptitudes (Group test 25), of manual dexterity (Cox tests), of mechanical aptitude (Cox and Vincent models) and spatial ability (Form Relations test). The Institute's work in the field of vocational guidance was of first-rate quality and importance; it provided a touchstone for vocational guidance wherever and by whomsoever it was conducted; and it laid the foundations for the procedures so successfully employed by the armed services during the Second World War.

[1] See *Human Factor*, V, VI, VII, X, XI (1931–7), for reports on follow-up investigations.

[2] For details see N.I.I.P. Report 5, *An Account of the Research Work carried out by the N.I.I.P. 1921–34.* Also A. Macrae *Talents and Temperaments* (1932); F. M. Earle et al. *Methods of Choosing a Career* (1931); A. Rodger *A Borstal Experiment in Vocational Guidance* (I.H.R.B. Report 78, 1937).

Finally, the Institute carried out educational work, both general and specialized. It did a good deal of general lecturing up and down the country; it continuously published a journal, named successively *The Journal of the N.I.I.P.* (1922–31), *The Human Factor* (1932–7) and *Occupational Psychology* (1938 onwards); it provided instruction in industrial psychology for the post-graduate diploma in psychology established by the University of London in 1922, and also, after the establishment of its Scottish office, in the University of Glasgow.

The private efforts of the National Institute of Industrial Psychology were throughout the inter-war period supplemented by the government sponsored Industrial Fatigue Research Board (renamed in 1929 Industrial Health Research Board). This body was a direct successor to the war-time Health of Munition Workers Committee and was established in June 1918 by a joint committee of the Department of Scientific and Industrial Research and the Medical Research Council under Sherrington's chairmanship "to consider and investigate the relations of the hours of labour and of other conditions of employment, including methods of work, to the production of fatigue, having regard both to individual efficiency and to the preservation of health among workers". Threatened by the economy cuts of 1921 its work was reduced in scale and transferred wholly to the Medical Research Council under whose auspices it continued until its disbandment with the reorganization of the psychological work of the M.R.C. after the Second World War. Between 1919 and 1947 no less than ninety reports were issued, many being documents of cardinal importance in the history of industrial psychology. Among the investigators working for the Board were H. M. Vernon, Eric Farmer, E. G. Chambers, S. Wyatt, T. Bedford, and May Smith. The Board also supported investigations carried out in university departments and by members of the staff of the N.I.I.P., for example, Mace's work on incentives, P. E. Vernon's on the assessment of personality, and the vocational guidance researches of Burt and of Rodger.[1]

The topics of investigation initiated by the Health of Munition Workers Committee – hours of work, environmental conditions (lighting, heating and ventilation, noise), methods of work (the physiology of work, time and motion study, the design of machinery in relation to the operator), accidents and accident proneness, and lost time – continued to receive attention; to these were added, particularly in the 1930's, studies of the more complex psychological responses to work,

[1] Reports 72, 83, 33 and 78 respectively.

e.g. monotony, psychoneurotic and psychosomatic disorders. Thus Wyatt and Langdon investigated the effects of repetitive work (Reports 77 and 82); May Smith and Millais Culpin studied telegraphists' cramp (Report 43) and the part played by 'The Nervous Temperament' (Report 61); while Bradford Hill looked into the incidence of gastric sickness among omnibus drivers (Report 79). Special mention must also be made of the work of H. M. Vernon who retired from the service of the Board in 1932 but who continued to write on industrial topics, particularly on environmental conditions, hours of work, and accidents.

The N.I.I.P. and the I.H.R.B. were the twin pillars of industrial psychology in Great Britain between the wars. There was some, mostly small-scale, research at the universities with well-established departments of psychology, particularly Cambridge, Manchester and Edinburgh, and in London at the London School of Hygiene, where Millais Culpin held a chair in Medical-Industrial Psychology, and to which several of the I.H.R.B. invesitgators were attached. With the exception of the Medical Research Council, government departments did not employ their own psychologists prior to the Second World War. Private industries were equally backward. Persons with psychological training were occasionally employed by firms as personnel or welfare officers, at times even as works managers. Some of the findings of industrial psychologists were applied through the services of the N.I.I.P. or as a part of the developing art of personnel management. But the only firm to set up a psychological department of its own was Rowntree's of York. Mr Seebohm Rowntree, a director of the firm, and chairman from 1925 to 1941, who had won recognition as a sociological investigator with his book on *Poverty* (1900), played a large part in the introduction of welfare services in munitions factories between 1915 and 1918, and was an early and continuous supporter of the N.I.I.P. His firm was a pioneer in improving the human conditions of industry, introducing a medical service in 1904, part-time day continuation classes in 1905, works-councils in 1917 and insurance schemes in 1920. In 1922 a psychologist was appointed to assist in the selection and training of workers. Mr Rowntree claims[1] that the introduction of selection tests reduced the wastage among girl workers from about twenty per cent to about five per cent, and also improved the selection of apprentices and clerical staff. The psychological department grew in size and scope, and was responsible for carrying out research into attitudes and satisfaction,

[1] B. S. Rowntree *The Human Factor in Business* (1935).

published as *Incentives and Contentment* (1938) by P. Hall and H. W. Locke.

The new-born industrial psychology of the inter-war period was marked initially by a concentration of interest on problems of fatigue and of selection – two problems which had come to the front in the First World War, and to which experimental psychology seemed to have most to contribute. In the early days it was, moreover, markedly influenced by the principles and methods of scientific management and of time and motion study, both movements which had originated in the U.S.A. at the turn of the century. The earliest accounts of industrial psychology, Muscio's *Lectures on Industrial Psychology* (1917) and C. S. Myers' *Mind and Work* (1920), though at pains to point out that the ideals of these movements were wholly economic, held that they might be regarded as component parts of industrial psychology and subordinated to the humane purposes of this science. And indeed there is a sense, as May Smith later pointed out, in which time and motion study at least can be regarded as "simply the psychology of habit-formation".[1] Nevertheless there was in this inclusion a subtle danger, which industrial psychologists by no means managed to avoid. Not all the investigations carried out in this area were founded firmly in psychological research; they often involved operational rather than psychological analysis; and psychologists were not specially, by virtue of their training, competent to carry them out. At the same time, because industrialists naturally wanted returns, there was a temptation to fall back on a line of country that promised fairly easy and quick productive increases. Writing in *Ten Years of Industrial Psychology* (1932) Welch and Myers pointed out that "during the last three years of the first decade of the Institute's existence the great majority of its investigations have been concerned, wholly or partly, with problems of planning and general organization".[2] This encroachment of psychologists into the field of scientific management was of doubtful wisdom, and today it has been rendered obsolete by the mushrooming of management consultants and work study engineers. Industrial psychology, too, in recognizing its own limitations and the need for interdisciplinary collaboration, has found its proper sphere in the problem of 'human engineering' and the study of human relations, together with the older topics of selection and training. The application of psychological techniques to advertising and market research, carried out on a small scale by the N.I.I.P. and some private

[1] May Smith *Introduction to Industrial Psychology*, (1943) 139.
[2] op. cit., 58.

firms in the 1930's, has also, of course, grown considerably since 1945, largely as a result of American influences.

No doubt the most serious shortcoming in the early industrial psychology was the absence of any real study of the social factors involved in industry, of working groups, workers' attitudes, and the general problem of incentives and contentment. Not until the middle 1930's did these topics begin to emerge above the industrial psychologist's horizon in any but the most rudimentary way. Myers in *Mind and Work* (1920) had briefly discussed industrial unrest, and its relation to mental worry and conflict; industrial relations were down on the list of matters falling within the province of the N.I.I.P. But interest in these questions remained academic. The change came in the middle 1930's, partly as a result of the publication in America of Elton Mayo's classic *Human Problems of an Industrial Civilization* (1933), a book which revealed the limitations of the older non-social industrial psychology, and partly as a result of the general emergence about this time of an empirical social psychology, freed from the shackles of McDougall's instinct theory and academic sociology. So we find in 1936 D. W. Harding discussing the social implications of industrial psychology,[1] Winifred Raphael investigating workers' grievances (1937),[2] Sheila Bevington in *Occupational Misfits* (1937) studying the social background of unemployed boys, and the Industrial Health Research Board beginning to consider the social background of work. A new dimension of industrial psychology, complementing the older lines of work, was clearly beginning to emerge.

## 5. In the Field of Mental Health

Today there is a recognized role for the application of psychology and for the clinical psychologist in the field of mental health. Though the possibilities of such a role had been envisaged, as we shall see, even in the nineteenth century, it was for practical purposes not much more than a dream until after the Second World War. Between the wars moves were made somewhat slowly and hesitantly towards a mental health service based on therapeutic principles and integrated into general medicine – moves which did not culminate till the passage of the Mental Health Act in 1959. In 1938 the great majority (93%) of the inmates of county

[1] D. W. Harding 'Some Social Implications of Industrial Psychology', *Human Factor* X. 84 (1936).
[2] W. Raphael 'Grievances: their ascertainment and alleviation', *Human Factor* XI (1937).

mental hospitals were still certified patients, and only in the smaller registered institutions were voluntary patients at all numerous.

The Board of Control, which was set up by the Mental Deficiency Act 1913 to take over all the powers of the Lunacy Commissioners, showed its own liberal tendencies in its annual report for 1918 when it recommended more voluntary treatment, psychiatric provision in general hospitals together with out-patient clinics, and the better training of psychiatrists. But the economy drives of the post-war period and the rapid evaporation of post-war idealism stopped the implementation of these suggestions. Before the Maudsley Hospital was finally opened in 1923 it needed special parliamentary legislation to enable it to treat voluntary patients. A year later a Royal Commission on Lunacy and Mental Disorder was appointed with special instructions to enquire into 'treatment without certification' among other matters. The Commission reported in 1926 and recommended that voluntary patients should be able to enter mental hospitals without having to be certified; they also recommended that the connexion of mental hospitals with the Poor Law should be terminated; that community care and out-patient centres should be increased. The Mental Treatment Act, 1930, embodied most of these recommendations, and also recognized a new class of 'temporary' patients who could be confined for a period of up to a year without formal certification. The Act replaced the old term 'asylum' by the term 'mental hospital', and the term 'lunatic' by 'person of unsound mind', and it authorized local authorities to set up out-patient clinics.[1] By the outbreak of the Second World War 177 such clinics were functioning in England and Wales and 10 in Scotland.

These statutory advances were supplemented by the work of several voluntary bodies, which in the field of mental health have played a major part both in the provision of services and in the education of the public. The oldest of these bodies, the Mental After-Care Association, had been founded as far back as 1879, and, operating mainly in the London area, concerned itself with the care of early cases of mental disorder, the provision of convalescent homes, and domiciliary visits to former patients. The Central Association for Mental Welfare (as it came to be termed) was established in 1913 to see that the provisions of the Mental Deficiency Act were put into full operation. Its work, however, soon came to extend beyond the sphere of mental deficiency alone, and under the active secretaryship of Miss Evelyn Fox it set up local

---

[1] The first out-patient clinic attached to Wakefield Asylum was established as early as 1893.

associations, and worked closely with local authorities in many parts of the country, developing occupation centres, training workers for mental health work, promoting after-care, and carrying out therapeutic activities. It employed its own social workers, speech therapists and, eventually, psychologists, of whom Miss Grace Rawlings, later secretary of the British Psychological Society, was one.

Just after the First World War these bodies were joined by a National Council for Mental Hygiene aimed at education in, and the improvement of, mental health in the broadest sense throughout the community. Associated particularly with the names of Maurice Craig, for many years its chairman, and Dr Doris Odlum, its honorary organizer and secretary, it carried out a great deal of useful work in promoting conferences, publishing a journal (*Mental Hygiene*), giving evidence before committees and lending support to developments in the mental health field. It was among the organizations which supported the child guidance movement in 1926-7, and the establishing of the Child Guidance Council.

By 1934 it had become apparent that there was a good deal of overlapping between the spheres of work of these various bodies, and after some preliminary discussions a joint committee was established in 1936 under the chairmanship of Lord Feversham to review the organization of the voluntary mental health services. The committee reported in 1939 and recommended that the voluntary associations should amalgamate in a National Association for Mental Health. The committee also made a number of important recommendations on the training of mental health workers and the provision of facilities for treatment and community care. Owing to the war it was not until 1946 that the proposed association was actually established, taking over the functions of the Central Association for Mental Welfare, the National Council for Mental Hygiene, and the Child Guidance Council, but not those of the Mental After-Care Association which remained independent.

Another voluntary body of a rather different kind was the Tavistock Clinic, originally established in a house in Tavistock Square, London, in 1920, largely as a result of the efforts of Dr H. Crichton Miller, its first medical director. "The clinic exists", stated an early prospectus, "to provide treatment along modern psychological lines for adults and children suffering from hysteria, abnormal fears and obsessions, neurasthenia, and various disorders of conduct, who are unable to afford specialists' fees. Coupled with thorough investigation of any physical defects, this treatment embraces all the known methods of psychotherapy, such as various forms of suggestion, re-education and mental analysis." A children's department was separately constituted in 1926, and, after Dr J. R. Rees became director in 1934, an assistant director was appointed to administer the considerable educational activities associated with the clinic which had been made possible by the move to larger premises in Malet Place in 1932. These educational activities included training courses for medical practitioners in psychotherapy, and for psychologists in educational and, later, in clinical psychology. Ideologically the Tavistock has always been closely associated with the psychoanalytically derived dynamic viewpoint, and has, indeed, been the headquarters of the eclectic psychotherapy which has found special favour in this country. From early times, too, the Tavistock has been interdisciplinary in its approach, a psychiatric social worker being appointed in 1925, an educational psychologist (Miss C. Simmins) in 1928, and a child psychotherapist (Miss A. T. Alcock) in 1933. Of course, a very considerable amount of effort before the war had to be spent on raising funds, fees from patients amounting to less than half the clinic's expenditure. This prevented much research being carried out until the late 1930's when grants from the Rockefeller Foundation and the Halley Stewart Trust enabled Dr A. T. M. Wilson to carry out research on peptic ulcer, and Dr E. Wittkower on hay fever, heart burn and ulcerative colitis. Not until after the Second World War did the incorporation of the Clinic into the National Health Service in 1948 remove financial worries. At about the same time the Tavistock Institute of Human Relations was independently established to undertake research into the social aspects of human behaviour.

The personnel and outlook of the Tavistock were from the first closely linked to the Medical Section of the British Psychological Society, which sprung from its parent body in 1919. Like the Tavistock the Medical Section was a by-product of the interest in psychotherapy generated during the First World War. Rivers was its first chairman, and its members were mainly medical men with some experience in psychotherapy, and with a sympathy towards, though not necessarily a strict adherence to, Freudian doctrines. The common factor among them was their belief in the dynamic unconscious, and in the *British Journal of Medical Psychology* which was founded in 1921 to express their views more than three-quarters of the articles between 1921 and 1934, when T. W. Mitchell was editor, were pure psychodynamics. Though the section was not wholly medical in its composition and included psychologists like Burt and Flugel, and later lay psychotherapists, clinical psychologists and psychiatric social workers, the overwhelming majority of members, whatever their provenance, were analytically orientated, and the non-analytic fields of psychiatry were never strongly represented. The section in fact came to represent a forum where psychodynamic thinkers of various schools, Freudian, Jungian, Adlerian and eclectic, could meet together, each school having besides its own special sanctum, the British Psychoanalytic Society and Institute of Psychoanalysis (Freudian), The Analytical Psychology Club (Jungian),[1] and the Medical Society of Individual Psychology (Adlerian).

In their psychodynamic bias neither the Tavistock nor the Medical Section were in fact really representative of British psychiatry, which was and has remained predominantly anti-Freudian. Sir John Macpherson in his ninth Maudsley lecture asserted[2] that Freud was "embarrassing to psychiatry", adding "the field of psychiatry is infinitely wider than that covered by the Freudian doctrines, and its relations with the medical and cognate sciences are too intimate to allow the possibility of the new psychology superseding it". This point of view would have been echoed by a large number of British psychiatrists. There was a temporary flirtation with psychoanalysis in the period immediately following the First World War, which in the case of most psychiatrists rather rapidly cooled off. E. Mapother (1881–1940), the first superintendent of the Maudsley Hospital, and London's first Professor of Psychiatry, was in this respect typical. His early attachment to Freudian views later turned into a conviction of their utter inadequacy, and he became a stout opponent of psychoanalytic doctrines. D. K. Henderson (born in 1884), Professor of Psychiatry at Edinburgh, the holder of the only other full-time chair of psychiatry in Great Britain before the Second World War, was far more influenced by the psychobiological ideas of Adolf Meyer than by the theories of Freud, which he regarded as difficult to integrate into medicine.

British psychiatry itself, however, produced no dominant school of thought. As W. Line, the Canadian psychologist, pointed out, "the story of British psychiatry is essentially one of persons rather than of schools or systems".[3] This is not surprising considering the inadequate academic provision for psychiatry prior to the Second World War, and

[1] The Analytical Psychology Club was formed in 1922 to propagate Jungian ideas. The professional Jungian organization, the Society of Analytical Psychology which concerns itself with training, etc., was not established until 1946.
[2] *Journal of Mental Science*, 1928.
[3] W. Line 'Some Impressions of British Psychiatry', *Am. J. Psychiat.*, XIV (1935).

the large number particularly of the older psychiatrists without any formal specialized training. Indeed the Diploma of Psychological Medicine was not instituted until 1911, when as a result of the initiative of the Medico-Psychological Association the Universities of Edinburgh, Durham and London (to be followed later by Leeds, Manchester, Cambridge and The Royal College of Physicians) introduced this qualification. There was among British psychiatrists, if not anything as definite as a school of thought, a proclivity to prefer the objective approach to the study of mental disorder; to agree with Mott as to the importance of genetic influences; to stress the role played by toxic and biochemical factors in the aetiology of the psychoses; and, when in the 1930's physical methods of treatment (convulsion therapy, insulin therapy, leucotomy, etc.) were introduced from the Continent, eagerly to adopt these new panaceas.

The ministrations of psychiatrists, however, ceased to be the only standby for the mentally afflicted. A number of new ancillary professions, of which clinical psychology was to become one, sprang up in the field of mental health. Steps were taken early in the twentieth century to transform the social worker, who in the nineteenth century had been an amateur usually inspired by religious or philanthropic motives, into a trained professional. The first university course for social workers was established in the University of Liverpool in 1904 and was soon followed by courses in other universities. There was, however, no specialized training for mental health workers for another quarter of a century. In 1929 the Commonwealth Fund of America assisted the London School of Economics in establishing a course of training for psychiatric social workers and offered a number of scholarships to students. The course under the direction of Miss Clement Brown, who had herself been trained in America, was the only course in Great Britain prior to the Second World War. In spite of this the profession grew steadily and the Association of Psychiatric Social Workers had a membership of 124 in 1937, employed for the most part in child guidance clinics and voluntary hospitals. The training of occupational therapists followed shortly afterwards, the first training school being opened in 1930 by Mrs Glyn Owens. In 1936 the Association of Occupational Therapists was founded.

It was against this general background in the mental health field that the demand for clinical psychologists first began to be felt. The possibilities of applying psychological techniques to assist in the diagnosis and assessment of mental patients goes back to the end of the nineteenth century. It is recorded that Galton himself visited asylums and was responsible for some experimental work on 'the prehension of idiots'. In 1892 W. H. R. Rivers, who had already supplemented his medical training by psychological study in Germany, was appointed clinical assistant at Bethlem Hospital. His duties, however, were medical rather than psychological, and it was only a year before he moved to Cambridge. At the turn of the century a department of experimental psychology, under W. G. Smith, was set up at the L.C.C. Asylum at Claybury, where R. Armstrong Jones (a founder member of the British Psychological Society) had gone as first medical superintendent in 1893, and F. W. Mott (another founder member) as pathologist in 1895. While at Claybury from 1901 to 1903 Smith carried out the researches on memory and association among mental patients which were published in the early volumes of the *British Journal of Psychology*.[1] Just before the First World War Spearman and Hart applied a range of mental tests to patients at the L.C.C. Asylum at Long Grove to ascertain whether intellectual functions were impaired in cases of dementia, and whether the impairments were general or specific (i.e. affecting Spearman's 'g' or his 's' factors), concluding that "in the main mental injury appears to be of a perfectly diffuse character and to constitute a lowering of the whole intellectual level".[2]

Between the wars the main development in clinical psychology was in connexion with child guidance. Work with adults was small in scale and mainly for purposes of research. The principal focus of such work was naturally the Maudsley Hospital. Here, as the results of an arrangement between Spearman and the medical superintendent, Mapother, Miss Studman was appointed to carry out psychological work. She concerned herself with studies of fluency, while W. J. Pinard worked on perseveration, almost entirely on adult subjects. From this time onwards there were always two psychologists employed half-time, one spending his or her time mainly in the children's department, the other being concerned with research mostly in the adult part of the hospital. Nancy Samuel, P. E. Vernon, J. Blackburn, and Gertrude Keir were among those holding posts at the Maudsley during the 1930's. At Bethlem, which moved to Eden Park in 1930, a psychological department was established under William Brown's direction with R. J. Bartlett as assistant director. In 1934 on Brown's resignation Bartlett took over the

[1] W. G. Smith *B. J. Psych.*, I (1905).
[2] C. Spearman and B. Hart 'Mental Tests of Dementia', *J. Abn. Psych.*, IX (1914).

direction, retaining it until 1942 when Bethlem became administratively joined to the Maudsley. During these years Bartlett spent two days a week at Bethlem engaged in diagnostic and therapeutic work with patients. At the Royal Eastern Counties Institution for mental defectives at Colchester L. S. Penrose in connexion with his studies in the inheritance of mental defect appointed J. C. Raven as a psychological assistant in 1934. It was while at Colchester that Raven devised and standardized the first version of the Progressive Matrices test.

It was from these small and rather sporadic beginnings that the psychological departments at the Maudsley, the Crichton Royal and elsewhere got going after the Second World War, and the new profession of clinical psychologist, now one of the major branches of applied psychology, came into being.

## 6. Crime and Delinquency

The extreme neglect of criminological studies in Great Britain has already been pointed out – a neglect undeniably strange in a nation whose almost morbid interest in crime is exemplified by its cult of the detective yarn. It has taken a lot to break down our amateurism and our academic indifference, and to establish the rudiments of a scientific criminology. The considerable increase, particularly in juvenile delinquency, and the contradictory conclusions of such enquiries as were carried out, made clear the need for more research. But the final impetus came from abroad. It was Hermann Mannheim (born in 1889), a refugee German judge, who built up the study of criminology at the London School of Economics, where he taught from 1935 to 1955, and L. Radzinowicz (born in 1906), a Pole who came to England in 1938 to investigate the English penal system on behalf of the Polish Ministry of Justice, who became Director of the department of criminal science at Cambridge (1949) and Professor of Criminology (1959).

The growing official concern with the problems of crime and delinquency was shown between the wars in a series of departmental committees – on sexual offences against young persons (1925), on the treatment of young offenders (1927), on persistent offenders (1932), on corporal punishment (1938) – and in a Children's and Young Person's Act (1933), which aimed at making the offender rather than the offence the first consideration, extending the jurisdiction of juvenile courts, and reorganizing remand homes and what came to be termed 'approved schools'. The Criminal Justices Bill (1939) had to be abandoned because of the war, and eventually became law in 1948. This Act, which gave the

British penal system a thorough overhaul, also enabled the Home Office to spend money on the psychological examination of offenders and on mental treatment.

Burt's investigations, which commenced soon after his appointment as L.C.C. psychologist in 1913, brought to bear for the first time in this country the concepts and techniques of psychology upon the problems of delinquency. The thoroughness, breadth and balance of his treatment have not yet been surpassed. His book *The Young Delinquent* (1925) in which the results of his enquiries are described was preceded by an article on 'The Causal Factors of Juvenile Crime',[1] in which the origin and scope of his investigation are more fully set out. Burt, while emphasizing and illustrating "the fact of multiple determination" – the fact that "crime is assignable to no single universal cause", but to "a multiplicity of alternative and converging influences" (genetic, social physical and psychological), so that "each delinquent child is the product of nine or ten subversive circumstances" – nevertheless insists that in the last resort crime is a psychological phenomenon.[2] "Every cause and every influence, no matter what its special form may be, is found to operate and can only operate through its inner psychological effects. Conduct and misconduct are always in the last analysis the outcome of mental life." [3]

In comparison with Burt's *Young Delinquent* other enquiries between the wars were less thorough and sometimes less balanced. Thus A. Royds in Oldham (1936) and J. H. Bagot in Liverpool (1937–8) placed the main emphasis on unemployment and poverty, factors which postwar experience has clearly shown not to be primary. These inter-war investigations have been fully summarized by Mannheim in *Young Offenders* (1942).[4] The joint enquiry also reported in this book was largely carried out before the war and involved the statistical comparison between delinquent and control groups in several areas, the main positive finding being the preponderance of abnormal family situations in the delinquents. But it was clear that there was no inevitable association between delinquency and social conditions, and 'stray delinquency' could occur among those brought up in apparently normal conditions.

The protagonist in this country of the psychoanalytic approach to crime has been Edward Glover (b. 1888), who had early become interested in crime through his contact in 1911 with James Devon, an enlightened prison medical officer, and author of *The Criminal and the Com-*

[1] *B. J. Med. Psych.*, III (1923).   [2] *Young Delinquent*, 602.   [3] op. cit., 608.
[4] A. Carr Saunders, H. Mannheim and E. C. Rhodes *Young Offenders* (1942).

*munity* (1912). So when Freud began to plumb the unconscious roots of guilt Glover became a responsive disciple. In 1922 he addressed a meeting of women magistrates on 'The Roots of Crime',[1] in which he emphasized that crime went back to infancy and that "the normal baby is for all practical purposes a born criminal". This shocked even Mrs St Loe Strachey, the midwife of child guidance clinics, who exclaimed, "But, doctor, the dear babies! How could you say such awful things about them." The lecture, states Glover, fell flat, and probably, he adds, did more harm than good! However, Glover's interest enabled Grace Pailthorpe, a psychoanalyst, to obtain support from the Medical Research Council and the Home Office for an investigation on female prisoners, and this investigation, which pointed to the practicability of the scientific diagnosis and treatment of crime,[2] provoked the discussions which led to the establishment in 1932 of the Institute for the Scientific Treatment of Delinquency (now known as the Portman Clinic). Glover,[3] together with Hadfield and others, was a leading figure in the founding of the Institute, which from small beginnings and an annual case load of around 166 before the war now deals with something like 900 cases a year. The clinic has always dealt with both adults and juveniles, and has selected those that seemed suitable for psychotherapy, all types of psychotherapy being employed. Prior to the war it was estimated that almost forty per cent of cases receiving treatment were likely to remain 'non-delinquent'. The difficulty, of course, is to assess how many would have remained crime-free without treatment, and how many subsequent delinquencies, if any, were undetected. So the figures must be accepted with some reservation.

Within the prison service a cautious advocate of the psychological approach was Norwood East (1872–1953), a prison medical officer, who eventually became a Commissioner of Prisons. East had been impressed with the good results of psychotherapeutic interviews while a medical officer at Brixton Prison before the First World War. In 1934 when a Commissioner of Prisons and head of the prison medical service, he was instrumental in initiating a centre at Wormwood Scrubs for an experiment in the psychological treatment of crime. Prisoners under forty years of age undergoing sentences of not less than six months for sexual offences, arson, or other crimes suggesting mental instability, were

---

[1] Reprinted in E. Glover *The Roots of Crime* (1960).
[2] G. Pailthorpe *Studies in the Psychology of Delinquency*, H.M.S.O., 1929.
[3] E. Glover 'The Diagnosis and Treatment of Delinquency', in *Mental Abnormality and Crime* (1944).

transferred to Wormwood Scrubs and given psychotherapeutic treatment by Dr W. H. Hubert. In the joint report written by East and Hubert the authors were very careful not to claim too much.[1] They believed that most prisoners (at least eighty per cent) were psychologically normal, and that "the psychological treatment of crime has suffered considerably from over-propagandization and over-statement". Ordinary methods of punishment were in most cases appropriate. In selected areas, however, psychotherapy was indicated; and the report advocated the establishment of a special prison for the psychological care, study and treatment of these cases. Nearly a quarter of a century later this recommendation was implemented by the opening in 1962 of Grendon Underwood in Buckinghamshire.

## 7. The Psychology of Religion and Popular Psychology

The flood of books on religious psychology and the growth of popular psychology which followed the return of peace in 1919 was primarily the result of the Freudian impact on minds unsettled by war and social change. The foundations, however, had been laid much earlier. As far back as 1857, Frederick Temple, later Archbishop of Canterbury, wrote "our theology has been cast in a scholastic mould, i.e. all based on logic. We are in need of, and we are being gradually forced into, a theology based on psychology. The transition, I fear, will not be without much pain; but nothing can prevent it." [2] In this development four contributory streams can be traced back into the last decades of the nineteenth century. First, Galton initiated an experimental attack on the manifestations of religion with his famous 'Statistical inquiries into the efficacy of prayer', first published in the *Fortnightly Review* (1873), and included in the first edition of *Inquiries into Human Faculty* (1883), though tactfully omitted from later editions. Secondly, the anthropologists, Robertson Smith, Frazer, and others, had collected much data relating to the comparative study and the origins of religions. Thirdly, the theologians themselves turned to the neglected fields of mysticism and religious experiences. Dr W. R. Inge, later Dean of St Paul's, heralded the new era with his Bampton Lectures on *Christian Mysticism* (1899). Two lay theologians followed in his wake. Baron F. von Hugel, a Catholic of Germanic origin who lived from an early age in this country and wrote extensively on religious questions, produced a particularly important

---

[1] N. East and W. H. Hubert *The Psychological Treatment of Crime*, H.M.S.O., 1939.
[2] *Memoirs of Archbishop Temple*, vol. II. 517.

study of *The Mystical Element in Religion* (1908); and Evelyn Underhill wrote her well-known book *Mysticism* shortly after, in 1911. Finally, the Americans, beginning with Starbuck's *Psychology of Religion* (1899), systematized the psychological study of religion. The most famous of all works of this kind, William James's *Varieties of Religious Experience* (1902), was delivered as Gifford Lectures in Edinburgh. The ground was therefore ready, with the advent of the 1920's, for the burgeoning of religious psychology.

The development was a two-sided one, from psychology and from religion. Thouless in his *Introduction to the Psychology of Religion* (1923) broadly followed James's approach. He considered the various factors involved in religious belief, the part played by both conscious and unconscious processes, the role of instincts and the phenomena of prayer, conversion and mystical experience. The emphasis of the book, as Thouless has pointed out in the preface to a paperback reissue (1961), was on religious consciousness rather than on religious behaviour, and more attention was paid to case history material than to statistical and experimental enquiries. But its general conclusions, and its 'faith in the ultimate mysteries" Thouless was prepared to uphold forty years later. In the meantime Thouless had conducted some empirical investigations into 'The Tendency to Certainty in Religious Belief',[1] and had come to believe that "psychical research does provide impressive empirical evidence for the continuance of existence after bodily death".

Crichton Miller's *The New Psychology and the Preacher* which appeared a year after Thouless's book (1924) was a slighter, more immediately topical work. It applied psychoanalytic findings to religion, discussed the influences of conflict, compensation, projection, phantasy, autosuggestion, sex, the 'mother complex', and symbolism generally on religious experience and practice. Miller held that religion could be purged and purified by means of psychoanalytic concepts, and at the same time that the materialistic bias of psychoanalysis could be counteracted by religion. In a rather similar vein J. A. Hadfield, who turned to medicine and psychotherapy after a theological training at Oxford, stressed in *Psychology and Morals* (1923) the essentially moral and spiritual nature of many psychoneurotic problems.

The theologians, partly no doubt because they were thicker on the ground, wrote even more profusely on the psychology of religion. Only a few of the key works can be referred to here. They came from most of the main sects: from the Anglicans, F. R. Barry and L. W. Grensted; from

[1] *B. J. Psych.*, XXVI (1935).

the Methodists, E. S. Waterhouse and L. D. Weatherhead; from the Congregationalists, W. B. Selbie and T. H. Hughes; and later from the Catholics, R. Hostie and V. White. There was, not unnaturally, much doubt, hesitation and ambivalence in the first tentative theological flirtations with the new psychology. Psychology, stated Barry, "is an ally, but a dangerous ally, to the Christian thinker".[1] Psychology in many Christian minds aroused "a feeling of prejudice amounting to repugnance", noted W. F. Halliday of Selly Oak College.[2] Indeed J. C. M. Conn, a Presbyterian minister who had studied psychology under Watt and Thouless in Glasgow, later wrote a book on *The Menace of the New Psychology* (1939); while A. C. Headlam, the formidable Bishop of Gloucester, warned against psychology's "extravagant claims" and lack of "sound scientific principles".[3] In spite of this opposition, however, there was a growing number of enlightened Christians who held with Barry that basically psychology, so far from being antagonistic to Christianity, was a "republication from the scientific standpoint of essential religious truths".[4] And indeed so august and authoritative a body as the Lambeth Conference of 1920 urged that ordinands "should be equipped by training in psychology, and be given some acquaintance with methods and principles of healing".

There were, in fact, as the Lambeth resolution suggests, two sides to the theological interest in psychology. There was an interest in the light which psychology could throw on the nature of religious experience, and there was an alliance between psychology and religion in the practical tasks of healing.

The most scholarly works of a theoretical stamp were those of W. B. Selbie, Principal of Mansfield College, Oxford, *The Psychology of Religion* (1924) delivered as Wilde Lectures in Oxford, and of Canon L. W. Grensted, Professor of the Philosophy of the Christian Religion at Oxford, *Psychology and God* (1930) delivered as Bampton Lectures in Oxford. Canon Grensted was sufficiently knowledgeable in psychology to be elected a Fellow of the British Psychological Society. Both were somewhat critical of the psychoanalytic emphasis on the unconscious mind, and preferred as a basis for the psychology of religion the systems of Ward and Shand. Thus Selbie maintained that religion is not an instinct, but a sentiment; not something that can be relegated to the un-

---

[1] F. R. Barry *Christianity and Psychology* (1923).
[2] W. F. Halliday *Psychology and Religious Experience* (1929).
[3] Preface to W. B. Selbie *The Psychology of Religion* (1924).
[4] F. R. Barry op. cit.

conscious, but something essentially normal and reasonable. Grensted also took Ward as a basis for a psychology of religion which knew its own limitations and did not destroy "those values which have meant so much to man". Oddly enough it was Jung rather than Freud who came in for Grensted's heaviest objurgations. We must remember however that Jung, whose 'perversity' in interpreting Christianity in terms of solar mythology Grensted objected to, did not write his *Psychology and Religion* until 1938, and it was only during the 1930's that he rediscovered the psychological value of the numinous and the sacred.

The alliance between psychology and religion in the work of therapy was preceded by a revived interest in spiritual healing in the Christian churches towards the close of the nineteenth century. An extreme manifestation of this revival was, of course, Christian Science, which from its Boston home began to colonize Britain about the turn of the century. By 1910 there were 58 Christian Science churches in Great Britain, by 1925 there were 148, and in 1960 over 300. Within the Anglican communion there were movements, less radical in their beliefs, with partly similar aims: the Guild of Health to promote spiritual healing, and to study the interaction of the spiritual, mental and physical factors in well-being, was founded in 1904; and the Guild of St Raphael, with rather more exclusive emphasis on the spiritual, in 1915. Clearly psychotherapy had a close connexion with these movements; on the one hand spiritual healing was a form of psychotherapy; on the other religion might well prove to be in itself a psychotherapeutic force. It seemed not unreasonable, therefore, to suggest that psychiatrist and pastor should work together, that the pastor should receive some psychological training, and that he might even undertake certain forms of psychotherapy. To promote this co-operation further the Guild of Pastoral Psychology, Jungian in its predominant outlook, was established in 1936. Even before this, however, individual ministers had been practising pastoral psychology: J. G. McKenzie (1881–1963), a Nottingham Congregationalist, for example, and most conspicuously, Leslie Weatherhead, a Leeds Methodist who after his translation to the City Temple in London in 1936 established a City Temple Psychological Clinic with medical collaboration. The general interest in psychology of other faiths was shown by the starting of a Catholic Psychological Society in 1936, with E. B. Strauss the psychiatrist as their first president, and of a Church of Scotland Committee on Psychology in 1937.

This ecclesiastical concern with psychology ran concurrently with, and was in part no doubt a function of, the growing popular interest in the subject. Psychology, of course, has attracted, at least from the time of Mesmer, an 'eccentric' fringe of followers. This fringe broadened after the First World War, and began to be 'exploited' by commercially interested persons who themselves had no recognized, or only very marginal, qualifications in psychology. 'Practical Psychology Clubs', imported from America in 1923, aimed at propagating a popular understanding of 'the basic principles that govern our lives'. In 1933 at the eleventh annual convention of the Federation of Practical Psychology Clubs of Great Britain a body named The British Union of Practical Psychologists was formed to co-ordinate their activity. In the same year (1933) another quite distinct organization, The British Institute of Practical Psychology, was established to run courses, on a commercial basis, in 'autopsychology'. The motto of the institute was 'I can . . . and I will'. Its advertisements claimed that "you can reconstruct your subconscious mind – this you can do yourself, in your own time, with our help and guidance. . . . Do not be deluded by that now proved false excuse 'heredity'." In addition to these and other organizations several popular psychological journals began to appear in the 1930's, *The Psychologist* in 1933, and *Psychology*, published by The Psychology Publishing Co. of Marple in Cheshire, in 1937, an illustrated magazine which claimed to be "the standard publication of practical, inspirational and applied psychology" and aimed to "call people forth from the bogs of ignorance, self-satisfaction and animal stupidity to the sublime heights of new-born being". This could be done by learning 'The Realization System of Practical Psychology' in twelve lessons costing seven guineas with a 'money back' guarantee of success.

These popular psychological movements are, of course, themselves interesting social psychological phenomena, pointing we may suspect to some failure on the part of the churches and of the medical profession to fulfil their healing missions. The growth of interest in eastern cults, theosophy, for example, and yoga, was symptomatic of the same malaise; and as Geraldine Coster demonstrated in her interesting study *Yoga and Western Psychology* (1934), there are many instructive similarities between yoga and analytical therapy; "both the candidate for analysis and the candidate for yoga enter upon their undertaking because they are, more or less self-consciously, dissatisfied with their own adaptation to life".[1] If so, we might predict that with the increase in the facilities for psychiatric treatment within the framework of the National Health Service both the more popular and the more esoteric cults and movements

[1] op. cit., 35.

should decline. And, although exact figures are not available, this would seem to have happened during the 1950's. The best safeguard against credulity and its exploitation is the progress of a broad and soundly based psychology, theoretical and applied. And since the Second World War steps in this direction have certainly been taken. From a century of effort, the British contribution to which this book has outlined, a science and a profession of psychology are beginning to take shape.

# Select Bibliography

NOTE: This bibliography makes no attempt to provide a list of the publications of British psychologists between 1840 and 1940. The more important books and articles have been mentioned in the text, and are not listed again. The bibliography aims (i) at indicating sources of reference where fuller information can be obtained; (ii) at giving some guidance to further reading.

## General

No work on British psychology as such has appeared since T. Ribot's *La psychologie anglaise contemporaine* (1870; trans. *English Psychology* 1873), but there are, of course, accounts in the general histories:

G. S. Brett, *A History of Psychology* (3 vols. 1912; abridged edition in one vol. ed. by R. S. Peters, 1953)

G. Murphy, *An Historical Introduction to Modern Psychology* (1929)

E. G. Boring, *A History of Experimental Psychology* (2nd ed. 1950)

J. C. Flugel, *A Hundred Years of Psychology* (2nd ed. 1951)

For the philosophical background consult:

R. Metz, *A Hundred Years of British Philosophy* (1938)

J. Passmore, *A Hundred Years of Philosophy* (1957)

A useful work of reference on general scientific developments is:

J. T. Merz, *A History of European Thought in the XIX Century* (4 vols. 1896–1914)

## Chapter I

G. M. Young, *Victorian England; Portrait of an Age* (1936, Oxford paperback edition 1960), gives an excellent picture of the social, political and intellectual background.

For associationism and utilitarianism consult:

T. Ribot, *English Psychology* (1873)

H. C. Warren, *A History of Association Psychology* (1921)

J. Plamenatz, *The English Utilitarians* (1949)

S. T. Coleridge, *Biographia Literaria* (1817), should be read in the original: also the extracts from his notebooks, edited by K. Coburn, *Inquiring Spirit* (1951). See also I. A. Richards, *Coleridge on Imagination* (1934).

For the emergence of psychology as a separate discipline:

J. S. Mill, *System of Logic* (1843) (particularly Part VI, 'The Logic of the Moral Sciences'), and W. Hamilton, *Lectures on Metaphysics* (1858) (particularly Vol. I, chaps. VIII–X).

J. S. Mill, *Autobiography* (1873), gives a classic account of the intellectual life of the progressives of the period.

## Alexander Bain (1818–1903)

Apart from *The Senses and the Intellect* (1855) and *The Emotions and the Will* (1859), Bain's principal psychological writings were *The Study of Character* (1861), *Mind and Body* (1872) and *Education as a Science* (1879). The last three contain little that was not already included in the two earlier works. The book on education is particularly long-winded and tedious. The first half of *Mental and Moral Science* (1870) contains an arid summary of the two volumes of 1855 and 1859. Although shorter it is far less worth consulting than the original works. Bain's contributions to *Mind* were reprinted in *Dissertations on Leading Philosophical Topics* (1903). Many of these are forceful and good. Bain was also the author of a two-volume *Logic* and a number of works on English grammar and composition. Besides his own posthumously published *Autobiography* (1904) he wrote biographies of *James Mill* (1882) and *J. S. Mill* (1882). Together with J. S. Mill and George Grote he edited a new edition of James Mill's *Analysis of the Phenomena of the Human Mind* (1869) which contains a good many notes and comments by Bain himself.

A recent study of Bain is contained in two articles in the *Australian Journal of Psychology* by J. A. Cardno, 'Bain and Physiological Psychology' (*A. J. Psych.* VII. 1955), 'Bain as a Social Psychologist' (*A. J. Psych.* VIII. 1956).

## Chapter II

For the material covered in Sections 1 and 2 W. B. Carpenter's *Principles of Mental Physiology* (1874), and his shorter book *Mesmerism, Spiritualism etc. historically and scientifically considered* (1877), give a reliable contemporary account. For the older material on mesmerism and hypnotism consult J. Milne Bramwell, *Hypnotism, its History, Practice and Theory* (2nd ed. 1906). J. Braid, *Neurypnology* (1843), was reissued as *Braid on Hypnotism* (1899). H. G. Atkinson and Harriet Martineau in *Letters on the Law of Man's Nature and Development* (1851) explain the hold which theories such as mesmerism, phrenology and spiritualism had at the time.

The literature on phrenology is large. George Combe's *Essays on Phrenology* (1819) were reissued as *A System of Phrenology* (1825. 5th ed. 1843). This was the leading work by a British phrenologist. As late as the beginning of the twentieth century Bernard Hollander was attempting to correlate the doctrines of phrenology with modern physiology: see *Scientific Phrenology* (1902).

The early history of spiritualism is dealt with in F. Podmore, *Modern Spiritualism* (1902).

W. B. Carpenter, *Nature and Man* (1888), contains a memoir by his son, J. Estlin Carpenter, and a collection of his principal scientific and philosophical essays and addresses.

An abridged edition of H. Maudsley, *Natural Causes and Supernatural Seemings* (1886), was published in 'The Thinker's Library' (Watts, 1939). References in the text are to this edition. On Maudsley himself refer to Aubrey Lewis, 'Henry Maudsley, his work and influence', *J. Ment. Sci.* XCVII (1951).

D. Leigh, *The Historical Development of British Psychiatry.* Vol. I, 18th and 19th centuries (1961), contains accounts of John Haslam, J. C. Prichard and John Conolly.

K. Jones, *Lunacy, Law and Conscience, 1744–1845*, deals with the background of early lunacy reform.

# Chapter III

P. G. Fothergill in *Historical Aspects of Organic Evolution* (1952) gives an account of both pre- and post-Darwinian theories of evolution. B. Glass, O. Temkin and W. L. Strauss in *Forerunners of Darwin, 1745–1859* (1960) deal in more detail with Darwin's immediate precedessors.

For a brief account see J. W. Judd, *The Coming of Evolution* (1910).

The centenary of the publication of Charles Darwin's *Origin of Species* (1859) led to a spate of books on Darwin and evolution, including:

J. Maynard Smith, *Evolution* (Pelican, 1958)
S. A. Barnett (ed.), *A Century of Darwin* (1958)

C. Himmelfarb, *Darwin and the Darwinian Revolution* (1959)
C. D. Darlington, *Darwin's Place in History* (1959)

Darwin's life has been fully documented in *The Life and Letters of Charles Darwin* (3 vols. 1887) ed. by his son Francis Darwin. This includes an autobiographical chapter, which was reprinted separately in 'The Thinker's Library' (Watts, 1929).

T. H. Huxley's evolutionary writings are extremely readable, particularly *Man's Place in Nature* (1863) and *Collected Essays*, Vols. I and II (1893).

There has been an almost complete dearth of interest in and writing about Herbert Spencer during the last fifty years, except for some discussions on his sociology. His psychological writings have been totally neglected in spite of Flugel's observations on "the breadth and magnificence of Spencer's vision" (*A Hundred Years of Psychology*, p. 116).

### G. H. Lewes

Lewes' principal psychological work, *Problems of Life and Mind*, consists of five volumes issued between 1874 and 1879. The contents of the volumes are:

*Series I* (2 vols.)
The part of most interest to the psychologist is that on 'Psychological Principles', in the Introduction, Vol. I, pp. 107–95.

*Series II The Physical Basis of Mind* (1 vol.)
Problem 1. The Nature of Life
Problem 2. The Nervous Mechanism
Problem 3. Animal Automatism
Problem 4. The Reflex Theory

*Series III* (2 vols.)
Problem 1. The Study of Psychology, its object, scope and method
Problem 2. Mind as a Function of the Organism
Problem 3. The Sphere of Sense and the Logic of Feeling
Problem 4. The Sphere of Intellect and Logic of Signs

The significance of Lewes' philosophical viewpoint is discussed in an article by J. Kaminsky, 'The Empirical Metaphysics of G. H. Lewes', *Journal of the History of Ideas*, Vol. XIII (1952), pp. 314–32. The second edition of Ribot's *English Psychology* (1877) contains a chapter on the earlier volumes of Lewes' *Problems*.

The second volume of Lewes, *Physiology of Common Life* (1859), is largely devoted to psychological questions.

T. H. Green, *Works*, Vol. I (1888), contains critical essays on Spencer and on Lewes.

## S. Butler

For the differences between Darwin and Butler, refer to B. Willey, *Darwin and Butler* (1960), and for a critical discussion of Butler's evolutionary views to the chapter on evolution in P. N. Furbank, *Samuel Butler* (1948).

# Chapter IV

## Francis Galton

An indispensable book of reference for the work of Galton is Karl Pearson's four-volume *Life, Letters and Labours of Francis Galton* (1914–30). It contains detailed accounts of his psychological, statistical and other work, and lists nearly 250 publications. Of these the books most important for the psychologist are *Hereditary Genius* (1869; reprinted 1952), *English Men of Science; their Nature and Nurture* (1874), *Inquiries into Human Faculty and its Development* (1883; reprinted in a cheap edition by the Eugenics Society, 1951) and *Natural Inheritance* (1889). Galton's own *Memories of My Life* (1908) is somewhat anecdotal. For references to articles consult Pearson's *Life of Galton*, and for a general survey on Galton's psychological work:

E. A. Peel, 'The Permanent Contribution of Francis Galton to Psychology', *Brit. J. Educ. Psych.* XXIV (1953)

## Karl Pearson

A selection of papers from the series *Mathematical Contributions to the Theory of Evolution*, together with some other important early papers, has been published under the title *Karl Pearson's Early Statistical Papers* (1948). The papers are highly technical. An account of Pearson's life and work with a complete bibliography of Pearson's writings will be found in *Karl Pearson: an appreciation of some aspects of his life and work* (1938) by his son, E. S. Pearson. See also Karl Pearson's 'Notes on the History of Correlation', *Biometrika* XIII (1920), pp. 25–45. *The Grammar of Science* (1892; reprinted in Everyman's Library 1937) is of only indirect interest to the psychologist.

# Chapter V

## Queen Square Neurologists

For a general history of the National Hospital see *The National Hospital, Queen Square 1860–1948* by Sir Gordon Holmes and *Queen Square and the National Hospital 1860–1960* (foreword by Sir Ernest Gowers). The main source for Hughlings Jackson is *Selected Writings of John Hughlings Jackson* ed. J. Taylor, 2 vols. (1932). Vol. I deals with Epilepsy, Vol. II with the Evolution and Dissolution of the Nervous System, Aphasia, etc. A biographical memoir by J. Taylor is prefaced to *Neurological Fragments* (1925), a collection of short articles published by Hughlings Jackson in *The Lancet* between 1891 and 1909.

Ferrier's *Functions of the Brain* (1876) summarizes most of Ferrier's research. The second edition (1886) was extensively revised. For a brief appreciation of Ferrier's life and work see the article by Sherrington in *The Dictionary of National Biography*. Bastian's *The Brain as an Organ of Mind* (1880) is a useful survey of the knowledge and controversies of the day, and contains an appendix on the muscular sense.

## Cambridge Physiologists

For the general background see Sharpey-Schafer's *History of the Physiological Society 1876–1926*. A memoir of Michael Foster was published in Vol. 35 of the *Journal of Physiology* (1907).

Summaries of the work most relevant to psychology are contained in W. H. Gaskell, *The Involuntary Nervous System* (1916); J. N. Langley, *The Autonomic Nervous System* (1921); and K. Lucas, *The Conduction of the Nervous Impulses* (1917). The original articles were mostly in the *Journal of Physiology*.

## Sherrington

A complete bibliography of Sherrington's writings is contained in the 1947 edition of *The Integrative Action of the Nervous System*. This work, which originally appeared in 1906, is the best account of the main principles of Sherringtonian neurophysiology. But for Sherrington on the muscle sense see his article in Schafer's *Textbook of Physiology* (1900). An account of the later work of Sherrington and his school is contained in *The Reflex Activity of the Spinal Cord* (1932) by Creed, Denny-Brown, Eccles, Liddell, and Sherrington, and in *Selected Writings of Sir Charles Sherrington* ed. Denny-Brown (1939). In a more reflective vein are Sherrington's Gifford Lectures *Man on his Nature* (1940; Pelican edition 1955).

A review of Sherrington's life and work by E. G. T. Liddell is contained in Vol. VIII of *Obituary Notices of Fellows of the Royal Society*; a briefer appreciation by R. S. Creed in *Brit. J. Psych.* XLIV (1953). Also see Lord Cohen of Birkenhead, *Sherrington, physiologist, philosopher and poet* (1958).

## Head

*Studies in Neurology* (2 vols. 1920) collects together papers by Head and various collaborators on sensation. These originally appeared in *Brain*. Head's other major work is *Aphasia and Kindred Disorders of Speech* (2 vols. 1926).

For criticisms see F. M. R. Walshe, 'The Anatomy and Physiology of Cutaneous Sensibility; a Critical Review', *Brain* LXV (1942); Weisenburg and McBride, *Aphasia* (1935); Oldfield and Zangwill, 'Head's Concept of the Schema and its Application in Contemporary British Psychology', *Brit. J. Psych.* XXXII–XXXIII (1942–3).

For Head's life see the accounts by Gordon Holmes, *Obit. Not. F.R.S.* Vol. III, and C. S. Myers, *Brit. J. Psych.* XXXII. Also *Henry Head Centenary Essays and Bibliography* (1961) by K. W. Cross, R. A. Henson, Macdonald Critchley, Russell Brain.

# Chapter VI

Biographical material on the early British comparative psychologists:

J. B. S. Haldane, 'Introducing Douglas Spalding', *Brit. J. Animal Behav.* II (1954)

H. G. Hutchinson, *The Life of Sir John Lubbock* (2 vols. 1914)

G. Romanes, *Life and Letters* ed. Mrs Romanes (1895)

Lloyd Morgan, *History of Psychology in Autobiography* ed. C. Murchison, Vol. II (1932)

J. A. Hobson and M. Ginsberg, *L. T. Hobhouse: His Life and Work* (1931). (Includes a memoir by Hobson; an account of Hobhouse's work by Ginsberg; and selected articles and essays by Hobhouse himself)

# Chapter VII

H. E. Barnes, *An Introduction to the History of Sociology* (1947), contains a section on Spencer, and a chapter of English sociology since

Spencer, with special emphasis on Hobhouse and Geddes. J. Rumney, 'La Sociologie anglaise' in *La Sociologie au XXme siécle* (ed. G. Gurvitch, Paris, 1947), contains a good deal on the nineteenth-century background. A. V. Dicey, *Law and Opinion in England During the 19th Century* (1905), is valuable on the changing climate of opinion.

**On Bagehot**

A. Buchan, *The Spare Chancellor: The Life of Walter Bagehot* (1959)
St John-Stevas, *Walter Bagehot: a Study of His Life and Thought* (1959)

**On Buckle**

Giles St Aubyn, *A Victorian Eminence* (1958)

**On Spencer**

J. Rumney, *Herbert Spencer's Sociology* (1934)

**On Geddes**

P. Mairet, *Pioneer of Sociology; Life and Letters of Patrick Geddes* (1957)

**On Socialism**

M. Beer, *A History of British Socialism* (2 vols. 1914–20)
C. Raven, *Christian Socialism* (1920)
E. Pease, *History of the Fabian Society* (1916)

**On Social Anthropology**

T. K. Penniman, *A Hundred Years of Anthropology* (1935)
R. K. Marrett, *Tylor* (1936)
R. A. Downie, *James George Frazer* (1940)

**On Graham Wallas**

A brief appreciation by Gilbert Murray was prefaced to Wallas, *Men and Ideas* (1940). See also Zimmern's article on Wallas in the *Dictionary of National Biography*.

# Chapter VIII

N. G. Annan, *Leslie Stephen* (1951), gives a most readable account of the struggle between religion and agnosticism, centred round the life of Leslie Stephen. For a fuller general account consult A. W. Benn, *A History of English Rationalism in the 19th Century* (2 vols. 1906); M. H.

Carré, *Phases of Thought in England* (1949), chap. IX, 'Naturalism and Idealism'.

A. W. Brown, *The Metaphysical Society* (1947), throws a very valuable searchlight on mid-Victorian intellectual controversies, and on the beginning of professional philosophy in this country.

On religious reactions see W. Ward, *W. G. Ward and the Catholic Revival* (1893); C. C. J. Webb, *A Study of Religious Thought in England from 1850* (1933).

On Scottish philosophy:

A. Seth, *Scottish Philosophy* (1886)
S. A. Grave, *The Scottish Philosophy of Commonsense* (1960)
A. C. Fraser, *Biographia Philosophica* (1904)

On idealism:

A. Aliotta, *The Idealistic Reaction Against Science* (Trans. from Italian, 1914)
R. Wellek, *Immanuel Kant in England 1793-1838* (1931)
J. H. Muirhead, 'How Hegel came to England', *Mind* XXXVI (1927)
J. H. Muirhead, *The Platonic Tradition in Anglo-Saxon Philosophy* (1931)
G. W. Cunningham, *The Idealist Argument in Recent British and American Philosophy* (1933)
T. H. Green, *Works*, Vol. III (1888), contains a memoir by R. L. Nettleship
W. H. Fairbrother, *The Philosophy of T. H. Green* (1900)
R. Wollheim, *F. H. Bradley* (Pelican, 1959)

For Bradley's psychological writing see:

F. H. Bradley, *Principles of Logic* (1883, 2nd ed. 1922) and *Collected Essays* (2 vols. 1935)

# Chapter IX

J. Sully, *My Life and Friends* (1918), is Sully's autobiography. J. Ward, *Essays in Philosophy* (1927), contains a memoir by his daughter, Mrs Campbell. F. C. Bartlett writes on Ward in *Amer. J. Psychol.* XXXVI (1925). See also A. H. Murray, *The Philosophy of James Ward* (1937).

A memoir on G. F. Stout by J. A. Passmore is contained in Stout's *God and Nature* (1952). Obituary notices by C. A. Mace appeared in *Proc. Brit. Acad.* XXXI (1945) and C. D. Broad, *Mind* LIV (1945).

In addition to Stout's major psychological works *Analytical Psychology* (1896), *Manual of Psychology* (1898, 5th ed. 1938), and the briefer *Groundwork of Psychology* (1903), there were several papers on psychology reprinted in *Studies in Philosophy and Psychology* (1930). The articles on 'Herbartian Psychology' appeared in *Mind* XIII–XIV (1888–9).

# Chapter X

## The Management of the Insane

Montague Lomax's *The Experiences of an Asylum Doctor* (1921) gives a vivid picture of the conditions which obtained in some asylums during this period. See also Mercier, *Lunatic Asylums, Their Organization and Management* (1894), and the report of the committees on the status of British psychiatry and of medical officers published in the *Journal of Mental Science* LX (1914), 667–93. Also the article 'Psychiatry in England', *Lancet* 1912, I. 1717–18, and the correspondence which followed. General reference: Kathleen Jones, *Mental Health and Social Policy, 1845–1959* (1960).

## Psychiatric Thought

In addition to works mentioned in the text, see article 'Insanity' in XIth edition *Encyclopaedia Britannica* (1910), and the attached bibliography.

## Mental Defect

*The Report of the Royal Commission on the Care and Control of the Feeble-Minded* (1908) is the key document. See also the early editions of A. F. Tredgold's *Mental Deficiency* (1st ed. 1908, 2nd ed. 1914).

## Crime and Delinquency

For a general background consult L. W. Fox, *The English Prison and Borstal Systems* (1952), and for the earlier period S. & B. Webb, *English Prisons under Local Government* (1922); on juveniles, Mary Burnett, *Young Delinquents* (1913) (a study of reformatory and industrial schools), W. Clarke Hall, *The State and the Child* (1917); on adult criminals, Havelock Ellis, *The Criminal* (1890), and Charles Goring, *The English Convict* (1913).

## Psychical Research

The *Proceedings* of the Society for the Promotion of Psychic Research (founded 1882) provide copious information on the development of psychic research. A brief history of the society by W. H. Salter was published by the society in 1948. F. W. H. Myers' *Human Personality and its Survival of Bodily Death*, published in 1903, was issued in an abbreviated one-volume edition in 1906.

## Havelock Ellis

Two rather unsatisfactory studies of Havelock Ellis were published during his centenary year (1955). A proper appreciation of his scientific and literary achievements remains to be carried out. *Studies in the Psychology of Sex* is now available to English readers in a two-volume edition published by Heinemann. The short one-volume *Psychology of Sex* (1933) is a concise introduction to, rather than a summary of, the larger work. Ellis's posthumously published autobiography, *My Life* (1940), both reveals and conceals. In style and content it contrasts strikingly with Freud's *An Autobiographical Study*.

## Psychoanalysis

For the early development of psychoanalysis in England see Ernest Jones, *Free Associations* (1959) and his article 'Reminiscent Notes on the Early History of Psychoanalysis in English-speaking Countries', *International Journal of Psychoanalysis* XXVI (1945), 8–10. There are also references in his *Sigmund Freud, Life and Work*, especially in Vol. III (1957). Obituary tributes and a paper on Jones's contribution to psychoanalytic theory are contained in Vol. XXXIX of the *International Journal of Psychoanalysis* (1958). For a complete list of Jones's writing up to 1957 see *The Index of Psychoanalytic Writings* by A. Grinstein, Vol. II (1957).

# Chapter XI

The original papers of scientific pioneers like Young, Wheatstone, Clerk Maxwell and Rayleigh are worth referring to in the original. The simplicity and directness of their approach to problems forms a valuable basis for the understanding of subsequent developments. See T. Young, *Miscellaneous Works*, Vol. I (1855); Wheatstone, *Scientific Papers* (1879); Clerk Maxwell, *Scientific Papers*, (1890); Rayleigh, *Scientific Papers* (1899–1920). For further details of colour vision consult Mary Collins, *Colour Blindness* (1925).

The following contain interesting information about some of the departments and personalities:

F. C. Bartlett, 'Cambridge, England 1887–1937', *Am. J. Psych.* L (1937)

H. Head, Notice of W. H. R. Rivers, *Proc. Roy. Soc. B.* XCV (1924)

C. S. Myers, 'The Influence of the Late W. H. R. Rivers on the Development of Psychology in Great Britain', *Brit. Ass. Reports* (1922)

Notice of C. S. Myers, *Obit. Notices F.R.S.* (with bibliography), V (1948)

H. J. Watt, Biographical account prefaced to *The Psychology of Dreams* (1929)

Accounts of University Departments in the *Bulletin of the British Psychological Society*:

R. C. Oldfield, Psychology in Oxford, *Bull. 9 and 10*

T. H. Pear, Manchester University Department of Psychology, *Bull. 26*

J. C. Flugel, One Hundred Years or so of Psychology at University College, London, *Bull. 27*

R. Knight The Department of Psychology in the University of Aberdeen, *Bull. 47*

Several psychologists contributed autobiographical accounts to a series published in *Occupational Psychology*:

T. H. Pear, *Occupational Psychology* XXII (1948)

James Drever snr., *Occupational Psychology* XXII (1948)

May Smith, *Occupational Psychology* XXIII (1949)

A. W. P. Wolters, *Occupational Psychology* XXII (1948)

**Obituary Notices**

J. C. Flugel, *Brit. J. Psych.* XLVII (1956)

Carveth Read, *Brit. J. Psych.* XXIII (1932)

J. C. MacCurdy, *Brit. J. Psych.* XL (1949)

S. F. J. Philpott, *Brit. J. Psych.* XLV (1954)

Beatrice Edgell, *Brit. J. Psych.* XXXIX (1949)

Victoria Hazlitt, *Brit. J. Psych.* XXIII (1933)

**On Societies**

Beatrice Edgell, 'The British Psychological Society', *Brit. J. Psych.* XXXVII (1947)

C. S. Myers, 'The Development of Psychology in the British Association', *Brit. Ass. Rep.* (1931).

## Chapter XII

A complete bibliography of McDougall's writings is contained in the notice of his life by May Smith and Major Greenwood in Vol. III of *Obituary Notices of Fellows of the Royal Society*. May Smith also wrote a biographical account in *Brit. J. Med. Psych.* XVIII. See also *History of Psychology in Autobiography*, Vol. I.

The 'hormic' theory is most clearly set out in *An Introduction to Social Psychology*. For an early discussion of the instinct question see the Symposium on 'Instinct and Intelligence', *Brit. J. Psych.* III (1910); and the more recent symposium 'Is the Doctrine of Instincts Dead ?', *Brit. J. Educ. Psych.* XI–XII (1941–3).

For accounts of McDougall's main position consult F. Fletcher, *Instinct in Man* (1957), and F. V. Smith, *Explanation of Human Behaviour* (2nd ed. 1960), chap. VI. Also C. Burt, 'The Permanent Contribution of McDougall to Psychology', *Brit. J. Educ. Psych.* XXV (1955).

## Chapter XIII

### Spearman

A complete bibliography of Spearman's writings is appended to Godfrey Thomson's account of Spearman in *Obituary Notices of Fellows of the Royal Society*, V (1947). Spearman's own account of his life is contained in Murchison's *History of Psychology in Autobiography*, Vol. I. The accounts by Flugel (*British Journal of Psychology* XXXVII, 1946) and Burt (*Psychological Review* LIII, 1946) are also worth consulting.

For the early factor controversies see Brown and Thomson, *Essentials of Mental Measurement* (1921); also Thomson's *The Factorial Analysis of Human Ability* (1938). For Burt's later versions of the origin of factor analysis see his articles in Vol. II of the *British Journal of Statistical Psychology* (1948) and the *British Journal of Educational Psychology* XIX (1949). Also his review of Spearman & Wynn Jones's *Human Ability*, in *Brit. J. Educ. Psych.* XX (1950), and his contribution 'The Factorial Study of the Mind' to *Essays in Psychology dedicated to David Katz* (1951). For Burt's earlier version see, for example, *Psychological Tests of Educable Capacity* (Board of Education, 1924, chap. I) and *The Factors of the Mind* (1940).

A somewhat uncritical account of Spearman's doctrine as a whole is contained in F. C. Thomas's *Ability and Knowledge* (1935).

**Burt**

A bibliography of Burt's writings up to 1951 compiled by Dr. Hannah Steinberg was published in *Brit. J. Educ. Psych.* XXI (1951). Autobiographical accounts are contained in *History of Psychology in Autobiography*, Vol. IV, and *Occupational Psychology* XXIII (1949).

In addition to the articles, books and reports mentioned in the text the following are of special importance:

'The Mental Differences Between the Sexes' (with R. C. Moore), *J. Exp. Ped.* I (1912)

'The Mental Differences Between Individuals', Presidential address to Brit. Ass. Sect. J., *Reports of Brit. Ass.* (1923)

*The Subnormal Mind* (1935), a systematic review of the main types of mental subnormality, and perhaps the fullest account of Burt's general psychological position

'The Analysis of Examination Marks', in *The Marks of Examiners*, ed. Hartog and Rhodes (1936) – a fairly technical review of factorial methods

'Correlations between Persons', *Brit. J. Psych.* XXVIII (1937) – again fairly technical

'The Relations of Educational Abilities', *Brit. J. Educ. Psych.* IX (1939)

# Chapter XIV

**Philosophical Background**

*The Revolution in Philosophy* (1956) by various authors with an introduction by Gilbert Ryle is brief and non-technical.

J. Passmore, *A Hundred Years of Philosophy* (1957), and C. A. Mace (ed.), *British Philosophy in Mid-Century* (1957). Many articles with a bearing on psychology appeared in *Mind* (edited by G. F. Stout from 1891 to 1920) and in *The Proceedings of The Aristotelian Society*.

**Trends in Psychology**

F. Aveling, *Psychology: the Changing Outlook* (1937) summarizes the main trends as they appeared from London in the 1930's. C. A. Mace and P. E. Vernon (eds.), *British Psychology in Mid-Century* (1953), contains some references to pre-war British psychology.

## F. C. Bartlett

His autobiography is to be found in Murchison's *History of Psychology in Autobiography*, Vol. III (1936). There is some autobiographical material in *Thinking* (1958).

## Experimental Psychology

Most of the experimental material produced by British psychologists between the wars was published in the *British Journal of Psychology* (general section and Monograph Supplements).

The standard experimental textbook in use in Great Britain between the wars was C. S. Myers and F. C. Bartlett, *Textbook of Experimental Psychology* (3rd ed. 1925). (The first edition by Myers alone appeared in 1909.) An elementary text by Mary Collins and J. Drever, *Experimental Psychology*, was published in 1929.

## Statistics

R. A. Fisher's original papers were reprinted in *Contributions to Mathematical Statistics* (1950) which also contains a biographical note.

## Aesthetics

C. W. Valentine, *The Experimental Psychology of Beauty* (1962), contains many references to British work between the wars. On non-experimental aesthetics, however, consult I. A. Richards, *Principles of Literary Criticism* (1925), Herbert Read, *Education Through Art* (1943), and Graham Hough, *Image and Experience* (1960), among other works.

## Physiological Developments

The 'Recent Advances' series is invaluable as an historical record:
*Recent Advances in Physiology* (1st ed. 1925 to 6th ed. 1939)
*Recent Advances in Neurology* (1st ed. 1929 to 4th ed. 1940)

On early work with E.E.G. see Gray Walter's articles in *Proc. Roy. Soc. Medicine.* XXX (1935) and *J. Neurol. Psychiat.* n.s. I (1938).

## Social Psychology

K. Mannheim, *Man and Society* (1940), contains an extensive classified bibliography, not, of course, confined to British authors. There are also bibliographies in F. C. Bartlett, M. Ginsberg, E. J. Lindgren and R. H. Thouless (eds.), *The Study of Society* (1939). W. J. H. Sprott, *Social Psychology* (1952), makes references to pre-war studies.

On the anthropological side:

T. K. Penniman, *A Hundred Years of Anthropology* (1935)

A. R. Radcliffe-Brown, 'The Present Position of Anthropological Studies', *Report of the British Association* (1931); *Method in Social Anthropology* (1958) (contains Radcliffe-Brown's collected essays and five chapters of a book on Social Anthropology not previously published)

R. Firth (ed.), *Man and Culture* (1957) (an evaluation of the work of Bronislaw Malinowski)

**Psychoanalytic Derivatives**

J. A. C. Brown, *Freud and the Post-Freudians* (Pelican, 1961), contains a chapter on 'The British Schools'; N. Walker, *A Short History of Psychotherapy* (1957); J. E. Nicole, *Psychopathology* (1st ed. 1930, 4th ed. 1946), contains a useful bibliography.

**Psychical Research**

See the bibliography in G. N. M. Tyrrell, *The Personality of Man* (Pelican, 1946).

# Chapter XV

**World War I**

The official sources of information on 'shell-shock' are *Report of the War Office Committee of Enquiry into Shell Shock* (Chairman: Lord Southborough) (cmd. 1734) (1922) and *History of the Great War Medical Services: Diseases of the War*, Vol. II (1923). There is a chapter on 'Neurasthenia and War-neuroses' by Lt.-Col. R. G. Rows, and a chapter on 'Medical Aspects of Aviation' which contains some psychological material.

C. S. Myers withheld his account of *Shell Shock in France 1914–18* until the outbreak of World War II. It was published in 1940.

No account of 'H.M.S. *Crystal Palace*' has yet been published. *The Final Report of the Health of Munition Workers Committee* (Ministry of Munitions, 1918) summarizes the work of the committee from its inception. *The Report of the British Association* (Manchester, 1915) contains a 60-page report on 'The question of fatigue from the economic standpoint'.

A good deal of this wartime material was incorporated into books by H. M. Vernon, *Industrial Fatigue and Efficiency* (1921), and P. Sargant Florence, *The Economics of Fatigue and Unrest* (1924).

**Psychological Tests**

For the immediate post-war period consult:

*Psychological Tests of Educable Capacity* (Board of Education, 1924) (Ballard, Burt, Myers and Spearman were associated with the preparation of the report); and *The Select List of Books No. 3* (Board of Education, 1928) which contains a full bibliography on testing

For the later part of the inter-war period:

F. C. Bartlett et al., *The Study of Society* (1939), contains chapters on: 'Intelligence Tests' by J. M. Blackburn; 'Questionnaires, Attitude Tests and Rating Scales' by P. E. Vernon; and 'Some Methods of Assessing Temperament and Personality' by C. J. C. Earl

P. E. Vernon, *The Measurement of Abilities* (1940), contains a list of current tests

Works on individual tests are mentioned in the text.


**Educational Psychology**

A good deal of the background material necessary for understanding the development of educational psychology is to be found summarized in Board (Ministry) of Education reports:

*The Education of the Adolescent* (Hadow Report, 1927)
*The Primary School* (1931)
*Infant and Nursery Schools* (1933)
*Secondary Education* (Spens Report, 1938)
*The Curriculum and Examinations in Secondary Schools* (Norwood Report, 1943)

The *Year Book of Education* contains many articles of a psychological nature.

A *Cumulative Index of Volumes I–XXX* (1930–60) of the *British Journal of Educational Psychology* was issued separately in 1961.

Obituary notices of Ballard, Adams, Nunn, Hamley, Thomson are to be found in *Brit. J. Educ. Psych.*

For C. W. Valentine see *Brit. J. Educ. Psych.* XXVI (1956) which contains a 'List of Publications of C. W. Valentine' compiled by L. B. Birch and an article by Burt, 'The Contributions of C. W. Valentine to Psychology'. Valentine's own *Psychology and its Bearing on Education*

(1950) contains many references to the work of himself and his pupils.

An article on 'The Contributions to Education of Sir Godfrey Thomson' by P. E. Vernon was published in *Brit. J. Educ. Studies* X (1962).

## On Progressive Education

J. Adams, *Modern Developments in Educational Practice* (1922)
L. B. Pekin, *Progressive Schools* (1934)

## On Educational Research

R. R. Rusk's books *Experimental Education* (1919) and *Research in Education* (1932) deal with the early period; F. J. Schonell's articles 'The Development of Educational Research in Great Britain' (*Brit. J. Educ. Psych.* XVII–XXII (1946–51) and C. M. Fleming, *Research and the Basic Curriculum* (1946), with later developments
See also A. M. Blackwell, *A List of Researches in Education and Educational Psychology* (Nat. Council for Educ. Research, 1950)
On the Scottish Council: *The Scottish Council for Research in Education: its Aims and Activities* (S.C.R.E. Report XXIV, 1947)

## On Child Guidance

There is a good deal of historical material in the Ministry of Education reports:

*Report of the Committee on Maladjusted Children* (Underwood Report, 1955)
*The Health of the School Child* (1958) (which contains a review of the school health service for its first fifty years)
G. Keir, 'A History of Child Guidance', *Brit. J. Educ. Psych.* XXII (1952)
C. McCallum, 'Child Guidance in Scotland', *Brit. J. Educ. Psych.* XXII (1952)
M. Collins, 'Modern Trends in Child Psychology' in *The Study of Society* (1939) ed. F. C. Bartlett et al.

The history of special education has recently been written by D. G. Pritchard, *Education and the Handicapped 1760–1960* (1962).

## Industrial Psychology

The reports of the Industrial Health Research Board are nearly all out of print and difficult to obtain. The *Eighteenth Annual Report* (1938) contained a summary of 'The Results of Twenty Years' Work'. E. G.

Chambers also summarized the Board's work in 'Industrial Fatigue', *Occupational Psych.* XXXV (1961).

The early work of the National Institute of Industrial Psychology is reviewed in C. S. Myers' *Ten Years of Industrial Psychology* (1932) and in *Industrial Psychology* (Home University Library, 1929) ed. C. S. Myers.

## Mental Health

Feversham Committee, *Voluntary Mental Health Services* (1939)
*Report of the Royal Commission on the Law Relating to Mental Illness and Mental Deficiency* (1957)
K. Jones, *Mental Health and Social Policy 1845–1959* (1960)
M. Ashdown and S. C. Brown, *Social Service and Mental Health* (1953)
H. Devine, *Recent Advances in Psychiatry* (1st. ed. 1929, 2nd ed. 1933)

## Crime and Delinquency

For historical surveys see in particular:

E. Glover, *The Roots of Crime* (1960) (which contains an historical outline of the investigation and treatment of delinquency in Great Britain from 1912 to 1948 from a psychoanalytic viewpoint)
A. M. Carr-Saunders, H. Mannheim, and E. C. Rhodes, *Young Offenders* (1942)
Norwood East, 'Delinquency and Crime', in *Recent Progress in Psychiatry* (*J. Ment. Sci.* (1944))

## Psychology and Religion

For a recent survey see G. Stephens Spinks, *Psychology and Religion* (1963)

# Index of Names

# Index of Topics

325